MANAGING THE WEALTH OF NATIONS

Political Economies of Change in Preindustrial Europe

Philipp Robinson Rössner

BRISTOL
UNIVERSITY
PRESS

First published in Great Britain in 2023 by

Bristol University Press
University of Bristol
1–9 Old Park Hill
Bristol
BS2 8BB
UK
t: +44 (0)117 374 6645
e: bup-info@bristol.ac.uk

Details of international sales and distribution partners are available at bristoluniversitypress.co.uk

British Library Cataloguing in Publication Data
A catalogue record for this book is available from the British Library

ISBN 978-1-5292-1122-1 hardcover
ISBN 978-1-5292-1124-5 ePub
ISBN 978-1-5292-1123-8 ePdf

Cover design: Qube Design
Front cover image: Professor Erik S. Reinert – © The Reinert Collection
Bristol University Press use environmentally responsible print partners.
Printed in the UK by CPI Group (UK) Ltd, Croydon, CR0 4YY

FSC
www.fsc.org
MIX
Paper | Supporting
responsible forestry
FSC® C013604

Contents

List of Figures and Tables

Figures

Tables

Acknowledgements

This book is, as usual, the product of a few years of labour and input from colleagues and friends, among whom I would like to thank in particular Carl Wennerlind, Mark Casson, Xuan Zhao, Stefano Locatelli, Georg Christ and Gerardo Serra, for having read either the complete manuscript or select chapters in draft. Thanks also to one anonymous reviewer, for having read the entire draft manuscript. Special thanks for invaluable help and support over the years go to my friends and colleagues Carl Wennerlind, Prasannan Parthasarathi, Francesco Boldizzoni, Patrick- Karl O'Brien, John J. McCusker, Markus A. Denzel, Wolfgang Drechsler, Erik S. Reinert and Nuno Palma. I have also learnt a lot from discussions with Keith Tribe, Ere Nokkala, Marten Seppel, and Juha Haavisto. Erik S. Reinert's comments and answers to my numerous questions have proved especially influential to my work. I am indebted to Paul Stevens at Bristol for being an exemplary editor and shepherding this project from start to finish. Guillaume Garner (Lyon), Arnd Reitemeier (Göttingen), Hans-Carl Hauptmeyer (Hanover), Suzanne L. Marchand (Louisiana State University), Volker Gehring (Hanover), and Karl Schünemann (Adenstedt) for providing advice on specific matters, sources and images. As usual I dedicate this book to my family and loves of my life, Britta, Ailidh and Marit Rössner.

1

Inventing Dynamics: Political Economies of Money, Markets and Manufacturing, 1300s–1800s

A tale of two models: the *Wealth of Nations* reconsidered

'[C]ommerce and manufactures gradually introduced order and good government', wrote Adam Smith in what eventually became an intellectual building block of economic modernity, *An Inquiry into the Nature and Causes of the Wealth of Nations* (1776, Book III, Chapter 4), 'and with them, the liberty and security of individuals, among the inhabitants of the country, who had before lived almost in a continual state of war with their neighbours, and of servile dependency upon their superiors'.[1]

This Enlightenment sentiment about 'commercial society' and the origins of civility has remained a powerful yet essentially abbreviated story of economic modernity in the West. It is founded upon principally selfish individuals tamed by commerce and trade as the key foundations of power and prosperity. Without civilized trade based on increasingly refined human taste, society would remain stuck in perennial conflicts and wars, and civilization well-nigh impossible.[2] Smith grounded his narrative in the historical example provided by the late medieval city states of Italy. Since the commercial revolutions of the Middle Ages, republics like Venice and Genoa had emerged as commercial societies dominating European trade and economic life. Enlightenment writers often used them as templates for good governance and the foundations of the wealth of nations.[3] The Enlightenment model of 'commercial society', as capitalism became known in the 18th-century Anglosphere,[4] in turn morphed into a common origin story of economic modernity.

In its anachronistic modern readings – and certainly the *Wealth of Nations* has had its fair share of such readings – virtue and wealth thus seemingly came *before* the state. Once cultural and economic progress were set in motion, all else would fall in place almost automatically: modern states, responsible government, accountable politicians, peace and prosperity. A closer look behind the scenes, however, reveals a different story. Medieval commercial republics featured modalities of statecraft commonly associated with rogue economic interventionism, mercantilism, protectionism and other forms of rogue state craft known from much later times.[5] The developmental policies of the late medieval Italian commercial republics were emulated by post-1400 territorial and later on fiscal-military European states. They shaped processes of industrialization and economic growth by the 1800s, only to return again, but now in more globalized and transnational shape, in 19th- to 21st-century variants often known as 'neomercantilism'.[6] Many later writers, while drawing on similar templates as Adam Smith, in fact came to fundamentally different conclusions.[7] But even at Smith's time, there were nuances: 'Civil and domestic liberty, introduced into Europe by the dissolution of the feudal form of government, set trade and industry on foot; these produced wealth and credit; these again debts and taxes; and all together established a perfectly new system of political oeconomy', argued Sir James Steuart, a contemporary of Smith's and another key figure of the Scottish Enlightenment.[8] Steuart pointed out feudalism as a key hindrance to economic development: in societies where the nobility (and other rent-seekers) controlled social and economic life, there was little scope for either freedom or capital accumulation, or any of the other signature features of modern economic development. This was what we may call a 'continental' view of economic development (in England, feudalism had vanished by the 1600s; in Scotland it lingered on a bit longer, in some branches of economy into the 1750s and beyond, but not in the way experienced on the continent). Like Smith, Steuart had toured Europe, but unwillingly. Exiled in 1746 upon becoming involved in the last Jacobite Rebellion aimed at bringing back the Stuart monarchy to the British throne, Steuart had a somewhat closer grip on continental political economy, due to his encounter with cameralism.[9] He had spent the mid-1750s in the southern German university town of Tübingen in Württemberg, a mudhole 'small, ill built, and entirely unprovided with any of the Elegances of Life'.[10] The cameralist model of economic modernization shared with Smith and other Scottish Enlightenment thinkers envisioned a generally positive outlook on competitive markets and self-interest as virtuous forces of economic development; but above all the continental model emphasized *order* as the beginning of the wealth of nations. Order was a way to overcome feudal privileges, rent-seeking and other infringements of the market process.

In this book I argue that the German-speaking lands had their own idiosyncratic ways to capitalism through the cameralist model of political economy, and that capitalism and market economy, rather than representing foreign language to continentals (as has often been claimed, see next section), just looked different from Anglo-Dutch templates of early economic modernity, which are all too often taken as historical norm templates by scholars, giving rise to distinctly skewed visions of world history, and Anglocentric narratives on long-term economic change and global divergence that in many ways not even nearly capture the 'European' experience. The continental model saw markets as dynamic processes – not merely institutions facilitating economic exchange; competitive markets had to be constructed and constantly maintained. Above all, cameralists acknowledged the role of manufacturing, creativity and useful knowledge in the making of the wealth of nations. This was state-building through market-building, something which Smith seems to have bothered less about. In continental cameralist political economy order was conceived as primarily set up by princes and monarchical rulers. There is some reminiscence of this in the *Wealth of Nations,* Steuart's *Principles* and other English-language political economy works of the Enlightenment, through their somewhat ubiquitous use of 'statesman' as a concept, referring alternatively to the ruler, government, administrative apparatus or, simply, by way of abstraction, 'the state'. Smith provided a very intelligent model of how value was *distributed* in a commercial society optimizing workflows according to the principles of division of labour; but gave less attention to the question of how value was *created* in the first instance, and the role played by the state creating and maintaining competitive markets and price systems marked by systems of private ownership of the means of production with the aim to generate profit (what 'capitalism' is usually about).[11]

In the British case the state had been proactive in promoting economic development early on. It became increasingly interventionist after the Civil Wars had given way to the Restoration of the Stuart monarchy in 1660; others would emphasize the Glorious Revolution (1688) as a landmark change.[12] During the Enlightenment 'mercantilism' and economic interventionism reached new heights; during the 19th and 20th centuries, states increased their grip even further on people, markets and economic activity.[13] Since medieval times political actors had interfered with the economic process – production, commerce and consumption – often with emphasis on manufacturing or industry, in Europe as well as other world regions.[14] Rationales varied over time and across space, as did the ways that such policies were applied *in situ*; in practice they often boiled down to central authorities aiming to repatriate value-added activities to raise the wealth of the common weal (and the fisc). Occasionally simplified by scholars as the 'standard model' of European historical economic development,[15] key features included strategies later on known as 'infant industry', 'import substitution' or, more recently, 'mission-driven' policies,[16] or a 'German' or 'Renaissance' way of doing development.[17] Popularized by Friedrich List in his classic *National System of Political Economy* (1841) the model entailed a mix of competitive laissez-faire and interventionism aimed at constructing comparative advantage and generating positive economic change.[18] Policies typically included protective tariffs on certain manufactured imports (but never across the board, as a truncated definition of 'protectionism' occasionally implies); bounties, tax breaks and other incentives encouraging specific sectors of domestic industry, but also active support of states picking up public overheads, promoting schooling and education, literacy and useful knowledge; all key ingredients to economic development.

An alternative view of bad economic governance had been known since pre-Biblical times, vividly discussed and depicted in the medieval and early modern political and economic literature.[19] It was based on violence and war, confiscation, irregular taxation, and inflation by currency debasement. Such policies carried a high social cost, because they were bound to create market asymmetries reducing the common good, increasing taxpayers' opposition, often resulting in popular unrest, uprising and revolts.[20] Since the Middle Ages an understanding emerged that such bad governance be avoided at all cost; together with the notion that economies could be *managed* in ways that *simultaneously* increased the well-being of citizens *and* state, without having to resort to predatory policies; and that there were rule books that could help kings and princes facilitate this process: policies that would generate economic *dynamics, changing* the status quo. These policies, embodied in contemporary princes' mirrors and various other literary genres constituting what is today known as political economy, often worked on the concept of *stewardship*. Rulers had a duty to *manage* what they had been given, to promote the well-being of their subjects, people and the common weal. This is the crucible upon which our modern terminology of 'economy' and 'economics' was forged. Based upon the Latinized *terminus technicus* for 'steward' – *oeconomus* (οἰκονόμος in the Greek original) – originally referring to someone managing a large household or farming estate, Renaissance and then cameralist political economy came to reconceptualize concepts of (political) *oeconomy* now applying them to bigger frameworks of state. This included increasingly dynamic visions; implying rulers who had the duty not only to preserve but *increase* what they had been given. Thus was born the concept of economic development. Some Enlightenment thinkers but especially modern readings thus occasionally put the cart before the horse, leading to a confusion of the original cause–effect mechanisms. Historically things usually happened the other way round. *Order and good government established commerce and manufactures in the first place. Then economic development took place.*

In this book I want to draw attention to some historical strategies and conceptualizations of managing the wealth of nations in the contemporaneous sense of oeconomic stewardship; zooming in on aspects either under-focused or misrepresented in historians' narratives on the origins of modern growth. (Detailed engagements with the literature, specific narratives and debates will be provided in individual chapters, so as not to overload the introduction and unnecessarily bore the reader.) 'Managing' the wealth of nations entailed careful and prudent allocation of resources. Subject to considerable reconceptualizations over the last two millennia, 'economy' – or, as it was known in its contemporaneous early modern form: *oeconomy* – has made it into the modern age as perhaps one of the most contested concepts:[21] today nearly everything evolves around 'the economy' and 'economics', including pandemics, politics, economic embargoes and wars to name but a few; 'management' and managerial principles have made wider inroads into culture and society, including higher education.

My aim is not to simply to 'bring the state back in' to stories of historical economic development,[22] because this has been done in recent years, with scholars debating mercantilism and protectionism as engines of growth and global divergence.[23] Another approach has been to study states through political and economic institutions considered beneficial or useful for economic growth, such as participation, parliaments and property rights, leading to limited government. In Chapter 3 I discuss some of the more problematic aspects inherent in this literature, especially regarding the underlying assumption of principally predatory states which has, essentially, given rise to what I would call the 'myth of the myopic state'.[24] From an intellectual perspective the deeper history of economic interventionism has also been reconstructed.[25] Few nowadays endorse the somewhat counterfactual proposition (given the abundant evidence to the contrary) that Britain industrialized *despite rather than because of* its high level of state interference.[26] In recent years scholars interested in the role of the state have moved focus from the *degree* of state interference to the question of *directionality* of economic change: were the areas targeted by preindustrial economic governance useful for raising productivity, incomes and employment in a sustained way?[27] Some deploy a concept of 'Renaissance economics' or 'Schumpeterian growth', positing innovation-based development as the 'true' source for the wealth of nations, while traditionally historians' interpretations have more commonly grounded upon 'Smithian' growth (extensive, division of labour) as a guiding concept.[28] I will discuss the implications of this in Chapters 3 and 8. Economic historians occasionally tend to dismiss Europe's preindustrial history and heritage altogether when explaining the origins of economic growth, on the (relatively trivial) assumption that prior to the Industrial Revolution economic growth occasionally happened but was never sustained.[29] To the present day economic history occasionally tends to be written *teleologically*, from front to back, as summarized in an excellent recent synthesis whose first chapter is aptly entitled 'Why, When, and How Did the World Become Rich?'[30] While not specifically addressing the question of growth as such, or its causal origins, I occasionally come back to these themes, because of the book's focus on three key institutions and processes supporting historical economic development: money, markets (institutional framework) and manufacturing (process).

Can the German-speaking lands – a region missing from most global narratives on the origins of growth – offer anything new, specifically the history of political economy, 1350s–1850s? Can German histories add to narratives about economic change that have often focused on climate, resource and factor endowment,[31] culture,[32] geography and geopolitics,[33] states defined as military-mercantilist,[34] or politics setting the frames for economic development chiefly through laissez-faire, transparency, credible commitment and inclusive institutions? The 'usual suspects' often chosen as proxy for 'Western' development and the origins of capitalism are England/ Britain and the Netherlands; but these two were the absolute outsiders, deviances from the historical European norm; and it is not clear why they should constitute prime choice a priori when trying to understand historical economic dynamics in a comparative frame.[35] I think that bringing back the continental European experience through a German lens can add nuance to our picture. I aim to demonstrate this through case studies: on the conceptual history of the future as a key ingredient to capitalism and economic development (Chapter 2); the panopticon of economic governance available to continental cameralist states in the age of early capitalism, which was much more varied than usually claimed (Chapter 3); the deep history of market governance, where 'medieval' features survived way into modern industrial capitalism, somewhat underlining how inherently anachronistic modern capitalism really was (Chapter 4); monetary management and money's velocity, key areas where states could make a productive difference to economic lives (Chapters 5 and 6); and the conceptual and intellectual history of manufacturing (Chapter 7) through industrial policies (Chapter 8), which modern histories of growth often quite simply choose to ignore.[36] My evidence comes chiefly from the history of economic thought, and policies and practices drawn from the late medieval and early modern German-speaking lands known as the Holy Roman Empire, albeit especially Chapter 8 will adopt a wider European perspective; defocusing the story from the Anglosphere simultaneously avoiding doing the same through a Germanocentric perspective. As subsequent chapters will hopefully make clear, in a wider and long-term comparative perspective I can find very little specifically German about any of them. Therefore, this is emphatically *not* a history of German political economy; especially since cameralist political economy, a focal point in subsequent chapters, was profoundly transnational in the early modern period. If anything I would like this book to be about the political economy of economic development and change as seen through a 'German-speaker's' lens.

Like most other conceptually contested '-isms' (capitalism, mercantilism, liberalism …) 'cameralism' can be contested and ultimately is no less or more than a helpful yet immensely reductionist label, reifying ideas, theories and debates where contemporaries, at least until 1727 when the first two university chairs in economics or *Kameralwissenschaften* were established in the German-speaking lands, had no such closed system in mind. Nor would most people have been aware of (or even cared about) their writings contributing to a particular doctrine, ideology or school. Such schools or doctrines are usually products of the modern imaginary. In recent years scholars have resorted to the 'cameralist' label when studying historical political economy in a transnational perspective, from Sweden, Denmark and Germany down to Portugal and Spain, looking at early modern debates and discourses on *oeconomy* and thrift, natural science and economic development in the age of capitalism and the emerging Anthropocene.[37] Cameralism doesn't so much appear as a characteristically German discourse any more, nor a specifically German *Sonderweg*, and that seems to me a healthy development. Similar with time: some locate Europe's 'cameralist' moment between the Thirty Years War (1618–48) and the onset of industrialization in the German-speaking lands (1820s–1850s); by that time List, Marx and post-Smithian neomercantilism would have just begun to take to the scene. Other scholars following the old bibliography by Humpert or Zielenziger would adopt a more *longue durée* perspective, locating the origins of cameralism in the Renaissance.[38] Limiting the book to the 17th and 18th centuries, the Newtonian Revolution and Enlightenment, an oft-claimed heyday for cameralist political economy and transitory period before cameralism and mercantilism gave way to more liberal models of economy – an essentially Whiggish proposition – seems not particularly helpful to me, either.[39] It would imply mechanic economic histories, linear trajectories in political economy and potentially teleological narratives, writing history through the Hegelian *Weltgeist* on horseback. Mercantilist and cameralist political economy survived unscathed into the 19th century, at least on the continent; and occasionally resurfaced in the 20th and 21st (strictly *not* to be confused with an obscure modern niche ideology occasionally known as 'neocameralism' which has *absolutely nothing* to do with the political economies studied in the present book). As subsequent chapters hopefully clarify, key pillars of cameralist money and market theory had been applied since the late Middle Ages. Thus, in these pages I will try to avoid labels and boxes as much as possible and simply point to a broadly conceived 'cameralist' perspective on managing the wealth of nations between the Renaissance and the Industrial Revolution. This perspective put great emphasis on human–material improvement, positive economic change and many other aspects we often associate with modern capitalism as well as – perhaps most crucially – the idea that the forces of Mother Nature could be harnessed through clever management of markets, money and manufacturing landscapes. Needless to say – through paradigms of potentially infinite expansion – cameralism also contributed to the dark forces of economic modernity: inequality, environmental damage and the Anthropocene (notwithstanding that cameralists also developed concepts of sustainability).[40]

The history of economic governance can principally be studied through various approaches; common ones include history of political economy and related disciplines such as history of economic and political thought, conceptual history (*Begriffsgeschichte*), and the history of ideas.[41] While the history of political thought has occasionally led to canon-building centred on 'big' thinkers of each age,[42] historians of *economic* thought often zoom in on particular ideas and concepts borrowed from modern economics, looking for their 'origins' in deeper time. Schumpeter organized his posthumously published landmark work according to which ideas made sense to him personally;[43] Karl Pribram interpreted the history of economic doctrines based on the prevailing philosophies or epistemes of their time;[44] while Blaug, another famous economist interested in the history of his discipline looked for theoretical improvement over time.[45] To the present day the search for progress in the history of ideas continues,[46] even though some may label this a Whig way of interpreting history.[47] Recent studies in the deeper history of political economy have acknowledged the *longue durée* dimensions of capitalist regulation,[48] the role of concepts and discourse in shaping modern economic language and ideas,[49] the history of 'primitive accumulation',[50] or the strange history of free markets.[51] Less often a specific concept is traced over time, or across a specific set of writings (*Begriffsgeschichte*).[52] In the same light one can study the history of economic governance through applied economic policies, or institutions shaping economic growth. In the following I refrain from limiting my approach to one specific method, lest the exercise become biased and myopic. Chapter 2, for instance, will be based on concepts, because there hardly is a better approach than *Begriffsgeschichte* to understand capitalism's temporalities and future dynamics ('future' is important for capitalism, and future is, essentially, a grammatological phenomenon). Chapter 3 will focus on ideas in context, simultaneously capturing the potential (through theories) *and* limits of economic management (through policy and application on the ground), sketching a non-myopic 'space of possibility' (*Möglichkeitsraum*). Many ideas were applied in practice, and many practices impacted back on ideas and theories. Some were tried but never worked; others remained utopian. But even good ideas applied in bad contexts can serve meaningful lessons on the politics of economic change.[53] Chapters 4 on market regulation, 5 on monetary theory and 7 on the history of the manufacturing paradigm will again predominantly focus on ideas; while Chapter 8 provides a comparative survey on how ideas related to industrial policy as sketched in Chapter 7 translated into practice.

Chapter 6 on velocity combines *Begriffsgeschichte* with numismatics, using material evidence drawn from coin hoards.

In most cases my story begins somewhere in the late Middle Ages and Renaissance because that time witnessed economic transformations of fundamental importance for later evolutions of capitalism, also giving rise to important conceptual reconfigurations that were crucial for modern political economy.[54] If we're talking policy and political economy, this also means that subsequent chapters will draw on texts and other sources linked to the state: because they *discussed* the state, or were *produced* by people in close connection with states. This does not mean that I seek to downplay the virtues of transnational history, or the role of individual actors and their social networks.[55] Moreover, it may be valid to ask, what – or, rather, who – the state was, historically? Speaking of 'the state' (with the definite article) implies a reification and assumption of the state as a monolithic entity in the way conceptualized by modern sociology and political sciences after Max Weber; but of course, such states did not exist in Renaissance and early modern Europe. State structures and bureaucratic morphologies widely differed across time and space; for early modern England, work by Braddick and Hoppit has shown how economic statehood played out on very different layers of actors and institutions, from regional networks to parliamentary processes negotiating far-reaching economic change, which after the constitutional changes between 1660 and 1688 attained very peculiar dynamics.[56] 'German' economic statehood looked different, with princely states and, after 1648, quasi-absolutist rulers dominating, who operated their own structures and strictures manifested by councils and counsellors, later on state departments (*Konsesse, Kammern*) for commerce and economy, larger economic bureaucracies that implemented policies on the regional and national level. Many states had territorial estates ('parliaments'), which were seldom called; Württemberg in the south-west even had its own territorial 'constitution' dating from 1514, which devolved legislative powers and formal voice to the estates, consisting only of clergy and the bourgeois estates, as the nobility had been disenfranchised and excluded from the political process. As Eucken and others have noted, economic policy can also be done by the subsidiary layers and quasi- as well as semi-state bodies such as business associations, chambers of industry and commerce (*Handelskammern*), or the various East India and other trading companies known from the historical record.[57] Research has established the increasingly dense transnational connections of economic lives in the early modern age; trade, payments and policy during the mercantilist age were by definition multilateral, even between states formally at war or trying to outcompete one another (Britain, France, Netherlands).[58] The history of political economy, especially of cameralism can indeed be well written using a transnational approach, since cameralism was a pan-European discourse. Europe's 'culture of growth'

(Mokyr) worked through international networks of literati that became increasingly integrated since the Reformation; entangled world regions and cross-cultural technology transfer.[59] In a similar way some of the topics discussed in the book also speak to 'international political economy', where the historical origins of neomercantilism have recently been reconstructed using a transnational approach.[60] Some would even argue that on balance state structures did not matter as much anyway, since early modern states were hybrid, punctuated and weak (the 'paper tiger' interpretation), and smuggling and tax evasion accordingly endemic; trading outside the state umbrella would have been at least as profitable for cunning traders and state monopoly evaders.[61] This proposition is not completely wrong. But we have overwhelming evidence of cases where cameralist and mercantilist state frameworks made positive net-differences to economic growth, not only in Britain, where mercantilism – however defined – triggered history's first industrial transformation. Of course, economic governance can also be studied through a *regional* focus: economic activities unfolded (and still do) very differently across geographical space, often transcending political or state borders;[62] regional and trans-regional foci may sharpen our perspective. I am fully aware of all these caveats, and will be taking them into consideration as the discussion unfolds.

The major intervention of my book I guess is this. If it is fair to define mercantilism and its post-Smithian global resurrections under the label 'neomercantilism' through the 'goal … to boost the wealth and power of a state within an integrated world economy through trade restrictions of a selective kind that were strategically designed to support specific domestic economic sectors, particularly local industry',[63] this had by and large been a cameralist template of economic action, but with two important modifications. One was that an 'integrated world economy' was off the table before 1800. Still, the European economy became more connected during the early modern period, which cameralist political economy often used as an analytical point of departure. Second, the 'cameralist' view was about more than simply promoting economic growth for the sake of making a stronger state. Policies occasionally defined as 'neomercantilist' (implying they were either unknown or underemphasized in pre-Listian 'mercantilist' thought) typically include 'imported skilled labor, exchange rate policy, … more aggressive promotion of exports and local merchants in international markets; … the creation of state-owned firms (including banks), exchange rate policy, imported skilled labor'.[64] Such policies abound in early modern writings of the cameralist ilk. But it was cameralists' focus specifically on manufacturing and industry that made for a cutting-edge theory, something that recent scholarship more commonly tends to associate with post-Listian traditions of thought. In a way 'mercantilism' thus seems less and less ideal as a concept nowadays when reassembling historical political economy and historical conceptualizations of the wealth of nations as they shaped up over the last millennium.

Coal but no colonies: political economy in the German-speaking lands and Marx's missed opportunity

That policies, concepts and ideas discussed in this book will mostly be drawn from a 'German-speaking' context probably requires a few words of explanation, especially because Germany has often been seen as a latecomer to modernity, left out of most studies on global divergences and economic growth. Instead, German history has often been written into various *Sonderwege* narratives.[65] 'The market economy retained a bit of foreignness for those for whom English and, by extension, capitalism are second languages', argued one of the most distinguished historians of her age.[66] 'The capitalist system was born in England', wrote Meiksins Wood, a Marxist. Many, Marxists and non-Marxists alike, would subscribe to the notion of 'England [being] the first capitalist nation in the world'.[67] Marx himself (*Kapital*, vol 1) had developed his theory of original ('primitive') accumulation on the example of the English economy after the Black Death. Others trace the institutional origins of economic modernity in post-1688 England.[68] Only very few would go earlier, to the Civil War period,[69] or elsewhere, such as the early modern Netherlands.[70] England and the Netherlands went through a 'small' or 'little' divergence within early modern Europe with higher than average incomes and real wages early on, albeit recent scholarship has modified both the timing and extent, at least in regard to England's imputed early deviance from the continental trend.[71] This does not necessarily mean that the German trajectory conveniently maps on a *Sonderweg* template, as I will suggest; but the story has obviously influenced narratives on the rise of capitalism, Anglo-Dutch and Western European exceptionality. Recent explanations of the 'rise of the West' and the question of why the Industrial Revolution happened in Britain first and not elsewhere have hovered around colonies and coal, literacy, skill levels, the Enlightenment and cultures of growth, mercantilist policy, state capacity and institutions, the role, size and nature of markets – to name but a few.[72] By these standards, most ingredients identified as key to the British 'miracle' also applied in the early modern Germanies. Institutional frameworks were different, with feudalism prevailing, and most states ruled by some form of enlightened autocrats. But, as David Hume noted, autocracy was no state form discriminating against capitalism and successful economic development per se. In most German regions, living standards and real wages would have been lower than in Britain, which may have discouraged processes of substituting capital for labour.[73] Others have posited historical–institutional bifurcations between a more open trade-centred 'Atlantic' or Western Europe versus a more landlocked traditionalist East–Central Europe, where feudal modes of production put a lower ceiling on incomes, living standards and long-term rates of economic development.[74] These bifurcations – if we accept them as valid (the evidence casts some doubt on this[75]) – cut right through the German-speaking lands. Nonetheless the Holy Roman Empire is still allocated in most narratives to the 'landlocked' version of backward Europe, which obviously is a gross simplification.

The same goes for the 'invention' of modern ways of doing economy, which is especially problematic when it comes to ideas.[76] But Ashworth has found that in Elizabethan England 'the experienced armourers at Woolwich Military Academy were from the German states. German experience was harnessed to make domestic cannon and saltpetre; it was also instrumental in creating a wool-card industry'.[77] It was in mining technology above all where German engineers enjoyed a cutting-edge advantage since the early 16th century. In modern political economy the usual suspects named as progenitors include William Petty or John Locke, and the epigones of the Scottish Enlightenment, above all others David Hume and Adam Smith; apart from the French physiocrats relatively little space is given to early modern non-Anglophone writers, and certainly not to the cameralists who commonly have no place in the history of modern political and economic thought.[78] Into the 1870s political economy in the German-speaking lands remained a 'foreign science', claimed Marx; an import from the English and the French (Marx, postscript to *Capital/Das Kapital*, I, 1873). Marx, however, was neither original in this, nor necessarily correct. In 1716, German cameralist Ephraim Gerhard (1682–1718) had noted exactly the same in his concise volume on state prudence (*Staatsklugheit*, a contemporaneous German term for state administration): the German-speaking lands had hitherto known the art of political economy only through imported foreign-language works.[79] Mapped onto this, a myth emerged that saw the German economic tradition *Kameralwissenschaften* – cameralism as a university discipline and technique of administration – as reflecting a general state of backwardness of a *Nachzüglernation* (latecomer nation). Marx snobbishly derogated cameralism as a 'silly mishmash of practices and insights, and purgatory which the hopeful [changed in the fourth edition to *hopeless*] candidate for a bureaucratic career in the service of the state had to undergo'.[80] That was the end of story; he paid no further attention to it in *Capital*. No use was to be found in the study of cameralist writings, argued Marxist economic historian Jürgen Kuczynski (1904–97), a doyen in the German Democratic Republic (GDR) with a fame and reputation reaching far beyond the Iron Curtain.[81] Non-Marxist scholars would not take issue with this assessment generally. In *The Road to Serfdom* (1944), a key contribution to post-war Western neoliberalism, Friedrich Hayek specifically marked out German contributions to political economy: 'Whether it was

Hegel or Marx, List or Schmoller, Sombart or Mannheim', wrote Hayek, they all were antinomy to modernity and liberalism.[82] Again, this all seems to neatly fit into a bigger German *Sonderwege* narratology of failed or abortive modernization, reflecting backward models of society and economy and, in the extreme, high roads to dark modernity. From that viewpoint it has proven tempting to write German history as a trajectory directly leading from Kant to concentration camps, from Hegel to Hitler.[83]

But the German-speaking lands were no stranger to capitalism or economic development. Modern scholarship has rehabilitated German thinkers in the making of modern political economy, from *Kameralwissenschaften* to the *Historical School*, with figures ranging from Veit Ludwig von Seckendorff (1626–92), Johann Heinrich Justi (1717–71), to Friedrich List (1789–1846) and, as a representative of a slightly darker modernity, Werner Sombart (1853–1941).[84] Some of the leading thinkers who built medieval scholastic economic theory, used across western Christendom, were of 'German' origin, including Gabriel Biel (*c.*1420–95) and Martin Luther (1483–1546). Cameralist writings during the 16th to early 19th centuries teem with descriptions of capitalist practices, as well as recommendations to make markets more transparent; breaking the grip of guilds and facilitating capital accumulation in industry and manufacturing.[85] Mid-17th century cameralist writers regularly deployed *Kapitalist* as a *terminus technicus* referring to people using their capital to make a profit, usually connected to some form of manufacturing. There thus was an intimate connection and close historical link between cameralism, primitive accumulation and manufacturing capitalism.[86] Chapters 2 to 8 will provide case studies on how *Kameralwissenschaften* and 'German' economic thought thus contributed to the making, conceptual as well as practical, of modern political economy and the wealth of nations through transformative ideas about markets and market regulation, monetary management and manufacturing development or what modern usage knows as 'industrial policy'.

Since the dawn of the early modern age living standards and real wages across the Holy Roman Empire and East-Central Europe also held up rather well with the north-west, with the region enjoying 'a surprisingly high standard of living during the late sixteenth and seventeenth centuries'.[87] German cities were looked upon with admiration. William Temple, in his *Observations upon the United Provinces of the Netherlands* (1673) noted that in case of the Netherlands being under threat of being swallowed by another state – Temple speculated this may be England –

> they will first seek to be admitted as a Belgick-Circle in the [Holy Roman] Empire (which they were of old); and thereby receive the protection of that Mighty Body, which (as far as great and smaller things may be compar'd) seems the likest their own State in its main

Constitutions, but especially in the Freedom or Soveraignty of the Imperial Cities.[88]

(Just compare this to the current 2022 situation with Russia, NATO and Ukraine.) Similarly with urbanization, a measure often used to approximate economic growth for times without reliable evidence on per capita GDP (gross domestic product).[89] Historians often deploy a big-city threshold of 10,000 inhabitants measuring the urbanization degree of historical societies, and upon doing so it turns out that throughout the early modern period the Holy Roman Empire indeed ranged somewhere in the lower end, sporting an urbanization quotient of less than 5 per cent, together with Poland, Sweden, Norway and Finland constituting the somewhat less developed economic semi-periphery (or periphery, depending which area of Germany one is looking at).[90] Once the threshold is lowered, though, to a more historically sensible level of 3,000–5,000 inhabitants, the German map all of a sudden sprouts towns and cities like mushrooms after fresh rain. Very few of them ever approached in size bigger north-western *metropoleis* such as Amsterdam, Antwerp, Paris or London. But these conglomerates were highly unusual anyway and not at all representative of the European urban fabric.[91]

Commercial capitalism also flourished when Upper Germany, 1450s–1550s, became integrated into the nascent global economy. Lisbon-centred Portuguese overseas expansion into the Atlantic and Indian Oceans was financed by Germans, and a considerable share of the spice trades and global silver flows were channelled through the hands of Augsburg and Nuremberg financial tycoons.[92] Super-companies that went by the name of Fugger and Welser made their name as creditors to literally all important rulers of Western Christendom, including the English monarchs, and Emperor Charles V, a ruler over an empire on which the sun never set. The central European mining regions of Saxony and Tyrol experienced waves of industrial development, 1470s–1550s, in connection with global trade booms.[93] Since the mid-15th century capitalist wage–labour relationships had become the norm in many German industrial regions.[94] Large mining and smelting businesses had sprung up in response to changing global payment and commodity flows fuelling what became known as the *Saiger* industry (liquation plants), early examples of large-scale proto-factory capitalism.[95] Agrarian regimes in the adjacent countryside changed towards Smithian growth. The central German economic region that happened to be the heartland of Martin Luther and the Reformation during the 1520s triggered a flood of writings on price formation, markets and capitalism, by Luther and fellow intellectuals such as Sebastian Brandt or Ulrich von Hutten.[96] Until the 1720s and 1730s, similar to Portugal and Sweden, German economies held up comparatively well with other European regions, and through entrepôts such as Bremen or Hamburg connected with the emerging global economy.[97] German merchants and their copper, metal and linen products made an essential contribution to the goods flows that kept the British and French Atlantic economies going (including the slave and plantation systems).[98] As late as the 1740s, when the British commercial revolution of the Atlantic was in full swing, a large chunk of manufactures sold in the British plantations had originated in the Holy Roman Empire. During the 1740s contemporary voices claimed that most slave and poor men's clothing in the British Caribbean was of German origin.[99] David Hume noted that:

> Germany is undoubtedly a very fine Country, full of industrious honest People, & were it united it woud [sic] be the greatest Power that ever was in the World. The common People are here, almost every where, much better treated & more at their Ease, than in France; and are not very much inferior to the English, notwithstanding all the Airs the latter give themselves. There are great Advantages, in travelling, & nothing serves more to remove Prejudices: For I confess I had entertain'd no such advantageous Idea of Germany.[100]

Germany's industrial take-off also happened earlier than previously thought; key sectors such as railroads and other heavy industry managed to complete a full import substitution process within very short periods.[101] Without any doubt the German lands experienced a later transition towards modern economic growth than Britain; but differences between growth rates and timings of such 'small divergences' were smaller than older Rostovian models of a rapid economic take-off would have implied.[102] When talking capitalism and the history of political economy through a German-cameralist lens therefore, there probably was much less of a historical *Sonderweg*.

There were some peculiarities nonetheless, which help put cameralist visions on markets, money and manufacturing into perspective. Coin debasement and hyperinflation impacted the Austrian and German-speaking countries particularly heavily: a first hyperinflation occurred in Inner Austria towards the late 1450s; another one during the early years of the Thirty Years War (1619–23; *Erste Kipperzeit*[103]), yet another one towards the end of the 17th century (*Zweite Kipperzeit*),[104] and, arguably, the most famous one, in 1921–23. Inflation *angst* still represents a collective millennial trauma for Germans, and massively influenced conceptualizations of money from the Middle Ages into the modern period (Chapters 5 and 6). The ur-catastrophe of the Thirty Years War shaped political economy after 1650; it gave rise to distinct nuances in conceptualizing the future (Chapter 2), not only in those parts of Germany that had seen Swedish occupation during the war, or formally belonged to Sweden (like Pomerania).[105] In Wehler's *Sonderweg* model (Wehler was one of the main protagonists in the *Sonderweg* debates) the peculiar development of German culture and polity reflected German failure to partake in lasting imperial projects and oceanic expansion before 1800.[106] The devastating long consequences of the Thirty Years War had perpetuated a long-term bifurcation in modes of production, contrasting a 'backward' Germany east of the River Elbe with more advanced western Rhineland provinces and states, where society, politics and productivity regimes came closer to the Atlantic model, and these bifurcations lived on into the age of Bismarck, the *Junkers* and the second industrial revolution during the *Kaiserreich*.[107] Recent research has challenged most of these notions, as we have already seen (especially regarding the timing of Germany's industrial take-off), and Malthusian forces seem to have vanished by the early 18th century, about hundred years earlier than the traditional dating by German historians would imply.[108] Still, especially in early modern Europe, including the German-speaking countries, governance was principally autocratic. But rulers were often weak, competing for social powers with their nobility and, occasionally, urban oligarchies estates as represented upon the territorial diets or estates (*Stände*). Outside the major towns and cities noblemen owned the majority of farmlands and forests – the main means of production (and forestry was one pillar of early modern state formation).[109] A bewildering variety of agrarian regimes and feudal modes of production prevailed, ranging from manorial and demesne economy (*Gutsherrschaft*) to free yeomen farming.[110] In the towns, guilds and corporations sometimes tried to canvass production.[111] These created peculiar social and political configurations to which 'cameralist' economics was the response.[112] Still German-speaking political economists often came to principally similar conclusions to those found in Anglophone writings on key matters regarding the virtue of markets and political economy.

On the continent – not only in the German-speaking lands – rulers, princes and their administrators usually looked towards currency and coins, market regulation and manufacturing when trying to establish good economic governance and raise the wealth of the polity.[113] Before the 13th century and the emergence of territorial states, such economic regulation would have been taken care of by the Empire, church or cities; and until the eve of industrialization aspects of 'territorial' economic governance remained contested between rulers, administrators, clergy and church. Local and regional economic actors carrying 'powers of state' included city councils, guilds, and artisanal or professional corporations; even supra-regional confederations like the *Reichskreise* (imperial districts): created in 1500 and surviving until the empire's dissolution (1806) the districts were, theoretically, in charge of monetary policy, as well as some aspects of public regulation and taxation (they collected taxes for imperial defence, initially called *Reichspfennig* or Common Penny).[114] By the later 17th century there even was a revived attempt to coordinate industrial and trade policy on the imperial level, labelled as *Reichsmerkantilismus* ('imperial mercantilism') by historians.[115] The Holy Roman Empire was fuzzy and flexible and all but dead. Even after the Treaty of Westphalia 1648 the trend towards state consolidation was anything but linear. Nevertheless, political economy as embodied in late medieval and Renaissance scholastic works, 16th- to 19th-century 'mirrors for princes' and 'cameralist' manuals on how to successfully administer a flourishing state usually evolved around frameworks of order managed by some sort of princely state. This order came increasingly to be conceptualized as a source of *dynamics*. Unordered, fuzzy, contested economic spaces were no use in generating a wealthy common weal. Cameralists looked towards markets as conceptual, virtual and physical spaces, and their need of regulation to promote the common weal. When evoking the idea of 'development', texts often spoke of *manufacturing* as the 'true gold mine' – less often silver – when referring to the wealth of nations.[116] By means of allegory, reference was made to Spain and her proverbially rich silver mines around the Cerro Rico in what is nowadays Potosí in Bolivia, which at times accounted for more than half the world's annual silver supplies. And still Spain had grown poor on the curse of an overabundant precious metal supply, deindustrializing and falling behind other Western nations during the 17th century.[117]

Cameralists aimed to create wealth, substituting manufacturing for silver mines as sources of the wealth of nations: productive subjects, well-governed markets, cohesive states and integrated market economies. (Some of these projects remained unfinished, and some utopian.) Oriented at state formation *and* consolidation[118] this entailed the spatial ordering and regional subordination of economic peripheries.[119] Cameralism also aimed to reduce social powers and privileges of the nobility. Some have gone as far as defining cameralism 'as an alternative to the mercantilist system in conditions where colonies are lacking, and borders among the many small German states relatively porous'.[120] But this only holds if we take mercantilism to have been the norm and cameralism its variant; in fact it was the other way around. The interpretation only works under the premise that mercantilism was fundamentally about trade, not production (again: it was exactly the other way round).[121] Some have pointed out that cameralist thought was specifically geared toward self-sufficiency, as visible in Sweden's great intellectual Linnaeus and his way of classifying biology and natural resources as economic utilities of national autarky.[122] But arguably cameralism was more. Cameralists knew (and sometimes practised) aspects of *Schumpeterian* development (after the Austro-American economist Joseph A. Schumpeter: intensive economic growth based on innovation and technological development that moves the productive frontier out rather than moving along it), where to the present day most historians still associate early modern European economic life with the chances and limitations posed by *Smithian* growth (after the model sketched in Smith's *Wealth of*

Nations: growth through specialization and market deepening; moving along rather than pushing out a given productive frontier, but with little or no technological change or innovation). We will come back to this in Chapters 7 and 8. And in terms of the institutional framework, cameralists occasionally drew upon older, medieval and Renaissance templates of market regulation (Chapter 4) or monetary policy and management (Chapters 5 and 6), which makes the 'cameralist' vision of political economy look somewhat hybrid; but still principally dynamic in vision and scope. It thus has a lot to offer when studying the origins of the wealth of nations.

There thus was a link between cameralism and the 'standard model' of European development presented so concisely by List. From the 17th century onwards Portuguese,[123] Spanish,[124] Swedish,[125] Danish-Norwegian,[126] Russian[127] or German[128] economic writings belonging to the cameralist spectrum began to systematically address the origins of the wealth of nations through a combination of natural discovery, useful knowledge management, the promotion of people's happiness and a proactive role of the state in shaping the process through well-governed monetary and market regimes. With hindsight, this proved crucial also for capital accumulation – important for economic growth not only in Marxist models; as well as technological development and demographic growth (the latter two are often named as key forces explaining modern economic development; but they were also part of the cameralist programmes).[129] True, cameralist texts on *oeconomy* could be bewilderingly eclectic: they often had something to say on good rulership and the management of public happiness, then went on to discuss morals; good behaviour (should people be allowed to curse or duel in public?); the nature and quality of church sermons on Sunday; public health and quarantine regulations (two weeks to a month in the case of bubonic plague); fire and insurance policies (should roofs on houses be made of straw, thatch and wooden shingles, or should people be compelled to use brick tiles instead?); before turning to more mundane matters, such as curfews, street lighting, monetary policy, market regulation, taxation, import substitution and infant industry protection.

What has been missing in the story of the wealth of nations? A summary of the argument

Following this introductory chapter, Chapter 2, 'Governing the Future: Capitalism's Early Modern Temporalities and the Origins of Growth' looks at a neglected conceptual history of capitalism's temporalities.[130] Knowing about the future has been one of the key ingredients of economic modernity. In modern capitalism the future is unknown but principally open, plannable and manageable. At least that is the illusion – the conviction that humans equipped with instruments of reason, rationality and science may make reasonable forecasts about their future. Notions of an economic future have existed since the Middle Ages. The commercial revolutions in business, banking and commerce that had paved the material foundations of the Italian Renaissance cannot be imagined without some sort of future vision. But these were limited to specific actors and types of activities. Post-1600 models were different. They extended the realm of actors and number of individual open futures, desacralizing the human future from the general biblical context, within which most future visions before 1600 had firmly rested. Around the same time people developed the idea of *infinite growth*, by discovering the right techniques and deciphering the working laws of Mother Nature. In the German context, it arose out of the devastating circumstances of the Thirty Years War. Sweden, a major power during and after the war, experienced similar models often connected to pan-European circles of scholars such as Sophopolis or the Hartlib Circle. Many of these new future visions and growth models originated within a cameralist frame of mind, with a strikingly Swedish-German connection.[131] Language and linguistic notions of economic order and dynamics played together in a close and intrinsic relationship. As yet the German language had no word for 'future' in the modern sense, denoting an open, manageable and potentially foreseeable (forecastable) human-economic future. In fact, the early modern German word for 'future' (*Zukunft*) until the 1700s usually referred to the Second Coming of Christ. But after the mid-17th century, writers embarked upon some important reconceptualizations, developing a new and increasingly dynamic syntax of growth based on the concept of multiple contingent open oeconomic futures. This desacralization of the human future and its remodelling as an economic sphere thus made a signature contribution to the making of capitalism and economic modernity.

Chapter 3, 'The Myth of the Myopic State: Governing Economy and the Politics of Economic Change, 1250s–1850s', contrasts policies with ideas offered for managing the wealth of nations. It revisits capitalism's rise through a fresh look at the contribution made by medieval and early modern states. What states were and what they did obviously changed over time. But the available menu of strategies governing capitalism was more comprehensive than acknowledged in the modern literature, particularly for the medieval and early modern period. And states grew better at it over time. Measures promoting welfare and happiness included: an ample supply of good coin; sound monetary regulation; ordinances regulating trade and exchange on urban markets; stabilizing food supply; a fair layout of market stalls; clean air; safety on roads; and good sermons in church. The ultimate goal was a good-spirited common weal. Invariably this included the promotion of manufacturing, creativity and originality in crafting, designing and shaping things – all tools that significantly contributed to the making of our modern 'culture of growth'.[132]

Having thus laid the conceptual groundwork the discussion proceeds focusing on market design and regulation, monetary exchange and manufacturing as key processes and institutions supporting market economy and capitalism since the Renaissance. Markets are an age-old institution. They can be documented long before capitalism, and in world regions where capitalism never took hold, or did so very late. But they had grown in importance since the Renaissance (Chapter 4). The same goes for money: 'invented' long before capitalism, it became increasingly vital as a tool of economic development as capitalism unfolded 1200s–2000s. Money was shot through with social and political dynamics, as well as painful asymmetries that gave rise to social conflicts (Chapter 5). Money could also be deployed as a tool promoting the quickness of economic life (Chapter 6). Manufacturing and manufactories were key to these processes of dynamics, representing key pillars of capitalist development since the Renaissance. Similar to the webs of finance and exchange (financial markets will not be studied in the present book), colonialism and overseas trade, also marked out by historians as 'drivers' of preindustrial economic expansion, these key tools drove, shaped and configured capitalism and European development. Retreating from a history focused on the individual consumer involved in various 'industrious'[133] or 'consumer revolutions'[134] as necessary preconditions for capitalism and the imputed European miracle, or about colonization and financial innovation as the keys to early modern wealth, we should turn our attention back to the real economy when studying the origin of the wealth of nations: creativity and the creating of things (Chapters 7 and 8).

Chapter 4, 'Configuring Free Markets: A Deeper History of Laissez-Faire', takes a long-run view on how preindustrial political economy conceptualized and designed markets in the age of capitalism's ascendancy. Drawing on select treatises from the scholastics to later ordoliberalism, the chapter examines how people framed and configured the market economy and capitalism over the longer run. Often these entailed a physical-spatial dimension, from the layout of market stalls to the hours of market access and trading times. Features of these long-gone political economies continued to shape European economic practices to the present day.

Chapter 5, 'Money and the Rise of Modern Capitalism', studies money as a fundamental tool in the market process. Money was an agent of social power, but also a tool empowering the velocity of economic life. Beginning with medieval models of money's political, social and economic functions, dating back to Oresme's *De Moneta*: texts that represent the 'origins of political economy',[135] the chapter studies policies and writings on monetary management in the preindustrial world. From the Middle Ages until the 1870s, monetary theories shared common elements only given up when the concept of money's purchasing power was decoupled from its metallic value (since this happened fairly late, during the 20th century, it won't concern us much). Currency stability and inflation management were known to preindustrial authors and rulers as tools promoting economic development.

When Adam Smith, in the second book of *The Wealth of Nations* (1776) suggested that 'Parsimony, and not industry, is the immediate cause of the increase of capital',[136] he broke with a long European tradition of thought, which had lasted half a millennium before him, that had claimed exactly the opposite. A prime cause of economic underdevelopment characteristic (as Marx claimed) of 'Asian' modes of production was *hoarding*; hoarding also haunted European political and economic thought since the age of the Renaissance. Recent studies have identified an early modern political economy paradigm also known as *oeconomy*, which followed a conceptual notion of *thrift* as a way of optimizing material wealth and breaking out of the shackles provided by Mother Nature's limitations on natural resources.[137] Since the Middle Ages moral and economic debates indeed evolved about concepts of parsimony, frugality, avarice and thriftiness, often with a negative undertone. Chapter 6, '*Velocity!* Money, Circulation and Economic Development, *c.*1250–1850', speaks to these debates, zooming in on money and its circulation, extending the argument in Chapter 5 by taking a dynamic perspective on materiality and coins. It provides an intellectual archaeology of an economic variable which to the present day is either enigmatic, or somewhat taken as a residual: *velocity*. I suggest that in historical times velocity was conceptualized more dynamically, as an independent variable with lots of economic agency. Combining archaeological and numismatic evidence with conceptual framings of velocity from Martin Luther and the humanists in the 16th century to John Locke and cameralists and economists of the so-called Historical School of the later 19th century, the chapter extends our view on the functionality of early modern markets through the lens of money. From the end of the Middle Ages, states developed an increasingly sophisticated toolkit of using the dynamics of monetary circulation in the economic process, preventing people from being parsimonious and overly thrifty. 'Money makes the world go round' thus attains a completely new meaning through a new methodological approach to coins and capitalism.

Chapter 7, 'Creating Wealth: *Homo Manufacturabilis* and the Wealth of Nations', moves on to the third field of empowering capitalism in the preindustrial age, looking at origins of creativity in manufacturing. It does so through a focus on economic writings and ideas. During the Renaissance, manufacturing became conceptualized as the main source of the wealth of nations. Somewhat unoriginally – given that many other authors had used the example as a case in point before – Smith's *Wealth of Nations* (1776) commences with the example of a (pin) manufactory. But rather than discussing the full implications in terms of value-added and creativity, Smith chose to proceed by demonstrating that the true origin of wealth lay in the division of labour, improving the distributional efficiency of the existing market systems. But even for a preindustrial economy – Smith's template of analysis – this wasn't completely the case; political economy had much more in stock. Smith thus missed a great opportunity – where did the wealth of nations originate?

Chapter 8, 'Manufacturing Wealth: Industrial Policy and the Rise of the European Economy, 1350–1850s', returns to policy and empirical- or archival-based histories, zooming in on a now all but forgotten type of business venture once characteristic of the preindustrial oeconomic landscape as a case in point: the very same large centralized workshop or manufactory (*Manufaktur*) that Smith had used in the opening chapters of *The Wealth of Nations* to illustrate his point about division of labour, stopping short of a full explanation of how the origin of the wealth of nations through the virtuous forces of manufacturing *really* came about (the difference between Smithian and cameralist – or Schumpeterian development – just a nuance, but of world-historical dimensions). Since the 16th century it was consensual among European writers to see manufacturing or the crafting of things as a main source of national prosperity. Manufacturing embodied skills, value-added, curiosity, learning and creativity so much more so than other economic activities such as farming, finance or trade. Studying the history of industrial policy with a focus on *Manufakturen* or manufactories in the Germanies, Scotland, Sweden, Austria and France, the chapter surveys how discourses examined in Chapter 7 reflected back upon and interacted with medieval and early modern economic practices, providing the foundations for capitalism, industrialization and the wealth of nations.

Europe's manufacturing heritage drew on age-old templates and examples (Chapter 7) which in the case of Britain (and in the 19th century its continental catchers-up) led to successful industrial transformation and global economic predominance. There was no necessary connection between 'good thinking' and 'good practice', and we should avoid mechanistic explanations of a cause–effect nature, implying economic failure where ideas were not applied to full extent, or 'wrong' practices prevailed because ideas were wrong.[138] There are too many unknowns in the equation, as Chapter 3 will discuss in more detail. This occasions us to reconsider the history of the wealth of nations in a deeper-history time frame, through continental contributions often left out from modern narratives on the origins of capitalism, global divergence and economic modernity.

2

Governing the Future: Capitalism's Early Modern Temporalities and the Origins of Growth

Working for posterity

'*Wir arbeiten für unsere Nachkommen!*' (We work for posterity!), exclaimed Daniel Gottfried Schreber, professor in cameral sciences from 1764 – as political oeconomy was known in the German-speaking lands at the time. Working at the University of Leipzig in Saxony, Schreber wrote this in the preface to his German translation of Anders Berch's textbook (*Introduction to Household Economics, Principles of Policey Science, Œconomic and Cameral Sciences*).[1] Berch had held the first chair in cameralism established in Sweden, at the University of Uppsala (1741). In the Holy Roman Empire, such professorships had been endowed at the Prussian Enlightenment universities of Halle/Saale and Frankfurt/Oder by 1727. Berch's book, concise compared to many contemporary German works on cameralism, was quite a success. It continued to be used in Swedish university teaching until the 1830s.[2] We know less about how well-acclaimed Berch was in Germany; but certainly Schreber, his translator, was over the moon about his Swedish cameralist colleague. As one of the lesser-known oeconomists of his time, more copycat than cameralist, Schreber made his name chiefly as a translator of Swedish books on useful things (*oeconomy*), and as editor of a multivolume work entitled *Daniel Gottfried Schrebers Neue Cameralschriften*, essentially a compendium of useful knowledge and useful things. With this he actively contributed to European's 'culture of growth'.[3] As did many of his fellow cameralists, Schreber oscillated comfortably yet from a modern viewpoint eclectically between various genres including political economy, *oeconomy* more traditionally framed – as an Aristotelian science of household management merging with early modern conceptualizations of 'thriftiness', botany, chemistry, metallurgy, alchemy and what German historians know as 'popular enlightenment' or *Volksaufklärung*.[4] As part of Germany's oeconomic enlightenment, cameralism was notably dynamic, containing signature features of modern capitalist practices and thought.[5] But it has been left out of most narratives on the making of industrialization, future and modern economic growth. The present chapter is aimed at recovering and reclaiming some conceptual bits of this lost story and introduce *Begriffsgeschichte* as a useful concept for a history of dynamics and managing economic change; before Chapter 3 will link Renaissance and early modern cameralist thought to broader practices and possibilities of historical economic development.

The present matters also in another regard: the *temporalities of capitalism*. With his exclamation, Schreber betrayed an attitude characteristic of the enlightened optimism of his age: the vision of *an open future horizon* – a signature feature of the modern economic condition.[6] By no means was this future forward thinking something that only arrived on the scene around the mid-18th century as some have claimed.[7] In 1564 southern German military surgeon and Renaissance humanist Leonhard Fronsperger had published a little-known treatise sporting an argument that became familiar much later as the Mandeville Paradox, usually associated with Dutch-English physician Bernard de Mandeville: the proposition that humans are naturally self-interested, but that through leaving them unconstrained pursuing their self-interest they automatically drive capitalism and humanity forward.[8] Using expressions about the world being 'preserved *in future*' (my emphasis), discussing social, cultural, religious and economic implications of self-interest translating into positive human development, Fronsperger essentially offered a dynamic world view and forward-facing model of the human–oeconomic condition, based on the concept of competitive allocations of labour, land and capital. Fronsperger used the example of an organ with its set of pipes as an analogy explaining how individuals cooperated in the marketplace by the virtuous forces of spontaneous coordination: 'just like an organ which has many sorts of pipes, long and short, big and small; none of which are sounding equal and alike. But from all these uneven voices rises the sweetest musical harmony'.[9]

About 150 years later the theme was picked up again by Mandeville, a physician like Fronsperger (many early modern oeconomists were trained as medics), in the *Fable of the Bees* (1714). Employing essentially the same analogy – 'this, as in music harmony, made jarrings in the main agree; parties directly opposite, assist each other, as it were for spite'[10] – Mandeville finally became famous for the argument that had enjoyed common currency centuries before his birth.[11] Both Fronsperger as well as later on Mandeville (and many others at their time) thus conceptualized an open human-oeconomic future long before its common location in the Koselleckian *Sattelzeit*, the crucial phase in history when European society and economy were neither here nor there yet. Modern industry, liberalism and human

24

rights were somewhat in sight and sketched at least as a possibility through the French and American Revolutions, but most people, politics and institutions remained vested in older, more traditional, political cultures and modes of production, working according the motion laws dictated by the *anciens régimes*. Conceptual historian Reinhart Koselleck used the suggestive metaphor of a rider saddled on a horse, looking left and right, facing both traditionalism and the new future commonly known as modernity – an axial age that would have seen landslide changes in political terms, but also brought about new timescapes, with human actors now consciously separating the future from the present and the past; and new academic disciplines taking to the stage, including history and its auxiliary companions aimed at verifying and validating historical evidence found in the sources, including palaeography, codicology and numismatics.[12]

This gives us ample occasion to reconsider capitalism's temporalities,[13] and related concepts in historians' grander narratives on economic development.[14] Paul Slack, a self-confessed 'Whig' historian, explicitly marked out early modern England as the place where a concept of *improvement* was initially invented, before spreading to other countries and cultures: 'By the beginning of the eighteenth century the quest for improvement distinguished England from other countries. It had become part of the collective mentality, and it made England distinctive. It might also be said to have been one of the things that made England modern, or more accurately early modern'.[15] Slack connects the breakthrough of this new culture of improvement to the British Civil Wars and the disruption caused in the political, social and economic framework, which would have somewhat facilitated open-ended non-soteriological future thinking:

> These political events were important to the character and plausibility of an improvement culture because they showed that there could be no rapid route to perfection, either in revolution with its expectation of an imminent millennium, or in total restoration of some earlier golden age. That left improvement – gradual, piecemeal, and cumulative progress – in command of the intellectual field. A radical change in economic circumstances had a similar effect.[16]

That attitude, however, never was particular to Britain or just England; certainly not during the early modern period – not least because most intellectual endeavours featuring such modern forward-facing cosmologies like Cornucopia or the Hartlibians were transnational networks and projects stretching across many Western European countries and cultures.[17] Right at that time there were wars overturning the current status quo almost everywhere – and the British Civil Wars may not even have been the harshest: the German-speaking countries, especially, were ravaged by the

Thirty Years War. This war also acted as a political, economic and conceptual game-changer in many ways. In fact it is this war which offers interesting transnational connections between English, Swedish and German oeconomic futures and cultures of forward-facing improvement. Moreover, the mere notion of ideas being 'invented', either by particular actors, in peculiar locations, or at distinct points in time is problematic, to say the least.[18] Again (see Chapter 1) we should be careful not to adopt Anglocentric *Sonderweg* hypotheses when explaining historical change.

Conceptual history or *Begriffsgeschichte* provides an excellent way to underline this point.

Concepts of growth: *Begriffsgeschichte* and early modern capitalism

From the 1970s it became fashionable in the social sciences to call for an *end to growth*; intensified in recent years based upon an improved understanding of the connections between capitalism and environmental change in the Anthropocene.[19] But before that a mercantilist-cameralist lust for growth had laid the important conceptual foundations of the Anthropocene in the first place. The cameralist-mercantilist vision also gave rise to a new economic language, which still needs to be studied in closer detail.[20] Key economic-linguistic switches and changes in meaning of key terms and concepts included 'capital' and 'capitalists'; 'industry',[21] 'increase' and 'growth' (*Wachstum*, *Mehren* in German), or 'velocity', 'vivacity' and 'circulation' (*Kreislauf* in German). Some of these terms came to attain a fundamental role in the modern capitalist syntax and will be considered in more detail in Chapter 6. Here I want to focus on conceptualizations of the open future as they shaped up in early modern German discourse suggesting a gradual change in gear and increasingly smoother road taken toward dynamic visions of economic development.

Knowing the future – or better: believing to do so – belongs to the key features of economic modernity.[22] Writers of the cameralist and mercantilist ilk were marked by a sheer unbound optimism of what the future could bring – if the forecast was rational, based on reasonable scientific means (definitions of 'scientific' changed, of course), and the choices taken in consequence were commensurate with the evidence. Managing the future was to manage the oeconomy in an expansionary way, augmenting people's incomes and whereabouts and the material world of goods. The emerging cameralist oeconomic future was distinct from earlier and alternative models and methods, such as fortune telling, sorcery and millenarianism; but rested upon the notion that the future was plannable *and* manageable; earlier on, medieval and Renaissance models of the future had often adopted a more pessimistic, millenarianist or Armageddonist outlook. While such futures were open and, to an extent, plannable, too (it was quite certain that the End Was Nigh as people waited for the Second Coming of Christ), fully 'manageable' as in modern Anthropocene capitalism they weren't quite yet. The new cameralist-mercantilist future of the post-1600 era on the other hand came closer; moreover, it was now 'oeconomic'; with a look toward improving, *in a quantitative sense*, the material-economic conditions of humankind,[23] using science, nature and philosophy. These reconceptualizations coincided with – and reflected – changes in the linguistic and semantic framings of political economy. Thus was born our modern vision of economic growth.

When locating the birth of the modern future, historians of concepts have commonly focused on post-1750 high Enlightenment political writings which prepared the ground for the French Revolution and its accompanying political reconceptualizations. Often following Koselleck's influential hypotheses on temporality and historiography during the age of Europe's *Sattelzeit*, but usually disregarding the broader economic context,[24] accordingly mercantilism, cameralism and political economy more generally have played a minor, if non-existent role in these debates. To the present day, cameralist and mercantilist theory are implicitly reckoned as the Dark Side of Enlightenment.[25] Some would see them as aberrations from the 'true' capitalist faith (embodied, according to some, in classical liberalism and modern economic thought), based on the proposition that modern economic reasoning was above all founded by Adam Smith and the Scottish Enlightenment philosophers. But as we have seen, and will see in further chapters, cameralism – to which we may reckon Enlightenment writers such as James Steuart or Johann Heinrich Justi – was a widely shared economic ideology across early modern Europe supporting development in ways principally reconcilable with 'enlightened economy' or even 'modern' ways of doing growth.[26] What comes up with remarkable clarity from many books and prefaces in particular of the cameralist ilk after *c.*1600 is a notably future-oriented dynamic vision of market economy that broke with older visions of *oeconomy* and scholastic models of the market process. As research has barely commenced in this field, the following only sketches the bare outlines of this epistemic shift, hoping for deeper level future studies.

Conceptual history (*Begriffsgeschichte*) is an excellent way of tackling these matters, and we should take it seriously, especially regarding the history of global divergence and long-term economic growth. To the present day, most exercises have tended to focus on *real, measurable* or performance-driven variables such as real income, GDP per capita, productivity, interest rates and so on, in other words: metrics of market performativity. On top of that, scholars have emphasized geography and resource endowment, institutions and state involvement in the economy as causes for regional and global divergences in income and wealth. When other factors such as economic culture enter the equation, they usually do so by ways of *institutions* or 'rules of the game', which are then held to account for regional or global variations in economic performativity.[27] Much less attention has been paid to *other* cultural factors, such as *temporality and concepts* (zooming in on historical actors and their sense of how past, present and future were connected); or concepts and ideas, including semantic and moral assumptions about how economic activities such as production, trade and consumption can be described, modelled and thus made sense of in the 'Grand Scheme of Things'; and how this played out in shaping markets in the longer run, making and breaking the wealth of nations.

While it is clear that institutions, social and cultural norms can be important when it comes to *structuring* historical economic reality by means of informal institutions through actors' *expectations*, they tell us little about people's *interpretation of the prevailing cosmological order*, and thus ill-*predict* economic behaviour and development. Some argue that humans adapt their belief structure regarding the cosmological order to *prevailing* or *changing* material-economic conditions.[28] Potentially this may even lead to *an improved understanding* of the world; the post-1660 Newtonian knowledge revolution is a good example of this.[29] But we can equally argue the other way round: since improvements in the knowledge of the *how-to-do* don't tell us much about their deeper meaning, that is, the reasons that guarded people's choices in each circumstance or – as in the case of subsequent chapters – when adopting certain strategies of economic regulation which sometimes remained remarkably similar over time, we don't know *why* these choices and institutions originated in the first place. Thus, the common historians' focus on performativity, asking which countries grew faster over time, or which states exhibited modern economic growth first, goes a long way in *describing* processes of development and divergence, but essentially short-circuits the ultimately bigger and more important question of how to *causally explain* economic change. To understand the managing of the wealth of nations, we should take a look at the underlying concepts, theories and ideas.

The Great War, cameralism and the origins of prospective thinking

Conceptual historians (*Begriffsgeschichte*) have argued that an epistemic change towards a discovery of the future took place in the days of the Koselleckian Axial Age (*Sattelzeit*) around 1770; others have dated such discoveries to the 1600s, even earlier.[30] While the debate has focused on aspects of cultural and general early modern history, there is a notable gap in historical scholarship on how new conceptions of the future since *c*.1600 impacted upon, and interacted with, new visions of political economy. One trace leads to Sweden and its role in the Thirty Years War, although this would be by no means the earliest nor most significant location point for this conceptual reframing.[31] But it ties in with a common scholarly notion of cameralism and German economic backwardness, which is true at least in terms of the economic, social, cultural backlashes and personal suffering caused by this ur-catastrophe pushing back German economic development by a century or so.

The Great War – 'Europe's Tragedy'[32] – had wrought havoc in the minds and souls of those living through the age, as Andreas Gryphius's beautifully gruesome poem *Tränen des Vaterlandes* (*Tears of the Fatherland*, 1636) alludes:

> Wir sind doch nunmehr gantz, ja mehr denn gantz verheeret!
> Der frechen Völcker Schar, die rasende Posaun
> Das vom Blutt fette Schwerdt, die donnernde Carthaun
> Hat aller Schweiß und Fleiß und Vorrath auffgezehret.
> Die Türme stehn in Glutt, die Kirch ist umgekehret.
> Das Rathhauß ligt im Grauß, die Starcken sind zerhaun,
> Die Jungfern sind geschänd't, und wo wir hin nur schaun,
> Ist Feuer, Pest, und Tod, der Hertz und Geist durchfähret.
> Hir durch die Schantz und Stadt rinnt allzeit frisches Blutt.
> Dreymal sind schon sechs Jahr, als unser Ströme Flutt,
> Von Leichen fast verstopfft, sich langsam fort gedrungen,
> Doch schweig ich noch von dem, was ärger als der Tod,
> Was grimmer denn die Pest und Glutt und Hungersnoth,
> Dass auch der Seelen Schatz so vielen abgezwungen.

> Full now – yea, more than full – behold our devastation:
> The frantic drum beat, and the brazen horde,
> The thundering siege gun, and the blood-slick sword
> Devour all diligence, and sweat, and careful preparation.
> The church is overthrown; our mighty men are slain;
> The town hall lies in dust; our towers burn;
> Virgins are raped; and everywhere we turn
> Are fire, plague, and death to pierce us – heart and brain.
> Down walls and through the town runs always fresh-spilled blood
> For eighteen summers now, our river's yearly flood
> Near-choked with corpses, has pushed slowly, slowly on
> But nothing will I say of one thing – worse, I know,
> Than death, more grim than plague, or fire, or hunger's woe:
> Those pillaged souls from whom even hope of heaven is gone.

At a time of global crisis and climate change, did the aftermath of this war stimulate a particularly German delusional obsession with order?[33] Debates about a rise of well- or less well-ordered police states after 1648 abounded. They have been connected to historians' debates about 'absolutism', 'social norming' and such.[34] On paper they seem fully compatible with broader claims of Germany's *Sonderweg* hypotheses, that is, assumptions that German history took a historical special path, apparently even before 1945, 1848 or 1789. But as we saw in Chapter 1 such *Sonderweg* hypotheses are overall problematic.[35] The basic frameworks and concepts of economic order developed in post-1648 cameralist discourse and *Policey* regulation – regulation aimed at a establishing productive, competitive and well-ordered Common Weal in the many German states of the time – had shaped up centuries before the war. They remained in place long after, and into the age of high industry, as we will see in more detail in Chapter 4. As Bernard Harcourt and others have shown notions of order (and coercion) have remained fundamental for the market process and capitalism.[36] But in the German states, there was indeed a significant upswing in economic regulation after 1648, which will be more closely examined in Chapter 4, and one scholar at least has speculated about a possible causal link between regulation, market integration, market performance and post-1648 German economic development.[37]

A major player in the war, Sweden emerged for a time as a northern European imperial power, almost turning the Baltic into a Swedish inland ocean (*Stormakstiden* / Sweden's Age of Greatness, *c.*1648–1721). German libraries were ransomed and taken to Sweden. Skokloster Castle near Uppsala, built in the 1650s for the great Swedish commander Carl Gustav Wrangel, for a long time held one of the most comprehensive collections of German-language works outside the Holy Roman Empire.[38] To the present day, the university library at Leipzig where Swedophile Schreber, whom we encountered earlier, was professor, holds a significant number of 18th-century Swedish oeconomic works.[39] As Wennerlind has shown, the Swedish Age of Greatness begot a wave of scientific discovery and transnational networks of natural science, alchemy and political oeconomy, with networks around figures such as Bengt Skytte, Chancellor Oxenstierna and many others involved with scholarly circles as far west as the Hartlib Circle in England.[40] The bibliometric evidence of translations of economic treatises from and into Swedish between 1650 and 1800 suggests there were considerable dynamics in Swedish economic reasoning, which may also have transmitted into other economic cultures,[41] but the process also worked in the reverse. Many authors associated with a more 'liberal' spectrum in Swedish mercantilism including Christopher Polhem (1661–1751), not only drew on Johann Joachim Becher's and other German scholars' works, but were later reimported into German economic culture.[42] Lars Magnusson, for instance, points out close parallels in structure and composition between iconic *Staatenkunde* and *Kameralwissenschaften* works such as Johann Dithmar's *Einleitung in die Oeconomische Policey- und Cameralwissenschaften* (1729/1745)[43] and Berch's *Inledning*, which became 18th-century Sweden's stock-in-trade university textbook in political oeconomy.[44]

With the quotation that opened this chapter, Schreber had put in a nutshell what many cameralists believed in; he also professed an economic faith that had been in the making long before the war: useful knowledge and proactive, *prospective* thinking, or, in short: *thinking about the future* as key to oeconomic improvement. Let us consider some of the implications regarding the history of political oeconomy, and the 'cameralist' strategy of managing the wealth of nations.[45]

Meanings of 'future' in early modern Europe

A basic Ngram analysis performed upon the Google Books corpus of works printed 1500–2000 for the word 'future' including both the substantive as well as adjective form – an important difference[46] – yields an interesting hypothesis. An upswing in English-language frequency of use during the second half of the 17th century with a peak around 1700 was followed by a secular decline to 1800, and a much less dynamic trajectory thereafter (Figure 2.1).

The chronology and cycles or *Konjunktur* for the equivalent German term *Zukunft* look very different (Figure 2.2).

After an initial boom during the first three decades of the 18th century came decline, and then an upward dynamic between the 1750s and 1850s, followed by another trough during the second half of the 19th century (the 20th century saw an upward trend again, interrupted by the three major crises: the First and Second World Wars, and the post-1973 crisis of European capitalism, the ending of the 'Golden Age' and the coming of neoliberalism). Even though more advanced distant-reading techniques exist, the prima facie intuition allowed by Ngram suggests notably different linguistic geographies and fluctuations of the conceptual uses of 'future' in post-1500 thought. In the German-speaking lands the trend was up at the same time when the English record went down. The German peak in the use of 'future' coincided with the Enlightenment; strikingly, the Anglophone corpus didn't – even though Anglophone Enlightenment writers including David Hume, Sir James Steuart and Adam Smith – are commonly heralded as forefathers of modern economic thought.[47]

By the early 1600s for instance it was perfectly normal for English-language writers to speak about '*the* future' with a definite article, in the substantive. Many financial treatises on usury and the taking of interest were naturally modelled upon the idea of future yield and of discounting value,[48] using the word 'future' for what it was, the unknown open and indefinite human timescape after the present. German-language works on the other hand may have had a more uneasy start prima facie with the corresponding German term *künftig* ('future' in the adjective), let alone *Zukunft* (the modern equivalent of the English future in the substantive). *Künftig* rarely appears in pre-1760 German-language economic texts; by then indeed usually referring to 'future things to come'.[49] But when used in the substantive and

Figure 2.1: Ngram of *future*

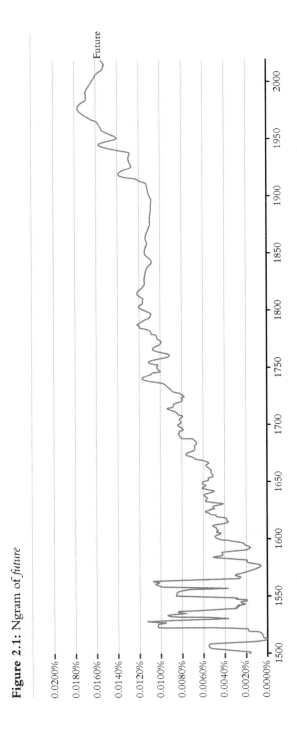

Figure 2.2: Ngram of *Zukunft* (All)

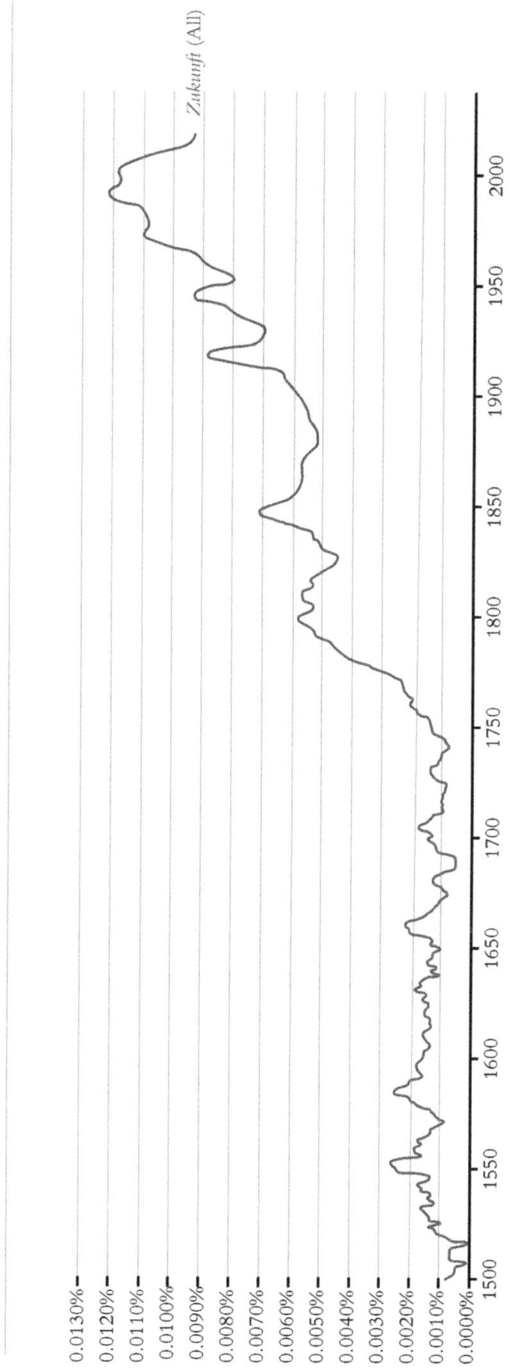

capitalized, *Zukunft* until the end of the 18th century in most cases denoted the traditional meaning, that is, the 'advent' of something – most commonly the Second Coming of Christ.[50]

Europeans had known certain ways of modelling the future, long before the open future of the Koselleckian Axial age around 1750–1850. Common strategies of foretelling the future included astrology, haruspicy (knowing the future from inspecting the entrails of sacrificed animals), augury (telling from the flight of birds), aeromancy ('by means of the air/winds'), alomancy ('by means of salt'), capnomancy ('ascent or motion of smoke'), chiromancy ('lines of the hand'), geomancy ('by tracing points or lines in the earth') and necromancy; all more or less belonging to the toolkit commonly known as 'magic'. To them came *utopias*, a literary genre known not only since Thomas More. As imaginary futures, often with a political undertone, utopias emphatically were not projections of what realistically *could* be achieved or what *was* expected to come; they were meant to tell people where things went wrong. Magic pertained to the realm and fate of individuals, but not society at large. In any case most societies and humans do have a vision of the future *of some sort*, in the same way as they share collective histories of the past: past, present and future are connected in a narrative about the world, including myths, fables and fairy tales, but also cosmologies and philosophies of history. These do not have to be linear; even in modern Europe non-linear time models are quite common still.[51] But until the 17th century in Europe most such visions of the future were commonly embedded within a Christian soteriology of the Second Coming of Christ.

What about financial markets and commerce, where we can perhaps most easily locate models of future, even in times when Germans as yet had no word for it (because the financial business, since ancient times, has been contingent upon temporality: usury and interest are fundamentally about 'buying' time)? Medieval European maritime trade and commercial insurance business, double-entry bookkeeping, bills of exchange and cashless payment – widely practised since the 12th-century commercial revolutions – all built on techniques that were future-oriented. The mere idea of credit – a centrepiece of any market economy – is: *credere* means 'to believe', and this far exceeds trustworthiness and what the early modern German business language had as *Trew vnd Glauben*,[52] good reputation – but also the belief in a future that would repay capital investment made in the here and now.[53] They rested on the idea of buying and selling time through putting a monetary value on future time. For the bill of exchange this was discounting, that is, selling a bill before its due date at a reduced price. For capital loans it was the interest rate. Since Aristotle the buying of time had been considered *chrematistic* and a violation of the just or godly order. But life rents and annuities, the stock-in-trade of medieval financial markets, were likewise based on elements of rational calculus and future prognostics and precisely those elements that moral philosophers abhorred, because they tended to trade something that belonged to God alone (and thus could not be sold).[54] Some have even gone so far as to state what seems a paradox, that is, that medieval prognostications of Armageddon may have represented the origin of modern scientific-rational approaches to the future.[55] Others have seen a Renaissance origin of an early modern European 'culture of growth'.[56] The commercialization processes of the 12th and 13th centuries gave rise to a growing culture of contractualization, with contracts, law, new forms of banking and marine insurance providing a distinctly new type of future vision towards a timescape that became more and more manageable.[57] In combination with the rise of Purgatory and the bill of exchange as the foundation of European financial markets and cashless payment, it was the Church, most particularly the Papacy, that stimulated such new forward-facing business techniques investing in the future *nolens volens* – by becoming progressively permissive of circumventing the usury laws and the buying of time.[58]

One way of framing the future thus belongs to the realm of soteriology. By criticizing indulgences as a means of buying oneself out of Purgatory – the only realm of the Ever After that was temporary or chronologically limited, Martin Luther in 1517 provided another blueprint for a new human future. He gave up the notion of Purgatory and indulgences, but only long after his Reformatory Breakthrough (around 1531). He substituted notions of commercializing the future in the Ever After with a more immediate relationship between the sinner and God. This freed monetary and financial resources for real investment in the market economy. Capital for investment, consumption and welfare provision for the poor by means of the Common Chest (*Gemeine Kasten*) that had been spent on soteriological investment (indulgences) before, could now be put to future use in what we call the 'real economy'.[59] But many 16th-century cultural visions and religious discourses retained a teleological and backward-facing vision of time. The human future before the Apocalypse was either short, bleak or generally predetermined by the past. The world as they knew it was deemed, or doomed, to end. True, a lot of it was rhetorical device, to drive home one's point and recruit followers to the Reformer's cause which eventually (and initially inadvertently) became geared toward a complete reconfiguration of the societal, soteriological and politico-economic landscape, as treatises such as Luther's *Address to the Christian Nobility of the German Lands* (1520) or Michael Gaismair's *Tyrolean Utopia* (1526) show.[60] We should not forget, either, that irony and hyperbole represented a stock-in-trade item in the Reformers' and Humanist rhetoric tool box. Texts of the Reformation era should not be read literally every line. The Reformation was, in essence, a public media event.[61]

Since the later 13th century, authors as diverse as John Duns Scotus or William of Ockham had propagated visions somewhat at variance with the prevailing scientific *Weltbild*.[62] Theorizing, as a heritage of antique Greek thought (Euclid), now became important in what later became known as physics and other sciences. Mathematics was increasingly resorted to in the explanation of physical and astronomical processes; two of the finest monetary theorists of the 14th and 16th centuries, Nicole Oresme and Nicolaus Copernicus, also wrote important treatises on physics and astronomy. Empiricism gave rise to practical and mechanical gadgets: gadgets to gauge time, harness the powers of water and wind, for mills and energy conversion; and, last but not least, experimenting with human flight. Leonardo da Vinci's aircraft models are well known; less well-known are the attempts at applying them in practice. We know of one, perhaps fictitious, used by an Italian alchemist in 1509 during the reign of Scottish king James IV (b 1473, r 1488–1513). This man is reported to have flown himself with a self-constructed aircraft from the walls of Stirling castle, the royal residence, down into the kingly gardens (legend claims he survived). It does not matter so much, however, whether such gadgets 'worked'. What is much more important is that people were *convinced* they would work. And that there was a virtue in trying them out in practice. There were people who believed that natural-scientific discovery would open a whole array of new human possibilities to control, tame and harness the forces of Mother Nature, in the same way as the 17th-century Swedish 'infinity' theorists around Skytte and the Hartlibian Sophopolists believed. Science was conceived as a means of discovering the hidden beautiful plan that God had had in mind during the process of Creation. The Renaissance paradigm entailed the notion that scientific discovery and human curiosity should know no boundaries, in the same way as God's creation and its beauty knew no borders: Religious zeal and active 'rational' scientific discovery were thus perfectly compatible. The latter principles were all shared by Swedish oeconomists during Sweden's Age of Greatness, who by the 1650s had developed a fully fledged theory of infinite growth.[63] From this it seems a comparatively small step in logic to derive the conclusion that, ultimately, there was a future out there that could be managed, planned and worked.[64] Could it be possible that *Homo* lived in a world that saw futures other than Armageddon?

Until the end of the early modern age some people kept looking for hints and signs that the end was nigh. They knew the word *Zukunft*, but this word mostly referred to the Second Coming of Christ (*newe Zukvnnft*).[65] As we have seen there was, in the German language, no genuine word for *future* written in the substantive yet; or at least contemporaries were not completely at ease with its modern grammatical use and meaning.[66] As late as the 1770s Ludwig von Hess, in his 'Promiscuous Thoughts' on economy, sexuality and society kept referring to *die grosse Zukunft* or 'grand future', literally the Return of Christ;[67] while elsewhere using the more familiar phrase *in Zukunft*, when referring to an edict by the Swedish king that 'in the future' bodies should be buried outside the city walls.[68] In Luther's economic vision (*On Commerce and Usury*, 1524),[69] one of the 16th-century economic bestsellers, there still was little place for the open future or economic *development*, either, in the sense of conscious human effort and *agency* directed at future betterment. Nor had scholastic economics left much room expressively for prospective and proactive economic development, choosing to focus on matters of market regulation, exchange rates and price formation instead. And even though Luther certainly was no scholastic – he abhorred scholastic 'sophistry' – his concept of economy in many ways borrowed from the medieval churchmen and those of the contemporaneous Salamanca School.

But even though 'future' was not quite yet framed in the modern way linguistically, from the 1600s contemporaries began to change semantic strategies of dealing with the human economic future. They identified new ways of how humankind could become the epicentre of future change, how *Homo* could proactively intervene in shaping their own future and make it more open.[70] Francis Bacon's essay *On Innovation* (1623), another bestseller,[71] encapsulated the new spirit thus:

> if time stood still; which contrariwise moveth so round, that a forward (meaning perverse) retention of custom, is as turbulent a thing as an innovation; and they that reverence too much old times, are but a scorn to the new. It were good, therefore, that men in their innovations would follow the example of time itself; which indeed innovateth greatly, but quietly, by degrees scarce to be perceived.

Research on the hyperinflation or *Kipper und Wipper Inflation* in the 1620s and the subsequent 'smaller' or second Kipper inflation of the 1680s has shown how perceptions in the public discourse also changed. While authors during the 1620s often tended to attribute causation to the wrath of God, in the later *Kipperzeit* they increasingly recurred to monetarist explanations of inflation. This matches with a gradual decline in chiliasm during that time,[72] and a more pronounced use of history to predict an unknown future by looking for parallels not providence.[73]

New literary genres emerged on the scene, including newspapers or the empty-page calendar, a personal diary with blank pages for future events – a key indication that people viewed their futures as open and contingent. The second half of the 17th century saw a blossoming not only of such printed empty calendars but also of almanacs, newspapers, gazetteers and other genres reporting events considered worthy of interest, such as wars, military campaigns, plague and other strange happenings, on a more or less yearly basis. Attention was increasingly drawn to *living* persons and open-ended events, especially events that *actually did happen*, rather than picking on things that *ought to* or *should have* happened. Possibly this reflected a more modern concept of linear-discrete time (but as we have seen, 'linear' time is no marker of modernity). Periodicals began to appear, regularly reporting about current events, for an emerging mass market and public sphere.[74] We find them in the shape of the *Relation aller Fuernemmen und gedenckwuerdigen Historien*, one of the earliest periodicals or newspapers that appeared weekly in Strasbourg from 1605; or in the Brunswick *Aviso, Relation oder Zeitung* (1609), later on the *Hildesheimer Zeitung* – the oldest newspaper that still exists to the present day. An initial attempt by the Augsburg citizen Samuel Dilbaum of the so-called *Rorschacher Monatsschrift* launched in 1597 had proved abortive. In 1618, the first example outside Germany can be found in the Netherlands. Whether this development was 'German' is a moot point, but one aspect that certainly helped promote this was the Thirty Years War – after Luther's Reformation the other great 'publicity event' (*Medienereignis*) of the early modern age, captured in thousands of pamphlets and prints intended for an increasingly public sphere. By the 1630s there were more than 30 weekly newspapers in the Holy Roman Empire alone.[75]

A genre had thus developed that grouped together news and information relating to actors, events and developments that were initially completely unconnected. New ways were devised to knit together threads of events and multiple times in a spatially and socially synchronized chronology. Previously information relating to a specific purpose had been distributed through distinct and exclusive channels, across specific and very limited networks of actors. Merchants acted as emissaries and ambassadors to rulers and courts at those foreign places with which they had business, thus mingling their economic or commercial interests with a decidedly political role. Larger companies – such as the giant firm of the Fugger family of Augsburg – by the 1570s operated their own networks of communication and news management using handwritten business newsletters (*Fuggerzeitungen*). These were primarily meant to stay *within* the firm, processing information reserved exclusively to members, partners, associates and other agents *of* the firm (but according to a recent reinterpretation, information contained therein may also have served diplomatic purposes, and would have been widely shared, even 'sold' to political agents).[76] By the 1600s, however, general-purpose news and information was now increasingly collected for its own sake and for distribution and sale across wider public audiences. A wider and more open-access *market* for news had emerged. While earlier in the 17th century newspapers had focused on wars and politics, some of the new types of enlightenment periodicals, such as the *Intelligenzblätter*, focused on the more basic themes in *oeconomy*, especially useful methods in husbandry, or second-hand sales of household items, rather than the big-bang campaigns or possibilities of Armageddon. The Second Coming receded as the only viable canvas against which future spaces could be painted. People began to understand the material world more and more as a space of contingency, in which catastrophes – such as war, coin debasement, inflation and other Horsemen of the Apocalypse could strike out of the blue, but were human-made, not God-made – meaning they could potentially be *managed*.[77]

These developments have been summarized by two leading cultural historians as the 'birth of the *present*' (Landwehr) or discovery of the *future* (Hölscher).[78] They gradually gave rise to a reconceptualization of economy and economic attitudes towards the future. The idea that the world could and – this is the crucial second step – *ought to be* changed gradually began to gain ground. With this came new semantics and a new economic mind map after *c.*1600 which fundamentally altered the epistemic basis of economic analysis.

Modelling the oeconomic future and early modern capitalism

Early modern political economy often hinged on *order*, and we need to understand the close connection between notions of order and conservation, and notions of dynamics (which prima facie seem opposites). Cameralist economic anthropology built upon the idea of *Homo imperfectabilis*,[79] torn between her passions, innate fallacies and personal interests and the urge to altruistically promote the common good. Contrary to the British case, where monarchy was never absolute and feudalism had vanished since the early 1600s, the market process on the continent started with the Prince. Only a strong absolute ruler would create the free market, because only a strong and politically and fiscally independent ruler could curb rent-seeking by private individuals and the nobility, and thus lift the prerogative veil that aristocratic rights and privileges, so-called private 'freedoms' and exceptions and jurisdictions, laid over the workings of the market process. When continental voices called for 'order' they therefore did not mean this in a static sense, but in an ordered process of dynamic forward-facing development that lowered barriers to market access, reduced chances of usury, asymmetry in exchange and rent-seeking, creating a capitalist framework of exchange. Joachim Georg Darjes, who made his name more as a philosopher than professor of cameralism, but whose textbooks in natural law and philosophy (*Institutiones iurisprudentiae universalis*) were read, taught and republished in places as far away as Copenhagen in the 1764s,[80] was known for his stubborn belief in the cultural progress of humankind, in society as an organism of rational individuals. But the smoothest way to Public Happiness – the cameralist societal state of bliss – was not through possessive individualism, but community (the state). Every person, as an individual was a tool in the state-promoted process of maximizing common welfare and happiness. This *Homo* was, in Darjes's word, 'industrieuse'. The vision of material oeconomy was progressive, expansive and dynamic.[81] But progress had, by definition, to be built on order.

It had been since much earlier times. Georg von Obrecht (1547–1612), one of the so-called 'older' cameralists,[82] was a professor of law at the Strasbourg Academy. In his *Discursus Bellico-politicus* (1604) Obrecht discussed the virtues of manufacturing and value-added that should be captured by domestic processing rather than exporting raw materials .[83] With reference to Jean Bodin, Obrecht adopted a mercantilist-cameralist trope on cities, manufacturing, economies of scale and adding value popularized by many authors in the 17th, 18th and 19th centuries, from Antonio Serra (*Breve Trattato*, 1613), Veit Ludwig von Seckendorff (*Additiones* to the *Teutscher Fürsten Stat*, 1655/1664) to Friedrich List (*Das nationale System der Politischen Ökonomie*), Daniel Raymond or Alexander Hamilton.[84] In his *Politisch Bedencken*, first published in 1617, Obrecht developed a characteristic early modern conception of the fiscal-military state with a 'German' imprint. The survival of the state or body politic (*in corpore civili*) – which could be a 'republic', principality, duchy or large city (*Fürstenthumb / Graffschafft / Herrschafft / vnd in fuernemen Staetten*) – depended on a well-functioning capitalist economy (*Geld vnd Gut die nervi, und instrumenta, ohne welche kein Respublica, angericht / gebessert / vnd so wol zu Friedens Zeit / als in Kriegs Emporungen / vnnd anderen hochbetrangten Zustaenden / erhalten werden kann*).[85] The prince, regent or king should do everything in his power to keep the common weal healthy, and goods, money and services circulating. Duties, taxes and imposts should be modest and limited, wherever possible, to non-essentials. We will study the conceptual ramifications and implications of circulation further in Chapter 6.

The language used by Obrecht and others at the time was still couched in conservative terms, focusing on what early modern and modern German language knows as *erhalten*, literally 'to conserve' or 'preserve'. But far from being static, conservativist language was deployed to sketch models that were inherently dynamic. Often authors would choose a distant past as an ideal for best practice or how things should be. Since the Reformation, Luther and other revolutionaries had applied the concept of *re-form*, that is, the return to an imputed ancient state of good order, as a persuasive device to implement what others may consider revolutionary, that is, an overturning of the current politico-economic status quo. Such ancient states of true or just order probably never existed. Everyone knew they never had. *Re-volution* on the other hand meant the divergence from an initial state of being, followed by subsequent *re-turn* to the initial state, that is, full circle (which no one wanted). During the German and Austrian Peasant Wars 1524–26, such conservativist rhetoric was used by reform blueprints including Michael Gaismair's Tyrolean *Landesordnung* (1526). These visions were revolutionary precisely because Gaismair and contemporaries reclaimed an ancient state of being; a state that had never been.[86] The present and the future were presented as fields of action and spaces of possibilities; worlds that could be bettered by reference to a better past and conscious choice or management ensuring that such states could be reached again.

Another semantic trick of building a collective open future was to deploy an 'if–then' rhetoric. Terms such as 'adventure', 'propose', 'scheme' and, of course, 'projector' entered the economic lexicon, denoting a fundamental reconceptualization of past, present and future. The 1752 *Proposals for carrying on certain Public Works in the City of Edinburgh* by the Convention of Royal Burghs in Scotland identified 'Private men, who adventure to propose schemes for the public good, are *no longer* ridiculed as vain projectors' (emphasis added).[87] The scheme went on to suggest, among other things, erecting a merchants' exchange or bourse following the London (1566) example, a representative building for housing the legal and historical records of the nation, as well as a new town for new moneyed men. *If* such a new quarter was built, *this would* also increase the number of the lesser ranks living in the cramped quarters of Edinburgh's Old Town. It would promote commerce and advance the commercial spirit, as well as 'consumption … and a more rapid circulation of money and other commodities, the great spring which gives motion to general industry and improvement'.[88] We will return to the issue of circulation in Chapter 6. Reflecting the *lamentos* of an industrially underdeveloped nation, Scottish political economy of the 1730s often worked along similar if–then mechanisms ('if we do this, then our linen industry will be bound to flourish', and so on).[89] Such language of conditionality can also be identified as a cornerstone of 18th-century German cameralism.[90] 'Industry' at that time usually still referred to 'industriousness' more than manufacturing. But it began to gradually incorporate, and soon to fully adapt, notions of manufacturing in workhouses or factories, which added another dynamic, as manufacturing and manufactories were widely understood to be a dynamic tool for economic development, which we will revisit in Chapter 8. Johann Joachim Becher (1635–82) – physicist, mercantilist and alchemist – became famous for his ambitious project of setting up an East India Company for the Counts of Hanau, some third- or fourth-rank princes in the Holy Roman Empire.[91] As illusionary perhaps was the Scottish West Indian company project at Darien, yet begotten in the same spirit, with the same optimism and future prospectivism, crushed by the English Navy in 1698 shortly before the parliaments of the two nations finally agreed to merge kingdoms in 1707.[92] Debates about the Anglo–Scottish Union of the Kingdoms in 1706 had, in the years preceding the final Act and Treaty as of 1 May 1707, seen vivid depictions of multiple possible futures along the if–then line of argumentation.[93] They represent important new linguistic strategies of projecting an open human-economic future.

This new economic grammar and syntax established a powerful claim to the human future. It comes across beautifully in a pamphlet written by Sir John Clerk, one of the main negotiators of the Anglo–Scottish Treaty of Union, 1706–07.[94] Among other things, Clerk highlighted the virtues of a customs union with the Auld Enemy, as a result of which Scots would become required to bury their dead in woollens, as was common practice in England; rather than using linens, as they had for ages in Scotland. Yes, furnishing the dead according to the English fashion would potentially damage Scotland's stock-in-trade industry, Clerk argued, and thus jeopardize the wealth of the Scottish nation. But a new export market would arise in the English and soon-to-be British West Indies instead. The subsequent history of the Anglo–Scottish Union and Scottish trade proved Clerk right. Clerk called the Union a 'Project that will abide the Test of our Posterity'.[95] Other such projects included land bank schemes – essentially money creation backed by some stock of landed assets, as well as the first national bank schemes. For Scotland, there was the 1706 proposal to set up a national bank to coin half the nation's stock of silver plate and add, to the new coins, as much copper and base metal as commensurate to the task of preventing the outflow of money. The outlines of this proposal included the important clause: 'and for the future to prevent the exorbitant Sums of Species which are yearly carried out, without any hopes of ever returning'.[96] There thus had emerged a fundamentally changed conception of time as an open-ended flow of events; of risk and chance entering the human equation and, most importantly, the new vision of the *future as a manageable entity*.

How did political *oeconomy* fit the bill? By the 1750s it was perfectly normal for cameralists to argue, as Darjes,[97] did in his main work *Erste Gründe der Cameral-Wissenschaften* (1756):

> The main aim of Policey Science is to teach us, how a state [polity] should be furnished, whose inhabitants were not only to preserve their yearly income, but in fact make them reasonably *grow*. ... The Policey science has wealth as its main aim, to avoid poverty and increase people's well-being.[98]

This definition extended models proposed in Berch's or Justi's works, which had employed a concept of eudaimonia or Public Happiness (*Glückseligkeit*) to prove the ruler's duty to promote Public Happiness. *Glückseligkeit* included, alongside good church service on Sundays, a well-governed Christian common weal, decent incomes and possibilities of employment, a flourishing system of goods and monetary circulation, low levels of interest, a positive trade balance and a proactive state supporting manufacturing as a source of economic dynamics.

Johann Christoph Christian Rüdiger (*Ueber die systematische Theorie der Cameralwissenschaften*, 1777) emphasized cameralism's potential to empower people and effect 'change to the benefit of all humankind'.[99] Since Seckendorff's *Princely State* (1655) cameralist texts abounded with concepts of increase and growth (*Wachstum*), but still embedded within more traditional linguistic framings. Seckendorff's preface to the *Fürsten Stat* (1656 edn) gives away the epistemological and methodological rationale of cameralism:

> Der Allmächtige GOTT / der beherrscher des erdbodens / und oberster regent aller hohen häupter und obrigkeiten / wolle mit seiner göttlichen Gnade ihme das Höchste Haupt / und die fürtrefflichen Glieder unseres Teutschen Vaterlandes / befohlen seyn lassen sie zu immerwährendem kräfftigen *Wachsthum* in erwünschter Zusammenstimmung erhalten. [My emphasis]
>
> [GOD the Almighty, ruler of the earth and supreme king of all kings, may come with his grace upon our German fatherland and its limbs – meaning the individual rulers and territories – and incense them to perennial growth in the desired harmonious order.]

Of course, the translation of *Wachsthum* here is crucial; 'growth' still referred to 'flourishing', in a sense of a tree or living plant that grows and springs anew year after year. Seckendorff would be taught and read and re-edited hundred years later still; his *Fürsten Stat* has made it into a list of pre-1850 economic bestsellers.[100] In the 1737 edition by Andreas Simson von Biechling the preface specified that the supreme goal of state was to promote 'harmony, happiness, true wealth and welfare' of the population.[101] Improvement (*Verbesserung*) had become exposed more clearly, with 'growth' now specified in the cameralist vocabulary through chances of betterment and innovation – of production processes and techniques, such as porcelain making and the right chemistry and technological improvement in industrial processes (Schumpeterian growth). Johann Joachim Becher regularly deployed terms including *Auffnehmen* or *increase* (in contrast to *Abnehmen* or *decrease*), of the populace and its *Nahrung* (subsistence) and *Handl und Wandl*, trade and commerce, but in a dynamic meaning: economic activity in motion, a circular-dynamic process, but growing in sum.[102] More research is needed on the cameralist lexicon of economic development; it may help shape a more nuanced intellectual genealogy of the European capitalist mindset.

Cameralist visions of growth also included an increasingly nuanced conception of velocity. These will be considered more fully, and placed within longer timelines of thought, in Chapter 6. Cameralists thus conceptualized a dynamic world marked by an increase in economic speed and social dynamics. It could even make the hormones spin: Ludwig von Hess (*Freymüthige Gedanken*, 1775) emphasized the virtues of extramarital sex, condemned under the traditional moral values of the Christian faith. If adultery served the need to canalize hormone overshoot and help increase the economically active population, so be it, Hess concluded. (We may speculate how much of this came from Hess's hormones running amok.) But still: risk-taking, forecasting and rational calculation of chances and risk were important epistemic paradigms on the Cameralists' mind.[103]

Curiously, a superficial reading of cameralist (and occasionally mercantilist) political economy has often suggested exactly the opposite. Cameralists have been described as advocates of social conservatism and economic stasis. Terms such as the ubiquitous and emblematic *Ordnung* (variously translating as order, arrangement, ordinance, classification), or *Stand* (social status, estate, rank), cornerstones of cameralist linguistics, are words which in English and modern German ears ('order') probably sound more conservative than initially meant to be. There is what one economist has once called the 'Goethe barrier' in German economic discourse:[104] before Goethe reshaped the German language, lyrics and poetry, most economic texts of the Baroque genre sound awkward and are occasionally difficult to read.

Words are important. Just because German economic language before the mid-18th century rarely used future in the substantive to denote the modern sense of term, we should not mistake this linguistic gap for a static vision of economy and society. Dynamics were captured in other ways, for instance through phrases such as *Auffnehmen* (literally meaning 'to begin' or 'to commence', or 'increase', as well as 'adopt' or 'lift something up') and *verbessern* (literally: 'improvement'). They were often framed within a larger context of 'order' (*Ordnung*). *Ordnung* could have many semantic dimensions, including market and monetary regulation, as in *Münzordnung* (coin ordinance, monetary regulation) or *Marcktordnung* (market ordinance or market regulation), genres we will take a closer look at in Chapters 4 and 5.

In late 16th- and early 17th-century Germany, there had been hefty debates about the tension between Christian morality, the common weal and self-interest and how these could be reconciled transforming the human future landscape. Leonhard Fronsperger's (1564) book on self-interest *On the Virtues of Self-Interest* (*Vom Lob deß Eigen Nutzens*) encapsuled a late Renaissance view which saw the two as complementary rather than mutually exclusive. In his *Politisch Bedencken vnd Discurs* (1617 edn), quoting the usual range of learned sources from Jean Bodin to Giovanni Botero, one of the 'early' cameralists, Georg von Obrecht concluded that regents and kings should promote 'seafaring and seaborne commerce', and lend out money from the princely treasure chests to enterprising merchants at favourable rates of interest (no more than 5 per cent per annum) and thus stimulate economic life.[105] Such visions of state and market process were dynamic not static. They were forward-facing and carried a future-prospective element that became characteristic of later, mainly post-1648 cameralist writings.

In the *Additiones* (1664 edn) to his *Princely State* (1655) Veit Ludwig von Seckendorff – the 'Adam Smith of Cameralism' (Albion Small) – formulated a set of rules or principles similar to those later suggested by Philipp Wilhelm von Hörnigk (1640–1714). Wilhelm von Schröder, in a phrasing also used by Hörnigk in *Austria Supreme if Only It So Wills* (1684), discussed how nations could become great by manufacturing, 'if only they wish' (*Fürstliche Schatz- und Rentkammer*, Ch. 87). This 'if only' was precisely the rhetorical device denoting future dynamics as a possibility, contingent upon deliberate and independent rational choices made in the here and now. Alongside silver and gold mines, as well as methods of smelting, manufactures were among the principal ways of making a nation rich, Schröder argued. A first principle was (Ch. 87) that manufacturing added value to unprocessed or raw materials, transforming, improving and embodying useful knowledge and work, giving rise to industry and employment. Florence, Venice, Naples, Valencia and Holland were named as historical examples of such dynamics; referring to the Brothers de la Court and their important book on *Interest van Holland* (1662).[106] A prince should take care to promote manufacturing growth (Chs 88, 89 and 90) using careful planning and wisely designed policies of industrial policy and import substitution. 'Be sober and watch out because your French adversaries go around like roaring lions, searching for ways of devouring the German lands', Schröder continued, very close to the phrasing of Becher and Hörnigk.[107] Germany lacked neither material nor people to surpass Holland, England and Italy, 'if only it so wills'. Alongside the conditional phrasing 'if only (it so wills)', and on top of evoking the distant past as a frame of comparison and opportunity to conceptually delineate 'future', rivalry[108] with superior trading nations represented a third discursive strategy of reframing the economic future(s) of the nation. As Hörnigk noted in the preface to his bestseller *Austria Supreme if Only It So Wills*, knowing about good principles was one thing; translating them into practice was another. There was every reason to believe that people had not yet chosen the right path. But Hörnigk provided them with a model of future dynamics.[109] He cited the negative example of the Holy Roman Empire which lost specie in return for French imports and thus got impoverished by the day. Hörnigk then formulated his iconic 'nine rules of economic development', a grammar of how to make a nation rich in the future through means of careful management, import substitution and industrial policy which we will examine more closely in Chapters 7 and 8. These rules were 'no invention of a speculative mind', but, as Hörnigk admitted in the very first paragraph (my italics):

> I have taken it upon myself to prove that *Austria could be supreme if it only so wished*. … And, according to another right of all men, I want these words to contain a promise, hence a harbinger. … The *supremacy* on

which the whole question turns *I place on a surplus of human requisites and comforts*, in real goods, gold and silver, *a surplus independent of other nations, whether actual in the present or even a possibility*. … And God willing, if Austria would so easily allow its natural gifts and advantages to be infused with the will to their proper benefit, it will be easily and manifestly proved that its salvation and elevation truly uniquely and alone, after God, rests in its own hands.

This was essentially a dynamic vision of economic development as an entirely open-ended process. The invocation of God was a rhetorical device, conceptualizing what the German oeconomic language had, as yet, no exact word for in the substantive: *Zukunft* or 'the future'. The later 17th century also saw the birth hour of economic statistics and national 'income' accounting, even if what was counted was still, essentially, uncountable and did not yet correspond to the units used in 20th-century national income accounting.[110] The post-1600 period represents a remarkable time in the history of economic reasoning. There was an explosion of economic writings comprising different genres as late scholastic economics, *Hausväter-* or *oikonomics (œconomy)* literature, but especially the new genres of mercantilist and cameralist economics.[111] The older demesne management or household management literature (*oikonomics* or *œconomy*) known by its German name as *Hausväterliteratur* blossomed in many European countries, including Germany, England and Sweden but became reconfigured and gradually merged into political (o)economy.[112] While initially drawing upon a classical economic Greek tradition,[113] it was now subjected to important reformulations: drawing on balance sheets and accounts, and the quantification of input and output data for production processes, introducing rationality – and future plannability and manageability.

Schreber's 'working for posterity' had begun to take visible shape, supported by the territorial states which likewise began to shape up more visibly, using a variety of policies and strategies that built upon the dynamic human future thus 'discovered'. Many continued to rest upon age-old templates of oeconomic governance, however, that had been developed centuries before. Again this underlines the problem of temporality in capitalism (and the anachronisms inherent in economic development as a practical problem faced by those concerned, either as politicians and administrators entrusted with making development a possibility, or the common people facing options that belong both to the present and the past, occasionally leading to irreconcilable conflicts and paradoxes). The next chapter will discuss some of these deeper histories of European economic governance from the Middle Ages to the onset of industrial capitalism.

3

The Myth of the Myopic State: Governing Economy and the Politics of Economic Change, 1250s–1850s

Prologue: Potatoes, stewardship and kings

Let's begin with a picture (see Figure 3.1).

This is Frederick 'the Great' of Prussia (b 1712, r 1740–86); a king on the road, massively admired during his lifetime (and beyond), in Prussia (and abroad). The painting, albeit not nearly contemporaneous, epitomizes what kingship meant within an early modern political-economic context. Kings were considered, for good and bad, 'fatherly managers' of their countries, conceptualized initially as extended kingly households. As 'the father of his fatherly duty is bound to care for the nourishing, education and vertuous government of his children: even so is the King bound to care for all his subjects', claimed James VI and I of Scotland and England in *The true lavv of free monarchy*, a programmatic pamphlet written in the tradition of early absolutism and the divine right of kings.[1] In the present case the king (Frederick) travels across the dispersed Prussian provinces, with only a small entourage,[2] in his likewise proverbial uniform of a common soldier, eagerly enquiring about his subjects' methods of production. We are obviously talking potatoes; essential for rescuing 18th-century Prussia from the Malthusian trap. This was a not uncommon trope. Across early modern Europe and Asia, emperors were often depicted behind ploughs; in the Chinese case this developed into a full political ritual.[3] During the Middle Ages and early modernity kings and rulers were conceptualized in the political literature as supreme 'oeconomists': as managers or *stewards* of their nations' wealth; merchants occasionally became described in similar terms, as in Thomas Mun's classic *England's Treasure by Foreign Trade* (1620/60).[4] The conceptual

Figure 3.1: *Der König überall* (*The King Everywhere*), Robert Müller (aka 'Warthmüller') (1886)

analogy was deliberate and intended, signifying an increasingly entangled evolution of politics and capital, something also noted in Marx, *Capital* and modern historians' narratives of 'fiscal-military states'.[5] Historically levels of economic wealth seem to have correlated with fiscal capacity, which in turn can be taken as a proxy measure of state capacity.[6] During the early modern age, Prussian state capacity and per capita incomes lagged behind, especially when compared to Sweden or England.[7] Rulers like Frederick tried all they could to be portrayed as omnipresent and omnipotent but were in fact neither.[8] In the Holy Roman Empire especially, political powers were decentralized, fuzzy and fragmented. The nobility with their exaction of feudal levies and other rents including compulsory labour services directly infringed upon peasants' productive capabilities *and* thus state capacity: rulers had a comparative advantage but no monopoly on violence and social power.[9] Literally anything not regulated under statutory law could be considered unregulated; even post-1648 'absolutist' states remained paper tigers.[10] This left, potentially, a lot of room for laissez-faire, but not necessarily in a good sense.

But what matters more is the *oeconomic* message behind the image. As we will see in this and subsequent chapters, there were certain areas where cameralist or *oeconomic* states could and did make a notably positive difference, if policies were chosen well. The idea of a benevolent-proactive ruler as their country's *oeconomus* or steward still stands in the modern German technical term *Volkswirtschaft* that variously translates as 'economy', 'the economy' and, by extension, 'economics' (depending on context). Initially based on classical and then Biblical ideas of management and stewardship of the heavenly treasure,[11] in early modern Europe stewardship became reframed in the *Hausväter* or oeconomy literary tradition: texts that told people how to lead a good life by diligently and prudently managing a large agrarian estate or demesne (or agribusiness in modern terms); often with reference to Aristotle and Xenophon, whose writings continued to enjoy popularity as early modern economic bestsellers.[12] But gradually 'stewardship' became reconceptualized, coming to comprise territories and economic management. Works and genres written in a cameralist fashion now included statistics, *Staatsklugheit* – an ill-translatable term approximating something like 'prudent governance and politics', Natural Law and *Staatenkunde* – likewise difficult to render in English; perhaps 'political geography' would be the best way of rendering this *terminus technicus* to an Anglo-phone audience – and increasingly macro models of economy, while keeping extended chapters on the more traditional matters of *oeconomy*, discussing everything from managing plants, gardening and manure up to how to keep ducks, pigs and geese. But far from being limited to the notion of thriftiness, economizing and enlarging the bounties awarded by Mother Nature,[13] an idea emerged of *managing the economy*, now with a definite article (*the*) and an ever-closely circumscribed territorial frame of competitive market-based exchange. After 1800, cameralism – in Schumpeter's timeless words 'laissez-faire with the nonsense taken out' – became reconfigured as 'national' economics, or *Volkswirtschaftslehre*, morphing into its modern conceptualization of (macro) 'economics'.[14]

To be sure, not all rulers lived up to such lofty claims as these. They waged war, and occasionally debased currencies, defaulted on state loans, or turned out to be 'borrowers from hell'.[15] This assessment represents common currency in modern interpretations of preindustrial economic statecraft; another one goes that states hardly made an impact on economic life at all (because they either couldn't, or wouldn't); this will be given some consideration later. A third interpretation would follow Foucault's views on governmentality and biopolitics and study early modern discourses and practices of economic governance as manifestations of emerging absolutist states trying to become omnipresent and omnipotent; with rulers and ruling classes attempting to control, domineer and exploit their subalterns.[16] As we will see later in this chapter, and in Chapter 4 (where I more specifically engage with Foucauldian musings), neither of these narratives matches particularly well with the historical evidence, often mistaking exceptional and grotesquely exaggerated Machiavellian features of premodern economic statesmanship for their historical norm templates. In this chapter I will consider strategies and *ideas* of economic statecraft as they unfolded under their given parameters and political and cultural institutions of their time, sketching the potential room of possibilities open to states managing the economic common weal. These were much more comprehensive and potentially benevolent than the modern historical political economy literature usually allows. Subsequent chapters on markets (Chapter 4), money (Chapter 5) and manufacturing matters (Chapter 7) will further zoom in on specific examples of historical market design and monetary management, primarily through the lens of ideas. Chapter 6 will return to concepts (akin to Chapter 2), while Chapter 8 will lean more towards actual policies. Far from being principally predatory and bellicose, late medieval and early modern economic statecraft could be actually quite dynamic and proactive in governing economy in peaceful ways.

In this way the chapter addresses some of the bigger historical questions: about tensions between markets, morality and states,[17] or historical state capacity and origins of good government,[18] state formation,[19] military revolutions[20] and fiscal-military states;[21] or the rise of 'effective states'.[22] What constitutes good government?[23] Scholars have questioned that before industrialization states even *could*, let alone *should* have played a proactive role in the economic process altogether. Following a common misinterpretation of Smith's *Wealth of Nations*, some would consider states' primary functions to simply provide basic regulatory frameworks and property rights security, within which market activity should be left more or less to itself (aka 'nightwatchmen states').[24] This goes against the available evidence on both the history *and* historical theories of economic statecraft.[25] Other recent interpretations imply that early modern economic policy could be reduced to a second-order spin-off of fiscal policy; within a conceptual framework focusing on how *effective* states emerged that could raise public finance through providing the right economic and political institutions (aka good conditions for business) in return for more taxes or low rates on public debt, or both.[26]

While all these models certainly have their merits, the premodern states that emerge from this record appear decidedly myopic.

Benevolent or bellicose states

Following Tilly's (in)famous pun that 'states made war and war made states' a literature has emerged that has come to interpret historical statecraft in the light of the tension field between hapless monarchs poised against helpless subjects spending most of their economic lives desperately trying to escape the predatory state.[27] 'War was the main preoccupation of medieval and early modern European states' according to a most recent synopsis.[28] Others argue that:

> Rulers in early modern (1500–1800) Europe built state capacity in the pursuit of state power and victory in war. Prosperity and economic

development were largely means to this end; they did not anticipate the possibility of modern economic growth. Many of their policies were destructive in the short-run. Contrary to the claims of heterodox development economists … there are few clear-cut examples of successful state-led 'industrial policy' in this period.[29]

'The tasks of government were minimal', writes a widely-acknowledged historian of early modern Europe, 'to maintain the proper relationship between elites (that is, to secure order and protect property), and to defend the commonweal'.[30] Another fashionable fable holds that 'Historically, rulers sought to achieve many goals: raising tax revenue, conquering territory, basking in their own glory, providing protection to their subjects, and giving favours to their constituents'.[31] Translated into trade language by a leading scholar, 'Attempts by predatory nations to plunder and tax richer and more successful economies were common and constituted negative-sum games that reversed previous episodes of expansion. Internally the greatest threat was rent-seeking by local rulers and elites, through confiscatory taxes, expropriating wealth, the sale of monopolies and repudiating debts'.[32] This reading has made it into stylized comparative global histories of economic change, where a Western or European model of governance is often reduced to aggressive warmongering but otherwise hands-off nightwatchmen states that were laissez-faire simply because they couldn't be otherwise (because bureaucracies were small and states' grip on their denizens comparatively light), and kings' main concern being constant competition with their native elites for dynastic survival.[33] Niccolò Machiavelli is occasionally invoked as vouching for this interpretation: 'A prince should therefore have no other aim or thought, nor take up any other thing for his study, but war'.[34]

But there is a rich record of preindustrial practices and thought – we can say the mainstream – that points in exactly the opposite direction. As Walser Smith has recently noted, the Pinker thesis of a secular decline of violence does not hold, in particular for the German-speaking countries (one of those European regions most severely ravaged by the Thirty Years War): in the early modern age, peace years far outnumbered those marked by violent conflict.[35] True, wars and violence were endemic in preindustrial Europe (as they were elsewhere), and without doubt a connection existed between the rise of the fiscal-military state, bureaucracy, war and modern capitalism. But neither in terms of scale nor scope does premodern warfare even come close to the level of violence inflicted by 20th-century industrialized warfare;[36] especially from a politico-economic viewpoint, Tilly's Theorem is simply wrong. In 1718 German cameralist Bernhard Julius von Rohr (*Einleitung zur Staats-Klugheit* / Principles of Politics), in a work conceived in the mirrors for princes (*Fürstenspiegel*) tradition, explicitly adhorted his readers that 'all measures taken to improve the state must strictly remain in line with the commands of the right and reasonable *lest they smack of Machiavellianism*' (my emphasis).[37] This echoed countless earlier writings sporting a strictly anti-Machiavellian thrust when conceptualizing economic statecraft. Machiavelli's book was a strange work on many counts;[38] possibly a satire, but definitely an anti-*Fürstenspiegel*, a template exactly on how *not* to do it. Since the Middle Ages, political economy had framed good governance through the benchmark of how subjects' happiness could be *raised* by *avoiding* war *and* overtaxation; through peaceful means, or in other words: economic development.[39] Cicero, a classical writer often invoked in Renaissance and Enlightenment political theory, had outlined this in Book I of *De Officiis*. The state ought to take 'care for the good of the whole citizen body to such a degree that, in everything they do, they devote themselves solely to that end'.[40] Allegories of good versus bad government included the frontispiece to the 1718 edition of Wilhelm von Schröder's *Fürstliche Schatz- und Renkammer* (original published in 1684), one of the pre-1850 German language economic bestsellers: good rulers *sheared* their sheep or taxpaying subjects; bad rulers *fleeced* (that is, skinned) them.[41]

Medieval and Renaissance states were proactive far beyond establishing the minimal base frame of good government of not fleecing their sheep.[42] In 1439 the rulers of Siena declared that given the sheer wealth generated from the industry that it were an 'honorable and very useful thing to ensure that the said silk manufacturing grows and increases as much as possible'.[43] Other Italian cities and states at the time including the Duchy of Tuscany, Milan, Florence applied a classical mercantilist-cameralist template of industrial policies, including tax breaks on vital raw material imports and other privileges, import prohibitions on competing manufactures, and encouraging knowledge and technology transfer. True, in the case of Genoa and Lucca this still included extreme measures such as bounties on killing skilled industrial fugitives.[44] From a deep-historical point of view, industrial policy, 'entrepreneurial' and 'developmental states' represent very old hats.[45] Since the Renaissance political economy provided increasingly refined models of economic governance aimed at keeping a fair balance between generating revenue and simultaneously keeping citizens well, happy and flourishing; in those cases where such policies could be implemented, outcomes were often measurably positive.[46]

Nevertheless modern scholarship has often chosen to define the key remits of economic intervention through trigger-happy warmongering rulers careful not to default, to pay back their debts and not confiscate their denizens' private property.[47] It is unclear where the idea comes from (apart from Tilly's intuition), because even evidence of states regularly going bankrupt or habitually confiscating their denizens' property is hard to come by for early modern Europe.[48] But limiting the role of the state to the provision of public goods and a baseline of inclusive institutions necessary for business to flourish and capitalism to flow smoothly is similarly reductionist: this was the main vantage point of economic policy neither in today's nor past societies.[49]

Thus let us take a look at the oeconomic morphology of preindustrial states, to get a more accurate picture of their possibilities and limitations.

Princes, mirrors and happiness: oeconomies of statecraft from the Renaissance to the Industrial Revolution

There are many problems with using modernisms and abstractions such as 'state' or 'economy', neither of which exist in a tangible form, but are embodied in their respective political and economic actors (politicians, business people, bureaucrats), their networks of power and systems of meaning, giving rise to distinct policies; ways of classifying social reality and gathering information about it, for instance by means of statistics. Moreover, the state may not be the only or even best-suited institution to do economic policy; as Walter Eucken, grand doyen in post-war German neoliberalism noted in his classic textbook on economic policy, there were three principal 'powers' (*Potenzen*) or sources of economic order: the state, the arts and sciences, and the Church. Below these one could imagine subsidiary layers, such as commercial and professional associations, trade unions, chambers of commerce and so on, upon whom the state could devolve certain matters of policy and regulation.[50] And both 'state' as well as 'economy' underwent considerable conceptual modifications as we walk across deep-historical time.[51] In medieval times 'state' usually equalled 'ruler': a king, a prince or a noble who, by virtue of the feudal pyramid held some prerogative powers of potentially unlimited but factually quite closely circumscribed rights over people and land, the most important production factor in the medieval and early modern economy. In the Middle Ages kings were conceptualized as supreme judges. During the early modern age more and more abstract concepts of state emerged: of states that became increasingly fiscal and military, territorially circumscribed, sporting ever-more complex bureaucracies, a comparative advantage on violence, legislation, executive and jurisdiction; in those cases where they did not manage they are occasionally classified as failures.[52] Modern concepts of state capacity and statecraft, especially when applied to medieval and early modern European polities, only go a short way, however, as not even the most modern polities of their age (say, post-1688 England or the Netherlands) even came close to state modernity as defined through a modern social sciences lens. Looking for evidence of states becoming increasingly democratic, parliamentary, centralized or transparent, where no concepts of democracy, parliament, centralized administration nor transparency in the modern sense existed represents dangerous fallacies known as presentism, anachronism and teleology, or tracing Hegel's *Weltgeist* upon horseback across deep-historical time. Similarly with political economy and 'the economy' as a tool to study and promote the wealth of nations. As a self-contained sphere of human interaction that could be modelled following its own working laws, and tapped (taxed) as a source of wealth, as a concept 'the economy' gradually began to emerge during the 17th and 18th centuries, when models of *oeconomy* shifted toward a more 'macro-scopic' outlook now increasingly comprising 'modern' economic variables such as prices and wages.[53]

Economic governance, especially in the case of the German-speaking lands, faced numerous problems on the ground; most pressing perhaps was the issue of territorial fragmentation and problematic modes of agrarian production. Medieval and early modern German agriculture knew hundreds of different patterns and regional variations ranging from serfdom and demesne economy (*Gutsherrschaft*) to *Rentengrundherrschaft* and other forms of commercial, tenant or free farming; states had very little grip on the countryside. There the nobility usually owned the major factor of production (land) which also entailed important executive and judicative prerogatives which the modern view usually associates with the state. As the early modern period wore on states took more and more competencies in influencing economy and citizen's economic lives. Economic governance focused on cities and towns that often retained some form of semi-autonomy or self-governance (and imperial cities were politically autonomous by definition);[54] on the countryside communal models of mutual obligation and self-governance prevailed.[55] Cities tried to control production, economic circulation and allocation in their surrounding hinterlands, often in the way that later states would.[56] Taxes (and thus data on economic activity) were still predominantly generated within cities and towns. Cities represented the vantage point of political economy; they were the points where cross-border traffic was monitored, recorded, documented and taxed.[57] In the wake of the Thirty Years War (1618–48) rulers became, on paper at least, more and more absolute; the 18th century saw the rise of 'enlightened despotism', with a theoretically benevolent ruler on top, and a branched-out and increasingly complex administration directly interfering with denizen's economic lives, promoting industry, commerce and agriculture and a general sense of improvement. Even here the reach of monarchical state power remained limited, and urban corporations such as artisan and trade guilds remained important in organizing daily economic life.[58]

In the German-speaking lands state-forms were many, but the majority of territories were ruled by some sort of monarch; republics were all but absent (if we discount the small medieval northern German peasant republic of Dithmarschen, and the Swiss confederation), but there were some cities ruled by oligarchies claiming a status of semi-independence, often resembling republican patterns of governance.[59] Proper city states (called free imperial cities) such as Hamburg, Frankfurt (Main), Augsburg and Nuremberg represent special cases; far from resembling the Republican model cherished for their political and economic 'liberties', they were often governed through commercial oligarchies, and less tolerant about matters of religion (which has been claimed as a prime marker of economic development) than the princely territorial states.[60] Other German types of ruler comprised princes, bishops, prince-bishops, prince-abbots, counts, dukes, electors or kings, to name but the most common ones; there were even a number of 40-odd so-called *Reichsdörfer* (imperial villages), hamlets strewn across (mostly) the south-west that had no feudal lord or territorial affiliation but were directly subordinate to the emperor, a strange relic of medieval times.[61] The Holy Roman Empire alone contained more than 300 territorial or princely states and a much larger number of further state-like entities, mini-polities, institutions and individuals such as Imperial Knights that went into the thousands, who were still classified as independent, because similar to the imperial villages and the *Reichsfürsten* (imperial princes) such as the Kings of Bohemia or the Margraves of Brandenburg, their only direct feudal superior was the emperor. State boundaries were fluid and fuzzy, with enclaves and exclaves everywhere.[62] Then there were supra-state bodies, including the medieval currency unions (*Münzvereine*) and other confederations such as the *Reichskreise* (imperial districts) founded after 1500.[63] In monetary matters the *Reichskreise* replaced the medieval currency unions and other regional associations of rulers and territories, with the aim of creating a common currency. Potentially this opened entirely new fields of economic governance, but it is unclear to what extent the Imperial Districts really succeeded in creating unified monetary regimes.[64] For a short time during the second half of the 17th century, German industrial and trade policy was even delegated from individual states to the highest possible level; known under its label 'imperial mercantilism' (*Reichsmerkantilismus*) this proved that at least in terms of ideas the Empire wasn't dead yet.[65] Overall, economic statecraft continued to be multilayered and polycentric and by no means focused exclusively on individual monarchical rulers.[66]

This provides the frame within which Renaissance and early modern states could operate. The nature and mutual relationship between good governance and good economy had been addressed by writers since times in the deep past, in Europe and beyond. Good kings had to constantly mitigate for human folly. As tales of ancient India argued: there was 'no problem in the world for which the Creator has not carefully invented some solution. But when it comes to countering a wicked person's way of thinking, it seems ... that even the Creator has failed in his efforts'.[67] Good kings could be judged by what they achieved in the light of such folly. Their main function was to protect individuals from violence, theft and bodily harm. The Kalhaṇa's Rājataraṅgiṇī chronicles written in the 12th century AD described lands 'so free of robbery, that at night the doors were left open in the bazaars, and the roads were secure for travelers'. 'When this legal authority was far off', the mid-15th century historian and poet Jonarāja, argued, 'the bloodsucking feudal landholders, like jackals, ate up even the innards of the people, without remainder'[68]. A similar critique of the nobility featured in many political economy works especially of the cameralist ilk since the 17th and 18th centuries.

In terms of what states *ought* to do, a time-aged precedent was set by Thomas Aquinas (1225–74), perhaps the most influential European thinker of the Middle Ages whose works continued to be read into modern times. In his treatise on good government (*De Regno*) Aquinas had defined the good or 'virtuous life' for the community as the supreme goal of policy. Since God was the only being that existed out of itself and as a goal in itself, everything else – including the state and the material-physical world – was subject to God's careful design. In Aquinas's vision government thus included a potentially *proactive and dynamic* vision, because:

> to govern is to lead the thing governed in a suitable way towards its proper end. Thus a ship is said to be governed when, through the skill of the pilot, it is brought unharmed and by a direct route to harbour. Consequently, if a thing be directed to an end outside itself (as a ship to the harbour), it is the governor's duty, not only to preserve the thing unharmed, but further to guide it towards this end.[69]

Potentially this passage can be read both ways, arguing *for* an interventionist ruler, *as well as* allowing a degree of laissez-faire. But, 'since the beatitude of heaven is the end of that virtuous life which we live at present, it pertains to the king's office to promote the good life of the multitude in such a way as to make it suitable for the attainment of heavenly happiness'.[70]

Such claims were repeated time and again in the mirrors for princes and early modern cameralist political economy from Germany to Denmark, Sweden and Norway.[71] Good rulers were expected to be mild to their subjects, and lavish to the poor; because that would, in the words of the Elector Friedrich Wilhelm von Brandenburg (1620–88), gain them invaluable heavenly treasure. Earthly treasures would diminish and decay, or be dug out by thieves; heavenly investment paid eternally. But for this some material investment, or hard cash, had to be expended by the government first.[72] Based upon an Old Testament command (Deuteronomy 17) which forbade kings to 'hoard money and silver', Reformation and early modern political economy put a special premium on spending and spreading money around as tools promoting economic development.[73] We will return to this important idea in Chapter 6.[74] True, Martin Luther and other religious reformers, apart from contributing to a streamlining of economic administration raising possibilities of long-term economic development,[75] also introduced the concept of 'deserving' versus 'idle' beggars, and voluntary and involuntary poverty. Where medieval scholastic theory had identified poverty and charity as important pillars of piety, in the early modern age poverty and begging were reconceptualized as voluntary states of mind and activities that directly reduced the nation's wealth. State theory in the age of 'primitive accumulation' invented the workhouse as part of an emerging European governmentality of discipline and punish,[76] and darker visions emerged of humans and nature as exploitable economic resources in the relentless nexus of infinite economic expansion.[77]

But overall political economy came to emphasize that rulers and princes should be generous, fair and proactive in *promoting* the common weal, refraining from war and excessive taxation. This had manifest consequences on economic development, as King James VI of Scotland's *Fürstenspiegel* known as *Basilikon Doron* (1599) seems to suggest: 'to prop the weale of your people, with prouident care for their good gouernment, that iustly ... and yet so to temper and mixe your seueritie with mildnes'.[78]

For this end, kings ought to collaborate with the businessmen of their realms. Merchants, albeit often known to 'enrich themselues vpon the losse of all the rest of the people' and to be 'also the speciall cause of the corruption of the coyne', were essential in provisioning the country with goods. The state had to take care and control the foreign trades 'so shall ye haue best and best cheape wares, not buying them at the third hand'.[79]

While the remark on 'corruption of the coyne' in the *Basilikon Doron* may seem somewhat abrupt and out of tune, it was in line with the more general context of the genre and a focus on monetary matters as a practical field of economic intervention. A good example is provided by Erasmus von Rotterdam, spearheading figure of the Renaissance, author of one of the most influential princes mirrors ever, the *Institutio Principis Christiani* 1516. Perhaps conceptualized as a response to Machiavelli's *Principe*, Erasmus emphasized that the first duty of a king was to *avoid* making war. In a chapter on economic policy Erasmus argued that a prince had to take care of his realms (*regio*) like a yeoman would of his farm, or a good man and housekeeper (*vir bonus*) of his inherited estate as he had received it from his parents: ideally he would leave it in an improved condition, that is *better off*.[80] There is a notion of economic development through good stewardship implicit in this passage (*ut acceptam reddat meliorem* in the Latin original), important in a wider sense: it presented *outlines* of a potentially dynamic model of economic statecraft. Renaissance economic thought put an increasing emphasis on human improvement and *homines* that became increasingly *economici*.

Erasmus also deployed the characteristic and at his time ubiquitous concept of *publica utilitas* (common weal, German *der gemeine Nutzen*). For Erasmus material goods came second after people's moral and spiritual demands had been taken care of. Economic policy was thus part of a larger set of morally framed goals of state. But Erasmus then digressed, abruptly turning his attention to coins and currency debasement: these were manifestations of the biggest tyranny imaginable.[81] From a modern reader's point this seems rather bewildering: why such an abrupt move from higher morals specifically to money? As a member of the rentier bourgeoisie, dependent on rent payments, annuities and other financial income streams, Erasmus's sentiments would have found open ears among an urban audience. But unstable money also remained a major cause of inflation and social revolts elsewhere.[82] England and the Netherlands were exceptional, with practically stable currencies after the mid-16th century and almost no debasement into the industrial age, a factor that without doubt supported long-term economic development.[83] As late as 1761 the leading German economist of the Enlightenment, Johann Heinrich Justi argued that nothing was so badly out of line with stately prudence as coin debasement.[84] And as we will see in Chapter 5, such sentiments had been on the table since the days of Oresme in the 1350s.

As a term, 'common weal' increased in use frequency in English-language texts from *c.*1450, supplemented from the 16th century onwards by the concept of *commonwealth*. Its German functional equivalent, *der gemeine Nutzen*, gained common currency during the peasant wars of the 1520s, but likewise sported a medieval heritage.[85] As a political–discursive concept it was part of an older vector of terms including, in the Germanies and beyond, *bonum publicum*, *bonum commune*, *salus publica* and *utilitas publica* (French: *comun profit*). 'Such phrases had their roots in Aristotelian texts, circulated in Roman legal theory, and were early infused with Christian teachings'.[86] Over the early modern period they became reconfigured, now including public goods, the building and repair of bridges and roads, or the regulation of water supplies.[87] Blickle has speculated about origins in medieval *communal* (cooperative) politics before it became adopted by state administrators aiming to legitimize territorial governmentality.[88] In the Peasant War(s) of 1524–26 'common weal' or *der gemeine Nutzen* was contrasted with avarice, greed and other morally abhorrent economic practices commonly reckoned by medieval theology to the seven deadly sins. In radical visions such as Michael Gaismair's *Tyrolean Constitution* (1526), a political utopia written in the aftermath of the Peasant War, *der gemeine Nutzen* even incorporated propositions of abolishing private property and adopting proto-communist modes of production.[89] Jurists of the 16th-century, such as Johannes Eisermann (Ferrarius), a principal of the University of Marburg in Hesse, defined 'Respublica oder gemein nutz', as a town, commune or commonwealth being in good order (*nit ander ist, denn ein gemein gute ordenung einer statt oder einer andern commun*).[90] But from 'being a term for the common good for most of the 1450s, it began, in the next few decades, to denote an almost tangible entity, associated with laws, principles, and consultative tradition, and denoting the welfare of the people',[91] under the auspices of the emerging territorial fiscal-military states.

A safe way of capturing early modern paradigms of oeconomic statecraft would be by looking at a text reflecting the mainstream, written by someone who already in his lifetime had acquired a reputation as bestselling polygraph (doubters may claim he was an auto-plagiarizer), and whose works were translated into other languages including Spanish, Russian and Dutch.[92] This was Johann Heinrich Justi (1717–71), contemporary of James Steuart and Adam Smith, arguably the most prominent figure of the German economic enlightenment.[93] Justi's cameralism built on influences far beyond the Germanies (such as Montesquieu) and older models often reaching back to the Renaissance, providing a general theory of economic development in the Age of Enlightenment. According to Justi, the first goal of state was to raise people's happiness (*Glückseligkeit*). As a political economy concept, *Glückseligkeit* had ancient pedigrees; it became reconfigured within the economic enlightenment, and continued as late as 1841, in Friedrich List's *National System of Political Economy*, as a superordinate economic reason of state.[94] In the Enlightenment model, public happiness, individual wealth and state power were intrinsically linked. Healthy, wealthy and happy subjects would pay taxes sufficient to maintain powers of state. Rulers should use all powers of diplomacy to avoid war. Food should be available in sufficient quantity. Roads should be safe; justice administered properly and equitably; industry and commerce should be closely monitored in the interest of the common weal. No class of people (*Stand*) should suppress others politically, socially or, through the market, economically; the state should make sure its citizens were well-mannered and well-behaved. This included curfews but also price and quality controls in key markets and industries. Foreign trade should be encouraged, as should be mining, especially of silver, and the velocity of monetary circulation (we shall delve more deeply into these in Chapters 4 to 6). Weights and measures ought to be properly regulated, to safeguard private property rights and economic stability. Immigration and population growth should be encouraged; skilled tradesmen and other 'useful' immigrants should be exempt from taxes. Medical police should watch apothecaries, and public health ought to be promoted through clean air in clean cities.[95] Markets were to be located at appropriate spaces in the cities, to keep the streets free from congestion and bad odours. Customs and tariffs should be moderate but designed in ways encouraging manufacturing exports. Imported manufactures should be discouraged. Particular interest was to be directed towards mining and metallurgy, and natural discovery and useful knowledge were to be encouraged across the board, to make the nation prosperous and its denizens industrious. Laziness was to be discouraged, good work to be supported using bounties, subventions and other incentives. Effective laws preventing bankruptcy, financial legislation and ordinances regulating cashless payments by means of bills of exchange added stability, credibility and optimism to traders, investors and customers alike. Markets, trade fairs and urban craft industry ought to be well-ordered and regulated to facilitate a smooth flow of goods. Monopolies and other market distortions were strictly to be avoided. Guilds and other associations that potentially harmed commerce and economic activity ought to be watched with caution and, better, be abolished. People should be empowered to become affluent, and business people entitled to decent profits. Markets should be as lightly regulated as possible. Noblemen should be encouraged to take up business and trade. No nobleman ought to use their prerogatives of birth in the common way by sucking the blood out of their feudal subjects; best would be to abolish noble privileges altogether. Tax farming – the practice of handing over the administration and collection of taxes to private entrepreneurs in return for lump-sum annual payments of cash – should be aborted. The state apparatus should be slim and bureaucracy effective. The state could borrow money but must always be a safe and reliable creditor. Any ruler who failed on this was to be considered a tyrant.[96]

Similar principles were put forth by German, Swedish and other authors of the cameralist ilk in the 17th and 18th centuries. Cameralism continued to be taught at many German and Swedish universities into the 1830s and beyond. They had built on earlier, partly medieval, templates in turn, especially regarding monetary theory and management. Justi's model of good economic governance and economic development thus represented stock-in-trade political theory at its time, with a long life into modern industrial capitalism.[97] Building upon classical origins (such as Plato and Aristotle), philosophers, jurists and natural theorists including Georg Wilhelm Leibniz (1646–1716), Christian Thomasius and Christian Wolff developed the idea further into comprehensive models of states actively *engineering* social and economic development: models of states that could do a lot of harm (if policy was bad), but also good, if rulers choose their policies wisely. Society thus framed became increasingly conceptualized as commercial and civic.[98] Public oeconomic happiness (*Glückseligkeit*) thus entailed a principally dynamic world view, including the possibility of economic development.[99] Kings, princes and states were assumed to *proactively* promote economic development, with the aim of creating open economic futures (Chapter 2). Among other things *Glückseligkeit* was achieved by promoting 'circulation' and 'vivacity' of goods and money, topics we will pick up in more detail in Chapters 4 to 6.[100]

Holle der Deuffel lieber meine zeitliche wohlfardt als daß so viell leutte Betler werden und ich reich – 'I'd rather the Devil snatch my earthly possessions than so many

60

people turn into beggars and I become rich', snorted the proverbially grumpy sociopath Friedrich Wilhelm I of Prussia (b 1688, r 1713–40).[101] The 'soldier king' did not mince words about his denizens, many of whom, including those living in the provinces of Cleve and Mark, he considered 'as dumb as oxen and as malicious as the Devil'. Still in his view a good ruler promoted oeconomy in his dominions as best as he could, not only in order to generate wilful taxpayers. Promoting manufacturing and value-added (see Chapters 7 and 8) were crucial in order to make the common weal flourish.[102] His son Frederick the Great of Prussia (b 1712, r 1740–86) emphasized that cities should be free and have self-elected magistrates. Peasants and farmers should also be as free as possible. In *Anti-Machiavel* (1740), he endorsed lavishness and luxury as promoters of civility, industriousness and economic development. He echoed a common fashion of his time that viewed possessive individualism as the key to economic development, including the poor who partook in consumption through numerous trickle-down effects. The story had been developed in contemporaneous writings by Anglo-Dutch émigré Bernard de Mandeville (*Fable of the Bees*, 1714), Scottish Jacobite and cameralist Sir James Steuart, *Principles of Political Oeconomy* (1767, Book II, Ch. 20 on luxury) or, most famously, Smith's *Theory of Moral Sentiments* (1759, Part IV, Ch. 1), where the nobility through their desires for vanity and luxury gave rise, through an 'invisible hand', to further industry thus increasing employment of the poor.[103] In his 1752 *Testament* Frederick II committed to establishing as many industries in the country as possible, to avoid losing money to foreign nations. Increasing the size of the labouring population, stimulating manufacturing and industriousness, and making cities populous were understood as key tools effecting capital formation and make the nation better off. In the end, Frederick assumed that these strategies would also eventually increase workers' standards of living, and the poor people's consumption.[104]

In early modern visions of the market process 'mercantilist' and laissez-faire principles were part of the same parcel; they cannot be meaningfully disentangled. Only for lack of a better word may they may be subsumed under the cameralist label – suboptimal in any case, but whose common utility has nevertheless been asserted by scholars.[105] The cameralist vision of development entailed an essentially dynamic vision of the human future and the common weal; Renaissance economic philosophy firmly rested upon the idea of improvement and 'growth' (or 'increase'). Cameralists considered markets as organic, not mechanic, and thoroughly embedded within morals, politics and culture. They accepted laissez-faire in principle, under the condition that the state had the duty to intervene whenever fair market conditions were violated (this included market imperfections, such as usury, rent-seeking and monopoly). They were concerned with *creating*, rather than destroying or simply redistributing someone else's wealth. To this end they favoured manufacturing and industry over agriculture and services, as manufacturing was considered the most promising branch of production, in those days, in terms of generating positive returns to scale.[106]

Such politics of development ought to be principally pursued by peaceful not warlike means. 'Peace nourishes, but war destroys (*der fride ernehret, Der krieg aber verzehret*)', noted Frederick William, ('Great') Elector of Brandenburg and Duke of Prussia, 1620-1688, in his *Political Testament* (1667).

What could states do in the age of capitalism's rise, 1250s–1850s?

Today most states above all tax, spend and invest: in infrastructure, schooling and literacy, the broader welfare state, and public goods. They pay attention to growth and development, employment, inflation, competition within industries, competitiveness on international markets, exchange rates and balance of payment deficits.[107] Especially in times of pandemic and war emergency, spending increases far beyond the limits allowed by textbooks for competitive market economies, but even in economies following the liberal-capitalist model, the share of state expenditure in total economic activity seldom falls below 40 per cent and approaches 60 per cent in social democratic or corporate state capitalist nations such as Sweden or Norway.[108] Since the Keynesian Revolution in policy and economic analysis, such interventions came to be understood as legitimate, reinforcing rather than violating the working principles of the 'free' market. Post-1945 German ordoliberal thinkers even managed the intellectual balancing act of positing the free market as a providential scenario of God's chosen economic world order of 'coordinated anarchy' whose perfect working conditions could only be guaranteed by continuous state intervention.[109]

If the definition of 'state' is a difficult one historically and a bit of a moving target, framing and assessing state policy and economic development for historical times is even more so. Today the nature and quality of states governing the economy are readily asserted using key performance indicators such as tax revenue, state expenditure and per capita income. Where unavailable, proxies such as real wages or urbanization rates can be used instead; state activity and quality can be proxied using interest rates on public debt, the frequency of parliaments, or coin debasement as historical barometers of institutional quality and good economic governance.[110] There are a number of methodological and conceptual problems with such approaches, however. Economic growth, commonly defined as per capita GDP growth is not an ideal measure of economic well-being (especially not when used for international comparison); and prior to the mid-19th century literally all figures are guesstimates rather than estimates.[111] Even nowadays per capita GDP does not capture distributional effects and income inequality, which may be much more skewed in some countries (say, the modern US) than others (say, Scandinavia or continental Europe), while still resulting in broadly similar per capita income levels.[112] State capability, access to economic, social and political resources, property rights, healthcare, sanitary facilities and a general increase in life expectancy are likewise measures of economic well-being but not particularly well-captured in the broad-brush stroke figure GDP. Nor does it tell us much about the *directionality* of economic change: is productive activity based on primary/decreasing-return/low-innovation sectors, or on manufacturing/increasing-return/high-innovation sectors?[113] As we saw previously, early modern political economy knew these items under the rubric '*happiness*', which is largely lost from modern standard concepts of economic development. Moreover, as productivity changes may give rise to changes in the weight of the innovative sectors within a specific economy, per capita income may either understate or overstate economic dynamics over time.[114] Within states and territories economic growth also takes place unevenly across space.[115] Early modern political economy occasionally made a point about manufacturing being *predominantly* located in cities. Cities were more productive, and product and labour markets were more dynamic; in cities the nobility had no political influence that would have hampered qualities of life and competed with the claims to governance by the emerging territorial states.[116] Nor were pre-1900 European national markets necessarily well integrated.[117] Furthermore the non-market and non-monetized sectors of economy (there is a difference between the two) may be significant in terms of their contribution to overall economic activity, too, but cannot readily be factored into assessments of growth, performance and productivity dependent upon the use of monetary aggregates.[118] Fiscal data can also be shaky, especially when based on using grams of silver for reducing different currencies to a common denominator (a highly problematic assumption, because in Asia silver was an altogether different commodity compared to Europe, with a purchasing power twice as high when measured in terms of gold than in Europe). This all makes historical quantifications and comparisons of state activity and state efficiency difficult.

There is an even more serious problem. Conceptually historians are not always explicit about what economic performance means historically (other than an increase in per capita GDP). There are at least two competing models offered in the historical literature; both relating in some form to the *directionality* of economic change. One is often known as *Smithian* (after Adam Smith); the other *Schumpeterian* (after Joseph Schumpeter) growth. We will take a closer look at them in Chapter 8. But directionality matters: based on the idea of *transformation*, about new ways of using markets and Mother Nature radically redesigning the possibilities provided by the material world, early modern cameralism, especially with its principally optimistic outlook towards the future and the possibility of redesigning markets and nature along more productive lines, in many ways matched criteria of Schumpeterian more than Smithian growth.

Another problem. While every state has an economic policy of some sorts, *nolens* or *volens*,[119] it is more difficult to formulate causal arguments about policy and economic development, especially in a deep-historical perspective. To what extent is one particular economic policy successful, and how do we measure this? One of the most important hindrances to effective economic policy was the resistance of stakeholder groups on the ground, such as local artisans or trade guilds, or other vested interests.[120] In the German states, a full implementation of cameralist market reforms would have required, essentially, an abolition of noble privileges and complete restructuring of agrarian property rights. In effect this would have amounted to abolishing feudalism altogether; and for towns and cities, the complete removal of local prerogatives, monopolies and special freedoms enjoyed by local stakeholders.[121] Elsewhere the situation was not radically different. In France around 1700 A.D. merchants in the seaward provinces lobbied for free trade with England, while those of the more inland manufacturing provinces strongly argued in favour of retaining tariffs on British manufacturing imports.[122] Spain was similarly fragmented institutionally.[123] When does a particular strategy stop being cronyism or rent-seeking defended by some pressure group and start becoming a national 'policy'?[124] There also may be a lack of sources that precludes us from knowing everything the state or ruler or government did, or intended to. We do not always know how long it takes for a specific policy to finally be successful, which multiplier effects to use and which transmission mechanisms to assume, and it may also be difficult to assert the precise number of economic sectors and enterprise units that this or another specific economic policy measure may have affected, positively or negatively. (This has become obvious from the perennial difficulties faced by historians estimating the contribution made by transatlantic slavery to British economic growth.)[125] A policy's lateral linkages or spillover effects across the economic spectrum may remain unquantifiable, but still be all the more significant than its more direct forward (direct productivity effects) and backward linkages (demand for inputs).[126] And: what has been left in archives, in terms of written sources on policy and revenue, only represents a snapshot of historical economic reality. Who are we to assert this snapshot's overall representativeness?[127]

With all these caveats in mind and avoiding being overly apologetic or agnostic, the following list thus captures the most common strategies of states developing or governing the economy since the Middle Ages. We need them for closer analysis of specific policy tools in Chapters 4 to 8. They should also serve as evidence to comfortably dispel the previously discussed myths of the myopic premodern European state.

Above all, *states set the rules*, creating legal or institutional frameworks that could turn out – in the modern historical economist's view – to be 'inclusive' or 'exclusive'. This was a medieval notion lingering on in post-1945 conceptualizations of economic statecraft: ordoliberal thinkers including Walter Eucken (1891–1950) still claimed that there were only two fundamental remits of proactive economic governance: establishing a framework of economic order (not interfering with it), and prevent monopoly, cartels and other market infringements reducing competitive laissez-faire.[128] Many modern narratives argue that states did this above all in order to generate tax, but as we have already seen such claims are probably exaggerated. The share of taxes in total product determines whether state activity generates protection rents and will turn predatory (that is, the state charging more in value terms from its denizens than it gives back to them), or whether this protection rent is reinvested in less utilitarian and more benevolent aims. This will create a framework of incentives or disincentives to certain types of economic behaviour, with knock-on effects on key metrics of economic development such as capital formation and the distribution of the social surplus generated each year by profits and rents. The number and design of special freedoms, government monopolies and so forth will tell us about the distribution of profits and society and whether or not profits are reinvested in productive activities that generate income and employment for others, or will simply contribute to conspicuous consumption by the rich.[129] Governments could use their surplus to wage war or enforce protection rents.[130]

States created infrastructure for production, trade and economic life. This could range from the mere establishment of permanent markets and country fairs,[131] often by special privilege, to promoting the establishment of stock and other exchanges, regulating brokers and other middlemen needed to decrease transaction cost and improve market integration. As Gelderblom and others have noted this could make or break the fate of trading places and thus economic development.[132] Since the Middle Ages polities also got involved in regulating other aspects and areas influencing market performance, including water supply, and sexual and food hygiene, and early modern cameralist *Policey* governance extended to regulations of dirt, waste removal and clean air, even quarantine at times of pandemic.[133]

States cared for the provisioning of goods and stabilized markets to keep the capitalist engine going. Since the Middle Ages, city governments and territorial rulers regularly engaged in stabilizing food supply, at times of crisis, through various means such as public storage facilities, export prohibitions, customs rebates or directly overseeing that certain arable land capacities were reserved for grain cultivation. States also mitigated for climatic variability and its effects on markets. What has often been named a marker of early modern Chinese good governance had, by the 18th century, become a common feature all over continental and northern Europe, from Prussia to Norway: the public granary or grain store.[134]

States policed the economy (but not in the modern Foucauldian sense of the concept, as we will see in Chapter 4). Market regulation laid out the framework of legal behaviour on markets in order to keep the capitalist machine running. This included the organization and scheduling of recurrent countryside fairs, and monetary ordinances regulating money markets, which happened to belong to the earliest forms of state intervention known since Antiquity and earlier. Working from medieval templates[135] they often continued unabated into modern capitalism – and were used verbatim into late-19th century, hundreds of years after first being drafted, as Chapter 4 will show. Policing thus framed was understood as a strategy of empowering the market, and represented one of the precocious few areas where governments *could* make a difference, in promoting economic development. Occasionally governments would engage in price control, by setting upper limits or threshold prices; but overall grain markets, as most others, functioned more or less according to the laws of competitive price formation.[136] The early modern Chinese state is often said to have followed more Physiocratic or laissez-faire attitudes regarding market regulation,[137] but Chapter 4 will show how European policies were, in effect, not far off that mark, either.

Later on, political economy developed increasingly refined tools of analysing market forms and failures. Examples include Martin Luther's *On Commerce and Usury* (1524) or Johann Joachim Becher's massive volume on the *Origins and Causes of Cities, States and Republics* (1668 [*Politischer Discurs: Von den eigentlichen Ursachen deß Auf- und Ablebens der Städt, Länder und Republicken*]). Becher discussed the nature and virtues of market regulation and economic principles known in the modern economist's literature as Say's Law.[138] He proposed different forms of market failure, most prominently monopoly (*Monopolium*), ruinous competition (*Polypolium*) and forestalling (*Propolium*).[139] Uppsala cameralist Anders Berch (1711–74), whom we encountered in Chapter 2, argued that no landsman should be engaged in forestalling (Pt II/4, Ch 9, §3); he called for licensing food merchants; regulation of marketplaces and hours of trading (§6), and so on, as most other political economists of his time and age usually would. As they continued to be used in academic teaching into the 1830s and beyond, political economy writings such as Berch's *Inledning* (1747) laid important intellectual foundations for modern capitalism.

Monetary policy was conceived as policy of market order, once again a medieval strategy and one of the most promising areas where government intervention was likely to make a difference. We will consider this in more detail in Chapters 5 and 6.

States watched the economy – or economic activity of subjects, usually taxed (or with the aim of taxing) – by counting, auditing and reporting, usually tax revenue. A most important by-product of this were the ubiquitous port books, customs accounts and other records derived from taxing economic activity and traffic and flows passing through the gates of market cities. In England and Scotland, continuous series of customs accounts and port books have survived from the 13th century onwards; similar records were produced elsewhere, but not usually at the same quality and coverage of information. From the 1690s data contained in the port books were used to compile national trade statistics, first for England and Ireland (1696), then Scotland (1755). Such records have been used by historians to reconstruct fluctuations in trade and payments.[140] Demographic censuses containing information on the number of households and often on taxable wealth are known from mid-16th century Spain and Saxony. In the 18th century, industrial censuses became more common and are known from France, Prussia and Austria, to name but a few. In Scotland the Board of Trustees for the Fisheries and Manufactures was established in 1727, with the aim of monitoring linen production; it has left us with yearly production statistics on marketed Scottish linen differentiated by type and quality.[141] In Austria the so-called *Kommerz Konsesse* were established that monitored an increasing number of industrial branches (1749: Styria and Lower Austria; 1752: Bohemia, Moravia and Upper Austria; 1757: Inner Austria and Vorarlberg; 1763 Tyrol). Watching and counting the economy represented the start and end point of prudent state policy, representing a key foundation of the making and breaking of the wealth of nations; even if contemporary figures and statistics were not necessarily accurate in a modern sense, and subject to political manipulation.[142]

Incentivizing the economy. Since the Middle Ages it had been common to grant privileges and monopoly rights to certain businesses and entrepreneurs. Very often these would have been purely fiscally motivated, as shown by the example of Stuart pre–Civil War England, where according to a prominent historian, literally all manufacturing activity was tied to some form of monopoly.[143] Towards the 18th century and into the Enlightenment, however, states and their economic administrators adopted more laissez-faire ways of encouraging businesses to adopt more productive technologies, by awarding premiums and bounties and other subventions if need be and domestic demand and supply were sluggish.[144]

Since the Renaissance states were also concerned with getting the nation into the 'right business'.[145] Aimed at constructing comparative advantages to raise the nation's wealth such policies included the promotion of technology transfer, useful knowledge, the creation of learned academies and societies, but also the abolition of urban guilds and noble privileges.[146] Many such principles have made it into modern concepts of industrial policy and entrepreneurial states.

Integrating the economy. Cameralists of the 17th and 18th century were concerned with market integration and the creation of standardized realms of taxation. Many states in the early modern age were discontiguous composite monarchies, with sometimes – as in the case of Prussia or Austria – a bewildering range of countries, kingdoms and territories assembled or interlocking under one crown. Habsburg economic policies for the Kingdom of Hungary or Naples occasionally followed an import-substitution-policy-cum-market-integration approach, abolishing internal tariffs and getting independent provinces and kingdoms into their 'right' business, but only for as long as that business served the interests of the imperial superior (in that case the Austrian Hereditary Lands). Thus polities at the periphery had occasionally to sacrifice and subordinate their regional economic interest to the stronger political-economic prerogatives of the imperial core.[147]

Industrial policy and *import substitution* represent some of the oldest economic state strategies as documented in the historical record. Since the 14th century the Counts of Flanders pursued an active policy supporting domestic cloth industries, and it was common for medieval rulers to support specific industries such as mining and salt-making, on top of cloth; the cloth industries became the subject of 16th-century German imperial ordinances.[148] They went through a heyday during the 17th and 18th centuries, especially in France under Colbert, in England and Scotland under Sir Robert Walpole (and the Duke of Argyll), Austria and the Austrian Netherlands, certainly in the Holy Roman Empire.[149] The rationale for this was concisely analysed in Sir James Steuart, *An Inquiry into the Principles of Political Œconomy* (1767: Book II); but Steuart's model built upon centuries worth of theory (Chapter 7).[150] The post-1707 British customs system originally established at the Restoration (1660) reflected a rather stringent implementation of this rationale; it was considerably expanded, and by the end of the 18th century comprised close to 60 different duties payable on imports (and a much lesser range of exports); only some duties were purely fiscally motivated, but most show a developmental perspective of state, some even with proven success, as the example of early modern India's cotton industry shows: by the 1770s it had been priced out of European and then global markets through the mercantilist policies established since the 1660s and intensified during the Age of Walpole (*c.*1721–42).[151]

The state also acted, since the 16th century, often as an *entrepreneur of last resort*.[152] In continental Europe, especially during the 18th century, many manufactories and muster workshops were run by the state. Often this meant they were part of the ruler's own finances; in the 1550s, when the central German *Saiger* plants where the native argentiferous copper deposits were smelted and separated into their components of pure silver and copper were ailing in the face of the growing competition from Hispano-American silver, the Counts of Mansfeld took over the running of most enterprises. During the late 1530s and early 1540s, Martin Luther repeatedly became involved in such processes of industry 'nationalization'. In other cases, direct state involvement targeted key industries promoting the generation, acquisition and circulation of useful knowledge and the training of a skilled workforce. Often the goal was to produce what others did not, for example weapons, ordnance, uniforms for the military, or to substitute foreign imports for a wider reason of economic development, promoting productivity across the entire economic spectrum.[153]

Economic governance in the preindustrial period also extended to other areas more loosely defined but still relevant for managing the wealth of nations; including disease control, midwifery, apothecaries and *medicinal policey*,[154] staple rights, brokers and brokerage,[155] transport and shipping on local or regional rivers,[156] ceremonies and festivities, fires and firefighting, the prohibitions of duels, regulation of building and or sales of landed property. Public health was important.[157] Often monitored and enforced at the local level or by semi-autonomous cities, many such functions would later on become key remits of modern welfare states.

'Modern' forms of economic interventionism such as exchange rate management, anti-cyclical demand management (tinkering with interest rates, public expenditure, taxation and so on) were not completely unknown, either, as we will see in Chapter 5, but not usually practised in the age before industry. It would probably be anachronistic to look for parallels or resemblances of them in the historical record before the 1900s. And yet, during the six or seven centuries of capitalism's ascendancy (1250–1850) political economy developed an increasingly versatile menu of governing economy that was far from myopic, limited to, or even focused on, providing sound legal frameworks for business. States' menus of choice and fields of intervention were broader, more wide-ranging given all political constraints faced, such as the ubiquitous grip of the nobility on societal and oeconomic resources. We will now look at select aspects: market regulation (Chapter 4), currency (Chapter 5) and velocity (Chapter 6), and manufacturing (Chapters 7 and 8) to put more nuance to the picture.

4

Configuring Free Markets:
A Deeper History of Laissez-Faire

Moral debates in the age of the free market, 1890s

In 1888, a ravaging debate took place in the Munich *Landtag* (the Bavarian state Diet) concerning pedlars and hucksters. Hucksters had mushroomed across the Bavarian countryside. They went from house to house, offering cheap and shoddy goods (*Ausschussware*). Purchasing from the manufacturer (*Fabrikant*), they pressed these goods on to the rural customer. The latter, poor souls that they were, unbeknownst and often illiterate, for reasons of sheer fear often simply gave in, hoping the pedlar would then move on harassing the next-door neighbour instead. The poor were forced to 'buy to their detriment', because they were too afraid of the pedlar's revenge in case they insisted on a firm 'no' to the offered deal (*kaufen lieber zu ihrem Schaden, ... nur aus Zwang ..., um der Hausirer los zu werden, weil sie die Leute fürchten, voll Angst und Schrecken sind, und um sich von den peinlichen Plaggeistern und deren Rache zu befreien*). The hucksters began with charming and praising their goods. If that were to no avail they would turn to swearing and threats, and, finally, if that didn't help ... begging! The source went on to lament the 'ferocious and dangerously cancerous phenomenon' that consumed rural society from within. It had to be weeded out (*Der verwilderte und gefährliche Krebsschaden und Auswuchs, die Schmarotzerpflanze, die dem seßhaften ehrlichen Bürger allen Lebenssaft entzieht, zerstört, frißt und schließlich tödtet und das Landvolk vollends ermattet*).[1] This rhetoric set a dangerous precedent for later, unholier ages, especially when directed against Roma and Jews.

Interestingly, in the present case the itinerant hucksters served as the prolonged arm of the capitalist-manufacturer or *Fabrikant* and wholesaler (*Grossist*). But by their shoddy selling and nature, they acted to the great detriment of the common weal. Such debates were not at all uncommon at the time. They never really had been. Justus Möser (1720–94) in his *Patriotische Phantasien* picked up on the dubious nature of sales 'forced' by the hucksters upon the innocent country people.[2] For centuries pedlars and hucksters had represented a common social stereotype in discourses on the common weal, the welfare of the nations, and the role played by markets.[3] Medieval market theory had *regrating* – peddling or huckstering writ large (=reselling) – as a potentially incriminatory activity, dangerously close to usury.[4] Early modern political economy remained similarly negative on peddling. Johann Heinrich Justi whom we encountered in previous chapters, included a separate chapter on peddling in his magnum opus (*Grundfeste*, 1761). Pedlars' wares and their quality could not be asserted. The common people had to rely on what was on offer in the village *in situ*. Hucksters undersold 'honourable' merchants, who risked their business in consequence (*so werden die ordentlichen Kaufleuthe an ihrer Nahrung sehr gehindert*).[5] Pedlars were especially bad with young immature lads: students were tricked into buying all sorts of unnecessary junk, often on credit (the real problem, according to Justi). 'Commerce is the big ocean that distributes itself into infinite number of smaller streams and brooks, generating wealth, prosperity and luxury (*Überfluss*) for all kinds of people and professions. Happy is a land like Tyrus, where merchants are like princes; destitute is the country whose tradesmen are poor', Justi wrote.[6] Only pedlars who bought up victuals unsold at urban markets were to be allowed (lest the food went waste), or those selling goods that no regular merchant would normally supply.[7] Ubiquitous in early modern rural Europe,[8] hucksters and pedlars remained part of the market landscape into the age of industrial capitalism. Werner Sombart argued that the *expansion* of peddling and huckstering was a sign of capitalism growing.[9] Peddling *deepened* goods markets (and thus people's access to merchandise); by meeting customers *in situ*, *nolens* or *volens*, pedlars and hucksters increased people's awareness, sensitivity and receptivity to capitalism's pleasures and new worlds of goods.[10]

In the 1880s Germany went through its second industrial revolution, marked by heavy manufacturing, chemicals and electrical engineering.[11] This puts the pedlar debates into perspective. They linked with ongoing discussions on tariff reform and the big question of the day: was Germany an agrarian or industrial nation? There were regions, such as the *Ruhrgebiet* or Upper Silesia, where heavy industry dominated economic landscapes in ways that made such quibbles almost obsolete.[12] But the image of the huckster was also used in contemporaneous British political debates (at that time Britain was the richest and leading industrial nation of the age): posters advertising tariff reform had the dangerous German manufacturer as a huckster peddling their wares to the innocent British granny.[13] But these debates also show a longer line in political economy of markets and trading. Political economy before Sombart had generally had little in stock for the itinerant trader.[14] Pedlars were here today and gone tomorrow. They could not be taxed. They literally carried their property on their back. They moved under the radar.

They remained outside the state's grip. Because you couldn't 'pinpoint' them physically in space and time they became identified as dangerous. In 1888, one petitioner in the Bavarian debate already mentioned asked the rhetorical question, 'What do we need the huckster for, since we've got railways, roads and modern means of transport?'[15] Many would have concurred with delegate Haberland, a craftsman, who recalled his contribution to the 1888 debate, which turned out to be a rather general rant: on salaries for civil servants (considered too low), the general economic conditions of the honest farmer and 'small people' (in a dilatory state) and the evils of Social Democracy at large. He identified hucksters and pedlars as 'vermin' (*verderbliche zerstörerische Ungeziefer*). They had to be uprooted.[16] On that occasion, however, Haberland apparently earned mostly laughter and jokes, as the protocol notes. He also received a stern warning from the chairman; not for his derogatory remarks on pedlars, but for his much more heinous allegation that the Bavarian government had inadvertently facilitated the rise of Social Democracy (seen by many Bavarians as equal to the Antichrist).[17] Interestingly, public discourse had also positive things to say on the itinerant trader: some would claim that hucksters and pedlars were important links within the distributive chain. Small tradesmen and shopkeepers regularly employed them to extend the outreach of their business.[18]

Debates continued beyond 1889, but according to State Minister Feilitzsch's speech 1889, complaints had been heard and first legislative measures taken since the 1870s.[19] One way to deal with the problem was to tax the huckster, something that had been tried (but to little avail).[20] The German *Reichstag* (Imperial Diet) had adopted a more liberal position towards peddling under the auspices of general freedom of trade (*Gewerbefreiheit*). The Bavarian Diet strongly disapproved of this.[21] Feilitzsch also urged people to distinguish between peddling and itinerant business by craftsmen and traders (*ambulante Gewerbe*). Such *ehrliche* or 'honest' hucksters were vital for the market economy. It would have been easier to prevent peddling in cities, where trading could be monitored and regulated (*eingehegt*) through the spatial-institutional framework of markets and emerging department stores. But in the countryside, with its dispersed villages, the rural folk were dependent upon the huckster.[22] Hucksters solved the problem that in order to engage with the market you would have to walk a few miles back and forth, at least a day trip's worth.[23] The cost was a lack of regulation, rule and quality enforcement possibilities, which made the countryside a much more fertile ground for rogue laissez-faire.

The debates of the 1880s came long after individual property rights had been assigned by ways of abolishing noble privileges over land and the agrarian and political reforms that had commenced in some cases even before the French Revolution but mostly between 1807 (Prussia) and 1861 (Russia), creating a class of individual land-owning tenants and a fully fledged land market.[24]

Simultaneously many such reforms aimed at the liberalization of urban industry and commerce, by abolishing (or trying to abolish) the monopoly of guilds on regulating market entry.[25] The Bavarian *Gewerbeordnung* of 1868 had, in the words of the same voice that lamented so graphically about hucksters, led to the 'apocalyptic catastrophe' (*himelschreienden Katastrophe*) of thousands of innocent small artisans, craftsmen and manufacturers who were thrown into the gaping jaws of avarice (aka free market capitalism), where people drowned in a 'Great Deluge', a possible Biblical allegory (*man warf mit Allgewalt ohne Erbarmen die so theuer erworbenen Rechte über Bord, so daß Hunderte und Tausende in den tobenden unbarmherzigen Wellen und Fluthen ihren Tod fanden*).[26] Many would see the same forces at work in the land market and contemporary rural society.

The debates on hucksters, however, were neither new nor peculiar to the industrial transformations of the later 19th century. Medieval and early modern political economy had sported essentially similar views. *Höken* or *Höker* (huckster), resellers or regraters, that is, economic actors purchasing more goods than needed, with the obvious aim of gaining a profit by cornering the market, failed to add any value to the common weal. Since the later Middle Ages and into the early modern period many came across in German-language sources as 'Scots'. Almost as a synonym *Scotus* in contemporary quotations indiscriminately referred to people of (supposedly) Irish, Scottish or northern English birth; but in early modern Germany the term had attained a standing reputation and life of its own, denoting the character of (shoddy) economic activity rather than ethnic origin.[27] In a letter to his wife Katharina (1540) Luther had referred in passing to *Schottenheller*, meaning completely valueless and useless small-change coins (*Heller* being halfpennies). In medieval English markets, 'hucksters, hawkers and regraters were closely watched, and authorities were anxious that they should not usurp the privileges of more permanent retailers'.[28] A 1726 market ordinance (*Marktordnung*) from the Saxon city of Leipzig, a city that also sported one of the biggest international trading fairs of its age, generally prohibited the reselling of victual and essentials, namely grain, chickens, geese, eggs, butter and fish, as well as timber for building and firewood for anyone apart from those who had registered and obtained a certificate for retailing.[29] These economic actors were only allowed upon the market after 11 am, giving the public the opportunity to meet demand without interference by the middleman; only surplus quantities were released into retailing. *Hökerey*, when carried out during the times and market slots reserved for direct interchange between producer and consumer, was considered incriminatory. A 1696 resolution by Leipzig City Council prohibited the forestalling of chickens, geese, eggs, butter, fish and other victuals, that is, *Aufkauff von hünern, gänsen, Eyern, Butter, fischen und anderen vicualien* (to which timber and firewood were later added) as unnatural: something that again harmed the common weal. This withdrew *der Bürgerschaft die Nothdurfft*[30]– an ill-translatable term roughly equal to 'communal economic entitlement of Leipzig citizens to a fair way of making a living'. Practices violating this moral economy had to be unconditionally prohibited. As an incriminatory behaviour, forestalling thus came close to usury.[31]

Two aspects are important in the present context. First, historians often assume premodern markets to have been guarded by tight moral rules and somewhat pre-capitalist norm templates, but this assumption is problematic; while there were some idiosyncratic regulations and discourses on markets, many of which seem lost to us today, this does not mean markets were generally over-regulated or working to non-modern or non-capitalist principles. In fact, medieval and early modern market intervention by the state (or temporal authority acting out powers of state, see Chapter 3) was largely limited to essentials traded on urban markets (today it is energy prices: even in capitalist societies the energy market tends to be densely regulated). Otherwise, authorities tried as much as they could to keep their hands off, and laws and ordinances were intended to *liberate* markets from economic and social asymmetry, such as rent-seeking, monopoly and similar such forms of distortion, which Martin Luther discussed in detail in *Von Kauffshandlung vnd Wucher* in 1524.[32] Second, we may question a Polanyian rupture between 'embedded' or moral economies before and beyond the French and industrial revolutions. Did markets become more laissez-faire after 1800? Had they been shaped by more non–market ideologies before; is it appropriate to think of early modern continental Europeans as people living in ages 'before capitalism'?[33] While it is probably fair to say that 'in the 18th century, economics, law and ethics were still closely tied together'[34] the same holds, *cum grano salis*, for the Middle and early modern ages, as much as it does today – but the ethics have changed, especially in some modern Anglo-Saxon varieties of capitalism. But also consider early neoliberalism and ordoliberalism of the 1930s and 1940s and their highly moralized competitive market theories.[35] The evidence does not support assumptions of either particularly 'demoralized' markets *after*, nor overly embedded markets *before* *c.*1750/1850, but generally competitive markets adjusted to the prevailing idiosyncratic conditions and requirements of their respective times and age.

In the present chapter I thus want to zoom in on markets as instruments promoting capitalism and economic development, followed by Chapters 5 on currency and 6 on velocity.

Of markets and men: modern models and market enchantments

Markets have been around for thousands of years, across the world.[36] But they are often reified or taken for granted; 'economic science has, until very recently, treated markets as naturally occurring loci for the exchange of goods and services and thus part of the assumptive world of economic thought, rather than as phenomena with contested origins which require investigation in their own right'.[37] Markets reduce transaction costs and facilitate division of labour, urbanization and extensive or 'Smithian' growth;[38] they were even more fundamental in Schumpeterian (or intensive) growth processes following a Renaissance strategy of development, often labelled the 'European standard model' as outlined in Chapter 1 (and to which we will return in Chapters 7 and 8).[39] Markets have been used as *explanans* in comparative global histories of income and purchasing power differentials, small and great divergences, or in stylized contrasts between comparatively (over)regulated *ancien régime* European market cultures on the one, and more laissez-faire China on the other hand.[40]

But the very assumption of markets as an explanans rather than explanandum in itself represents a modern form of enchantment.[41] Scholars employing a 'positivist' rationale occasionally apply a simplified understanding of economic performativity derived from modern economic theory, while others emphasizing the moral nature and quality of markets through a 'substantivist' approach would postulate that there were fundamental differences that separate premodern or preindustrial market societies from more modern modes of exchange, with various assumptions of historical transitions, for instance from 'moral' or 'before capitalism' to disembedded or 'capitalist' market economies.[42] It has also been suggested that there were specifically 'medieval' or 'early modern' outlooks on markets (implicitly suggesting that such outlooks somewhat radically changed again during and after the Industrial Revolution).[43] I would take all these as a given: in *every* time and age, economic actors produce their own specific political economies of markets.[44] Trivellato has proposed a middle way, arguing that premodern 'markets achieved a fragile compromise between elements of status and elements of contract, at least for the most protected categories of goods and workers', and that 'by insisting on this fragile compromise we come closer to an accurate description of how markets worked in societies of order in prerevolutionary Europe than by drawing from Thompson's concept of the moral economy'.[45] Medieval English property markets seem as competitive as later markets in modern capitalism, and the evidence for early 16th-century German capitalism points into similar direction, where markets were omnipresent and ubiquitous, which is also borne out by the rich economic discourse of the Renaissance and early Reformation age that evolved around issues of money, markets and salvation.[46] In the following I will argue that in many markets in the German-speaking lands, 'medieval' and 'early modern' market regulation survived into the later 19th century, that is, industrial capitalism. Still, these times witnessed highly moralized debates on markets. Another origin myth (which may be called 'neoliberal') has modern capitalism evolving through the *victory* of the market, through *deregulation* and a *retreat* of the state from the market process.[47] Landmarks include popular classics like Friedman (*Capitalism and Freedom*, 1962), or Hayek's *Road to Serfdom* (1944). Following this literature we would portray preindustrial European market governance as coercive, interventionist and regulatory, but this was only true occasionally for grain and food markets, usually during times of crisis.[48] Alternative modes of exchange and forms of allocation, including 'moral economy', common economy, 'civic society', reciprocity, gift exchange and redistribution (taxation), were also known to medieval and early modern market cultures, in the same way as they belong to modern industrial (and post-industrial) capitalism too: they did not necessarily represent forms of allocation that were mutually exclusive, but often supplementary or even complementary to market exchange.[49] On the other hand, early modern market models remained deeply embedded within late medieval practices and thought. In tune with the modern market-fundamentalist viewpoint Seabright,[50] for instance, has proposed an (inherently paradox) scenario of human freedom without order, and the idea that order in the market may obtain spontaneously *quasi ex nihilo*. The popular 'invisible hand' metaphor represents one of the most common invocations of Adam Smith by modern scholars.[51] But neither a positivist nor substantivist nor market-fundamentalist/utopian approach fully captures the dynamics and political economies of preindustrial markets.

There was a long tradition in European thought that dealt with market infringements and conceptually wrestled with competitiveness, regulation and the idea of free price formation. From the medieval scholastic authors to *Soziale Marktwirtschaft* and *ordoliberalism* in the 20th century, economic thinkers emphasized the virtues of free markets; but such freedom was based on order. Freedom and regulation represented two sides of the same coin, precisely to avoid market distortions, rent-seeking and other asymmetries in exchange.[52] From medieval scholasticism to the Enlightenment, from Italy to Scotland and Sweden-Finland writers and thinkers like Aquinas, Luther, Cesare Beccaria (1738–94), Antonio Genovesi (1713–69), Anders Chydenius (1729–1803)[53] to Adam Smith were aware of humans as sociable beings within their wider networks defined by moral norms, the Christian faith or simply the sentiments dictated by anthropology: creatures whose sociability unfolded on the marketplace through reciprocity; but these required baseline frames of regulation, lest some claimed too much of their own market freedom at the expense of others.[54] And if markets were, especially during the Middle Ages, circumscribed in terms of specific locations, actors and chronologies, with certain marketplaces – usually towns or cities – claiming regional monopolies on specific goods, this was not necessarily the outcome of a pre-capitalist mentality but, to the contrary, a sign of strong 'capitalist' systems of exchange in place, reflecting interests of regional or local elites manipulating market regulation in their favour.[55] Special 'freedoms' and tax exemptions enjoyed at the cost of society continued to be held by many noblemen by statutory law (this was no German exception; France was proverbial, and in 18th-century Scotland nobles continued to enjoy hereditary exemptions from certain duties on imported wines and other purchases for their own consumption); businessmen bypassed the market by purchasing privileges from their respective rulers.[56] 'Clearing' the market was thus potentially tricky business, as Martin Luther (*On Commerce and Usury*, 1524) or Johann Becher noted (*Politischer Discurs Von den eigentlichen Vrsachen / deß Auf- und Abnehmens / der Städt / Länder / und Republicken*, 1668). When left in a 'natural' state of competition, markets tilted towards monopoly, rent-seeking and other distortions.

Market equilibrium was the result of *political* intervention. This may entail the taking-away of merchandise at the closing hour of the market, or the assignment of discrete trading slots to specified types of economic actors as we have already seen. Or else, 'clearing' the market may mean people *cornering* the market through pre-emptively buying up goods with the aim of creating a shortage, only to resell at much increased prices to the public ('forestalling'). Far from representing natural or spontaneous arrangements they often resulted from conscious forward-planning, a key feature of a capitalist mindset (see Chapter 2). Markets emerged and disappeared in waves and cycles involving state action, as shown by the multiple English medieval country fairs established by privilege, some of which never came to see the light of day, or disappeared shortly after the charter was granted.[57] Such exercises in trial and error reflect a future-facing capitalist mentality towards markets as useful tools for economic development. In medieval England, peasant farmers tended to 'intensify production, specialize, and participate in the market exchange when they [had] to, and feudalism – through the extraction of their surpluses in various forms of feudal rent – obliged them to do precisely this'.[58] During the 17th century the Swedish Crown founded winter fairs in the Sami lands of Lapland, in order to draw the native transhumant Saami people into a cash-based system of market exchange; the primary interest behind this was not to serve a Smithian principle of facilitating 'truck, barter and exchange', but rather to control a population of subalterns, raise revenue and improve state consolidation by integrating indigenous modes of production into an increasingly commercialized (and imperialistic) Swedish polity during Sweden's Age of Greatness (*Stormaktstiden*, c.1648–1721).[59] Throughout European history, markets had proved vital for state formation *and* economic development. It is virtually impossible to keep the two apart.[60]

Our modern visions of the *market process* thus build on theories that are much older, reaching back to scholastic, mercantilist and cameralist roots.[61] Still these theories entertained certain conceptual, spatial and visual models of markets that were very different from ours, and the following section tries to uncover some of their underlying rationalities.

Markets, time and spatiality

German political economy has occasionally been associated with notions of strong order (this was not necessarily a peculiarly 'German' political economy feature, though).[62] During the early modern period, German language usage often subsumed such strategies of ordering markets – with the aim of making them competitive – under the term *policey*, a word that later became associated with a sense of rigid law enforcement, giving rise to conceptual confusion, for instance in Foucault's influential interpretation. A common shorthand interpretation would reduce '[p]olicy (*Polizei*) ... to a painful regulation of all social conditions of the citizens'.[63] Roughly translating as 'order' and the means, instruments, strategies and policies to establish order, *policey* was a catchword in many European languages and, alongside 'happiness', one of the central terms of early modern European political economy. In its practical ramifications it covered a potentially panoptic realm of intervention ranging from street lighting, sexual order, sumptuary law enforcement and market regulation to monetary systems and infant industry protectionism. Yet it was not meant to be universal or universally enforceable as modern usages of the term 'police' seem to insinuate. In many ways, *policey* remained a normative discourse. It framed the limits of the desirable without claims to comprehensive enforcement.[64] In the early modern age, it was used as a concept empowering economic actors and their freedoms on markets, with a view of generating economic dynamics – precisely because in the cameralist view *policey* also included notions of industrial policy, the promotion of domestic competitiveness and of useful knowledge, science and technology. As Johann Heinrich Justi, Germany's most prolific Enlightenment economist argued (*Moralische und Philosophische Schriften*, 1760), order was associated with empty spaces, or spaces that were *relatively empty*. To think of order within a *crammed* spatial arrangement was counterintuitive. We may invoke the allegory of a box or chest packed right up to the top with stuff: how can you find a particular item or piece within such an assemblage of objects even if the packing had followed a plan (that is, wasn't chaotic)? One could only assemble – that is *order* – objects in a regular pattern if there was enough empty space between them. Accordingly, a well-designed order of markets was inherent to any process of societal and economic development.[65] Order turned freedom, productivity and economic development into a possibility.

This entailed a series of very concrete spatial and chronological arrangements.[66] It began with the literal consideration of *where* markets should be located. Early modern German political economy requested that city streets and squares should be 'well spacious' (*genugsam geräumlich*). They should constitute a functional spatial-commercial system. This was important not least because only a generous spatial arrangement left enough room for 'stinking odours' (*Ausdünstungen*) to clear away. Too many people crammed into one spot represented veritable health and safety risks. Marketplaces and roads leading to the market should be 'spacious', set out in optimal proportion and well-connected to maximize the efficiency of market access. To prevent fires and let air flow freely, buildings should be no more than five storeys high; new buildings no more than three.[67]

Ordering markets also carried chronological implications. In mid-17th century Leipzig, the process of physically 'clearing' the weekly markets (*Markträumung*) had to be completed by 2 pm. Tone and content of these regulations usually reached back far into medieval times, and they were kept well into the 1850s and beyond, sometimes verbatim.[68] In 1656, market times were extended to three o'clock for country butchers (*Landfleischer*);[69] perhaps because they now had a longer way back and forth. Fruit and vegetable *Hacken* or *Höken*, that is, hucksters or resellers, should not be allowed to enter the market before 11 am. This was because they were known to clear the market at their own speed, as the document said (*räumen*), that is before local customers had completed their purchases. Potentially this would create shortfalls in supply and drive up prices.[70] A tradition dating back to the 16th century, if not earlier, had it that such *Höken* must not be 'foreigners' in any case.[71] Fruit, vegetable and salad *Hacken* were also banned from selling their goods on Sundays.[72] Authorities should keep a close eye on them (*Soll man auff alle Haeckhen vndt Vorkauffer ein guth Auffsicht haben*).[73] *Hacken* were to be registered in person with their names and whereabouts; several lists from the later 1720s suggest that most of them were female.[74] In 1771 a census listed a total of 43 households engaged in *Troedlerei* as a main occupation (a total of 127 persons), an activity similar to peddling.[75] The boundaries between this form of retailing and straight forestalling were fluid. As a petition from 1739 suggests, many of the native or domestic *Höken* frequented the inns on the countryside outside the city gates, where they would meet with peasants, buying up victuals before they could reach the urban market.[76] The year 1739 was one of pan-European crisis and harvest failure, which exacerbated the situation; forestalling would have worsened the crisis.[77] The petition also called for a physical division of market stalls. *Höken* should be placed in separate streets from the 'peasant folk' (*Bauern Volck*), to remain identifiable by the general public. This gave farmers space and leeway to set up their stalls on the market at their own pace (*als wodurch dann die Höcken denn Bürgern nicht nur bekannter wurden, sondern auch dem Bauern Volck aif dem Marckt mehr Platz gegeben*).[78] It was hoped that this would reduce skirmishes, fights and other disputes (*viele Zänckerey und Unfug ausblieben*).[79]

Market stalls had to be arranged in a specific order. This mapped onto the social order of actors accessing the market, within a closely orchestrated chronological framework. Plans were drawn with the exact measures of market stalls, down to the precise degrees of angles and slopes of rooftops (Figure 4.1).

Fish markets were to be kept separate from flesh markets, and those in turn were usually to be held in quarters of the town different from where grain and vegetables were sold. This followed public hygiene conceptions in the same way as keeping a minimum threshold of economic fairness in the market. By the 1660s, Leipzig's weekly market had become one of the biggest of its day. It spilled out from the big central market square in front of the town hall, into adjacent closes and streets. The market took place under the open sky, continued into the roofed hallways, vestibules and vaults of the larger merchants' houses lining the market square, then on into adjacent streets such as the Grimmaische Strasse, up to the Naschmarkt. Leipzig City Council members also operated stalls and vaults from which goods were vended, in the same way as the canons of St Nicolas Church, but since the later 1400s most stalls were leased to local merchants.[80] One of the vaults of the City Hall hosted the office of the local mint guardian or *Wardein*, an official appointed by the Saxon rulers who supervised coin exchange and payment in the marketplace, putting the 'right' value on foreign coins and checking those sets of coins that had just sprung fresh from the local mint. A bewildering range of currencies, old and new, foreign and domestic (Saxon) origin circulated, most of which had been admitted as legal tender in the Saxon market economy.[81] We will look at the specific political economies of money closer in Chapters 5 and 6.

Sections 1 and 2 of a 1794 market ordinance for the city of Braunsberg (Braniewo) in Prussia similarly specified the physical locations within the city where buying and selling should normally take place. This included markets for victuals, including fish, cattle and horses; as well as other products such as textiles (woollen goods and so on). Section 3 of the same ordinance sketched the order of filling up the markets with carts; this should be done in straight and even lines, one after the other, in orderly fashion; enough space was to be left in the middle and on the fringes of the market for carts to pass and watchmen to be on their guard. The same order was to be kept on the river for incoming barges laden with grain. Its sale was limited to resident citizens for a period of 24 hours, before it could be offered to merchants, brokers and regraters; Polish grain remained free of such regulation.

Ordering markets in medieval and early modern Europe thus entailed a physical-spatial as well as chronological dimension. The wording and conceptualization of markets and market ordinances exhibited some remarkably constant (or reoccurring) features well into the industrial age. And what was common in the Leipzig and other urban markets around

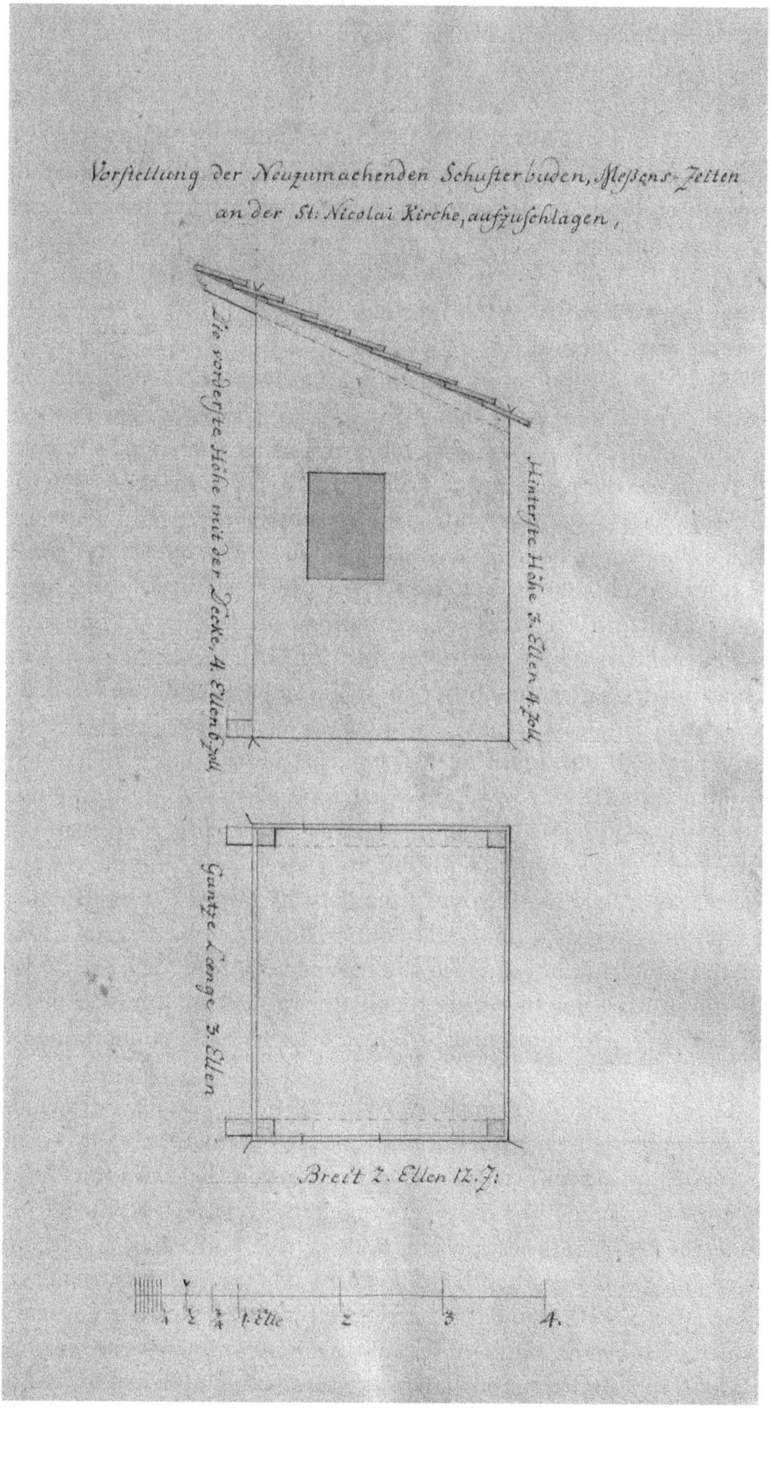

Figure 4.1: Sketch of a new market stall to be erected in the Leipzig weekly market (1765)

Source: STA Leipzig, Tit. LIV Nr. 18 Bl. 58 (16.02.1765). With permission by Leipzig municipal archives.

1600 or 1700 was still common practice in English markets in the early 1800s, with the first Industrial Revolution well under way.[82] Moreover, these regulations closely mirrored templates known from medieval trade regulation[83] and seem to have enjoyed common currency across Western Europe into the age of industry. Different time slots allocated to different market actors (locals, retailers, foreigners and so on) facilitated direct encounters between producers and buyers, increasing transparency. Brokers, retailers and profiteers were potentially looked upon with suspicion, especially on the countryside, where possibilities of monitoring and enforcing would have been more limited – and the market more laissez-faire in consequence.

Now, urban markets were neither the only nor necessarily the main spaces where market exchange took place; *ancien régime* Europe knew several types of market and systems of market exchange. On top of the system were the more abstract ones, tightly regulated and typified by the *exchange* (Ger. *Börse*; fairs and stock exchanges) where products were traded *in absentia* (that is, goods that actually weren't there, but located somewhere else, or goods that hadn't even been produced yet). Stock exchanges founded in Antwerp in 1631, Amsterdam in 1611 and London in 1571 traded handwritten paper notes, bills of exchange, stocks and financial obligations; on grain and other goods exchanges goods were traded usually by *muster* (sample, specimen) or otherwise endorsed by the seller's promise to guaranteed minimum quality standard and quantity.[84] Then came the regional country and city fairs, which took place up to four times per year; for goods acquired through long-distance trade; larger international trade fairs connecting regions with different levels of economic development were also crucial for European market integration.[85] Grants and patents establishing regional and local country fairs followed certain logics and rhythms catering not only for the regional economy but also considering the rhythms of neighbouring regional, national and international systems of exchange, thus integrating local markets into wider trans-regional circuits of exchange.

Then came the weekly markets, in pretty much any city or town, because that was one of the main economic functions of towns, usually documented by means of special privilege; markets were also held in some villages and in the countryside. Territorial rulers granted market privileges in return for taxes, fees, road tolls and other duties levied on activities in the market. These included fees and other dues charged in return for the trader's right to erect a stall (*Bude*), stand, or 'basket' in the market; or to keep a vault from which goods were vended.[86] Fees also accrued for paying the weighers who assessed and testified goods' correct type, quantity and quality.[87] And so on.

Since the Middle Ages, political economy would be written usually from an urban vantage point before attaining a more macro or territorial outlook towards the 17th and 18th centuries. This does not mean that economic exchange was limited to the cities and towns. Recent studies have asserted a relatively thorough commercialization of early modern German village society.[88] The problem remains that such transactions and economic networks have rarely been captured in writing, let alone survived in the archives. Peasants didn't usually keep written records (or, at least, these haven't survived).[89] If we want to capture 'the market' in early modern Europe – practically as well as in terms of political economy and economic thought, our focus is urban almost by default.

Well-ordered police states? The myth of over-regulated markets, 1250s–1850s

In his *Lectures at the College du France*, Foucault famously integrated early modern *policey* into his overall theory of early modern governmentality, as 'that authoritarian intervention of the state in the form of police, which controls the space, the territory, and the population'. This was part of a larger process of state formation, specifically 'an attempt at a general disciplinarization, a general regulation of individuals and the territory of the realm in the form of a police based on an essentially urban model. Making the town into a sort of quasi-convent and the realm into a sort of quasi-town is the kind of great disciplinary dream behind police'.[90] Echoing Bücher's old concept of city economy and stadial evolution of markets over time[91], Foucault claimed that premodern state administrations' main aim would have been subjects' 'total and exhaustive obedience in their conduct to whatever the imperatives of the state may be'.[92] Foucault's views were in tune with postmodern vibes of his age, which put a premium on individualism; to the present day postmodernism and neoliberalism are sceptical of the state.[93] But when trying to understand preindustrial European political economy, Foucauldian approaches can be profoundly misleading.

Let's look at some figures. The Frankfurt Max Planck Institute for European Legal History has produced an awe-inspiring compendium of (thus far 12) thick volumes of available archival sources documenting early modern German market governmentality between the 1300s to the early 1800s – *Policeyordnungen*, police ordinances – including those territories located within the Holy Roman Empire but under foreign rule, such as Swedish Pomerania.[94] This is the type of police that Foucault alluded to and which Adam Smith mentioned several times, including the posthumously published *Lectures on Jurisprudence* (1763).[95] Known in many European countries and languages, *Gute Policey* (German), Police (English), *bonne police* (French) and so on captured the baseline of early modern social and economic normative discourse about what was right and what wasn't, including sumptuary laws, behaviour in markets and other social regulation. As we saw in Chapter 3, and will again in Chapters 5 and 6, *policey* included the regulation of currency, weights and measures, food supply and public goods (such as clean water). Occasionally it would capture wider normative recommendations of what types of garment and cloth were considered appropriate to which sort of people or social group.[96] In a rough arithmetic exercise counting the uncountable[97] I estimated the number of ordinances issued in the Holy Roman Empire between 1450 and 1800 regarding the prohibition of forestalling or *Fürkauf*, a clearly defined market infringement: perhaps *the* most common violation of the free market principle identified in medieval and early modern sources on economic governmentality.[98] Forestalling most commonly referred to merchants buying up supplies of a particular commodity peremptorily, either at the point of production or even before (by means of a *future* option of purchase, for instance grain either still in the field or not even grown yet), or in any case before the goods reached the common market. Contemporary theory identified this behaviour as usurious, harming the common weal.[99] Since we cannot expect the actual type of incriminatory behaviour thus captured to have changed radically over time, the series seems standardized enough to bear out a *longue durée* view (see Figures 4.2, 4.3 and 4.4).

Figure 4.2: *Gute Policy* or total social control? Number of ordinances relating to forestalling (*Fürkauf*), Holy Roman Empire, 1450–1800

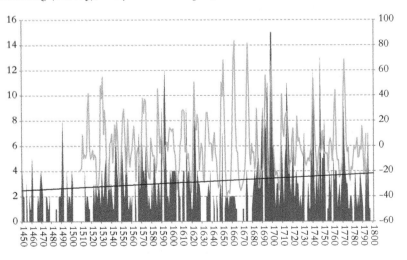

▬ Total nr of ordinances relating to *forestalling* (incl. imperial cities)

— Price Level Oscillation (Rye; deviation in percent from 25-year-moving AVE)

— Linear (Total nr of ordinances relating to *forestalling* (incl. imperial cities))

Figure 4.3: Trend lines for the number of ordinances relating to forestalling (*Fürkauf*) in imperial cities and the territorial states, Holy Roman Empire, 1450–1800

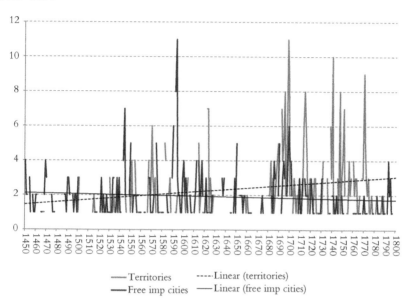

In the German-speaking lands the total number of ordinances dealing with *Fürkauf* thus circumscribed ascended only moderately between 1450 and 1800. The trend line was mildly negative for imperial cities (given all statistical uncertainties that go with this type of data), but interestingly more pronouncedly positive for territorial states, suggesting a somewhat clearer edge towards 'regulation' among the emerging fiscal states (see also Chapter 3). Yet, even in the case of the territorial states the increase was rather moderate. I could see no *significantly* large ascending trend over time. More importantly, intervention seems to have roughly mirrored grain-market fluctuations, measured as the percentage deviation from a 25-year-moving average of a price series for major German grain markets.[100] Therefore we may draw – even if the data doesn't lend itself to more formal quantitative modelling – the very tentative conclusion that in preindustrial Europe states neither had an interest (nor, to be fair, really the power) to regulate markets and society the way occasionally suggested in Foucauldian literature. German states *intervened chiefly in times of economic crisis (harvest failure), but tended to keep their hands off the market in normal times.*

This is a far cry from what modern industrial-bureaucratic and interventionist states could and would do to their citizens: contemporary

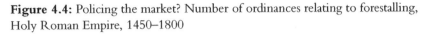

Figure 4.4: Policing the market? Number of ordinances relating to forestalling, Holy Roman Empire, 1450–1800

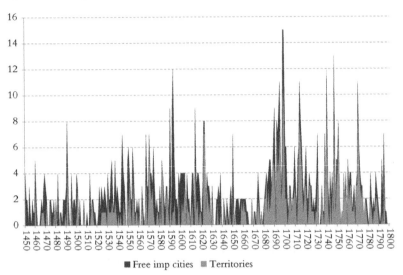

■ Free imp cities ■ Territories

(21st-century) states can potentially know almost everything about their citizens, from spending habits to tax evasion propensity.[101] Given that the modern literature has often gone the opposite way, peddling various myths of early modern 'absolutist' state governance, or transitions from *ancien régime* absolutist mercantilism to more liberal forms of economy and so on (see Chapter 3), with an increasing drive of early modern states to 'regulate' their denizens' lives,[102] it is striking to find so relatively little evidence of this in the sources on economic governance. *Economic regulation* was, during normal times, light touch – and probably meant to be; at least in the most important market of the time: foodstuffs. Other areas, such as manufacturing (which contributed a much smaller share to incomes and output) occasionally saw other and more rigorous forms of interventionism, and we will discuss the rationales and implications of this in subsequent chapters.[103]

This should give us some pause to reflect: as a discursive trope and powerful idea shaping modern capitalism, the free market co-emerged with Europe's transformation into the industrial economy over the past three centuries.[104] As the last harvest crises of the *ancien régime* type swept continental countries in the 1770s, it became fashionable to advocate deregulation and liberalization of grain markets (which at that time extended mainly to price controls), and thus improve welfare by introducing the supposedly free forces of demand and supply. As Rothschild and Kaplan have noted, however, these were not calls for *general* economic liberalization.

Writers of the physiocrat ilk, usually associated with a more liberal view on markets, seem to have been generally very happy with keeping high levels of regulation in other sectors of economy.[105]

The term 'free market' as such is an oxymoron, and has been long understood as such. It simultaneously represents the ultimate goal *and* paradox of capitalist societies.[106] Effective markets require rules, supervision and a balanced mix between forms of action commonly stylized in the literature as 'coercion' and 'laissez-faire'. (Neither label is helpful, because neither represent empirical forms of resource allocation. In history, polities and societies used mixtures of both, depending upon commodity class and type of good, the market segment, whether feudal, capitalistic or something else.) This was obviously understood by temporal authorities since early times, even as premodern states lacked the law enforcement capacities characteristic of modern bureaucratic-industrial capitalism.

Strategies of market order, 1250s–1800s

Since the later Enlightenment it became increasingly fashionable to interpret market processes as answering to mechanical logics and laws of physics.[107] Modern markets are thus characterized by 'rationality, computability, contract'.[108] Such markets required little interference by the state (other than designing a fair tax code). Individuals are assumed to act rationally, and information distributed symmetrically. But, of course, reality looks different, and throughout the ages political economy writers would consider that economic actors are somewhat irrational, not all the time, of course, but that markets were a good too precious to be left alone and unattended.

These were by no means 'medieval' or premodern templates. Just consider *ordoliberalism*, the German version of post-war economic neoliberalism. (The project was begun before 1945 during National Socialism, but it became the crucible upon which the post-war Western German success model of coordinated capitalism was forged.) Navigating a difficult strait between Western-Atlantic versions of market-fundamentalism on the one hand, and Marxist projects of remodelling society on the other, ordoliberalism's fundamental proposition was to establish a competitive capitalist market economy securing optimum welfare, surpassing scarcity and ultimately reconstructing the nation's economic wealth, retaining market fairness as well as the principle of individual self-responsibility. Perfect competition meant the absence of cartels and rent-seeking, which Schumpeter in *Capitalism, Socialism and Democracy* (1942) had identified as characteristic features of late capitalism. Ordoliberals were especially concerned with bad 'perfect competition' when market-fundamentalism was taken to its extremes. To prevent all this, a stable currency was essential, open markets, freedom to negotiate contracts, and the principle of full liability (*Haftung*).[109] The general price mechanism should serve as the main allocation mechanism. Markets should be open and transparent; private property was deemed as a necessary thing per se; especially for capital assets. The economy should not become depersonalized; every entrepreneur should take full responsibility of all the consequences of their economic activity, as emphasized by Walter Eucken, one of the leading proponents of this school. Economic policy and outlook should be congruent and coherent, providing stability of expectations. The state should consequently battle monopoly and other market infringements that gave undue control of economic power into the wrong hands; ordoliberals even called for minimum wages (!), if population pressure depressed incomes below feasible or 'just' or subsistence level.

We will look at the *longue durée* view on monetary stability in Chapter 5, but suffice to say that medieval scholastic and early modern mercantilist and cameralist authors from the 15th century to the 19th shared key elements of this market philosophy of coordinated competitive capitalism. Obviously history moved on, and physical-material environments changed along the way and occasionally required adjustment of some of the rules, so it would be wrong to claim that ordoliberals shared the same market ideology as Luther, the late scholastics or Johann Becher. But modern researchers have been able to trace references of some ordoliberal thinkers to late medieval religious and political theories of order, so the *longue durée* was not irrelevant in shaping 20th-century models of coordinated capitalism.[110] One business historian even offered the (somewhat anachronistic) hypothesis that medieval market theory contained all elements necessary for the formation of modern market theory.[111] This is problematic, because it requires a simultaneous disassembling of modern theories (which are multiple and diverse) and then their reconfiguration through reconstructions stage by stage over time, of the bits and fragments offered by late medieval and early modern monetary and market theory, proving direct influence in each instance (we will look closer at snippets of monetary theory in Chapters 5 and 6). We would especially need firm evidence, in the shape of quotations, personal libraries (of the 'big' thinkers studied), their academic circles, symposia attended and lecture notes over time – anything that would allow us to prove such longer-term connections and 'traditions'. From a purely methodological perspective even searching for such long traditions of ideas may be problematic; suffice it to point out some of the main morphological parallels.

Looking just at the main contents of market practices as captured by documented transactions and accompanying templates of regulation helps clear up the picture a bit. Reconstructing the history of market practices from the Renaissance to the Industrial Revolution is anything but straightforward. Evidence of actual transactions, prices and transaction volumes is much harder to come by than theoretical treatises on market exchange and political economy, especially for agrarian economies before the Industrial Revolution.[112] We can draw upon records produced by governments and their administrators trying to regulate economic lives, as well as documents from the private business sphere produced by merchants, lawyers, brokers and other middlemen.[113] None of these are unbiased. Government records reflect their idiosyncratic 'governmentalities' of 'seeing like a state'.[114] Merchants were notoriously prone to cheat and evade formal economic governance. The best evidence we have, however, seems to suggest that price formation on medieval and early modern markets was 'bifurcated'.[115] On the one hand we find, especially in urban food markets, *competitive* prices coexisting with sets of fixed prices or set rates for certain limited types of goods and transaction cycles. As we have seen, market intervention was usually off the table for government and temporal authority unless at times of crisis, that is, when intervention was considered necessary to stabilize the common good. So-called 'tax prices' (or wages in the case of labour), in German *Preistaxen* and *Lohntaxen*, were occasionally applied, setting maximum wages or price caps, minimum and threshold prices, or intervals and price spans within which prices were allowed to fluctuate. Evidence from 14th-century French towns suggests that such measures were more discursive than normative; price taxes were regularly circumvented, and there is little evidence of this having been fundamentally different in the German-speaking lands.[116] Municipal governments acknowledged that persistently 'wrong' price design, bypassing the 'free' market price would cause allocative problems (misallocation). Therefore, regulation and intervention *emphatically should not apply during normal times*; we must also acknowledge, however, practical limitations towards enforcing grain-market intervention, as monitoring and enforcement, public grain storage capacities and other market stabilization possibilities were underdeveloped and transport costs high.[117] In cities dependent upon export industries, prices for raw materials such as flax and hemp were occasionally regulated, salt, timber and other essentials, too. Supervision extended to quality and the monitoring of weights and measures, or the sampling of brews and baker's bread and so on. Occasionally, as the case of the city of Cologne (1495/98) shows, quite complex formulae were developed to get grain prices 'right'.[118] As bread prices were frequently fixed, the weight of bread was adjusted allowing fluctuations in the current market prices for grain, a phenomenon known in modern times as 'shrinkflation' (where price hikes are concealed by decreasing package size while keeping the price constant).[119] Compared to modern contemporary capitalism, where nearly every economic transaction outside the black market is heavily regulated – usually by means of invisible regulation preceding market access, enforcement of minimum standards and quality norms, or direct price intervention in the case of food and energy sales – medieval and early modern markets were decidedly laissez-faire.

Myriads of regulative templates, markets and monetary ordinances have come down to us through urban, municipal and territorial archives.[120] Grain markets are comparatively well documented; for most bigger towns and cities we have recorded series, often monthly, for grain and other vital raw materials. These have been used by historians in reconstructing market fluctuations and market integration.[121] To what extent did these fluctuations reflect competitive markets? This is difficult to assert, because institutional purchasers (and occasionally sellers) of grain, such as city councils and other public authorities – from which such historical price evidence is usually drawn – bought at favourable below-market rates, potentially influencing market outcomes and price formation. On the other hand, the price series we have for medieval and early modern Europe tend to exhibit exactly those fluctuations and changes we commonly associate with the textbook script of a competitive market. Historians of early modern governmentality have found state legislation, especially when it came to police/*policey* and the establishment of normative order, to be less about strict enforcement and more about discourses about what was right and what was not.[122] *Saying* things mattered as much to rulers as *doing* things, and the evidence presented in the previous section on forestalling has lent some tentative quantitative support to this argument. Regulation and enforcement were usually limited to clearly circumscribed market *segments*, often carrying concrete time signatures. An example is, again, given by a 1726 Leipzig market ordinance, a type of record we have already encountered. In terms of wording, composition and drive, this ordinance built on medieval legislative market semantics (and continued well into the later 19th century). So long as the market flag was up, retailers were prohibited to buy up goods in bulk; goods had to be sold by the piece. But as soon as the market flag was taken down (*nach gefallenem Wisch*), everyone – burghers, brokers, citizens, regraters – were free to buy at freely negotiable prices and quantity.[123] A similar regulation existed for meat. Butchers first had to put aside set quantities of meat for individual local buyers. After 9 am in the summer (and 10 am in winter time), however, they could offer all they had on a 'first come, first served' basis. Violations of this non-discretionary free market principle cost a fine of five *Thaler*.[124] After the circumscribed market segment for local purchases the *Marktzwang* was waived, and the market liberalized, for the sake of quicker turnaround. An earlier Leipzig market order from the mid-1650s had allowed traders from Austria, Hungary and Moravia to sell their merchandise directly to 'anyone who desired them' and allow them to hit the road again as soon as possible (*sollen sie nicht gezwungen werden, auf den Marckt zu fahren und feil zu haben, sondern jedermann davon zu geben, wer sie begehrt, auf daß sie desto eher wieder zur Ladung kommen, und sich wieder auf die Raise schicken koennen*).[125] A 1794 market ordinance from Braunsberg in Prussia knew a similar segmentation of the market. Until 11 am only native citizens could buy grain on the market; this market slot was reserved for the city and its subsistence needs (called *das Consument*). The idea behind this – safeguarding sufficiency or *Nahrung* for locals – dated back to the Middle Ages. According to Justi, 11 am was the common hour in most German market towns.[126] When flags were taken down after 11 am, the market was opened to the wider public, including brokers, retailers and wholesalers. Victual markets, especially, were regulated so as to leave purchasers and sellers in peace to freely seal their deals and agree upon a price without interference by another party (§12). Butter and grain measures were to be checked before these products could be put up for sale, to achieve standardization and prevent usury (§§8, 9). Anyone caught in violation of these acts would – if this was the first incidence – have their goods confiscated; if this happened repeatedly, fines and corporal punishment were the result (§§15–17). The ordinance was published by reading it out aloud during church sermon on Sunday (*von den Kanzeln zu verlesen*). Printed copies were to be put up at the Town Halls and the Town Gates (§23). Thus was the early modern free market conceptualized in cameralist political economy.

In Ulm, an ordinance of 1414 created the free market by lifting all quantitative and chronological restrictions on slaughtering; butchers were allowed to process as much meat as they wanted, at any time, at their discretion. A petition from 1470 had Leipzig citizens asking for a 'free market' in meat, allowing foreign butchers in. The recent monopoly enjoyed by local butchers had led to considerable adulteration of goods, bad (*böse*) quality and local meat fights (*zerren* and *ziehen*); the richer you were the better pieces of meat you got at the market. Here, a free market was achieved by lifting an existing monopoly, as a means of abolishing scarcity and *improving* the quality of provisioning. This extended to product quality. Fish to be sold on Leipzig's weekly markets had to meet certain minimum standards of weight and measure. Any small fish, crayfish and crustacean falling below these standards had to be thrown back into the rivers and lakes whence they had been taken.[127] Modern capitalism knows similar institutions, preventing monopoly, speculation, arbitrage and other market distortions, but also regulating quality, controlling for health and safety, especially for pharmaceuticals, victuals and electrical equipment. Safeguarding a critical minimum standard of goods belongs to the DNA of capitalist market governance.[128]

In early modern times notions of freedom in the market thus played out as notions of economic order. On one level this captured the physical-spatial architecture of the market; another conceptualized markets as virtual spaces of interaction; a third axis was time. For a market to be 'free' it had to be literally cleared of all obstructions. Buyers and sellers should be empowered to meet on equitable terms, physically as well as in terms of rules and the institutional framework. This entailed a principle of *supervision*, as we also saw in urban regulations relating to pedlars, brokers and other middle(wo) men. How liberal the premodern market order was in tune is perhaps illustrated in a comment to the official Prussian announcement (*Amtsblatt*) of the Breslau district government in 1811, which explicitly limited municipal market regulations to the Braunsberg urban market times: outside the specified market times everyone and everybody had the right to bring to market and buy and sell anything they wanted, at any time, and as much as they wished, and to freely negotiate prices and quantities of goods, inside and outside the city. Only during Sunday church sermons did commerce have to stop. Numerous other ordinances were produced to the same tune elsewhere, not only in the late 18th or early 19th centuries. None of them seem in any way peculiar or significantly different; they all reflect basically very similar philosophies of exchange. Their wording and structure changed surprisingly little between the 1400s and the 1800s.[129] Regulations of similar type were known all across western Christendom, be that in Rome (Campo de' Fiori), Paris or London.[130]

Beyond the Industrial Revolution and the moral economy: back to the 1890s

Some of the developments discussed previously coincided with an era of a landslide of political, social and economic changes brought about by the Enlightenment, the French and Industrial Revolutions and the rise of industry; a time once labelled by an influential conceptual historian as Europe's *Sattelzeit* (Koselleck) where people – like the rider on the saddle of the horse, could simultaneously look to the olden times (represented by the *ancien régime*) as well as the new fate ahead (represented by the industrial age), but with history and society still undecided about what course to finally take (Chapter 2).[131] Indeed such interpretations very much capture Hegel's *Weltgeist* on horseback, usually people on high horses – modern history of political concepts and ideas is notoriously biased towards high-fashion theoretical writings capturing views and interests of the elite – but not necessarily in tune with the economic worries and sentiments of the common folk. It can – and has – thus occasionally given rise to some conceptual and chronological fuzziness.

Around 1800 a series of agrarian reforms swept across the German lands (and elsewhere), introducing individual land ownership for those who had previously worked as dependent serfs or bonded peasants; this also was an age of the waning of merchant and craft guilds, accompanying processes of deregulation in the urban production landscapes.[132]

No servitude whatsoever, neither of the vassal to his lord, nor the dependent peasant to the proprietor of his land, of journeyman to master and so on, regardless how much such relationships may have changed or diverged from their original character of mutuality and reciprocity, can be compared to the relationship of the debtor to his creditor, in terms of its inherent dishonouring and humiliating nature[133]

wrote economic romanticist (and antisemite) Adam Müller, in his *Treatise on Money* in 1816. What Müller described was the transformation from an *ancien régime* corporate market economy to fully fledged capitalism with clearly defined private property rights following Roman law, and competitive markets that now tended to interpret land, labour and capital as increasingly mobile and marketable factors of production. In Müller's day and age this transition was still under way. The post-1807 Prussian reforms had aimed at abolishing serfdom, creating the free market and establishing 'commercial society' by abolishing old guild privileges in the cities and towns, and noble privileges in the countryside. To Müller and other sceptics of his age, this all smacked of 'Smithianism', a new fashion that had swept the continent and completely uprooted the social body politic.[134] Smith, in his 1776 *Wealth of Nations*, had based his analysis on an advanced-agrarian commercial society, a historically very peculiar model and exceptional case (see Chapter 1). The British economy had long been marked by comparative economic freedom. Elsewhere, agrarian production had remained embedded in manorial and feudal modes of allocation that often were only partially market-oriented, often cooperative and sometimes, as in the case of the urban craft and merchant guilds, worked according to the principle of incorporation. East of the River Elbe the manorial or demesne system had been particularly strong. The *ancien régime* social model of corporate estates (*Stände*) and demesne or feudalist economy had given everyone their firm place and a degree of protection from the worst vagaries of life, Müller argued. Abolishing corporatism, feudalism and the cultural-social ties that bound humans together in the human economic process all at once following Smith's rationale, Müller argued, would only lead to atomistic competition and a-personal individualism: the dark forces of economic modernity. It would create a lifeless and bloodless society, ridden by destitution, poverty and armies of proletarians unable to work sufficiently long to pay off the new debts incurred in return for the creation of private property according to Roman law (allodial property or individual ownership). It would bring back servitude leading back to the pre-Hobbesian state of nature of *homines homini lupi*. Müller thus made a startling case for old modes of agrarian production.

Müller and the economic romanticists, however, were marginal figures in 19th-century economic thought. Modern historians have occasionally interpreted economic modernizations post-1800 as policies by rulers and authorities trying to retain their traditional power base. The 'defensive modernization' hypothesis gained currency in regard to Prussia in particular, a state defeated by Napoleon after 1806; there was very little in it that initially smacked of modern laissez-faire capitalism.[135] However, as we have seen in the present chapter – and Chapter 3 – the cameralists had internalized the virtues of competitive capitalism long before the 1800s. The 'free' market had made inroads into people's economic lives centuries before, but very differently from modern conceptualizations. Some contemporaries around 1800 perceived the new world of industry, liberalism and modernization as anything other than 'brave'; not just because the grip of the state increased in the wake of the French Revolution, and the rise of global trade and industrial revolutions also occasioned important processes of state modernization. Not all would have shared Smithians' conceptualizations of private property and 'free' markets'.[136] And indeed preindustrial forms of economic organization lingered on into modern capitalism long after 1850. The preserved files and market ordinances kept in the Leipzig City Council archives only cover about two handfuls of folders for the time extending between the 1650s and the 1820s. When a new list of market fees and related documentation was compiled in 1824, the documents note that the last time such a list had been compiled had been in 1659.[137] The Leipzig market order from 1726 was applied at least till 1835, as the circumstantial documentary and palaeographic evidence suggests, especially the inserted handwritten comments and annotations.[138] With a 1726 *Marktordnung* that comprised 44 pages and remained in use for over 100 years, only covering essentials, this market was not precisely tightly regulated.

Nor does any of this, however, support the interpretation of radical departures in mainstream political economy regarding markets, or of moral economy giving way to capitalism, or of cameralist and mercantilist theory reflecting pre-capitalist or pre-liberal modes of exchange and premodern frameworks of market regulation. What certainly changed were the materialities of consumption and capitalism. With the industrial take-offs in Saxony, Prussia and elsewhere during the 1830s and 1840s, new worlds of work appeared in the German lands.[139] These occasioned new fields of economic intervention. Working women had no more opportunities to visit the weekly markets in the morning. This had now become a privilege reserved to the leisured classes who kept servants, as the Leipzig City Council noted in 1882.[140] Due to the new rhythms of the working week, factory workers could visit the market only after they had been paid, usually at the end of the week (Saturday evening).[141] But as we have seen, prices at the market differed, depending on whether goods were offered in the morning or afternoon, which, potentially, would create unfair conditions for those unable to enter the market at a time when prices were lower.[142] A resolution presented by the Leipzig chamber of commerce and industry (*Gewerbekammer*) on 28 September 1882 confirmed that times 'were a-changing'; the market did not at all look like it had in the olden days. Few producers nowadays marketed their goods directly (farmers); but if that were the case they usually entered the market in the early hours.[143] The rest of the day the market was dominated by intermediaries (*Höken*) who drove up prices. The working population were advised to buy consumables and essentials from the numerous shops and stores (*Productengeschäfte*) that had sprung up in Leipzig in the meantime instead. The Chamber saw no fundamental reason to keep the market – perceived to be a nuisance by those living close-by – open beyond 2 pm. The wholesalers on the other hand vehemently opposed this proposition, insisting on longer market hours. Most goods, including another new item on the menu: tropical fruit (*Südfrüchte*) had to be brought in on the railways each day which cost time, especially in the morning, they claimed.

Almost none of the wholesalers were Leipzig residents. Restricting market hours to the morning and early afternoon would have meant increasing transaction costs, especially for additional storage, staff and logistics. Traders claimed that it would have been too difficult to hire extra spaces in the city cellars and vaults during the times of the big international Leipzig trade fairs.[144] The chamber of industry noted that 'housewives' hesitated to frequent shops, still preferring the weekly market instead, because it offered a greater choice, especially with regards to butter, fruit and green vegetables.[145] Working-class women were unable to keep servants. For better or worse, they were occupied with housekeeping and other chores in the morning, and couldn't freely access the market either.[146] A compromise solution was offered reconciling both interests by stipulating that market hours should extend to 6 pm in summer (April–September), and 4 pm in winter time (October– March).[147] Leipzig City Council finally accepted the proposition submitted by the Chamber by decree on 5 October 1882.[148] Officially published in the *Leipziger Nachrichten* or *Amtsblatt* and major daily newspapers of Monday 30 October 1882, it was now announced that the *hiesige Wochenmarkt* outside the fair period was to be closed at 4 pm (and during the fair continued to 6 pm), that by these times all stalls had to be dismantled and all rubbish collected and disposed of, again upon hefty fines, possibly even incarceration of up to 14 days.[149] This was a compromise, as market times were reduced; but not as drastically as per the original proposition (to 2 pm). On 14 April 1883, it was decreed that during Leipzig trade-fair times the weekly market should remain open late until 8 pm.[150]

So, the moral economy never gave way to capitalism; but morals were reframed, attuned to the new signs of new times. These practices were also reflected in the theoretical writings of their time and age.

Markets in theory: a continental perspective, 1250s–1850s

Medieval and scholastic definitions of 'just' prices varied. But some approached later notions of competitive markets and price formation.

Aquinas and Augustinus had, in the 13th century, defined a good's price as determined by utility (*indigentia omnia mensurat*). Petrus Johannes Olivi (d 1298) and Buridanus or Bernardo di Siena added a notion of *virtuositas*, *complacibilitas* and *raritas*, considering relative scarcity (supply and demand), as well as costs, troubles and expenses incurred by the merchants in procuring and vending goods as factors influencing price.[151] Konrad Summenhart (1450/60–1502), rector of the University of Tübingen and one of the leading theologians of the Middle Ages, listed a total of 16 factors, including first cost or purchasing price, labour cost, transport and storage cost, or diligence expended in crafting a product (similar passages are found in Adam Smith's first two chapters of Book I of the *Wealth of Nations* 1776). Summenhart's list also extended to search and information costs, risk, transaction type, type and nature of the good under consideration, scarcity, utility or, if applicable, price caps set by the state. This list included items such as the social standing and reputation of the vendor or purchaser or the 'council of a wise old man'; compare this to the practice of price determining common in early modern Scotland known as Fiars Prices, where 'old wise men' from the local parish were consulted in documenting and recording prices from the preceding market period (this was a method of making the market more transparent by recording actual prices from previous periods based on transactions that had actually been taken place. These were also important in fixing the value of rent streams and similar incomes).[152] Johannes Nider (d 1438) had argued that the main factor influencing price formation was the relationship between demand for and supply of a specific good.[153] Roman law (*Corpus iuris civilis*) knew the concept of *multitudo civilis, prout scilicet in civitate sunt multa artificial ad quae una domus sufficere non potest*.[154] The scholastic model thus allowed for differentiation, specialization and division of labour in the economic process. Once a community had reached a certain threshold size, exchange became a necessity. And where there were many goods and buyers, there was competition.

The medieval scholastic view conceived markets as webs of interaction framed by social, moral and legal norms. To look for a simple formula guarding price formation would have been foolish. The Salamanca schoolman Domingo de Soto (1494–1560), a contemporary of Luther, made the point that the very posing of the question did not lead anywhere in particular, because, 'if someone asks you how much he can sell for, and you answer "What justice dictates", you tell him nothing that he did not already know'.[155] Still, scholastic norms provided enough flexibility within the bounds of the normative to keep the market economy running. Scholastics wrote their treatises on money and markets as part of handbooks for repentance. Meant to be used by priests taking the confession from merchants habitually known to stand with one foot in Purgatory (potentially moving on to Hell), they acknowledged changing realities of contemporary capitalism. The increasing flexibility offered in these handbooks points towards their nature as facilitators rather than inhibitors of capitalism in medieval and early modern Europe, and there were certain practices in late medieval monasticism supporting a capitalist outlook thus framed.[156] Other cultures knew similar propositions. In Buddhist economics, for instance, concern 'about the avoidance of suffering … [w]ealth and property are not bad in themselves. Buddhism offers the "middle path". Although that may look, from an outside perspective, to be a place between two extremes, it is not actually a compromise but rather a way of "getting things exactly right".'[157]

In his bestseller *On Commerce and Usury* (1524)[158] Martin Luther admitted that 'buying and selling are necessary'. He conceded that in most cases the factual price realized in the market should be considered the 'just' price. In this way, his notion came close to what earlier scholastics had identified as competitive market prices (discussed earlier). The state should only intervene when prices, profits and market practices violated the common good. Such practices Luther subsumed under the contemporaneous catch-all term 'monopoly',[159] including profiteering, forestalling, price dumping, futures trading, undercutting, using straw men, price cartels, ruinous competition, manipulation and adulteration of merchandise, or deliberate bankruptcy.[160] Governments had a duty to intervene to prevent such infringements, establishing the 'free market' in the first place. The 17th-century cameralist-alchemist Johann Joachim Becher, in his magnum opus on the rise and fall of the wealth of nations, knew similar distortions.[161] Different markets should be established for flesh, grain, wine and vegetables at different places in town. This was aimed at achieving a more even distribution of the population across urban space.[162] It was necessary for trade to be supervised in order to rule out 'fraud, overcharging, disorder, preference or bias in transactions' (*Betrug / Bevortheilung / Vnordnung / Haß oder Gunst im Verkauffe*; §2). Straw men should be prohibited (§3), something Luther had proposed in his *Sermon on Commerce and Usury* (1524; discussed earlier). The 'first come first served' principle should rule in the marketplace (apart from Jews; §4). All wares entering the markets must be inspected by municipal authorities (§5). Measures, weights and currency should be supervised by the municipal authorities; uses of false weights, measures and coins were prohibited upon punishment (§6). Becher continued with his famous topology of market distortions, comprising *Propolium* (forestalling), *Polypolium* (ruinous competition) and monopolies, as well as cartels and syndicates. It is no wonder that he also opposed serfdom and feudalism, both of which were incompatible with capitalism.[163] Contrary to later cameralists including Johann Heinrich Justi (whom we encountered in Chapters 1, 2 and 3), Becher was critical of hereditary monarchy, though. This form of state was anti-market, because unconstrained monarchs who inherited the throne were predatory and belligerent, prone to luxury and notoriously exposed to bad counsel by their administrators. He favoured republics (where rulership rotated) as well as 'mixed' constitutions such as the Holy Roman Empire with more of a balance between political interest of rulers, estates and elites.

In his inaugural lecture on the newly established chair in cameral sciences at the enlightened university of Halle an der Saale Johann Peter von Ludewig (*Die zu Halle 1727 neuangerichtete Profession in Oeconomie-Policey und Cammer Sachen*, 1727) emphasized the importance of standardizing and monitoring weights and measures as cornerstones of the free market (§ 33; *Gleichmachung von Ellen; Maaß u. Gewicht*). Metrology was crucial in the framing of property rights and transparent market processes.[164] Anders Berch, holder of the first Swedish university chair in cameral sciences established at Uppsala, confirmed forestalling – which we studied earlier – to be one of the biggest violations of the free market principle.[165] Marketplaces and hours of trading should be monitored by the authorities (§6), just as had been European practice for ages (as we have already seen). Berch also cautioned against monopoly and *polypolium* (ruinous competition), a concept introduced by Becher. Regulation was important but should be moderate; guild monopolies should be avoided. Zedler's grand economic encyclopaedia *Grosses vollständiges Universal-Lexicon Aller Wissenschafften und Künste* called for the state to secure market freedom and justice (*alles besorget und angeordnet ist, was zur Marckt= Freyheit und Gerechtigkeit diensam*).[166] Such freedom included the curbing of rent-seeking and usurious practices including, once again, forestalling, the forging of measures and coins. It defined 'market purchase' (*Marckt= Kauff*) as individual bargaining processes between respectable citizens (1281–82); Johann Georg Krünitz's *Economic Encyclopedia* (vol. 84) concurred. A contemporary of Krünitz's, Georg Heinrich Zincke, in his likewise voluminous economic encyclopaedia pointed to the nature of the market as a physical space;[167] its entry on *Marckt* featured a large overlap with Zedler, in the sort of shameless plagiarism characteristic of many an Enlightened writer. Market regulation represented a cornerstone of contemporary *Policey*. Krünitz's encyclopaedia, in the entry on *Markt* emphasized how a well-ordered spatially designed market prevented individual actors from usurious practices, fraud and other ways of putting others at a disadvantage.[168] Justi, a contemporary of Adam Smith, emphasized the notion of spatial order in the market. He included concrete examples of a *Marktordnung* and how the sanctioning of market distortions should work, including adultery of goods (§354), false measures and weights (§355), the introduction of fixed market hours and times for sales (10 am or 11 am), as well as effective supervision of those merchants travelling the countryside to purchase foodstuffs (§357).[169] Again, this mirrored age-old anxieties and templates of the market, matching – as we have already seen – actual practices on markets.

Order was the centrepiece of the establishment of economic freedom. Markets required regulation to allow individuals the highest possible degree of economic freedom *without harming or being harmed by others*, by means of usury, rent-seeking, arbitrage, speculation and other forms of market distortion. Continental market theory in this sense was *proactive* and dynamic. The free market was something that had to be continuously recreated. It could not be expected to emerge spontaneously.

Modern scholarship has asserted the importance of markets in the process of economic change, before and beyond the Industrial Revolution.[170] Obviously, such markets needed to be functional. To further underline this, and get deeper into the matter of how such functionality could be established and maintained, the discussion will now – in the next two chapters – turn to monetary policy as a further area of market governmentality in the age of capitalism's ascendancy, 1250s–1850s.

Money and the Rise
of Modern Capitalism

> As for the right of coinage, it is contained within the law-making
> power, for only he who can make law can regulate currency. This
> is illustrated in the very terms used by Greeks, Romans, and French
> alike, for the word nummus comes from the Greek nomos signifying
> both law and alloy. There is nothing of more moment to a country,
> after the law, than the denomination, the value, and the weight of
> the coinage, as we have already shown in a separate treatise.
>
> Jean Bodin, *On the true attributes of sovereignty*[1]

Early modern money's dirty hidden lives

Money lies at the heart of the economic process. It is dirty. When Saxon
polymath, medic and engineer Georg Agricola published in 1556 his much-
acclaimed mining handbook *De re metallica* – the first full translation from the
original Latin into modern English made by no less than Herbert Hoover,
later president of the United States – he was crystal clear about money's
dangerous origins in mining:

> The critics say further that mining is a perilous occupation to pursue,
> because the miners are sometimes killed by the pestilential air which
> they breathe; sometimes their lungs rot away; sometimes the men
> perish by being crushed in masses of rock; sometimes, falling from
> the ladders into the shafts, they break their arms, legs, or necks; and
> it is added there is no compensation which should be thought great
> enough to equalize the extreme dangers to safety and life.[2]

Silver mining was at the heart of the transitions (and subsequent decline) of
capitalism that swept central Europe during the age of the early Reformation.
Martin Luther, who wrote his main economic pieces on business and

usury, was not an ignoramus helplessly shouting against the rise of modern capitalism, but rather its decline; his works addressed late capitalism's perversions in the wake of the penultimate medieval mining boom that had transformed the economic morphology and turned the Saxon-Thuringian lands into engines of growth, with increasing inequality, peasant unrest and skyrocketing business profits made by some late medieval super-companies including Fugger and Welser that ran some of the largest mining and smelting works and practically controlled the Asian spice trades and global silver flows.[3] Environmental pollution and degradation were intrinsic by-products of this boom – and thus the process of 'making' money.[4] More important were its social, political and economic ramifications. In market economies prices, wages and economic values are usually expressed using some form of money, either real or money of account (sometimes called 'ghost monies'); in Europe during the last millennium coins represented the main means of daily exchange, and most debates about money usually evolved around coins.[5] Money also was an anchor of state formation and state consolidation,[6] albeit scholars have remained undecided what came first, money or the state.[7] Again Agricola (*De Re Metallica*, 1556):

> When ingenious and clever men considered carefully the system of barter, which ignorant men of old employed and which even to-day is used by certain uncivilised and barbarous races, it appeared to them so troublesome and laborious that they invented money. Indeed, nothing more useful could have been devised, because a small amount of gold and silver is of as great value as things cumbrous and heavy; and so peoples far distant from one another can, by the use of money, trade very easily in those things which civilized life can scarcely do without.[8]

This is the old Aristotelian argument of money as a facilitator of exchange; a well-known origin myth that has made it into modern textbooks as the 'coincidence of wants' argument.[9] The process between money and state formation was dynamic and symbiotic, and in the process both state and money became reconfigured all over again.

But money had its inner lives, which are not always readily acknowledged. It is a container of information, carrying and transmitting economic (price, value, purchasing power), political (power, governance: limiting actors' means of transaction), magic (spells, cures, curses[10]), or cultural meaning ('money stinks').[11] It can be studied as a semiotic phenomenon.[12] Global economic historians employ monetary metrics when comparing incomes and living standards using a common denominator – silver – based on the assumption that most small and medium-sized currencies in the world historically tended to be based on silver. But even *if* silver was a universally accepted means of payment, as Adam Smith once noted (and there is no real doubt about that), its value differed considerably enough across world regions and time. (This makes silver less useful as a global comparator of purchasing power. In early modern times silver was worth up to twice as much (in terms of gold) in India and China when compared to Europe, so incomes and payments between global regions, when reduced to grams of silver for comparison, would need to be deflated using the respective local gold–silver ratios in order to yield meaningful comparators.[13]) On the other hand, money can be a powerful tool promoting economic development through market participation, market widening and an increase in specialization and division of labour.[14]

But the real problems begin when we break down money and coin use from its abstract and aggregate levels (such as velocity, amount of money in circulation, price levels, transaction volume, or general theories of money's origin and purported use) to individuals' economic lives. Different economic actors and groups of actors used different moneys in the marketplace; in different frequencies and intensities over the years, due to differences in incomes sourced through the market; different forms of engaging with the market, different demands for cash to hold and so on. Even within premodern European peasant societies there was considerable differentiation in economic occupation and social stratification within the village, which resulted in fundamentally different forms and schedules of using money.[15] Coin debasement and other monetary manipulations by the state affected different groups of actors in the marketplace differently.[16] And while the 'common (wo)man' may be seriously disadvantaged, more powerful players in the market, such as merchants, may benefit from coin debasement and other such currency manipulations.[17] There is thus a political economy of medieval and early modern money, which yet needs to be more systematically written; for the early modern Germanies, only its basic outlines are hitherto understood.[18] There is an all-too-common habit of reading premodern money through the modern lens, or a 'positivist' view on money, which goes somewhat like this: 'A groat is a groat, and a penny is a penny' (meaning that all monetary parameters and relations given in the sources are readily comparable using the contemporary normative evidence – monetary legislation and currency edicts – on what such coin types and currencies should be worth). But in reality this was hardly ever true; if an ordinance of the time for instance said that 252 pennies made a florin, reflecting official exchange rates as state targets, the realities of monetary exchange could look very different. One groat here could equal a groat and a quarter somewhere else; in some cases, 20 groats made a florin, in others 21, 22 or 23; often in the same year, same territory, same market economy (say, the Saxon lands, c.1500). Premodern currency relationships were hybrid, fuzzy and principally negotiable, with coin values fluctuating wildly around target exchange rates set by the state. This gave rise to complaints, grievances, even social unrest and sometimes revolt.[19]

In terms of forms, shape and meaning, money in late Antiquity was not fundamentally different from money in the Middle Ages, or from money around 1870. Only when governments finally retreated from *metallism*, that is, the principle that money should normally embody its purchasing power by the weight and amount of precious metal it contained, moving to a *chartalist* theory of money, where money only represents but does not embody value, did the framing and configuration of money change for good.[20] In most European countries this process was fully completed only after the First World War, and in many ways lasted until the abolition of the Bretton Woods system by the United States in 1971. But there had been a long history of trial and error, with small-change currencies (pennies, farthings, groats and mites) containing elements of a fiduciary or chartalist character since the Middle Ages. Very few people would accept fiduciary currencies (Ger. *Scheidemünze*) which led, as we will see, to conflict and controversy when it came to defining (or rather negotiating) the purchasing power of small change against higher-value coins.[21]

In the following I will give some examples how money was conceptualized as an instrument of state and a tool potentially improving markets and economic development.

Money and political economies of state formation

In the Renaissance and early modern German lands, money and monetary policy were mostly contingent upon silver. Gold coins were used, but increasingly infrequently after the 1500s, chiefly by merchants settling accounts in long-distance trade (or for paying and maintaining armies in the field). Gold mines were far and few between; gold was usually sourced by means of trade. Some German states did generate revenue in gold (and thus obtained the means of striking gold coins), including the Dukes of Hesse who had inherited the County of Katzenelnbogen, whose counts had collected the Rhine tolls, payable in gold. But the currencies of the common man[22] were usually made up of low and medium denominations such as groats or *Kreutzer*, which consisted of mixtures of silver with base metals such as copper. From the later 15th century onwards, larger nominals of the silver florin or gulden type would be struck, first in the Tyrol (1486), then in 1500 in Saxony, substituting silver for gold in the high-denomination range of currency used in large and long-distance transactions, which had been hitherto limited to gold. This begot an entirely new period and monetary paradigm of state formation which will be given some consideration in this chapter.[23]

Silver mining (and thus minting) was an important and, in some territories, if we include related enterprises such as copper smelting and the *Saiger* process, *the* most important industry and economic activity outside agriculture before the Industrial Revolution.[24] Everyone could dig down into the mines, but needed to pay the ruler a fee for the permission to do so. Then any silver yielded had to pass through one of the princely mints and be turned into current money. Rulers used proceeds from free mining not only to finance state expenditure and repayment of loans, but also to keep monetary supply running, and construct and maintain order in what were to become economic hothouses with high levels of economic specialization and high-value added activities.[25] Mining and state formation required dense webs of intervention and regulation, ranging from the establishment of good order, law enforcement and regular church services, to the supervision of taverns and roads, the correct use of weights and measures, or the staking of claims in one of the local silver mines.[26] Since the 15th century, Saxon rulers actively intervened in the process of configuring and managing an increasingly dynamic and changing socio-economic landscape in the Erz Mountains mining regions, where cities such as St Annaberg had mushroomed and grown, during the last medieval mining boom, from a few hundred inhabitants in the 1470s to more than 20,000 in the 1490s.[27]

This would have had manifest consequences on monetary policy. The Leipzig Currency Reform of 1500 will be used as a case in point. By a monetary ordinance dated mid-May 1500, the Saxon duke and elector introduced a new large silver coin equivalent to a gold florin in the Saxon lands: a silver florin or *Groschen so ein gulden gilt* – shortly afterwards, this became known as *Thaler*. In the Middle Ages the Saxon lands had been divided between the Ernestine and the Albertine lines of the Wettin dynasty, one headed by a duke, the other by an elector (who, participating in the election of the German emperor, had a higher political status); but the Wettins operated a joint currency and, most of the time, coordinated monetary policy in line with such a common currency. This ordinance or 'reform' established the first proper silver currency in the German-speaking lands substituting for the *Goldgulden* or Rhenish florin. It signalled a decisive switch in monetary paradigm from gold to silver, as previously high-value coins in the German-speaking lands had almost exclusively been made of gold (there had been experiments with silver florins in Tyrol since the 1480s, but these had been short-lived and temporary). The new Leipzig ordinance also triggered long-term changes of considerable social and economic importance. The Saxon-Thuringian lands belonged to the commercially and economically most developed areas in the contemporary Holy Roman Empire. Silver mining was centred in the Saxon Erzgebirge, and smelting in the Thuringian lands. Silver and copper smelting was organized in large-scale plants or industrial enterprises known as *Saiger* huts (liquation plants, prototypes of the later factory). In these areas money payments for wages represented the norm; division of labour and functional economic specialization had advanced to high levels. Saxony-Thuringia was urbanized and industrialized.[28] It also lay at the crossroads of important long-distance roads. Important trade fairs were held at Leipzig and Naumburg. Monetary policy had to take these factors into account.

Even more or less resembling earlier medieval ordinances in terms of wording and set-up, the 1500 Leipzig Monetary Ordinance was nothing short of revolutionary. It laid the foundations of a completely new monetary paradigm, even though contemporary economic actors certainly would not yet have been fully aware of this. Substituting a large silver coin for the old gold florin was predicated on promoting economic life and stability, and credibility of the state in safeguarding property rights, indicative of a new vision of money, statehood and commercial society – all in the face of rapidly expanding levels of economic activity and prodigious streams of silver that had flown out of Saxon mines since the 1470s. The Leipzig ordinance introduced a six-tiered monetary system, centring upon the new silver florin (*Groschen so ein gulden gilt*, later on nicknamed *Thaler* after Joachimsthal, today Jàchymov in Czechia), which exchanged at 21 *Zinsgroschen* (the biblical 'tithe groat' according to Martin Luther's translation) and 252 *Pfennige* (pennies, d.). This system knew further subdivisions, including the *Schreckenberger* groat at 3 *Zinsgroschen* or ⅐ florin, the ½ *Schwertgroschen* (equal to ½ Zins groat), as well as the *Heller* (halfpenny) at $^1/_{504}$ to the florin or *Thaler*. The order specifically extended to lands beyond the Saxon realms; reflecting a way of monetary muscle flexing and hegemonic policy over weaker adjacent states whose rulers were considered subordinate to the Saxon elector and duke as suzerains, and thus forced – or 'asked' in contemporary legal language – to adopt Saxon monetary standards for their polities.[29] Monetary policy was thus conceived as hegemonic power politics embedded into contemporary logics and logistics of fiefdom and feudal tenure; but we also see an emerging and more nuanced understanding of the state managing the internal market process, especially the idea of government positively committing to social and economic stability through a stable currency. This currency was not predominantly configured in the princely interests any more (as a potential source of inflation tax), but now took into account the needs of expanding *market economies and quickening economic life* that increasingly fed on capitalist business practices. For many years after the 1500 monetary reform the Saxon dukes and electors refrained from charging seigniorage – the statutory legal 'profit share' due to rulers from all minting processes – on new Saxon mint runs, resisting the all-too-common temptation to fill the princely coffers by means of a tax by inputting less silver into the coins than they should contain, based on their nominally guaranteed face value. This was a deliberate step taken to signal a new commitment to economic stability in line with the new Saxon monetary philosophy during the age of price revolution (1470/1530s–1620s).

Money is also an instrument that lowers transaction costs in the market, by providing a reliable means of exchange, of quantifying value, a syntax and grammar for the language of the market, a means of storing value and of transferring purchasing power over time. Since early times coins – the main type of money until the 19th century – had usually carried images of the ruler under whose remit and licence coins had been minted. Coins thus communicated top-down relations, claims to power: personal, impersonal and spatial. They did so by the imagined realm of circulation, which since the Middle Ages took on an increasingly territorialized character and was, after the Treaty of Westphalia in 1648, complemented by the notion of discrete geometric territorial borders as frontiers denominating physical spaces of political power.[30] Coins could also communicate magic, good and evil. They were worn as necklaces to fend off evil powers. In the 14th century, French kings would use their 'healing touch', given to them by God, by placing their hands on coins that were then given away as amulets of good health. Two of the four canonical gospels mention a specific sum of money ('thirty pieces of silver') paid to Judas for the betrayal of Jesus; but the gnostic-apocryphal Gospel of Judas (written in Coptic), where Judas may even have been the 'good guy' (or a demon), turns the reward from 'silver' (that is, high value) into 'a few copper coins', that is, coins literally worthless, not worth his while, creating an entirely different narrational-eschatological arc when compared to the canonical gospels.[31]

But above all, money served as a powerful tool for ordering the market, empowering capitalism and economic development. Before moving on to a history of political economy perspective of what could potentially be done with money – from the point of view of the writings on money and monetary policy since the age of Oresme and the beginnings of political economy: works that influenced people's ways of thinking about money into the modern age – I would briefly like to take a look at the context of monetary policy *in situ*. We saw in Chapter 3 how abruptly Erasmus in his *Institutio Principis Christiani* (1516) moved from general principles of princely duties specifically to the evils of currency debasement. In the Middle Ages debasement had been one of the most frequent scourges pressed by governments and kings upon the common people. It immediately illustrates the double-faced Janus nature of medieval and early modern money as a tool, to either potentially do good – and promote economic development – or wreak havoc to the common weal, creating misery, poverty and economic decline.[32]

Coin debasement means that coins – the main means of currency, or 'money' in medieval and early modern Europe – lose some of their intrinsic value when the ruler or prince or whichever monetary authority operating mints and striking coins decide to issue the next run of fresh coins at a lower mint ratio, that is, containing less precious metal than previous mint issues.

During the Middle Ages and well into the 18th century, rulers and states often used debasement to prop up princely chests. A modern anachronism has this as 'inflation tax', to reap a temporary gain for the public fisc; but since in medieval and early modern Europe the boundaries between public finance and the princely chest were not yet clearly demarcated, such terminology remains anachronistic.[33] Sometimes debasement simply followed a change in silver's (or gold's) market price that required an adjustment in money's intrinsic value, lest coins became demonetized, that is, taken off the market (Gresham's Law). In that case, no one would have had any moral objections to debasement. Such manipulations were considered just, even from a canon law perspective. As European populations grew in the long run, c.1250s–1900s, much faster than the available supply of precious metal, which represented the foundation of monetary stock, per capita supplies of silver and thus effective monetary stock declined. This usually meant that new coins *had* to contain less silver (or gold) than formerly. But just how much was enough? The long monetary history of Europe in the age of capitalism's ascendancy effectively is a history of devaluation, that is, reduction in the circulating coins' precious metal content or intrinsic value. Revaluations or reinforcements of the currency (increases in the amount of silver or gold in the circulating coins) were not completely unknown, but were seldom, and usually came after major debasements, obviously directed at returning to a somewhat more 'normal' standard.[34] The political economy literature of the period ranging from Nicholas Oresmius and other late medieval scholastics to the early modern cameralists accordingly focused on debasement, considered as frivolous and damaging to the common weal (even though it was habitually practised; and as we shall see, there were some notable exceptions from that rule).

While rates of debasement varied over time and space, giving ample opportunity to coin arbitrage and speculation, rates of debasement for small-change currencies, that is, the money of the common man, were much higher than for middle-sized or larger full-bodied coins. Overall, in the German lands small-change coins declined by as much as 25 per cent in terms of intrinsic value (silver weight) during the 17th and 18th centuries. This was mild when compared to the 14th- and 15th-century average rates of debasement, which had been almost twice as high on average.[35] This clearly reflects a change in policy approaches, and as the early modern fiscal states developed, so did alternative means of raising finance, which lessened the temptation to use the currency as a source of government revenue. Over the very long run, however, that is, between the 1400s and 1900s, small change coins lost about 90 per cent of their original silver content, nearly twice or three times as much as the full-bodied silver thalers.[36] Debasement rates thus far outpaced the rise in silver's price caused by population growth and resultant pressures on available per capita monetary stock and levels of monetization. Rulers and their mint masters, who ran the mint and produced coins, often cross-subsidized the production of higher-type full-bodied coins by recouping some of their expenses through an over-proportional devaluation of the small-change currencies.[37] In fact, since the Middle Ages, there was something of a tacit consensus that small-change coins did not even have to embody their full purchasing power; they thus embodied elements of a 'fiduciary' or 'chartalist' character by default; but this was not usually openly communicated to the common man. In German such small change coins were called *Scheidemünze*, and their acceptance in payments could usually only be enforced up to a certain amount, after which sellers could ask for payment in full-bodied coin. As an official paradigm however, chartalism was never accepted (albeit there were infrequent experiments with proper fiduciary currencies before the 1800s; made or based on copper containing no precious metal whatsoever; experiments which usually proved abortive). But the public – village communities, urban craftsmen, working poor, who had to make do mostly with small-change coins in their daily lives – seldom got full-bodied silver thalers or Rhenish florins into their hands. They would not accept the fiduciary-money proposition readily, especially since their small-change coins were not accepted at face value, either, when handed over for the payment of taxes and other dues accruing to the state or feudal lords, as a closer study of monetary complaints during peasant uprisings between the Middle Ages and the early modern period has shown.[38] The problem continued until towards the end of the 19th century, when full fiduciary standards and new 'formulas' (Sargent and Velde) of money were implemented *across all segments of currency*, that is, small, medium and full-bodied or large-denomination coins.[39] Only much later on, the adoption of fiduciary money, banknotes and other means of cashless payment substitutes for coins would shift some of the problems (and create new ones in their stead).

In theory, governments, princes, kings and other rulers could have used gold and silver reserves, where available, to mint a fixed amount of coins that would then be put into circulation. This method, if it had been used, would have been similar to modern central banks trying to control the amount of money in circulation (not always effectively). Such measures may help meet some basic economic, social and fiscal policy goals; one of the principal aims of monetary policy up to the present day has been price-level stability (inflation control), and the smoothing out of business cycles. Governments may employ a policy of tight money to prevent the business cycle from overheating. Or they may print cheap money, extending monetary and credit supply within the economy thus lowering interest rates as a quick fix for a recession. In the Middle Ages and early modern capitalism, however, none of these options were on the table. Rulers were notoriously short of cash and powerless with regard to controlling the *amount* of currency in circulation. The public determined the amount of coins in circulation by the quantity of precious metal (including old coins that had been invalidated for payment) that individual actors chose to bring into the mint to be transformed into current coins. The state could only influence the process within narrow limits, for instance by commanding mint masters to limit production for certain types of coin, or by setting the 'right' parameters, that is, the 'right' price, luring enough silver and gold into the mint to cover the costs of minting while still yielding some seigniorage (income for the prince resulting from the activity of producing currency). Edicts and ordinances to this extent were published and put up in every marketplace where money was regularly used, stipulating what currencies and coins were accepted as legal tender, together with their official target exchange rates against other coin types.

From the Middle Ages a concept of 'territorial money' began to take some shape, albeit this was nowhere near fully implemented until the 1900s. But rulers increasingly tried to monopolize or restrict the applicability and convertibility of foreign coins, by specifying the type, age and range of domestic *as well as* foreign moneys allowed as legal tender within their realm. If foreign merchants came into a particular town or crossed a foreign territory on their way through, they were often required to have their 'foreign' money recoined into current domestic money. Foreign coins may be stamped (or counter-stamped) and tariffed, and thus admitted as part of the (usually very eclectic) overall mix of coins (old, new, foreign and domestic) allowed in market transactions. The concept of 'domestic' versus 'foreign' currency was quite different from the way we usually think of money nowadays; in particular, concepts like 'foreign' exchange, or 'legal tender' are difficult to apply in historical analysis, requiring some stretch of the historian's imagination. The resulting effects on the monetary landscape and market economy can be glimpsed from published data on official coin exchange rates in early 16th-century Saxony, where the Saxon dukes and electors such as Frederick the Wise, who later became a protector of Martin Luther, at regular intervals had tables printed, containing the legally fixed spot rates for all coins current and accepted as what we would call 'legal tender' in the Saxon realms. Around 1500 there were about 60 to 80 types of coin denominations, Saxon and foreign, normally admitted this way into circulation.[40] People didn't necessarily adhere to these official exchange rates set by the state, though. From the point of view of the public these were often considered recommendations or state monetary targets rather than actually enforceable legal exchange rates. I have collected evidence on how these rates were habitually evaded, casting some doubt on the existence of homogenous monetary spheres as prescribed in the monetary ordinances of the time – and most of the historians' literature.[41] It is thus difficult to imagine contemporaries around 1500 *not* having had a hard time when handling money, settling transactions, enforcing contracts and monitoring compliance. Conflicts about coins and bad money were ubiquitous. Social problems as a consequence of either a lack of money or a lack of good money were almost habitually voiced in late medieval and early modern German politics.

Rulers were not in control of money supply, but they could set important monetary parameters that worked towards stabilizing market behaviour, counterbalancing at least some of the worst effects of monetary fragmentation and hybrid monetary spheres. Looking at the process of how coins actually originated helps us understand some of the underlying political economy parameters.

Princely mints were usually leased to private entrepreneurs, who operated them as they would any other profit-making business or firm. Mint masters usually came from a mercantile background. They had extensive experience in finance and trade and insider knowledge of monetary markets and metallurgy, operating networks with other long-distance traders and merchant bankers. They were usually called upon by rulers as experts when it came to matters of monetary policy. Their expert opinions, where they have survived in the archives documenting the process history of such currency reforms, constitute an invaluable body of economic knowledge, providing us with insights into the dynamics of early modern monetary regimes and market systems, and how orders and ordinances – and thus views and ideologies of money and the market – became shaped, configured and reconfigured over time. During the process of minting, the costs of minting (brassage) and the cut taken by the local ruler (seigniorage) were deducted from the coins' intrinsic value. Consequently, the value of the silver or gold in coins was always less than the coins' nominal value or purchasing power, especially after debasement. Coined silver and gold thus enjoyed a premium over un-coined, and thus un-standardized, silver or gold bars, ingots or plate. Thus bearing a liquidity premium, coins made market exchange potentially more efficient, because this reduced transaction costs, avoiding barter and complex operations assessing the intrinsic value of the precious metal exchanged in return for payments of goods, at least in theory. Reality was more complex, as I have demonstrated elsewhere: people negotiated, renegotiated and sometimes even physically fought about coin values and spot exchange rates on specific transactions involving specific types of coin.[42] One obvious and easy policy fix for rulers would have been to strictly stick to a well-managed, stable monetary supply and system of circulation which would have simultaneously helped promote monetary, economic *and* social stability. The available circumstantial historical evidence shows that even in the 1400s many rulers were quite aware of this.[43] Yet, a contrary strategy was often chosen, especially before the 16th century, after which rates of coin debasement gradually came down.

This tells us something about a gradually changed understanding of monetary policy and state capacity. First, as we have seen, debasement was, especially in the Middle Ages, considered a way of generating state revenue. To do this, rulers set a fixed price at which the mint would buy precious metal, while hiding from the public the exact amount of precious metal that the new coins would contain.[44] The success of debasement depended upon how quickly the public found out about the deceit – if the actual amount of silver put into the coins was lower than suggested by these coins' officially proclaimed value on the market. Determining the exact fine silver or gold content of a coin required advanced knowledge in metallurgy and financial markets, as well as specialized testing equipment.[45] There was a time lag between concealed debasement and its first detection by experts, and it took much longer before the general public would have become aware. In the 1350s this process could take up to six months:[46] this was the time horizon that rulers and their mint masters could use to operate debasement with profit. In France, more than 120 currency debasements are known between the 1220s and the 1490s. That amounts to one major reduction in the coinage every other year. This practice was the pure embodiment of 'bad government' as framed in late medieval and early modern mirrors for princes studied in Chapter 3. As new forms of raising revenue were adopted during the age of the early modern fiscal-military states, the scourge of debasement receded, but never completely vanished. As late as the Seven Years War (1755–63) Prussian King Frederick the Great and his congenial mint mastermind Grauman used the coin press as a source of inflation tax.[47] Only England and the Netherlands experienced practically stable currencies and no debasement after the mid-16th century.

Debasement put those people who were in receipt of regular fixed income streams paid in money at a disadvantage, including rents and annuities, interest payments and credit instalments, all of which were usually payable in terms of a specified type of coin or currency. It was not usually easy to renegotiate existing contracts. Since prices charged in the market for consumables and other goods often rose out of proportion to the amount that coins were debased – sellers would try and protect themselves against the risk of inflation – this would exacerbate the negative effects of debasement. As prices rose, causing silver's purchasing power to decline, and as a mint's monetary manipulations became widely known, people had less and less incentive to bring bullion to the mint. At that point, the cycle of coin devaluation probably came to a halt.[48] To restore trust and stability, the existing currency had to be revalued and an 'old' or standard closer to pre-debasement be restored. Such revaluations or enhancements of the currency occurred in France in 1330, 1343, 1360 and 1436.[49]

Not all such manipulations, however, were necessarily or chiefly motivated by fiscal reasons. There were times and places when periods of acute coin debasement coincided with acute ebbs in economic activity. During these times, prices were also low and the regional economy stuck in a deflationary cycle. Royal merchant Jacques Coeur, who had whole galleon-loads of goods unsold in the Italian sea ports during the 1440s and 1450s, commented upon the brunt of this kind of commercial depression.[50] The debasements of the 1420s and of 1440–60 were particularly marked in the Hanseatic-Baltic area,[51] the Holy Roman Empire, Flanders, France and, to a lesser extent, in England, Aragon and the Italian cities. Here debasement coincided with monetary scarcity. Bullion stocks in Europe were depleted; silver's price increased (in line with deflation in general prices). This suggests some sort of correlation between general economic fluctuations and money supply.[52] At such times of crisis, the same amount of silver could buy more goods than before. Rulers were literally *forced* to devalue their currencies, lest these would be culled out of circulation.

Debasement and consequential financial market operations, however, affected coins of different types and currency segments differently.

Minting high-value coins such as florin, thaler, *cruzado* (the highest value coin in Portugal) and so on, was almost as expensive, from the point of labour and equipment involved, as minting a low-value one: regardless of the type of coin concerned, the labour and capital outlays, for tools, buildings, smelting and so on, practically remained the same. Accordingly, it was proportionally cheaper, that is more profitable, for the mint master to strike high-value coins compared to low-value ones.[53] The costs of minting small change pennies and *hellers* (German halfpennies) and so on thus had to be cross-subsidized: that is, the costs had to be recouped somewhere else. Using profits from minting larger coins such as shillings, *batzen* and groats, or ducats, florins and thalers, would not usually make up the difference. As larger coins were important for long-distance trade and the settling of large balances, as well as paying taxes, rulers refrained from the temptation to debase them, not least because such coins would flow back into the princely chest by means of tolls, taxes and other duties. As late as the 1770s, German poet, lawyer, cameralist and administrator Johann Wolfgang von Goethe urged his Duke of Saxe-Gotha-Eisenach to only accept full-bodied or high-value coins in tax payments.[54] It was naturally tempting to finance the minting of small coins by debasing them beyond proportion, to the point at which the mint master could make a profit from them. Or else, rulers would completely refrain from issuing small-change coins altogether, which could also pose problems: during the late medieval German peasant wars of the 1460s–1520s peasants usually complained about a lack of small change, as did Luther in a letter to his wife dated 1540.[55] People would try to renegotiate existing contracts whenever they found that too many 'bad' or 'evil' (that is, underweight) small-change coins were in circulation. Very often they agreed on spot exchange rates below the legal rate stipulated in the monetary ordinances. Whenever feudal dues or levies were supposed to be paid in 'good money' (high-value, full-bodied coins such as gulden, florins, or thalers) but payment was made in small change – debased coins such as pennies – the feudal noblemen and tax collectors would ask for a premium, accepting small-change coins offered for payment only at discounted rate. To give one example: in Southern Germany in the 1470s, the florin or silver gulden was officially worth 24 white pennies or *albi*. But existing contracts and rent payments were frequently renegotiated at rates of up to 27 white pennies or *albi* to the florin, whenever the actual coins handed over diverged from the 'old' or 'official' or 'good' standard of the *albus* groat at 24 to the gulden.[56] This increased transaction costs, because money had to be renegotiated and lost some of its function as a reliable store of value.

Peasant complaints during 15th- and 16th-century peasant revolts often specifically related to situations where there were too many different types of small-change coins around, of too many uncertain origins and provenances, minted under too many authorities and from too many time periods. These various types of coin had very different purchasing power, so that accepting one specific coin at face value might yield its bearer a financial loss, depending upon whom they faced in future transactions and payments. Attempts were made to centralize monetary policy and create a true imperial currency for the Holy Roman Empire during the first half of the 16th century. But these efforts came to naught.[57] The German lands therefore represent a good case in point about competition and institutional arbitrage, often considered beneficial for countries' economic performance and key to European superiority over other less politically fragmented world regions.[58] The history of money suggests the opposite. Monetary competition clearly harmed rather than helped German economic development during the medieval and early modern period. Coin debasement increased transaction costs, gave rise to conflicts and reduced overall welfare. Is it a coincidence that the two nations which became the 'first modern' economies, the early modern Netherlands and early industrial England, were also those countries whose currencies had been stable almost over the entire early modern period?

How, then, did contemporary political economy conceptualize and configure money's role in the market process?

Money supply and continental visions of market economy, 1500s–1900s

In times and ages when states were decidedly weak and 'soft' (M. Mann) one of the most likely and efficient areas of state intervention in the market process was through *monetary policy and monetary* management. Rulers and temporal authority did not control the amount of coin in circulation; but they had means of intervening in money's value and thus *ordering the market*. In some regards this comes close to what we regard as laissez-faire, where state intervention is reserved to the state providing the right set of institutions that help keep the market transparent, fair, equal-access and competitive. To post-1945 West German ordoliberals, monetary regulation and currency stability were key activities of state. Indeed, it is in the realm of monetary policy as a 'policy of order', which the German language still has as *Ordnungspolitik*, where we find a rich economic discourse on money in the capitalist process, with important roots in pre-1800 German and scholastic political economy.[59] We find competing paradigms on how the well-being of the common weal, later on the state, could be raised by a well-designed *monetary* management. This discourse has remained underexplored, both in regard to its possibilities of actively interfering with the market process and thus the promoting of the common weal, as well as in terms of its general contributions to modern economic reasoning.

Perhaps the best way to elucidate this point is by returning to the mid-14th century polymath and father of monetary theory Nicolaus Oresme, an origin figure in political economy.[60] Later mercantilist and cameralist writers continued drawing on Oresme's views, upon 'scholastic' models of money and the economy; theories that had been presented in condensed form, inter alia, in Oresme's *Tractatus de origine, natura, jure et mutationibus monetarum*, written between 1350 and 1358.[61] Although a direct link between Oresmius and post-1600 'German' economic texts is difficult to prove – authors before 1700 never bothered much about referencing and footnoting – we know that Oresmius was widely read across Europe until the end of the Middle Ages, and his arguments continued in use for centuries to come. Gabriel Biel (*c.*1415–95), one of Germany's most important scholastics, for instance was heavily influenced by Oresmius in his remarks on monetary theory and policy. Principal of the newly founded University of Tübingen, advisor to Duke Eberhard of Württemberg, Biel became actively involved in south-west German monetary policy. His fame and reputation in turn extended as far as the Spanish School of Salamanca: in the first half of the 16th century during the heyday of Spanish and Portuguese overseas expansion and economic high status within the developing early modern world economy, Salamanca and Coimbra (the latter a leading Portuguese university) both had chairs endowed explicitly for the exegesis of Biel's works. Biel was probably the first (or at least most prominent) voice in the German-speaking lands to promulgate Oresme's message that the currency – and thus monetary management – were *not* the property of the king or prince. Money belonged to the entire political nation.[62] This sounds quite radical, especially within a late medieval context, even more so when compared to money in the early modern German-speaking lands, where cameralist political economy theory habitually claimed money as the exclusive prerogative of the prince. Oresme's claim was, of course, written against the background of the absurdly high rates of French currency debasement in the 1350s (discussed earlier).[63] It nevertheless contributed to an important development in medieval and early modern conceptions of state and economy. Biel in turn proved highly influential to other 16th-century German writers, including Martin Luther. Nederman has concluded that 'By acknowledging and exploring the necessity of a symbiotic relationship between good government and the common wealth, Oresme maps out the rudiments of a route that would be travelled time and again in European political and social thought'.[64]

By negating the prince's (or king's) prerogative to alter the currency at will and emphasizing that promoting the common weal should have the highest priority for any ruler, Oresme captured the pillars of Renaissance and early modern Reason of State theory, as manifest in the contemporaneous *Fürstenspiegel* (mirrors of princes) literature and Giovanni Botero's *Ragion di Stato* (1589), upon which the mercantilist-cameralist conception of market processes built.[65] Since the 15th century excerpts of Oresme's treatise appeared in print: 1484 in Cologne, 1511 in Paris.[66] For these reasons we can be confident that early modern political economists would have been reasonably familiar with Oresme and his works.[67] With Biel acting as an important transmitter between Oresme and cameralism, and with early cameralist texts going back to the 16th century, we also have a connection with early modern reason of state theory, Enlightenment economics and cameralism-mercantilism.[68] Thus Oresme's *Tractatus*, although not usually specifically acknowledged as a source of inspiration by later authors, provided a baseline of early modern monetary theory. Still, it would be wrong to argue that neither mercantilists nor cameralists made any meaningful contribution to modern European monetary theory.[69] While cameralists borrowed heavily from medieval conceptions of money, they still devised important new departures in monetary theory and monetary management.

Well into the days and age of Johann Heinrich Gottlob von Justi (1717–71) or James Steuart (1712–80) political economists shared convictions as to what money should look like and what it could do in the marketplace. These conceptions extended chiefly to the axiom that its purchasing power should rest upon intrinsic content. The number of ounces of gold or silver each coin contained should equal the market value of these metals, with only a small allowance deducted, usually around 2 per cent, for brassage (cost of minting) and seigniorage (at that time the regal monopoly charge). There is little here that distinguished earlier voices during the 14th, 15th and 16th centuries from the post-1650 cameralist and mercantilist 'mainstream', including English writers such as Francis Bacon, Gerard de Malynes, William Potter and John Locke down to their continental counterparts such as Justi, even into the 19th century, when a commodity theory of money slowly started giving way to chartalism. This 'medieval' framework of analysis carried an important set of implications. A bullionist reasoning – bullionism denoting a sort of crude mercantilism with a generally rather undifferentiated emphasis on a positive balance of payments, not considering wider implications, such as particular trade balances which may be negative as long as the aggregate trade balance remained positive – ran across the epistemological boundaries of what could be called scholastic or neo-Aristotelian and then mercantilist and cameralist economics.[70] It can be found in European economic thought during the mid-14th century; and it has continued to reappear until very recently. Scholars have studied this hunger for bullion or 'fear of goods'[71] from various angles. John Maynard Keynes, in his 1936 *General Theory*, was among the few influential non-Germanic thinkers who was outspokenly positive about mercantilists' monetary views; arguing that a net inflow of money would have kept interest rates, and thus the costs of borrowing money, low, which should have helped stimulate incomes, consumption and employment.[72] Rather than looking for theories that are good or bad, right or wrong, we should try to contextualize those propositions in their specific historical times. What becomes clear from this exercise is that monetary theories I have described already transcended the relatively narrow remit of providing good property rights and the frame of a well-governed Christian market economy, towards achieving a more dynamic landscape that knew the principal possibility of economic development.

As we saw in Chapter 4, early modern cameralist political economy emphasized *order in the market*. In this model, good markets were defined as markets free of monopoly, ruinous competition ('polypoly' in the words of J. J. Becher), speculation, arbitrage and other forms of usurious exchange, or what Martin Luther in the 1520s and Cyriacus Spangenberg in the 1590s called *vngleiche hendel*: asymmetrical transactions involving money, in which one person lost because of imperfect market knowledge or lack of good money.[73] In this way German cameralists conceptualized economic order as a means to raise overall welfare. Early modern political economy also expressed a profound fear of *deflation*.[74] And that fear was often justified by the course of real-life events. Low prices reflected shortfalls of aggregate demand over supply, often caused by a lack of silver money that could, if worst came to worst, translate into economic depression.[75] Around 1500, Germany had exported about 16 tons of pure silver annually via Lisbon, Venice and Antwerp into the Baltic, Levant, Africa, India and China. Very often this equalled the entire yearly output of the German mines.[76] Prior to the influx of American silver (after the mid-16th century) Germany was the world's largest exporter of silver. Global price differentials in the gold–silver ratio offered merchants ample arbitrage opportunities, as silver fetched an greater price the further east it went, used in financing the East India trades.[77] This could have manifest impacts on trade cycles. Between 1470 and 1530 population increased, while silver supplies per capita decreased. This caused a fall in food and other prices, as well as general dip in economic activity in the German lands.[78] Accordingly, German political economy and economic theory evolved around rather peculiar lines. Martin Luther for instance, in his great economic treatise of 1524 *Von Kauffshandlung vnd Wucher* (*On Commerce and Usury*), lamented upon the emerging global trades of his day. He called them *auslendische kauffs handel*, literally 'foreign trades', which brought in 'from Calicut, India, and such places, wares such as costly silks, gold-work and spices, which minister only to luxury and serve no useful purpose, draining away the wealth of land and people'.[79] This concept of superfluous luxury was something Luther shared with other mercantilists, before later contributions occasionally developed a more relaxed stance, admitting that *bilateral* trade balances may be negative as long as the *aggregate* balance of trade and payments remained positive, sustaining a positive or net influx of bullion.

In a famous passage about the Frankfurt fairs as 'Germany's silver sink' through which silver left the German lands for good, Luther picked up the problem of *monetary contraction* and economic depression that haunted the Holy Roman Empire during the 1520s.[80] A similar argument was presented in his *Address to the Christian Nobility of the German Nation* (*An den Christlichen Adel Deutscher Nation*, 1520). Many other works, such as his *Table Talk*, bear out a classic mercantilist 'fear of goods'. In the same year that Luther's *Kauffshandlung* appeared, a small book was published by popular preacher Eberlin von Günzburg, titled *I Wonder Why There Is So Little Money in Germany*. Ulrich von Hutten, another influential thinker of the German Renaissance, struck a similar chord. In his *Vadiscus* dialogue (1519/20), von Hutten reported how Rome (meaning the papacy) daily devised new means of 'taking away' money from the Germans. People returning from Rome – mostly as pilgrims – only brought back 'bad conscience, an upset stomach, an empty purse'. At the eve of the Reformation, pilgrimages, not only to Rome, represented common practice and regular tasks to complete for pious Christians; they were seen as one of the main evils in contemporary political economy. This was because three things everyone in Rome desired: 'short Mass, good coins, having a good time'; pilgrimages drained the German lands of money, causing persistent monetary shortfall and balance of payment problems.[81] Here von Hutten hinted at Gresham's Law or *spontaneous debasement*:[82] when coins of differing precious metal contents circulated alongside each other at the same face value, rational economic actors would cull out the good money, substituting it with bad coins instead. The debates at the Imperial Diet in Nuremberg 1522 similarly lamented the export of 'good money', as did complaints of the imperial knights (*Reichsritterschaft*) in 1523.[83] Such discourses were not limited to the 1520s. The German *Reichspolizeyordnung* of 1548 (Imperial Policy Ordinance) contained a general export ban on raw wool, as well as the admonition to 'wear only domestically manufactured cloth'. The Imperial Resolution of 1555 featured similar restrictions.[84] Later cameralists, especially Philipp Wilhelm von Hörnigk (*Oesterreich über alles wann es nur will*, 1684) or Johann Heinrich Gottlob Justi (1717–71), but also 19th-century thinkers such as Friedrich List (1789–1846) or Gustav Schmoller (1838–1917) and Wilhelm Roscher (1817–94) all developed fuller theories about catch-up development through an infant industry model implicitly following some lines and hints laid in the monetary literature of the Renaissance.

From these late medieval and early modern discourses some interesting yet occasionally profoundly conflicting policy stances were derived in the monetary field. Economic stability could only be achieved, the first proposition claimed, by keeping money stable; another proposition had it that playing around with coins' exchange value by coin debasement would be allowed, so long as it was aimed at restoring export strength and thus the well-being of the common weal; a third strategy focused on money's velocity, something we will explore in a separate chapter (Chapter 6).

Advocates of stable money

In an occasionally well-written résumé of his political life as engineer of the post-war German economic miracle, the rotund cigar-smoking minister of economic affairs and later chancellor of the Federal Republic of Germany, Ludwig Erhard (1897–1977), did not mince words. Defining 'freedom of consumption' as the supreme right of the modern economic citizen, he concluded that 'social market economy cannot exist without a consequent policy of price level stability' [*soziale Marktwirtschaft ist ohne eine konsequente Politik der Preisstabilität nicht denkbar*]. This principle came to be firmly embedded within the logics of West German political economy. Upon the eve of post-war economic recovery, the 1949 currency reform gave birth to the Deutsche Mark, the German economic miracle and a subsequent ideology of currency stability, for decades to come.[85] Erhard – perhaps unwittingly, since his qualities as an economist and writer are said to have been limited[86] – placed himself into an ancient tradition of political economy. It went back to late medieval scholastic authors including Oresme and Biel, towering figures of medieval monetary theory. Price level stability had been one of its central tenets, and one reason why so many late medieval and early modern writers expressed continuous worry about coins and currency debasement. The latter was considered a main cause of inflation and the ruin of nations.

Oresme had argued that currency must not be tampered with,[87] unless the common good was in acute danger, for instance from an imminent foreign invasion. Then the prince was naturally entitled to collect 'inflation tax' through temporary debasement. But as a general principle, coin debasement harmed the common weal, because it increased economic instability, especially when negotiations over a coin's exchange value made contracts harder to enforce. Coin debasement was considered an unjust transfer of assets (effectively a tax) from the subjects to the king or whoever had the sovereign right to mint coins (*regalian* right). Sustained debasement would cause an outflow of good or full-bodied coin (Gresham's Law). An excess of bad over good money would depress imports, because no one would want to do business with a country where payments were made in bad coin. Domestic circulation and exchange would thus be hampered. Rents and all other types of fixed income specified in a certain currency would devalue, too, once this currency became debased. People adjusted coin values downwards as soon as they discovered the true nature of debasement. Money then lost its function as a means of storing value. Some people culled a profit from using coins of differential standard, substituting bad money for good, or vice versa, depending upon nature and motive for the transaction. Such currency arbitrage was deemed usurious, but practices were so ubiquitous that they were often picked up in common complaints.[88]

Gabriel Biel (*c*.1415–95) embedded his monetary theory within an overall treatise on theological matters (*Collectorium circa quattuor libros Sententiarium*).[89] Coin debasement was bad for the common weal and community of the realm, he said. Coins ought to contain precious metal roughly equalling their purchasing power. Only a small deduction was allowed to cover for the expenses of minting, that is, seigniorage and brassage; this remained standard monetary theory, into the 19th century. But if coins were manipulated to extract a *profit*, for example by reducing their silver beyond below the allowance for seigniorage and brassage, this would ruin the country, Biel claimed, echoing Oresme. Only a change in the silver price would make such manipulations legitimate. The bottom line was: 'Don't touch the coins'.

Nicolaus Koppernigk or Copernicus (1473–1543), Prussian churchman, theologian and astronomer, produced three memoranda on Prussian currency matters between 1517 and *c*.1526.[90] In the first memorandum dating from 1517,[91] he maintained that the coinage represented a measure to be fixed by the 'community'. An unstable or devalued currency would harm the common good. Copernicus differentiated between two sources of a coin's value: first its intrinsic value (roughly equalling its market value), derived from the physical amount of precious metal embodied within each coin; second, the coin's official exchange rate as set by the government.[92] Coins enjoyed a liquidity premium over un-coined silver.

Sir Thomas Gresham (1519–79), the English royal financial wizard, advanced a common monetary origin myth in his 1578 memorandum entitled *On the Rules of Exchange of Moneys*. Whereupon 'the exchaunge between man and man, that was in the beginning of one thing for an other, fell away, and policy drave every thing to be valued to a certayne portion of fyne sylver and fyne golde', man would find it convenient to transform precious metal into coins, because:

> every state fynding it was to confuse to waye and truye golde and sylver agreed on for every thing bowght and solde, they made them selves (according to the proportion of fyne golde and sylver) coyned moneis of golde and sylver & appoynted pryntes, standerds, weightes, and valewe all thinges by.[93]

Gresham used the word 'state' here in a sense of '(temporal) estate', that is, denoting a particular range of people, such as nobility, clergy or townsfolk. But he may have had something bigger in mind, as it turns out, because such moneys were, in Gresham's words again, 'fyne at the first but sore alleyedd afterward, because that the *states* had not fyne golde and sylver enough for the use of their subiectes' [my emphasis].[94]

From the Renaissance, Europe's economy grew and Europeans occasionally had to stretch monetary supply to extremes. Copernicus admitted that coins could contain a *little* less precious metal than their face value, and this difference must not exceed the cost of minting (brassage plus seigniorage). Then the value of the coin was to be considered 'just'.[95] Like practically every scholastic author since Oresmius and many others still to come, Copernicus thought it a matter of course that *devaluation* – meaning more than a little less – of the currency by means of coin debasement was a no-go. In his more detailed 1526 memorandum he identified four plagues of humankind: war, plague, hunger and ... again: coin debasement.[96] (Remember the similarly abrupt turn in Erasmus's book; see Chapter 3.) Contrary to the first three evils, which were obvious, coin debasement was less visible, leading to *slow* corrosion of the common weal (*quia non vno impetus simul, sed paulatim et occulta quadam ratione respublicas euertit*).[97] Bad coins made purely or chiefly of copper would cause trade to decay. No foreign merchant would sell their wares for debased coin. Debased coin would purchase nothing in foreign lands, either.[98] It would lead, Copernicus was convinced, to the utter ruin of the country: *ingentem reipublice prussiane ... in dies magis et magis supine negligencia miserabiliter labi ac perire sinunt*.[99] Goldsmiths, silversmiths and expert metal traders – the financial market speculators of these days – profited from debased money by sorting out and buying up the old coins, resmelting them and selling the silver back to the mints (Gresham's Law again).[100] This would only contribute to price inflation, in Copernicus's view: *Hinc illa vulgaris et perpetua querimonia Aurum, argentum, annonam, familie mercedem, opificum operam et quicquid in humanis vsibus est, solitum transcendere precium.*[101] Modern research on German price-level trends during the so-called Price Revolution (1470–1620) has confirmed Copernicus's caveat. Over the 150 years or so of this inflationary cycle prices quoted in pennies – the money of the common man – increased more than twice and sometimes thrice as fast as prices expressed in 'good' money such as florins and thalers.[102] Among other things this was a result of these coins' higher velocity of circulation. Heavily debased small-change coins were of little use in the medium to long run. People tried to get rid of them as soon as possible, because they were of no use for saving or storing value.[103] Copernicus was convinced that only those countries where good coins circulated would also do well economically. Countries with a weak currency would suffer from 'inertia' (*ignavia*), idleness, stagnation (*desidia*) and 'regression' (*resupinatio*), Copernicus argued.[104] Not everyone shared this view, as we will see.

The anonymous *Albertine* or Catholic voice in the Saxon currency debate (*Münzstreit*, 1530–31),[105] echoed Oresmius, Copernicus and the other medieval metallists. People receiving fixed income streams, such as interest, rent and census payments, suffered most from currency debasement, because their payment streams got eroded, and their coins thus received would only be accepted in purchases at a discount (*Aber die geringe Muentze beraubet von stundt den nehmer des zehinden pfennigs seins guths / vnd alles seins werths / vnd zuweylen mehr / das er zu auffgelde geben mus*).[106] It was not just the better off whose fortunes were harmed by bad coin. The entire common weal suffered.[107] Bad money increased prices for imports as well as domestic goods, since sellers adjusted their prices to the changed precious metal content of the coins offered in return.[108] The negative welfare effect of an underweight currency that kept the economy below full potential was also highlighted by the Saxon jurist Melchior von Osse (1506–57): Where good money circulated, business and economy flourished, which, as Osse argued, also bolstered the fisc.[109]

Georg Agricola (1494–1555), whom we have encountered in the beginning, reiterated a common argument about money facilitating exchange and a coincidence of wants. In *De precio metallorum et monetis libri III* (1550) he claimed that coins made it easier for prices to form and adjust.[110] The costs of transporting money were lower than payment in goods or barter. Money was needed to settle debts with people who will not take our wares in return.[111] Agricola picked up on one of the most prominent debates and pressing issues of the day, that is, whether coins should circulate full-bodied or debased (that is, overvalued), giving both pros and cons. The arguments given in favour of a full-bodied coinage were that coins represented a 'treasure' or 'investment'; they were worth their value everywhere, Agricola maintained. But debased coins had a higher value in those places where they were struck. In their native realms they would always contain a small *fiat* element, while in foreign nations they were likely to be given and taken *below* face value, that is, discounted.[112] Countries with bad or debased money were less favoured by merchants than countries where good (full-bodied) coins were struck. Customs and toll revenue would decline; investors and entrepreneurs would move to states offering a better currency.[113]

This common narrative about coins and the wealth and ruin of nations was rehashed in early modern cameralist writings. Georg von Obrecht (1547–1612) emphasized the need to mint a sound currency (*ordentliche Muentzen angericht*).[114] He advocated the foundation of a central clearing institution (*Wechsel*) dealing with foreign and bad (underweight) coins at just rates of exchange, protecting the populace from the adverse consequences of instable and underweight currency. Veit Ludwig von Seckendorff, the 'Godfather of Cameralism'[115] argued in his *Teutsche Fürsten-Stat* in 1655 [1720][116] that coins represented a standardized means of exchange. Therefore, they should always retain their 'just' intrinsic weight. As most authors before and after him, Seckendorff avoided a specification of *just how much* debasement was 'justifiable' or 'right'. He evoked a functionalist origin myth of money, that is, that money had been invented as societies became ever-more complex and moved from barter to monetized exchange. Scripture confirmed, in Seckendorff's view, that the use of money had been common in biblical times (this depends on the correct translation of respective biblical passages). Money made of precious metal fulfilled all the qualities for this purpose: it was scarce; it was highly estimated by the people; and it could be made to represent value and thus facilitate the exchange of different products of different amount, quality and so on, which would otherwise have to be bartered.[117] While Jevons and virtually all modern textbooks on monetary theory have copied this Aristotelian line of reasoning; classical archaeologists, cultural anthropologists and some monetary historians are in disagreement with this origin story of money, suggesting a state-driven process of money's origin instead.[118]

Precious metal had been transformed, Seckendorff argued, by princes into coins of varying design, shape, size and purchasing power. And since this regal privilege had been devolved to the hundreds of political authorities within the Holy Roman Empire, a considerable level of confusion of currencies had ensued.[119] Coins should not be tampered with or altered at will (*daß eine jede müntze in gold, silber und kupffer, ihr verordnetes, richtiges gewichte habe*),[120] as this would reduce people's trust in them. Transaction costs would rise. Seckendorff acknowledged that the state should have the right of striking *slightly* underweight coins, but only in recompense for expenses incurred in the process of minting (brassage). Perhaps this also included an allowance for seigniorage. As the labour and fixed capital outlays needed in minting (buildings, tools and equipment) were the same for each coin type regardless of their value or weight, the costs of minting small-change coins was proportionally larger compared to full-bodied coins in value term.[121] Small-change coins must be slightly debased, the logical conclusion went, lest their production became unprofitable. Seen in the reverse, this explains early modern mint masters' and rulers' temptation to issue heavily debased small-change pennies. Introducing a fiat element into small change to cross-subsidize for the cost of minting must not be confused with outright *debasement* as a deliberate political choice, that is, reducing the currency *significantly* below face value to increase state revenue. Seckendorff considered such debased coins 'abominable', 'fraudulent' and harmful to the people (*schaendlich, gemischten, betrieglichen, unwuerdigen sorten* by which *viel leute in schaden und armuth erbaermlich gesetzet warden*).[122] Later cameralists followed suit. Like most of his predecessors, Justi argued[123] that underweight coins reduced people's trust, increased transaction cost and depressed future expectations, thus doing harm to people's economic lives and the common weal.[124]

But not every writer agreed that debasing coins was a bad thing per se.

Advocati Diaboli: playing around with exchange rates

Six years after Luther's *On Commerce and Usury / Von Kauffshandlung vnd Wucher* appeared in 1524, an anonymous 'Ernestine' or heterodox (1530) voice in the Saxon currency dispute (discussed earlier) spoke up.[125] Like his Albertine counterpart he probably belonged to the Saxon merchant community. Choosing to remain anonymous, the label 'Ernestine' simply denoted that this man was in the services of the Ernestine branch of the Saxon lands.[126] But he made a surprising departure from the prevailing monetary mainstream, arguing that:

> the same kingdoms, countries and islands [referring to the Low Countries/Holland, England and France] have oriented their business, commerce, order of things, economic policy and practical economic activity thus that they export their and other countries' goods predominantly to us Germans, as well as Hungarians and Bohemians, thereby bringing our money into their country, which enriches them and makes their wealth increase.

And: 'Our domestic industry is geared towards accumulating and exporting money and wealth [silver being Saxony's main export commodity] and take manufactured imports in return. This enriches about a hundred people, while driving princes and the common man, numbering more than one hundred thousand, to ruins'.[127]

The Ernestine had a point. Saxon silver at his time contributed between 20 and 50 per cent of total European silver output.[128] In theory the Saxon rulers could produce the most stable currency of their age.[129] As silver was cheaper in Saxony than elsewhere, Saxon money ought to contain more silver than other currencies. This would have reflected the inverse relationship between goods prices and the price of silver money in Saxony, compared to lands lacking silver mines, and which had to rely upon foreign trade in turn to replenish domestic monetary stocks. But Saxon goods paid in full-bodied heavy money would have been less competitive on markets outside Saxony, where goods were paid in lighter money, that is, coins containing proportionally less silver than the 'good' and 'hard' Saxon currency. The Ernestine specifically named the overvalued currency as the prime cause of Saxony's lack of economic competitiveness (*den wirdigen / vberigen wert der Muentz / Vnd was ferner dem anhengig erfolgt*) because, as he claimed, an overvalued currency drove up prices for consumables and wages alike (*so doch die kauff wahr / das gesinde lon / vñ alle gemeine zerung vnd ausgaben / bey der wirdigen Muentz erhoehet vnd gestiegen*).

The recipe suggested by the Ernestine in consequence sounds somewhat surprising, as this is about the last thing one would expect from an author trained in scholastic theory. He straightforwardly suggested the Saxon currency be *debased*, by raising the number of coins struck out a silver mark (*c.*250 grams) from 8¼ to 10 Rhenish florins or silver thalers. This debasement in the order of 21 per cent would have led to an effective devaluation of the Saxon currency, because the public would try to give and take coins by weight not tale (i.e. face value), according to the known amount of precious metal contained in them. As Europe's monetary history shows, people adjusted their appreciation of devalued coins downwards. Within weeks or months after each new mint run, or as soon as the common man received reliable information regarding the new coins' factual intrinsic value, they would adjust spot exchange rates in day-to-day market exchange.[130] This would cause a downward adjustment of the domestic currency in terms of foreign coins (devaluation). This quick fix should, as the Ernestine expected, solve Saxony's economic problems of the day. It would have made Saxon exports cheaper. It would also reduce the demand for imports, as those would become more expensive. And more importantly: the money would remain in the country (*damit das gelt souil mehr ynn landen blieben*).

In a 20th- or 21st-century context such currency manipulations have occasionally been labelled 'neomercantilist'.[131] But most mercantilists and cameralists during the age of early capitalism, 1250s–1850s, abhorred the profoundly heterodox perspective offered by the Ernestine. Devaluation through deliberate debasement simply flew in the face of medieval and Renaissance monetary and social theory, which held that only a stable and trustworthy currency would keep the Christian common weal well-governed and intact.

Only a century and a half later we hear something of an unorthodox voice again. It comes from our infamous *Projektemacher*,[132] Johann Joachim Becher (1635–82; see Chapter 2). Polymath-alchemist Becher travelled widely in the Netherlands and England during the 1660s. He became acquainted with Prince Rupert of the Palatine, the Cavalier and Lord High Admiral of the Royalist army and navy during the English Civil Wars.[133]

In his 1668 *Politischer Discurs: Von den eigentlichen Ursachen deß Auf- und Ablebens der Städt, Länder und Republicken* [*Political Discourse on the Rise and Decline of Cities, States and Republics*], Becher once more argued that money's general function was to reduce transaction cost, in comparison with the counterfactual (and counterintuitive) scenario of pure barter exchange.[134] Money was the *nervus rerum* (*Nerv uñ Seel*) of things; the currency should be standardized and stable.[135] So far so good (and not much new compared to other cameralist writers and earlier scholastic theories of money). But then Becher made a departure from mainstream dogma, suggesting upfront that domestic currency may be minted *5 per cent* below the intrinsic value of foreign moneys, to prevent spontaneous debasement. As we have seen, such spontaneous debasement, also known as Gresham's Law, by which underweight coins are introduced as legal money circulating at par with full-bodied or higher-value coins, will incentivize people to withhold the 'good' money from the market, or export it to other places where they can make an arbitrage gain from this transaction. Only the 'bad' or underweight coins will remain in the country. Research on 16th-century German monetary history, combining numismatic evidence (coin hoards) with casual evidence drawn from records of everyday market exchange and monetary transactions (bills, receipts, account books) suggests that this working mechanism was alive and kicking, and that people perceived it as a social and economic danger.[136] One consequence of 'good money drawing out the bad' was that people started renegotiating spot exchange rates. As we have already seen, this caused numerous problems.

None of the previous authors, however, had dared quantify exactly *how much* divergence from the 'pure' currency standard was permissible. But Becher did! His proposition almost sounds reasonably moderate. It certainly was low by comparison with the 'Ernestine' devaluation of 21 per cent. By issuing underweight coins, Becher said, people's propensity to export money was reduced and a somewhat healthier amount of money retained for domestic circulation.[137] Domestically the money would circulate at face value with foreign coins. But everyone taking it abroad would incur a loss of 5 per cent on its exchange, as foreign markets would rate the coins based on their true (reduced) precious metal content. Becher called this manipulation a 'tax' on the export of money (*billige und rechtmaessige impost und zoll*).[138] All foreign exchange transactions should be cleared through an exchange bank (*Wechsel=Banck*) financed using the profits yielded from the debasement.[139]

Becher had realized one important thing here. People need a certain amount of cash to make market economy run smoothly, quite regardless of each coins' intrinsic value: money is an important economic resource in the process of capitalist development (notwithstanding alternative forms of payment, such as bills of exchange, used chiefly by merchants in long-distance transaction but never the common man on the street).

Monetary policy and economic life in the age of early capitalism, 1250s–1850s

Thus monetary policy was conceived since the age of the scholastics as a policy of stabilizing the common weal, facilitating economic interaction and commercialization. Stable money could provide just the institutional framework needed for business and trade to flourish, reducing usury and arbitrage opportunities and other financial manipulations harmful to the lesser, poorer people. Bad money made people poor. Stable money meant foreign merchants coming into the country, giving people jobs (such as weaving and other manufacturing) and putting food on people's tables. As the European population grew between the 1470s and the 1800s (with interruptions during the 17th century, due to war and climate change), more and more people lacked the opportunity to have a farm or gain a living from agriculture; outside the towns manufacturing and 'proto-industry' blossomed. Manufacturing in the countryside, usually decentralized, with small-scale production controlled and financed by wealthy merchant-capitalists who sold the goods thus produced across long distances, grew in importance. German and Silesian linens, after travelling downstream the big rivers such as the Elbe, reached the Caribbean and Brazilian slave plantations. In the cities, manufacturing was even more significant (and as we shall see in Chapters 7 and 8, certain types of manufacturing were, according to Renaissance and early modern political economy, *best* located in cities). Without the monetary web provided by the hundreds of independent princely states such processes would hardly have been possible. But money required constant steering. Fiscal and monetary capacity on the one hand and economic development on the other were two sides of the same coin.

There were other options of monetary management. We will zoom in on one in particular: velocity and the idea that money must go round (and not be kept, hoarded or locked away) in order for the nation to flourish.

6

Velocity! Money, Circulation and Economic Development, *c.*1250–1850

Burying money: hoarding as a danger to the common weal

Hoarding, as Marx argued in *Critique of Political Economy* and *Kapital*, was a 'completely senseless activity'. Quoting an impressive range of political economy writings from the ancient Greeks to Martin Luther and mercantilists such as Misselden, Genovesi's *Lezioni di Economia Civile* (1765) or Petty's *Political Arithmetic*, Marx characterised the hoarder as:

> a martyr to exchange-value, a holy ascetic seated at the top of a metal column. He cares for wealth only in its social form, and accordingly he hides it away from society. He wants commodities in a form in which they can always circulate and he therefore withdraws them from circulation. He adores exchange-value and he consequently refrains from exchange. The liquid form of wealth and its petrification, the elixir of life and the philosophers' stone are wildly mixed together like an alchemist's apparitions. His imaginary boundless thirst for enjoyment causes him to renounce all enjoyment.[1]

Marx was not the first economic writer to abhor hoarders. He had certainly read his Luther – one of the most ardent critics of hoarding – as borne out by the extensive quote from Luther's *Sermon on Commerce and Usury* (1524), buried in the footnotes of *Critique of Political Economy*. Luther in turn had drawn upon Scripture, as would other contemporary Renaissance humanists who likewise habitually ridiculed and condemned hoarders and their dangerous habits. Classical writers like Xenophon had critiqued practices of hoarding, too; defining them as harmful they for business and economic life.[2] As late as 1850 a popular book on *Lives and Anecdotes of*

Misers; or, The Passion of Avarice Displayed rehashed centuries-old tropes of hoarding's vices, parsimony and the 'ill-natured miser',[3] a ubiquitous figure in 17th- and 18th-century cameralist political economy. Dutch émigré and London-based medic-onomist Bernard de Mandeville, in his 1714 *Fable of the Bees* (defending the idea of private vices as the driving forces of capitalism), mentioned the problem of money locked away in the ground where it was of no use to economy and market exchange. Austrian cameralist Joseph von Sonnenfels (1732–1817), one of the most influential Austrian economists of the Enlightenment, held that the wealth of nations rose and fell with the level of monetary circulation: money hoarded, sent abroad (for capital flows, remittances), saved, buried underground, directly reduced the volume of economic activity and lowered the nation's wealth.[4]

Early modern political economy commonly expressed a profound aversion to hoarding as a principally unprofitable form of saving, at least since the Renaissance. Often this was framed morally and soteriologically: being covetous with your money meant you were not giving to the poor, potentially jeopardizing a chance to make thy neighbour happy (or sure she was well-fed), help the common weal flourish, and – most importantly – yourself potentially entering Heaven (as a pay-off to your good deeds). In Renaissance thought the argument connected with the bigger issue of indulgences, which Reformed theologians now defined as flawed forms of spending that were simultaneously soteriologically *and* economically dangerous: the reverse of hoarding but, when defined purely in terms of its economic consequences, similarly harmful. (The idea was that you literally could, by purchasing an indulgence letter, buy yourself out of Purgatory. The latter was an intermediate stage after death between Heaven and Hell, with a chance of entering the former still, by doing good works, repenting your sin and buying some nice little insurance letters that would reduce your time in this limbo – called indulgences; but Luther and the Reformers would have none of it.) Luther reiterated Oresme the scholastic, whose works we have encountered in the last chapter. Oresme, in his *Treatise on Money* written during the later 1350s, had in turn evoked a dictum ascribed to the Ostrogoth King Theodoric (*c*.451/6–526) that 'graves should be stripped of buried silver and gold treasure, as wealth that had been put away this way would prove of no use'.[5] Some of Luther's contemporaries were more hands-on and less fussed about morals when condemning hoarding. Imperial knight and Reformation intellectual Ulrich von Hutten habitually ridiculed men who 'buried' wealth, a phrase that Marx would later use as well. Money resting underneath the soil should rather be put to productive purpose above ground. Mandeville, in a later (1723) addition to the *Fable of the Bees* (Remark G), made a startling proposition about hoarding, crime and the ironies of some forms of contemporary criminal verdicts and punishment:

If an Ill-natur'd Miser, who is almost a Plumb, and spends but Fifty
Pounds a Year, tho' he has no Relation to inherit his Wealth, should
be Robb'd of Five Hundred or a Thousand Guineas, it is certain that
as soon as this Money should come to Circulate, the Nation would be
the better for the Robbery, and receive the same and as real a Benefit
from it as if an Archbishop had left the same Sum to the Publick,
yet Justice and the peace of the Society require that he or they who
robb'd the Miser should be Hang'd, tho' there were Half a Dozen of
'em concern'd.[6]

In 17th- and 18th-century German-speaking political economy, misers thus
hiding away their wealth without spending were identified as *Kapitalist* (plural
Kapitalisten) – 'capitalists'. In the *Fable of the Bees*, Mandeville thus picked
up an entirely common theme of his time, avarice, in words that would
not have sounded in the least unfamiliar to people like Hutten, Luther and
other Renaissance people:

the true Reason why every Body exclaims so much against it [avarice],
is, that almost every Body suffers by it; for the more the Money is
hoarded up by some, the scarcer it must grow among the rest, and
therefore when Men rail very much at Misers, there is generally self
Interest at bottom.[7]

The 'miser' came up again in Enlightenment Scottish political economist
James Steuart's *Principles of Political Oeconomy* (1767) and the story of the
travelling guinea (a high-value gold coin worth a little more than a pound
sterling at Steuart's time): every time it stopped, that is, at the point of
purchase or expense, 'it marks a want of desire to consume, in him who
possesses it. If therefore, in any country, there were but one guinea in
circulation, all consumption would stop (or barter would take place) the
moment it fell into the hands of a miser'.[8] Ferdinando Galiani, a leading
political economist of the Italian Enlightenment, in 1751 estimated the
value of hoarded silver and gold at three to four times the monetary stock,
which – if true – pointed to the gravity of the problem.[9] When Adam Smith,
in the second book of the *Wealth of Nations* (1776), titled 'On the Nature,
Accumulation, and Employment of Stock', offered the startling concession
(which modern economists have identified as a modern theory of saving)
that 'Parsimony, and not industry, is the immediate cause of the increase of
capital',[10] he literally broke with six centuries' worth of political economy
that had usually claimed exactly the opposite.

One way of interpreting hoarding is through the economist's lens: it can
be written as the inverse of *velocity* or money's propensity to go places,
to circulate and reverberate between individuals, maintaining chains of

economic transactions that keep the economy going. Velocity and circulation are the subject of the present chapter, building up on Chapter 5, but extending the view on money as a potentially transformative *oeconomic* tool. Combining conceptual history with some numismatic evidence I will try to shed new light on how between the 1300s and 1800s political economy reconceptualized money and its velocity as a means to dynamize the common weal. For early modern economic landscapes were chronically short of cash[11] and are commonly assumed (at least by many modern historians) to have known very few dynamics.[12]

Hoarding and velocity in the history of concepts and of economic thought

'The term circulation is, perhaps, one of the most expressive in any language, and is therefore easily understood. It represents the successive transition of money, or transferable commodities, from hand to hand, and their return, as it were in a circle, to the point from which they set out'.[13] Thus wrote Sir James Steuart, one of Scotland's leading Enlightenment oeconomists, in his bestselling *Principles of Political Oeconomy* (1767). During his travels in the southern German lands in the mid-1750s, Steuart had familiarized himself with cameralist political economy, which paid very specific attention to money and circulation as transformative tools. Probably neither Steuart nor the cameralists had *modern* conceptions of monetary velocity in mind when discussing aspects of vivacity of circulation or *Lebhaftigkeit des Umlaufs*: vivacity could equally refer to money and goods, or a general notion of increased economic turnover across the market system. Nevertheless, it is helpful for analytic clarity to briefly consider velocity in more formal terms, to understand the wider implications of these debates.

In modern economics, velocity can be defined as the number of times a currency unit (or the stock of money available at any one point in time) changes hands, that is, circulates. Velocity is elusive, certainly historically, because it is a residual. It cannot be measured but only calculated after *measurable* variables such as amount of money (M), price level (P) and economic activity (T or GDP) have been asserted with some degree of confidence (which is always difficult for historical times, as people neither knew the concept of GDP nor, therefore, bothered measuring it).[14] How can velocity be captured in historical times and from the historical record? And how did political economy come to conceptualize it as an economic tool?

In *Contribution to the Critique of Political Economy* (1859), Marx connected velocity with:

> the total character of the mode of production, the size of the population, relationship of city and country, development of means

of transportation, of greater or lesser development of labour, credit, and so on, in short circumstances, which all lie outside the simple circulation of money and are just reflected in it.[15]

Wilhelm Roscher (1817–94), alongside Gustav (von) Schmoller (1838–1917) one of the towering figures of the 19th-century German Historical School in economics, likewise held velocity to be a dependent *variable*. But it was culturally contingent. In Roscher's conception velocity followed distinct waves: during the process of development monetary stock would first increase and, when a certain per capita income had been reached and people had become accustomed to money use and adjusted their demand for money, velocity would decrease again.[16] This is interesting because, unlike Roscher, many historians nowadays tend to associate a declining velocity with a *decrease* (not increase) in economic activity (and vice versa). Cameralist political economist Johann Georg Büsch (1728–1800) had criticized Adam Smith, insisting it was not the division of labour that caused the wealth of the nation to increase, but circulation – of money and goods, and to be precise: money's speed of circulation.[17]

In his masterpiece on the *History of Economic Reasoning*,[18] historian of economic thought Karl Pribram proposed that velocity was 'discovered' as an independent variable by mid-17th century English writers, including William Petty or William Potter (*The Key of Wealth, or A New Way for Improving Trade*, 1650).[19] Schumpeter, in his monumental *History of Economic Analysis* (1954) agreed that velocity 'did not acquire substance until the last decades of the 17th century. This was a purely English achievement'.[20] But these assessments require revision. First of all, most historians would nowadays probably take issue with the notion that ideas or concepts are 'invented' or 'discovered' by specific actors at specific points in time and space; rather we would look for certain types of specimens of concepts and ideas, and how they are used, made use of and appropriated by certain actors in their distinct context of action, networks and debates. For the present purpose I am interested in how velocity – which differed in meaning and interpretation across writers, actors, spaces and time – shaped up within a wider perspective and more *longue durée* historical context of raising the wealth of nations. Is it accurate to claim that pre-Newtonian writers had no concept or knowledge of velocity? Or did they simply employ a different semantics when capturing it? Can these discourses be connected? Zooming in on *velocity* by means of case study thus tells us something bigger about capitalism.

Like many of the German cameralists, but also earlier voices such as Martin Luther and the Renaissance humanists, Potter conceptualized his observations on money and velocity against a 'decay of trade' or perceived depression.[21] Continental cameralists of the 18th century often used the term *Umlauf* probably referring to what Potter had as 'quick current' or 'revolution' ('re-volution' here meaning movement completing a full cycle of 360 degrees). Perhaps Potter's 'revolution' and the cameralists' *Umlauf* came close to what the modern monetary conception of the Fisher equation –after Irving Fisher (1867-1947), which posits that the amount of money (M) multiplied by its velocity of circulation (V) equals the total volume of economic transactions, T (or GDP) valued at current prices P – has 'monetary mass' (MV).[22] But modern labels and theories are not normally tailor-made for the past, especially not when that past is four or more centuries away. A Potterian 'quick current'[23] could be a sign of ample supply of commodities and low prices, that is, a glut in the market: early modern German market semantics knew this as the *wohlfeile Markt* (literally 'cheap market').[24] Because, as Potter went on, 'seeing for that we cannot increase money at pleasure to any quantity needfull; we have no feasible means whereby to quicken Trade, (as I said before) but by multiplying a firme and knowne credit amongst Tradesmen, fit to transmit from hand to hand'.[25] Potter thus connected money's velocity, credit and economic development in ways characteristic of its time and age, with a financial revolution and the idea of monetary alchemy, common in many proposals and projects about land banks and other forms of money creation *ex nihilo* prevailing during the later 17th century.[26]

John Locke (1632–1704), physician, philosopher and political economist sometimes reckoned to the proto-classical political economy spectrum, analysed the frequency and rhythms of payment and the duration of time that people would withhold money from the market.[27] Modern economists may find similarity with Keynes's concept of demand for money to hold, but again care is needed to avoid anachronism; suffice it to say there were resonances in political economy. Charles D'Avenant (1656–1714), Commissioner of the Excise and after 1703 Inspector General of the Imports and Exports for England, emphasized the necessity for 'A quick Stock running amongst the People'.[28] Petty (1661) clarified this by stating that the more hands a fixed sum of money passed through throughout the year, the higher would be economic activity and employment.[29] Petty also observed that different classes of people had different rhythms of cash utilization resulting in differing frequencies of payment. Artisans often sourced inputs and sold their final manufactures upon short-term credit; accounts were settled weekly. Long-distance and wholesale trade, on the other hand, ran along longer lines of credit, extending for months if not years. Irving Fisher, one of the founding fathers of modern monetary economics acknowledged such differentiation in payment habits as an important way of approaching overall velocity.[30]

Historians occasionally reckon Locke's concept to have been an 'innovation'.[31] But if we take a broader comparative view, this judgement requires revision. By looking to the continent, adopting a broader and long-term view, we can identify older and broader traditions that spoke to very similar questions but with models of velocity and circulation that did not quite match the modern ones. As Quentin Skinner and others in his wake have reminded us, no idea remains 'the same' in a pure or ontological sense, and ideas get reshaped, reconfigured, remoulded and reassembled as they change or move across different discursive and political contexts.[32]

The Spanish theologian-economists of the School of Salamanca, a late scholastic school of thought that flourished between the late 15th and mid-16th centuries, had, for instance, known a concept of velocity of some sorts, but broadly seem to have interpreted it as a constant.[33] Later authors would add a dynamic component. In 1664 Jean de Lartigue argued:

> The Prince's affairs must be put in order, his debts paid, … his treasury filled … and employed immediately for outlays and the needs of state, in fear that it [money] will languish and fail; if we do not keep the existing [stock] of money in circulation it is put in reserve and produces nothing. Instead, by passing from hand to hand it gives vigor to commerce of which it is the soul.[34]

German cameralists, especially during the later 18th century Enlightenment period, developed interesting modifications. Georg Gottfried Strelin's dictionary of the cameral sciences (1788) for instance knew a variable called *Umlauf* – perhaps the amount of money in circulation, perhaps monetary mass (velocity times the amount of coins in circulation), perhaps the transactions volume: *ex posteriori* it is difficult to know exactly what was being referred to. Strelin distinguished *Umlauf* (literally re-*volution* or *circulation*) from *Lebhaftigkeit* (vivacity), alongside coins' intrinsic value as another manifest economic variable determining money's utility in the market process (see Chapter 5).[35] A good *Umlauf* was characterized by low interest rates (*niedrige Interessen*), absence of 'mistrust' and a balance between the amount of goods and the total amount of money in circulation. The more money in circulation, and thus the higher the *Umlauf*, the lower the *Interessen*.[36] But how could monetary mass be stimulated? One option was through the creation of paper money (*Papiere*),[37] Strelin suggested. Earlier on the 1650s, 1670s and 1680s had seen an age of alchemists, 'projects' and project makers all over Europe, coinciding with the foundation of some of the continent's most venerable academies, such as the Royal Society, or the Albertina in Halle/Saale, which later on became the Holy Roman Empire's 'national' academy, founded in 1652; all important steps taken in the early age of Enlightenment.[38] Another way to promote the vivacity of circulation according to the cameralist view was to attract wealthy foreigners and producers of high-quality manufactures into the country, to increase manufacturing exports.[39] This was standard fare, most clearly laid out in

Philip Wilhelm von Hörnigk's 1684 bestseller *Oesterreich über alles wann es nur will* (*Austria Supreme if Only It So Wills*).[40] Cultural transfer would cause knowledge transfer and emulation and increase useful knowledge, which would improve the circulation of money and goods.[41]

What blood circulation was to the human body, a good monetary *Umlauf* was to economic life and exchange.[42] Commodities and money were 'drawn to each other' like blood contracted to the human heart, only to be released back again into circulation, when the heart pulse expanded: to attract new purchases and goods and restart the cycle over and over again, so that no 'beggar' and no *Kapitalist* – someone hoarding money for speculative or avaricious purposes – could possibly survive ('*und es würde kein Kapitalist und kein Bettler seyn*').[43] Money locked away in the *Kapitalist* vaults caused, literally, 'disequilibrium' ('*allein das Gleichgewicht hört auf*'), raising interest rates, which put the brake to economic activity. These would be reflected in higher prices charged by the producers who were dependent on financial loans for carrying on their business. England's generally low interest rates, Strelin noted, were the cause of this nation's wealth.[44] Modern research seems to agree that low rates on government borrowing were part and parcel of British economic development in the wake of the Glorious Revolution (1688) and the onset of early industrialization.[45] According to the cameralist model, vivacity of circulation may also be stimulated through population growth and a concomitant rise in domestic demand; through the expansion of manufacturing activities, especially exports.[46] Authors of the late cameralist school would further point toward division of labour, economic specialization and diversification within the economy ('*Manchfaltigkeit von Gütern, Nutzungen und Leistungen*') as factors upon which vivacity of circulation was contingent.[47] Banks (land banks, giro and deposit banks, extending credit and clearing bills of exchange; as well as 'foreign trading companies') were considered powerful instruments stimulating overall monetary circulation.[48] A rather long entry on 'Geld' in the first edition 1779 (2nd edn, 1787) of Krünitz's economic encyclopaedia – one of the mammoth projects of the continental economic enlightenment, on which large parts of later works were based almost verbatim, including Strelin's previously mentioned entry in his *Realwörterbuch* – emphasized that circulation would be stimulated mostly by 'useful and necessary goods', not luxury wares.[49] This is important to keep in mind, especially since later historians have often claimed that early modern policies were usually targeted at luxury and niche industries, without paying much attention to the 'real' needs of economy and people: a problematic claim at variance with the evidence, as we will further see in Chapters 7 and 8.[50]

Cameralists during the later 17th and into the 18th centuries paid increasing attention to manufacturing and how this could be stimulated across the board, encouraging general economic development. They thus extended an initially rather narrowly conceptualized view on *oeconomy* as prudent or 'thrifty' (in the word of one recent scholar) management into a wider conceptual analysis of the causes, nature and origin of the wealth of nations.[51] In *Grundsätze der Policeywissenschaft* (*Principles of Economics*, 1756) Johann Heinrich Gottlob Justi specifically called for government to ensure a good amount of money in circulation (*Umlauf*): a key variable in the economic process.[52] Justi established a functional relationship between *Umlauf* and the price level. If there was less 'circulation' vis-à-vis a constant amount of goods and services produced, prices would decrease, because silver-based currencies would appreciate in purchasing power. Goods would become cheaper, but employment and incomes would also fall. Government should take care that enough money was circulating at a 'healthy' velocity to avoid this and keep the economic process running at full capacity.[53] Justi was more afraid of falling prices than he was of inflation: a modest rise in prices may fuel a boom in economic activity, filling the order books, inducing the people to spend more, spiralling the whole system upwards. In a somewhat tacit reminiscence of cameralist monetary theory two hundred years later, federal German chancellor Helmut Schmidt is said to have quibbled he'd 'rather have five per cent inflation than five per cent unemployment'.[54] Justi's project was best achieved by putting more money into circulation. But this was difficult, if silver reserves were scarce – the somewhat default scenario in most German states bar those few that had native silver mines, and if currency debasement was to be ruled out as a political option (see Chapter 5).

Such tropes were no peculiar cameralist or exclusively German political economy fare. David Hume developed a dynamic theory of money, manufacturing, employment, wages and economic development; in this he also considered hoarding.[55] Uppsala political economist Pehr Nicholas Christiernin (1725–99) cautioned that:

> Wage earners would suffer immediately from unemployment and lack of income; the nation would suffer from the reduction in output. The reduction in incomes itself reduces aggregate demand, causing still further declines in income. In addition, the burden of public and private debt would be increased; and private debtors, constituting the entrepreneurial class, would be forced into bankruptcy.[56]

According to Anders Berch, an enlightened Swedish cameralist and oeconomic writer whose fame extended deep into the German realms (and whom we already encountered as a future-facing writer in Chapter 2), clever economic policy entailed avoiding a halting (*Anhalten*) of the monetary flow at all cost.[57] Capital must never lie idle.[58] Later writers of the historical school followed suit, connecting velocity with political stability, economic development, institutions, property rights security and fluctuations in the business cycle.[59] But to what extent was the cameralist conceptualization itself original?

Martin Luther's (1483–1546) sermons of the early 1520s are full of references to indulgences, luxurious chalices, monstrances, church bells and altar pieces and other ways that money was invested in economically as well as religiously unproductive ways.[60] This Reformers' viewpoint was shared by intellectuals who had occasionally professed similar sentiments even before 1517. Rather than giving the money to the Church for indulgences and other devotional purposes, the money should be allocated to those in need; the poor, the hungry.[61] In his *Sendbrief vom Dolmetschen* (*On Translation*, 1530), Luther quoted scripture on condemning the practice of hoarding money: 'Thus is why the master in the gospel scolds the unfaithful servant as a slothful rogue for having buried and hidden his money in the ground [Matt. 25:25–26]'.[62] Such voices were ubiquitous during the 1520s and 1530s. As I have shown elsewhere, coupled with debates about indulgences as the most unproductive form of hoarding (as the money was sunk within churches and cloisters), the intense anti-hoarding debates of the age constitute a centrepiece of 'Reformation economics'.[63] Luther and the early 16th-century Reformed theologians conceptualized money as an economic resource. Money was more than its *amount*: *velocity* mattered, that is, the number of times a particular stock of money would *circulate* within the economy. As we have already seen, this sentiment resonated in later economic writings and discourses well into the 19th century, in the German-speaking countries as well as elsewhere. 'Geld im kasten ist dem Lande ein schade', mused Wilhelm von Schröder, alongside Becher and Hörnigk another widely received political economist of the later 17th century.[64] Many cameralists were Protestants, or in the services of Protestant princes in their German lands, and would have naturally drawn on Luther's works in their visions of the economic and political process. Philip Wilhelm von Hörnigk, one of the few early modern authors of the mercantilist-cameralist ilk to quote Luther directly (*On Commerce and Usury*, 1524) was a Catholic even; but he was a convertite, and had adopted the Catholic faith to enter the emperor's service as a secret diplomat and economic attaché on a mission to reunify the German lands under a common Christian faith and, along the way, implement a common economic policy for the Empire labelled 'imperial mercantilism'.[65]

Thus, there was a longer line of political economy reaching from Renaissance humanism to cameralist political economy, English mercantilism to the German Historical School that conceptualized money's velocity as a means of economizing on money as a scarce resource and stimulating *Umlauf* or circulation, especially when the amount of money was scarce or declining.

Coins and the dynamics of capitalism

Thinking about the political economy of money's velocity opens up broader questions about capitalism and the long road of economic development. The history of materiality and of objects have been on the rise recently, but not usually connected with capitalism or historical political economy; coins, especially, have been omitted from most recent object-based cultural and social histories.[66] This is striking because if there was *one* everyday item commonly used in preindustrial Europe, by virtually everyone, people of lower and higher rank alike, it was money and coins. Of those studies that do indeed zoom in on monetary developments and their impact on price level and output in the premodern market economy, many tend to either casually omit velocity; mention it in passing, or simply assume it was a constant.[67] Often money supply is taken as the main independent variable when it comes to explaining economic change, and changes in output and living standards through a monetary lens.[68] There are conflicting assumptions about the causes, nature, size, trend and historical dimensions of velocity (Was it variable? Can we measure it? Did it change over time? Did it matter?), with Goldstone, for instance, proposing that 'in occupationally specialized linked networks, the potential velocity of circulation of coins grows as the square of the size of the network',[69] while Mayhew on the other hand would claim that 'in periods of growth in terms of money, prices and economic activity, velocity may be expected to fall rather than rise. ... Indeed, the increasing use of money usually seems to require an enlarged money supply which will actually permit a reduction in velocity rather than an increase'.[70] According to Mayhew an increase in velocity would be a sign of 'monetary distress', not good order, and as we have already seen with reference to Wilhelm Roscher, this proposition was not so out of line with some assumptions held by economists of the German Historical School towards the 1860s and 1870s.

The late John Munro pointed out another important yet often neglected detail. Different types of currency – silver or gold, small-change or full-bodied coin – have different velocities of circulation,[71] and as I have been able to show these different coin segments correspond to different social groups sporting different idiosyncratic patterns of handling money and rhythms of payment with considerable economic and political implications: the currencies of the common man in preindustrial Europe – small and medium coins (farthings, *hellers*, pennies, groats) – usually had a much higher velocity, for a number of reasons, most importantly being their often debased or dubious nature (see discussion in Chapter 5). They did not serve particularly well as stores of value, and would not necessarily be accepted at face value in market transactions or tax payments. In consequence people tried to get rid of them as soon as they could; resulting in a faster turnaround (and thus higher velocity) than for higher-level and full-bodied coins.[72]

On the other hand, there is no scholarly consensus as to what extent changes in monetary supply or 'monetary mass' – that is, the amount of money (M) as well as the frequency with which it is used in transactions (V) during a set period, usually a year[73] – impact on changes in output and employment; in the short or medium run, immediately or through indirect changes. Many hold money to be entirely neutral or a 'veil' that simply covers what goes on in the market process. The evidence presented here suggests a different interpretation. Money *did* matter, and so did velocity – in both directions.

That said, even though we do have some good figures for European silver and gold mining since the 13th century, as well as some basic trade data[74] allowing tentative hypotheses about the possible size and direction of monetary supply for certain European regions, much less is known on velocity. Even in contemporary national income accounting 'measuring' the income velocity of money remains problematic. Morgan has summarized the state of the art thus:

> So, measured velocity has three faces. On one side, it is simply the measured ratio between two things, each of which are determined elsewhere than the equation of exchange: because velocity has no autonomous causal connections, it provides for no measure of V that can be used for policy setting. On the second, it exhibits its own (autonomous) trend growth rate (sometimes unreliably so) which could be useful for prediction and so policy setting for the two elements from which it is measured. On the third, it has a relationship to the behaviour of money demand, a relationship which is both potentially reliable and potentially analysable, so that it could be useful for understanding the economy and for policy work, but here the focus seems to have reversed itself: understanding the determinants of velocity now seems to be the device to understand the behaviour of the money stock, even while the measuring instrument works in the opposite direction.[75]

Thus velocity *can* be an historical actor; but a profoundly elusive one. Surely it must be even more difficult to claim any better evidence for any period prior to industrialization? Perhaps the available historical evidence, if interpreted carefully, gives us a few further hints.

The Fisher equation of exchange ($MV=PT$) posits that changes in velocity of money, that is, the number of times a monetary unit changes hand in a given period, may principally affect the economy in the same way as a change in the amount of money does (M). Or, if the two develop in different directions, the trend in V may offset a positive (negative) trend in M. Finally, a decline (rise) in V may reinforce a contracting (rising) trend in M when both M and V rise or decline in tandem, which appears to have been the case during the late medieval economic depression in the Germanies, *c.*1350–1520, when M and V declined simultaneously.[76] The Fisher equation, however, does not tell us much about what is going on in the economy and why, and what drives observable changes in certain key variables on which it is based. But which of the four variables may take the lead in the game? It may therefore be more sensible to analyse the aggregate component or product MV or 'monetary mass' – Austrian cameralist Joseph von Sonnenfels seems to have called this the *kreislaufende Masse* – rather than keeping V and M apart from each other, as otherwise the historical picture of the market process will probably be incomplete.[77]

Let's illustrate this further by returning to some of the key conjunctures in early modern capitalism. As we saw in Chapter 5 around 1500 AD German mines were the main supplier of European silver (and thus payment and monetary stock). Political economy picked up on this problem. When brought via Lisbon and the Cape route into the Indian Ocean and the southeast Asian realms, silver's price, measured in terms of units of gold, increased by 50 per cent. It doubled in price when it finally reached China.[78] German and many other European merchants rushed to export an increasing quantity of it from west to east, *c.*1500–1800. After German silver mining had run beyond its peak towards the middle of the 1530s, initially fuelling the 'Price Revolution' and secular expansion of population and economic activity (but not per capita GDP[79]), after the 1550s the role was taken over by American silver. This allowed inflation to be reined in and prices to rise, vis-à-vis a decrease of per capita economic resources, 1470/1530–1620.[80] But *before* the American silver flowed, however, the story was different from the common neo-Malthusian model, which is often invoked, alongside a monetarist or quantity theory approach, to explain the Price Revolution (a revolution that was none, as the average yearly rate of inflation was 1.5 per cent, which is moderate by most modern inflation targets).[81] A neo-Malthusian model predicts that a decreasing per capita supply of resources (mainly foodstuffs and essentials: food, drink, cloth, shelter and heating/energy) should cause inflation in the general price level, with food prices rising faster than others (such as industrial inputs).[82] Between 1470 and 1530, however, the story did not quite go according to the predictions of a Malthusian approach, because the monetary stock that would have supported Malthusian signals in the price level was lacking. Population increased all over the Germanies,[83] while disposable incomes *and* real wages *and* silver supplies (cash) per capita *decreased simultaneously*.[84] This was mirrored by *deflation*, approximated using grain prices as those prices with the highest weight in the premodern consumer price index for the period concerned; only temporarily interrupted by a peak around 1515, years of acute harvest crisis.[85]

As shown in Chapter 5, silver-based currencies represented the general means of payment in the German territories. With the available amount of coined money per capita (units of silver) declining, V (velocity) undecided (on which, more later), and the total volume of market transactions potentially growing (as Chapter 2 has shown) people in the German-speaking lands faced declining prices as economic activity increased faster than the amount of silver available.[86] Price data from the period indeed show a downward trend between 1490–1500 and 1530,[87] as they would in the time around 1600–20, that is, the period immediately preceding the Thirty Years War[88] or the Kipper and Wipper hyperinflation of 1619–23, or around 1660–80, when wars against the Turks and the so-called Second Kipper inflation exerted monetary stress on the market economies. These were all times when per capita silver resources contracted, mostly because more of the incoming silver was exported to the Baltic and Asia; or because less silver than usual came into Europe. These times can also be identified as times of economic crisis.[89]

Curiously, these were also times when political economy produced some of its finest pieces on crises in religion and the markets, as we have seen in Chapter 5. There is good evidence of contraction in the urban market economies in upper and central Germany during the first two decades of the 16th century. This may serve as a reference point explaining Luther's comments on money, commerce and indulgences, money much better spent 'towards schools for the training of the poor children. That would be an excellent investment'.[90] In other words, what Luther and the political discourse of the years around 1517 *may* have referred to what *may* have been a monetary contraction caused by a simultaneous *decrease in velocity* as well as money supply, similar to the case of the depression in the market economies of the 14th- and 15th-century Renaissance.[91] In the German-speaking lands, the period between c.1500 and the mid-1520s represented the last phase of a series of general late medieval (to use John Day's phrase) 'bullion famines' only temporarily reversed during the Central European silver mining boom of the 1470s and 1480s.[92] The great inflation of the 16th century did not set in before the late 1530s, driven by the silver-mining districts around Annaberg in the Saxon Erz Mountains, followed by another peak during the 1540s fuelled by the mines of Marienberg (the boom of the 1470s and 1480s had been driven by Schneeberg); to this came a temporary revival in the Thuringia *Saiger* smelting industry, especially in the Mansfeld area, where Luther came from. The area was marked by high levels of trade dependency and market integration, and its wider implications will be discussed in Chapter 8.[93]

But back to coins and velocity.

Materiality, velocity and numismatics: a new approach to the history of capitalism

The numismatist has become an endangered species. This is sad because coins can be fundamentally important for studying the history of capitalism and economic life.[94] And yet at the same time coin hoards – the main 'data storage' that such histories can usefully draw upon – also belong to some of the most enigmatic type of historical sources that we have; trying to get them to 'speak' can be tricky.[95] Chapter 5 has presented the basic framework of monetary dynamics and politics in Renaissance and early modern Germany. Because we cannot know with reasonable confidence how much money was around, and what GDP was for the early modern German market economies, we may perhaps use the Cambridge equation for intuition instead, replacing the velocity of money with its inverse called 'demand for money to hold' (k), thus $V = 1/k$. K denotes the share of money held by individuals that is neither invested nor spent on consumption. Notwithstanding the anachronisms inherent to any such exercise interpreting history through the lens of modern theory, we can still search for possible historical illustrations and 'mirrors'.

One way of approximating the patterns of preindustrial individuals holding cash, and thus indirectly estimating velocity and its impact on capitalism and economic development may be provided by numismatics.[96] Numismatic data on coin hoards, documented in modern databases for Germany, the UK[97] and the Netherlands (and many other European portable antiquity schemes) may give us – under certain assumptions – an impression of the average level and trend of money withheld from the market, assuming that hoards captured in such databases tell us something about temporary withdrawals of money from circulation (meaning they represented declines in velocity but not the monetary stock as such). Numismatists date coin hoards by determining the age of the most recently struck coin found in each hoard. This gives us a tentative *post*-date or minimum age for the hoard. It also leaves room for criticism and reflection, working on the following assumptions:

1. Before the deposit of the hoard there was an opportunity to bury coin; this mostly applies to hoards, not single coins or stray finds.[98]
2. The owner of the hoard buried the money deliberately (which can be problematic, because coin 'hoards' as defined by numismatists usually refer to *any* deposit containing a minimum of at least two coins meaning such deposits also covered *casual* losses, that is, when someone worked in the field and lost a handful of pennies during the day).
3. Their owners were for some reason or another prevented from subsequently unearthing the hoard (that is, to remonetize it); this is what I would call the 'Squirrel Effect'. People may simply forget, after burying a coin hoard, where they did it. External markers initially placed at the site of deposit for later orientation and remembrance, such as stones, trees and so on, may vanish or be removed in the meantime by someone else and so on.
4. Instead the hoard was rediscovered by someone else, at a later stage.

5. The hoard has been captured, published or documented accurately in an indicative repository, portable antiquities scheme, or professional (academic) publication including a detailed description of its contents and material quality (meaning the coins can be reasonably confidently dated).

Another interpretation claims that the numismatic record on coin hoards only captures *failures*, that is, hoards that failed to achieve their initial purpose; since we neither know the number of recirculated hoards (that is, hoards that were buried but subsequently found again, unearthed and remonetized), nor hoards undiscovered by numismatists and treasure hunters, nor those found but not documented (for example, hoards retrieved illegally), the total figure for known hoards is likely to underestimate the true level of money burials, with an unknown ratio between undiscovered versus discovered hoards; this ratio itself may fluctuate over time. Coins from antiquity also tend to be preserved and documented in much better shape and frequency than, say, coins from the early Middle Ages, or even more recent times, due to their higher estimation among private collectors. Moreover, due to Gresham's Law (see Chapter 5) we may expect hoards to display a bias towards high-value coins.[99] Coin hoards also seem to appear much more frequently in the countryside than in urban areas. This seems odd because historians would commonly associate coin use and capitalism mainly with cities and urban markets. This, however, can be explained by differential patterns and subsequent layers of an area's built history; chances of coin discovery and excavation are much lower in an urban context than in the countryside (because they most likely happen when buildings are demolished and space is repurposed). Coins also commonly appear in the middle of rural fields, but not so much because people necessarily took them to work, but most likely because they were lost on the floor of a home, swept away during cleaning and then released into the fields together with other domestic refuse which served as fertilizer. Such *stray* finds give us very different stories about monetization and velocity than coin hoards.[100] Many factors may have been at work that influenced the pattern of hoarding, leaving the historian without much of a clue as to what really happened. But still the evidence we have points towards some sort of connection between the numismatic data on hoards thus defined, and politico-economic developments. Even failed hoards (total known hoards) tend to mirror patterns of politics and other disruptive events such as Martin Luther's Reformation, the American Civil War (1861–65), or the Great Depression of the 1930s.[101]

What, now, were the possible *reasons* that led people to bury money in the first place? These could include precautionary measures; especially important during times of political and social instability (war, conflict or revolt). Hoards could also be a means of storing or saving money in more normal times, especially for the common folk.[102] People may want to conceal money from someone else to protect it against theft. Since hoards are most likely generated where there is some base-level circulation in the first place and thus some sort of functional division of labour, perhaps even 'deep monetization',[103] we can expect coins from all monetary denominations to have made it, at one stage or another, in some place or another, into a coin hoard. This means, in turn, that we can derive from the number of coin hoards and their composition some tentative conclusions as to the state, nature and trends of monetary circulation for the market economies we are concerned with.

Yet numismatists are in notorious disagreement about all of this, as the debate within the Numismatische Kommission – the association of West German numismatists from 1954 – shows, which resulted in an unpublished yet immensely stimulating memo systematizing rationales for hoarding.[104] The coin hoard database then available to the Numismatic Commission showed no significant correlation for coin findings for the AD 200–1500 period with war-related campaigns and other elements of the 'political process' that we would expect to have influenced the level of hoarding over time.[105] But other interesting patterns surface. Spatially for instance, coin hoards clustered in areas with higher levels of commercialization (and possibly per capita income). Stray findings of single or a handful of coins are usually found along the main trading routes.[106] And where we find them within a built settlement – towns or cities – they often reflect 'piggy bank' patterns of hoarding, that is, the small (wo)man's savings. Merchants and capitalists would have other means of saving; they can be expected to have contributed to this pattern of hoarding money in a much lesser way, albeit findings from this social stratum are not unknown. When Martin Luther's house in Eisleben was excavated in 2003, items found included a wide range of coins from all types and ages, notwithstanding – or underlining? – the fact that Luther often joked how little money he had, and how bad he was on oeconomizing on cash.[107] Indeed, when unearthed within the urban environment, German coin hoards from the 12th to 19th centuries usually contain more higher-denomination coins than hoards from the countryside. Pennies dominated in rural finds, and by far the largest groups of hoards from the 1500–1800 period belong to the class of hoards containing less than a hundred pennies and other small-change coins.[108] Within a rural environment numismatists often associate such coin finds with economic occupations such as colliers, miners, hauliers and other transport workers, to a lesser extent with village tradesmen such as shoemakers, smiths, tailors and carpenters who may have kept more high-value coins in their hoards, pockets and piggy banks.[109]

Of course, the numismatic record is by its very nature dynamic. Databases on coin finds get constantly updated. Many unknowns are thus in the equation.[110] Given all caveats there still appear remarkable patterns and rhythms in hoarding, chiming with other empirical economic data, including political economy, which suggest that the available data – notwithstanding agnostics such as Holt[111] – may actually tell us something important. In the rural areas of the German-speaking lands for instance there seems to have been an increase in hoarding on the countryside from the 12th to the15th centuries, followed by a contraction (dis-hoarding) 1400–1600. In the 1950s the Numismatische Kommission explained this by referring to urbanization and the rise of the city economy. New evidence from Dutch archaeology suggests that the secular expansion of population and economy during the 16th century coincided with processes of dis-saving, when more money was released back into circulation and people literally smashed open their piggy banks in times of secular 'price revolution' that accompanied a general quickening of economic life. There is also ample evidence not only of population growth but also some urban recovery after the Black Death and into the 1490s, especially in the big trading cities and those adjacent to the silver mines in the Harz and Erz Mountains matching the known rhythms of coin finds as established by the numismatic evidence.[112] Potentially this gives us occasion to rethink Max Weber's influential hypothesis about Calvinism, the rise of Protestantism and economic thrift.[113]

For the German lands then, the quantitative record on coin hoards produced by the Numismatische Kommission can be captured as seen in Figure 6.1.[114]

As I have suggested elsewhere[115] the data in Figure 6.1 are consistent with the general pattern and recurrent cycles of monetary contraction during Europe's depression of the Renaissance (c.1350–1520), followed by the secular expansion of the 16th century ('Price Revolution').[116] The long-term linear trend in Figure 6.1 is negative, in line with common models explaining historical inflation.[117] In the long run an increasing amount of coined money was dis-hoarded and put back into circulation. Expanding mining and growing silver imports from South-Central America after c.1550 fuelled and supported this inflationary process.[118] Looking at the data in shorter intervals also suggest that they chime rather well with the known rhythms of European mint output and monetary circulation.[119] The upswings in hoarding around 1400–09 and 1440–59 coincide almost precisely with the respective periods of monetary contractions or 'bullion famines' identified by Day.[120] Similar monetary contractions and declining mint output have been documented for contemporaneous Saxony and most other regions in the Holy Roman Empire, so the numismatic evidence is again in tune with the monetary evidence from the archival record.[121] At these times more money than usual was held back from the market. This would have reinforced the contractive effect caused by declines in mint output. Moreover, stagnant or declining level of money's velocity – captured by the pattern of hoarding around 1500 – mirrored stagnations in urban growth across the Germanies on the eve of Reformation.[122]

Figure 6.1: Number of coin hoards buried per decade in the area of today's Federal Republic of Germany (1400–1600)

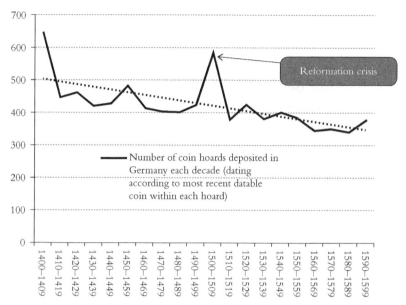

Source: *Datenbank der Numismatischen Kommission der Länder in der Bundesrepublik Deutschland e. V.*, accessed 23 December 2010

Last but not least, the data also fit the religious-economic discourses of the early 16th century that we have already encountered. These debates unfolded around problems of money either hoarded or buried, or spent on unproductive purposes such as indulgences – in the eyes of the reformers and humanists (discussed earlier), which amounted to the same effect: a decline in money's velocity. While the overall decrease in hoarding across the German lands (1400–1600) thus seems in line with a 'monetarist' explanation of the 16th-century inflation, there was one notable upswing in the series, representing a temporary trend reversal during the first decade of the 16th century, when hoarding levels returned to abnormally high levels, even allowing for statistical bias. The decade immediately preceding Martin Luther's 95 *Theses* (1517) thus appears to have been period of *increased hoarding*. This helps us put the evolution of Martin Luther's and the Reformers' economic thought in context; Luther's theology of indulgences and salvation, and the impact it had on politics and social lives in the 16th century, where the Reformer's monetary ideas would have met with open doors.[123] Would these discourses have unfolded the same rhetorical power and prowess if the monetary variables had moved in a different direction? Around 1517 people felt that things went pear-shaped, all of them connected to religious causes and circumstances: the climate was ripe for risings and revolts.[124] Economic debates often focused on money, the lack of it, and the habit of people using it the wrong way. In later times, those discourses came back, but in different context and use, as exemplified by the cameralists (who would have read their Luther) and their proverbial trope of the miserable *Kapitalist*.

Transforming oeconomy: velocity, urbanization and the manufacturing of capitalism

Reformation discourses on hoarding and spending had developed the idea that money was an economic resource. Money was more than its *amount*: *velocity* mattered, that is, the number of times a particular stock of money *circulated* within the economy. Later cameralists developed this idea further. Money must remain in circulation at all cost. It was a vital source that kept economic life going, and potentially conceived as a dynamic tool to generate economic dynamics.

Why does all of this matter?

Cameralists – especially those of the late Enlightenment – conceptualized economy and markets in ways that were increasingly transformative and dynamic. Living through the beginnings of the secular transformation that saw the surpassing of feudalism, the onset of industrialization and coming of factory capitalism,[125] cameralists like Sonnenfels and Justi felt the changing market dynamics of their day and age. This comes across in their writings on money and velocity. Capturing market behaviour through the means of exchange, specifically money and coins, cameralists addressed capitalist practices, capturing fraudulent manipulations such as forging money, currency speculation and arbitrage. In the cameralist vision these were crucial for the process of state formation and state consolidation, and the making of modern institutions supporting economic development. Cameralists built on contributions made by late medieval scholastic and Renaissance thinkers. Through deliberate ignorance of the cameralist heritage, Marx[126] and his followers thus missed a great chance when trying to reconstruct the intellectual genealogy of capitalism and the making of modern political economy.

These things matter in a more global context, as well. Goldstone has suggested that within early modern economies, velocity (that is, the frequency of payment) was functionally dependent upon the degree of urbanization.[127] In Goldstone's model, velocity varies overproportionately with changes in urbanization, that is, the share of people in society who live in cities.[128] This is apparently not so far off with some of the sentiments expressed by earlier authors in political economy. Georg Heinrich Zincke, in his 'Sketch of an Introduction to the Cameral Sciences' drew the analogy of cities as 'blood vessels' and 'nerves' (*Spann=Ader*) of state through which the products of the country were distributed, circulated, exported and 'transformed' (manufactured from raw materials).[129] Cameralists had a very clear notion of regional segmentation and economic geography: in the cameralist vision, town and countryside represented two fundamentally different yet entangled economic spheres with distinct modes of production.[130] An anonymous pamphlet *Bedencken von Manufacturen* (1683), ascribed to Johann Daniel Crafft or Krafft – a 17th-century Saxon 'project-maker' connected to Philipp Wilhelm von Hörnigk, possibly influencing the latter's magnum opus *Oesterreich über alles* (1684) – was clear-cut about it: 'Where cities decline and become desolate, the surrounding countryside will decline as well; but where cities are populous peasants will be rich'.[131] Rößig's *Treatise on Economic Policy* (1786) claimed that '*Industrie*' – at that time still referring to 'industrious, or value-adding economic activity' – was mainly to be found in manufacturing, an economic activity mainly located within cities ('*Gewerbsamkeit und den Kunstfleiß der Städte*').[132] Even though cities had higher wages and living costs (making them less attractive in terms of labour cost), the benefits of urban location – *Bequemlichkeit*, short communication, mutual synergies and dependencies promoting 'circulation' – outweighed these by the numerous stimuli they gave to occupations and professions that transformed and added value to products ('*Veredlung der rohen Producte*').[133] Competition and the confluence of economic actors, multitudes of buyers and sellers would thicken and deepen the market and thus further promoted the circulation of money and goods.[134]

Without doubt, rural manufacturing was important, too; it had stretched out widely into the European countryside since the late Middle Ages.[135] But dynamics of development were most likely to be found within cities. Cities were marked by functional specialization, mutual dependency ('*Je mehr sich die Mitglieder einander beschäftigen*') and division of labour that would greatly stimulate the 'vivacity of inner (meaning 'domestic') circulation' ('*Lebhaftigkeit der innern Circulation des Geldes*').[136] Justi had proposed that in 'civilized' societies ('*gesitteten und bevölkerten Ländern*') about half the population would engage in agriculture, the other half in 'transforming and manufacturing' non-essential goods. In other words, the presence – or lack – of manufacturing thus kept a natural ceiling upon nations' possibilities of economic growth.[137] The only way of escaping the trap of poverty, hunger and premature death was to promote urban development.

Not all cameralists agreed on cities being the linchpin of the making and breaking of the wealth of nations,[138] but broadly speaking the proposition represented the mainstream. 'City economy begins where nature ends', Darjes, another cameralist author pointedly had it.[139] We will look at this more closely now, in the next chapter on manufacturing.

7

Creating Wealth:
Homo Manufacturabilis and the
Wealth of Nations

Manufacturing capitalism: between concepts, policies and ideas

> Manufactures are of great use to the state. They create abundance, improve agrarian output, abolish poverty, purge the country of idlers and idleness, promote arts and sciences, bring comfort and ease to its inhabitants; fill the coffers of the fisc, and make us forget about the shortcomings and infertility of agriculture.
>
> Julius Bernhard von Rohr, *Einleitung*
> *zur Staats-Klugheit* (1716), p 1019

Our great origin myths often configure industry and the task of being industrious as part of a bigger Fall from Grace. Adam and Eve were expelled from Paradise because they had tasted the forbidden fruit. The consequence was an endless life of misery and toil (Genesis). When Cain, a farmer, slew his brother Abel − a herdsman (Genesis 4:1–18), you would hardly guess he'd come away so lightly.[1] Yes, human economy would in consequence be a life of endless toil: 'If you till the soil, it will no longer give you strength. A restless wanderer shall you be on the earth'. But Cain got rehabilitated, and even became forefather of industrial modernity. Cain's name in literal translation simply means 'metalsmith'. He founded a city and, by ways of his great-great-great-grandsons turns out to be the forefather of music, ironmaking and economic development:

> Then Cain went out from the presence of the Lord and dwelt in the land of Nod on the east of Eden. And Cain knew his wife, and she conceived and bore Enoch. And he built a city, and called the name

148

of the city after the name of his son – Enoch. To Enoch was born Irad; and Irad begot Mehujael, and Mehujael begot Methushael, and Methushael begot Lamech. Then Lamech took for himself two wives: the name of one *was* Adah, and the name of the second *was* Zillah. And Adah bore Jabal. He was the father of those who dwell in tents and have livestock. His brother's name was Jubal. He was the father of all those who play the harp and flute. And as for Zillah, she also bore Tubal-Cain, an instructor of every craftsman in bronze and iron. (Genesis 4:16–22)[2]

The first blacksmith, Tubal-Cain, allegedly gave his name to Vulcanus (Greek *Hephaistos*), the Roman god of fire and metalworking, as noted by Paul Jacob Marperger, German *oeconomic* writer and author of numerous manuals for merchants and political economy. These were the origins of industry and cities (where most industry was commonly located), which had provided humans with the tools necessary to work the land: iron spades, ploughs and scythes and, in the end, weapons, tools of war: tools to kill.[3] While according to the Book of Genesis economic modernity thus came at terrible cost, some later traditions were more amenable towards industry and development. Craftsmen were valued in classical antiquity, and Greek myths and epics abound with canny gods inventing automatic machines – the very same god of economic development, Hephaistos or Vulcanus, that Marperger linked to the descendants of Cain; or heroes like Odysseus who, when not engaged in fights or flights, would design, build and repair their palaces using their own hands, quite like the proverbial contemporaneous German *Häuslebauer*, who spends their free weekend in the hardware store always on set for the next home improvement project.[4]

Contrast this with the later Enlightenment. 'In their natural state', claimed Enlightenment Germany's star political economist Johann Justi in 1758, 'Humankind only tends to sloth. The Ancient Germans considered work dishonourable; like Baron Hollberg has shown in his History of the Danish and Norwegian people, Nordic people in ancient times conceived binge drinking, eating and idleness as the perfect state of bliss (*Glückseligkeit*)'.[5] At the time another and perhaps slightly more profane myth gradually gained ground. 'Agriculture is of all other arts the most beneficent to society, and whatever tends to retard its improvement is extremely prejudicial to the public interest. The produce of agriculture is much greater than that of any other manufacture',[6] wrote Adam Smith, in his *Lectures*, introducing two common yet dangerous confusions into the modern economic mind. It was one thing to throw agriculture into the same pot as an *art* – as manufacturing and crafts were labelled in 18th century French and German economic discourse.[7] This gave rise to a number of modern conceptual confusions, for instance the stubborn insistence of Anglophone financial linguistics which insists on calling the financial market sector an 'industry', as though it were a branch of economic activity that generated real or tangible added value. Another was the somewhat counterintuitive assumption of agriculture being equally productive as industry in terms of adding to the wealth of nations. Manufacturing and industry lend themselves to economies of scale, especially when employing technology, innovation and division of labour (average costs progressively decline when the scale of business and operations are extended), which is not the case with agriculture and most primary (and service sector) production processes.[8] There was considerable enthusiasm sported by economic writers during the 1770s about agriculture as the true basis for the wealth of nations, in an era that saw one of the last grave hunger crises of the old type sweep across Europe.[9] Historically, though, the origins of wealth had lain in manufacturing and manufactories as engines of capitalism; crucial to making the European industrial miracle and contributing to a Schumpeterian culture of growth.[10] As Thomas Mun, one of the early so-called 'mercantilists' had argued around 1620 (his book would not be published before the 1660s) that: 'The revenue or stock of a Kingdom ... is either Natural or Artificial. The Natural wealth is so much only as can be spared from our own use and necessities to be exported unto strangers. The Artificial consists in our manufactures and industrious trading with forraign commodities'.

Smith's *Wealth of Nations* (1776) opened with the example of a pin manufactory and how the wealth of nations could be raised using the principle of division of labour. Johann Heinrich von Justi (1717–71) had discussed the Smithian division of labour principle during the 1750s using a mint – where money was made – as a template; since the 1680s similar reference templates had been used for illustration in European political economy.[11] The 1750s French *Encyclopédie* project led by Denis Diderot featured many engravings of how the principle worked in practice, combining Smithian elements with a more Schumpeterian view of techno-economic development. Other continental projects included a German translation of the French Academy's *Descriptions des Arts et Métiers, faites ou approuvées par Messieurs de l'Académie Royale des Sciences* (*Schauplatz der Künste und Handwerke*, 15 vols, 1762–1805), or standalone oeconomic encyclopaedias by Zedler (*Grosses vollständiges Universal-Lexicon*, 68 vols, 1731–54) and Krünitz (242 vols, 1773–1858), collaborative exercises of the German Enlightenment that ran over hundreds of volumes (and several decades) and many thousands of pages, sketching a cornucopian world of infinite expansion based on useful knowledge and the idea of engineering economic growth.[12] As yet, the economic terminology of the day had not quite caught up with modern uses. In the economic vocabulary of the early Enlightenment 'factory' for instance could mean many things. One translation possibility referred to trading posts located within foreign territories, as in the case of the Portuguese chain of trading emporia across Western and Eastern African coasts and the Indian Ocean basin running into the South China Sea. Known from medieval trade (in Venice for instance foreign merchants had usually been hosted within specifically denoted quarters or buildings within the city known as *fondaco*, from the Arabian word *Funduk*), these emporia were in early modern use called 'factory' (*Faktorei* in German).[13] A similar case was with 'industry': a term used in English, German and French but still undecidedly moving between 'industriousness' and 'manufacturing' during the 1750s. At that time the German terms *Manufakturen* and *Fabriquen* began to denote different types of enterprise approaching the modern distinction between workshop or manufactory (*Manufaktur*) and *Fabriquen* or *Fabrik*, that is, factory proper, in the sense of an industrial production site using large-scale technologies, assembly lines and steam engines (and later on oil burners) for mechanical energy. Still the emerging industrial semantics remained contested. Künsberg's *Grundsätze der Fabrikpolizei* (1792) or Justi's *Abhandlung von den Manufacturen* (vol 1, first edn, Copenhagen, 1758) for instance defined 'manufactories' (*Manufakturen*) as places where people worked more with their hands (*mehr mit der Hand*); and *Fabriquen* ('factories') as places where 'hammer and fire' were used instead, that is, iron works and heavy plants using traditional forms of energy and technology that had been known for millennia (such as charcoal or coal, smelting ovens).[14] On the other hand Künsberg subsumed porcelain pottery manufactories (*Porcellan-Fabrik*) under *Fabriquen*. During the 1770s and 1780s, Künsberg's and Justi's age witnessed the early beginnings of the steam engine and the Industrial Revolution. Contemporaries wrestled with the conceptual challenges of integrating the new production regimes into an economic lexicon still fundamentally rooted in *ancien régime* modes of production.[15] These conceptual switches would deserve closer attention in future research; but we can draw on tentative interpretations in Conze, Brunner and Koselleck's eight-volume milestone on *Geschichtliche Grundbegriffe*.[16]

Manufactories and large workshops represented means of organizing production known since the commercial revolutions of the Renaissance and from medieval Italian trading cities such as Venice and Florence. Often called 'arsenal' they frequently had a military background in uniform and weaponry production. Well into the 19th century people used 'factory' (*Fabrik*) and 'manufactory' (*Manufaktur*) freely and interchangeably. Andrew Ure, a 19th-century chemist and economist, contended that

MANUFACTURE is a word, which, in the vicissitude of language, has come to signify the reverse of its intrinsic meaning, for it now denotes every extensive product of art, which is made by machinery, with little or no aid of the human hand; so that the most perfect manufacture is that which dispenses entirely with manual labour. The philosophy of manufactures is therefore an exposition of the general principles, on which productive industry should be conducted by self-acting machines.[17]

Marx used Ure's work as inspiration for his sketch of industrial factory capitalism. In Chapter 12 of *Capital* (Vol I) he discussed manufactories, the large workhouses deployed by Justi and Smith to illustrate 18th-century industrial modernity through the concept of 'relative surplus value' generated by capitalist-driven division of labour, as a crucial intermediary between preindustrial capitalism (primitive or original accumulation) and proper factory capitalism, where organic energy replaced wind, water, animals and humans. In the Marxist model the early modern period had seen an age of 'primitive' (better: 'original') accumulation, in which mercantilist or fiscal-military states actively supported the accumulation of profit in the hands of capitalist manufacturers, by policies supporting domestic industry, protectionism and the building-up of colonial webs of exploitation, slavery and unfair trade. Within this logic (original accumulation according to Marx's model also occurred in the agrarian sector) manufactories were usually run and financed by merchant-capitalists using privileges, monopoly and protectionism to vend their goods on world markets. This form of crony capitalism helped them accumulate the capital necessary for later industrial expansion.[18] To the present day Marxist historians interpret the age of manufactories as an advanced form of merchant or preindustrial capitalism but not industrial capitalism per se. Historians of early modern Europe have endorsed this interpretation unwittingly, often dismissing manufactories as unprofitable and misguided ventures of early modern absolutist rulers; enterprises whose contribution to employment, output and productivity would have been far too low to generate sustained effects on economic development. Manufactories are thus commonly written off as dead ends in histories interpreting modern development teleologically, through the lens of the already known end point.[19]

In the following I want to add something from a 'German' viewpoint, a perspective that has not featured that prominently in global histories of capitalism, divergence and economic modernity; by providing a sense of the main concepts and ideas that underpinned manufacturing since the Renaissance. This will lay the conceptual groundwork for the concluding Chapter 8. The conceptual framings and linguistic histories are important here. Why was manufacturing so important? It was the *Fabrikant* who 'trades in copious amounts of raw material from the agricultural producer (*Landwirth*), deploying thousands of human hands, giving a surprising number of people employment, by transforming and adding value to the products he received, creating trade, increasing monetary circulation and attracting foreigners into the country', as a late 18th-century voice argued.[20]

Cameralist Justi had produced an entire book on manufacturing. Karl Marx, in *Capital*, Vol I, Ch 22, linked the age of manufactory to the emergence of full-blown industrial capitalism. To Sombart (*Der moderne Kapitalismus*) manufactories likewise represented the epitome of early modern economic governmentality and the crafting of the wealth of nations.

Friedrich List, in *Das Nationale System der politischen Ökonomie* (1841),[21] and *Das Wesen und der Werth einer nationalen Produktivkraft* (1839)[22] defined the modern nation state as a manufacturing state. Manufacturing and industry were *conditiones sine qua non* which every country or national economy needed in order to grow rich. Smith (*Wealth of Nations*) had not developed this in similar clarity, implicitly suggesting that *all* economic activities were alike (implicit in his 'labour theory of value'). For List the wealth of a nation was not primarily dependent upon accumulated riches and treasure, but founded on the dynamic development of its productive powers. This was based on institutions, law and good governance, but especially *cultural* factors such as training and education.[23] Whereas List called agriculture 'lifeless' or sterile (in stark contrast to Smith or the physiocrats), it was manufacturing, with its higher capacities of market integration, utilizing human skill, knowledge and creativity; division of labour and potential capacity for productivity-enhancing innovation strategies that was best placed to generate economic growth. 'Manufactures', List argued in *Outlines of American Political Economy* (1827), 'moreover, are the nurses of arts, sciences and skill, the sources of power and wealth'.[24] Such phrasing – especially 'nurses of arts, sciences and skills' – would sound familiar to readers of Bernard de Mandeville's poem on the 'grumbling hive' which provided the groundwork for the later *Fable of the Bees* (1714). According to List, economic development required creating an integrated national market (*Volkswirtschaft*) as well as protecting key industries with 'educational' tariffs for as long as it took them to reach internationally competitive productivity levels (once again the Mandevillian 'nursing' metaphor). List was a free trader by heart. But the *timing* of free trade mattered for economic development.[25]

Such lines of reasoning became important later on, especially for transformative processes known as 'Schumpeterian growth' based on creative destruction and technology-intensive modes of production.[26] As Mokyr has shown, useful knowledge and Schumpeterian lines of thought mattered fundamentally in shaping economic development in early modern Europe.[27] The British community of Enlightenment philosophers were not isolated but part of a larger network of savants and discourses across early modern Europe.[28] Societies such as the Royal Society, founded in 1660 were strewn across the continent, and the first such national academy was founded in 1652 with the Leopoldina Academy of Natural Sciences in Halle/Saale in Prussia, which in 1687 became certified by imperial privilege as the 'national' or imperial academy for the entire Holy Roman

Empire. The German-speaking lands had their 'popular enlightenment' (*Volksaufklärung*), a more grassroots improvement movement from below, outside the academy, based on useful, not propositional, knowledge, to use Mokyr's classification of different types of knowledge and their contribution to modern economic growth.[29] The sheer explosion of a literary genre known as *Intelligenzblätter* since the 1730s – as the periodicals on practical day-to-day matters of *oeconomy* were called in the German-language context – which appeared in almost every medium-rank country town, covering an occasionally absurdly wide-ranging panoptic of tips and tricks, from animal husbandry to advertising small auctions, second-hand sales of household goods and other stuff suggests that what happened in Britain was not so far off the mark. This type of newspaper had started its career in France, and it was not unknown in England, either, as the *Public Advertiser*, founded in 1637, shows.[30] However, in the German-speaking lands, these 'Advertisers' – there may have been up to 200 towards the end of the 18th century – developed a life of their own, making their very own contribution to the German economic enlightenment.[31] As List himself admitted, his theory was not particularly original, but distilled centuries' worth of different voices, strands and streams in political economy into a manual fit for 19th-century industrial catch-up processes under conditions of globalization and economic imperialism – or the 19th-century 'European standard model', to use economic historian Robert Allen's phrase.

In the next section I would like to briefly sketch the broad outlines of this age-old discourse and explore the common ground List shared with his ancestors, before Chapter 8 looks at aspects of practical policy in more detail.

Mercantilism, manufacturing and the history of an old idea, 1500s–2000s

Two basic ideas were once held important in Europe's transition to capitalism, but got forgotten over time. These were, first, that manufacturing mattered and, second, that a proactive state was important to safeguard and nurture the precarious plant later known as *economic growth and development*. Names have been given to these ideas, as well as the theories embodying them, such as 'mercantilism', 'Colbertism'[32] (in France) or 'cameralism', denoting differences more of nuance and context-specific economic practice rather than principal content. Perhaps a more neutral term 'Economic Reason of State'[33] would be in order – with all '-isms' being inherently problematic, reflecting mutual interest and feedback processes between state and economy that influenced political economies of modern capitalism.

Such ideas were widely shared across Europe. Their pedigree was quite ancient. Looking at preindustrial Europe, we see many of the key practices and ideas identified as crucial to modern economic growth were already in it.[34] A strong manufacturing base? Known to 16th-century Italian economic writers. 'Schumpeterian' approaches to knowledge management, technology and science? Known to early 17th-century Swedish thinkers. The notion that infinite growth is possible in principle? Again, Sweden, around 1600. A strong state supporting private property and promoting growth and development?[35] This was the core feature of cameralist political economy. In a common set-up as a series of dialogues between a 'doctor' and a 'knight' accompanied by three lesser figures known as farmer, capper and merchant, the *Discourse on the Common Weal* – a manuscript work dated to 1549, first printed in 1581 and commonly ascribed to someone named either Thomas Smith or John Hales – described how Germany at that time was blessed with so many cities, and blossoming manufacturing exports. Curiously German economic discourse in the 1520s and 1530 had claimed exactly the opposite, enviously looking to England for their superior manufacturing.[36] The text identified three types of industry, only one of which was apt to dynamically increase the nation's wealth; others were luxury importers, and base-level occupations such as shoemakers, carpenters, masons and builders catering for the daily necessities and the country's physical infrastructure. Those occupations adding to the real or productive wealth of nations were the

> clothiars, tannars, cappers, and worsted makers. ... As for oure woll, felles, tinne, lead, butter and chese, these be the commodities that the ground beares, requiringe the Industrie of a few persons; and yf we should only trust to such, and devise nothinge ells to occupie oure selves, a few persons wold serve vs for the reringe of such things.

But if

> townes and Cities ... be replenished with all kind of *artificers* [my emphasis]; not only clothiars, which as yet weare oure naturall occupation, but with cappers, glovers, paper makers, glasiers, pointers, gold smithes, blacke smithes of all sortes, coverlet makers, nedle makers, pinners and such other; so as we should not only haue enowghe of such thinges to serve oure realme, and saue an infinite treasour that goeth now over for so manie of the same, but also might spare of such thinges redie wrought to be sold over, whearby we should fetch againe other necessarie commodities and tresours. ... Such occupations alone doe enrich enriche divers countries, that be els barren of theim selves; and what riches they bringe to the countrie wheare they be well vsed, the countrie of flaunders and Germany doe well declare; wheare, throughe such occupations, it hath so manie and wealthie Cities, that it weare vncredible in so litle grounde to be.[37]

Note the use of terms such as *barren* when referring to infertile lands focusing on marginal agriculture and low-level manufacturing, the introduction of pin-making as an exemplification of high-powered economic activity (compare Smith, *Wealth of Nations*), but especially the term *artificers* denoting precisely those higher-order manufacturers that added real value to the wealth of the nation, by making development a possibility. Such 'cameralist' visions of economy can further be traced in Giovanni Botero, Jesuit, ethnographer, geographer and author of key works on reason of state theory occasionally labelled as a 'common origin' figure for mercantilism and cameralist political economy. In Book 8 of his *Ragione di Stato*, originally part of his other opus magnum *Delle cause della grandezza delle città* (1588), but since 1589 included in the *Reason of State*, Botero concluded that:

> Nothing is of greater importance for increasing the power of a state and gaining for it more inhabitants and wealth of every kind than the industry of its people and the number of crafts they exercise. ... These crafts cause a conflux of money and of people, some of whom work, some trade in the finished products, some provide raw materials and others buy, sell and transport from one place to another the fruits of man's ingenuity and skill.

The virtues of industry lay in the art of transforming nature (raw materials) using labour, skill and capital (machines, technology). This would dynamically raise the wealth of nations through an increase in incomes, employment, value-added, technological improvement. Again Botero: 'Such is the power of industry that no mine of silver or gold in New Spain or in Peru can compare with it, and the duties from the merchandise of Milan are worth more to the Catholic King than the mines of Zacatecas or Jalisco'.[38]

As we saw in Chapter 5, in the German context Georg Agricola (*De re metallica*, 1556) had invoked a similar causal link with regard to the technical processes employed in large-scale mining. Mid-16th century German mining was widely considered to be at the top of its league, and German miners were brought in during the early 1560s to kickstart northern English ventures.[39] Botero's 'Peruvian goldmine' metaphor, describing the virtues of manufacturing and industry, remained popular in early modern economic discourse, cropping up widely in oeconomic writings of the German, Swedish and English tongues.

In Philipp Wilhelm von Hörnigk's *Oesterreich über alles wann es nur will* (*Austria Supreme if Only It So Wills*, 1684), it only took pen, paper and human reason to substitute economic development for silver and gold:

> How much easier it should be for us, given our present travails [...], to atone for our pride awhile by using our good Silesian, Moravian

and Bohemian cloth, and our Silesian, Upper Austrian and other domestically produced canvas; hence leaving in their own country the silken and woven goods, Dutch lacquers, Indian bombazine, the pestilential French fashions, sparing us them, if they are really so important, for just as long as it takes until we have learned how to imitate them in sufficient quantities? To bring this about we need neither armies, nor deep and far-ranging counsel and advice, nor unaffordable capitals. It can be done with paper, pen and ink without any expense, so long as the plan is stuck to. And then the Emperor would, in a few years, have gained a powerful kingdom within his lands without injustice, blood, flight and bad conscience, the land giving as much as a Peruvian mine now does to the Spanish monarchy.[40]

Hörnigk – like most other writers using the analogy of silver mines and manufacturing – referred to the mines of Potosí, now in Bolivia, once the world's largest producer and heart and engine of global capitalism.[41] In mid-18th century Spain it was thought so banal a truth that it hardly warranted any discussion: 'leaving to avoid verbosity, to the learned comprehension of your Excellency the utility which comes to royal interests and public utility from the establishment of manufactures in these kingdoms'.[42] In Portugal during the 1740s and 1750s contemporaries lamented the Anglo-French commercial treaty of Methuen in 1703. This treaty made it into later textbooks as the prime example of specialization through comparative advantage and why liberalized trade is good for everyone – in that case of English cloth in return for Portuguese wine. The Marquis de Pombal in the 1730s and 1740s, however, would have none of that. He argued that the export of a raw material such as wine (unfinished; no value-added, decreasing returns to scale) in return for manufactured imports of cloth (finished, value-added, and subject to increasing returns) would over time progressively enrich England at Portugal's expense. Economic development required manufacturing. In Germany, Justi wrote book after book after book, including *Staatswirthschaft* (first edn Leipzig: Breitkopf, 1755) and *Policeywissenschaft* (1756), that worked a very similar logic. In Scotland it was through pamphlets written in the 1720s and 1730s by people like James Lindsay and many other anonymous writers, but most clearly exposed in James Steuart's *Principles* (1767).[43]

The importance of adding value and creating employment had been noted by Veit Ludwig von Seckendorff (1626–92). Occasionally hailed the 'Adam Smith of Cameralism',[44] Seckendorff was a jurist and state official in the services of Ernest I 'the Pious' of Saxony-Gotha since 1645, one of the mini-states of the Holy Roman Empire, badly hit by the disastrous consequences of the Thirty Years War. In the *Additiones* to his magnum opus on the *Teutsche Fürsten-Stat* (*The German Princely State*) published in 1665 after a visit to the Netherlands, the 'first modern economy'[45] Seckendorff argued that employment and incomes were only likely to rise where wages were high. These were the foundation of the wealth of nations, and the art of development was to find activities that would put people in the position of attaining high standards of living.[46] This somewhat runs contrary to Marx (*Capital*, Vol I) who, dismissing cameralism (as we saw in the introduction) reckoned mercantilism to be a handmaiden of bourgeois capitalism, supporting capitalists' conspiration to keep labour's wages down. But more importantly, Seckendorff stressed the importance of industry and *adding value*[47] using the negative example of pastoral farming. Where the focus was on the production and export of raw wool, only the sheep owners, carriers, haulers and merchants trading the raw wool earned something on top of the value generated in pastoral agriculture. The general income multiplier effects, so to speak, of this activity were low. But where the wool was processed *within* the country using domestic manufactures and factor employment, 'ten or twelve men might be nourished for one year', Seckendorff maintained.[48] One sector where this virtuous cycle was most likely to be achieved was woollen manufactures,[49] an activity also particularly highlighted in Philip Wilhelm von Hörnigk's *Oesterreich über alles wann es nur will* (1684). Economic activity (*Nahrung*) should be 'free' (*frey*), Seckendorff went on, meaning free from guild incorporation and other restrictive regulations characteristic of *ancien régime* Europe restrictions on output and business competition.[50] The beneficial aspects of guild incorporation – caring for the poor and widows; keeping up good order in the respective trade and trader's communities, ceremonial and burial arrangements – were far outweighed by the negative effects, especially the tendency to create monopoly.[51] These harmed the common good. The editor of the 1720 edition of Seckendorff's *Fürsten-Stat*, Andreas Simson Biechling, reminded readers that 'to concede a permanent monopoly would be as wrong as, even worse than, the artisans' and craft guilds' themselves;[52] endorsing a cameralist pledge for a competitive market. Valuable raw material imports should be taxed lightly (if at all); and no commodity that could be produced at comparable quality at home should be imported from foreigners.[53] Manufacturing should be located in cities. Where cities were populous and flourished, manufacturing would flourish, and industrial by-employment on the countryside (proto-industrialization) would wither away.[54]

An anonymous report *Bedencken von Manufacturen* (1683), commonly ascribed to 17th-century Saxon entrepreneur and *Projektemacher* Johann Daniel Crafft or Krafft[55] emphasized the multiple linkages and multiplier effects generated by a well-managed urban industrial landscape ('where cities decline and become desolate, the surrounding countryside will decline as well; but where cities are populous peasants will be rich') (see Chapter 5).[56]

This became a recurring figuration in contemporary economic discourse. Philip Wilhelm von Hörnigk summarized this in his famous 'Nine Rules of Economics' (*Austria Supreme*, 1684). All corners of the land, both above the earth, as well as subterranean, should be surveyed carefully and put to productive use. All raw materials that could not be used or consumed domestically should be processed into manufactures domestically because their value-added surpassed their initial value by 'two, three, ten, twenty, in fact a hundred times' (*zwey / drey / zehen / zwantzig / auch wol hundertfach*). Hörnigk speaks of 'transformation' or 'transmutation' (*Inländischer rohen Güter oder deren Verwandelung in Manufacturen*) when relating the qualities of industry; practical examples included the process of turning quicksilver into *sublimat, praecipitat und Zinober,* using other chemicals (industries on which Venice and Amsterdam flourished); or wool from Pilsen (nowadays in Czechia) that was processed in Saxony (Vogtland) into proper woollen stuffs; or Annaberg and Dutch *Spitzen,* a high-grade fine linen garment made from Silesian yarn whose final value increased by more than a hundred times in turn. Population growth was to be encouraged; idleness not. Technology transfer should be promoted by hiring foreign experts. All native precious metal reserves should be mined, dug up and brought into circulation. No money was to be spent on unnecessary imports. Foreign imports should be minimized and limited to the absolute minimum necessary. Imports from abroad should be limited to raw materials. Exporting specie in payment for imports should be avoided at all cost. No goods must be imported that could be produced domestically. It would be better to spend two thalers on a domestically made good, even if lower in quality, than spending one thaler for importing a better substitute.

The Hörnigk strategy represented mercantilism at its crudest and most brutal stage; Hörnigk was fully aware of this, but called for 'rough measures as times were rough'.[57] During the 1660s to 1680s the Austrian lands had been badly hit by the military campaigns of the Ottoman Wars, and French industrial production had been ramped-up under Colbert (Chapter 8), creating high barriers to market entry for other competitors engaging in high-end manufacturing. Once Austria's manufactures had become competitive enough, Hörnigk argued, less restrictive trade policies and more laissez-faire could be adopted.

Wilhelm von Schröder, another widely read Austro-German cameralist who had travelled England and Scotland extensively and become associated with the Royal Society,[58] based his magnum opus on the 'Princely Treasure Chest'[59] on the proposition that countries lacking much productive land but sporting flourishing commerce and manufacturing were better placed than countries with good natural endowment and flourishing agriculture but lacking industry. A pound of unprocessed bar iron fetched very little value on the market; but when turned into a clock or any other mechanical gadget, its value increased by a hundred times if not more.[60] ('A hundred times' seems to have been a common multiplier employed in cameralist visionaries of economic growth.) In his *Staatswirthschaft* or 'Principles of economics',[61] Johann Justi adopted a shotgun or sprinkler approach (to formulate it more lightly) to economic development: a flourishing common weal required *all* types of manufacturing at the same time, that is, as broad an industrial portfolio as possible.[62] Similarly to List later on (*National System*, 1841), Justi claimed that the state should support manufacturing enterprises for as long as it took them to offer their products to the domestic consumer at the same prices as foreigners.[63] Here 'useful knowledge' comes into play again, that is, the generation of innovation *within* the system (as already discussed). Introducing new industry meant increasing economic vivacity and monetary circulation, as we saw in Chapter 6. But in order for these processes to work, all areas of economic activity should be empowered. State regulation should be as light as possible. Justi called for an abolition of guild privileges (he preferred to have guilds altogether abolished). The state should also establish statistical offices monitoring industrial development keeping records of output and productivity for strategic or key industries (so-called *Manufactur-Collegia*). It was the state's role to enforce baseline standards of quality.[64] Export commodities should be inspected by government officials (*Auffseher*) before sale; good-quality work fit for export would be marked or stamped accordingly.[65] Such practices were known in many German territories of the time, but also Scotland (and Ireland) after 1727.[66] More examples of such industrial policy will be given in Chapter 8.

Moving away from a focus on agriculture still inherent in the late bloom of the *Hausväterliteratur* around 1700 in the German-speaking lands and Sweden,[67] Justi and others thus developed cameralism into a full-blown theory of economic development within a framework of dynamic international competition. Justi acknowledged that difficulties were likely faced when trying to catch up with neighbouring countries such as the Netherlands, England, and France (the *Welschen*), and to substitute native commodities for imports. The key to creating a competitive domestic landscape was to create new worlds of goods, to stimulate new fashions; develop new techniques.[68] *Erfindungen* (inventions) should be turned into useful applications to get people into employment and mouths fed (*das, was sie täglich erfinden, zu nutzen, und ihnen Gelegenheit zu verschaffen, daß sie ihre gute Nahrung dadurch finden können*). Government should be risk-taking, accepting losses in certain cases to promote a general climate of invention, because 'who doesn't dare win's nothing' (*Wer gar nichts wagen will, der wird auch sein Vermögen niemals vergößern*).[69] Only the good-quality pieces should be exempted from excise and customs duties upon export. Premiums and bounties should be granted on well-made piecework. Foreign experts and expertise should be lured into the country; if need be by means of industrial espionage.[70] Justi specifically called for the state to take an active role in encouraging and promoting learned *conversations* between craftsmen and learned scholars (*Gelehrte*), to facilitate a general culture of emulation and improvement.[71]

To what extent was this a feasible proposition? The following section will offer some tentative answers before Chapter 8 turns to a concluding round-up on creativity and the manufacturing of the wealth of nations.

Lost in translation? Culture, popular enlightenment and the powers of space

Culture and geography thus mattered in shaping the evolution of capitalism. This comes across particularly clearly from the margins of economic development.[72] When Leipzig Professor of Cameralism Daniel Gottfried Schreber, a persona we encountered in Chapter 2, edited his translation of volumes 5–13 of the grand French oeconomic encyclopaedia *Descriptions des arts et métiers* – a monumental project by the Royal French Academy of Sciences commenced under the auspices of the great economic wizard Colbert – he was struck by the considerable number of metal trades then current in the German lands that the learned professors in the original French edition had quite simply ignored.[73] Inter alia these included a list amounting to 24 individual trades, including minting, the making of church clocks, turners (*Bratenwender*), scales, chirurgical instruments, coffee and pepper grinders, barrel hoops, and ... wait, marten traps (*Mardereisen*).[74] To proceed with the German edition, Schreber had consulted with a local Leipzig master locksmith ('der hiesige Schlossermeister, Hr. Johann Christian Schwarze der ältere') to check on some of the technical details of what turned out as quite idiosyncratic modes and processes of production that did not easily translate from French into German.[75] We may ask ourselves how many German locksmiths were expected to even want to (let alone could) read these translations, and what sort of audience Justi (who had edited the first four volumes) and subsequent editors would have in mind for the translated *Metiers*, which appeared in Germany as *Schauplatz der Künste und Handwerke* (*Theatre of Arts, Crafts and Trades*)? Members of the learned classes, including literati such as Schreber and contemporary cameralists would have been fluent in French anyway. But Justi, in his preface to the first volume in the project (1762) had called for this work to be read by the common workers.[76] Many 18th-century craftsmen were indeed literate.[77] The encyclopaedia would have been part and parcel of the 'popular enlightenment' project, with an increasing number of practically oriented publications ranging from animal husbandry to arts, crafts and trades, addressed at practical women and men. A 'culture of growth',[78] in which people had begun to taste the sweet scent of improvement bettering the human oeconomic condition had to come from below, not lofty philosophers such as Christian Wolff, David Hume and Adam Smith.

The *Metiers*, Schreber commented, included lengthy discussions of tools and professions that were either irrelevant for a German context, or had by now become obsolete ('außer dem Gebrauch gekommene Arbeiten sind im gegenwärtigen Werke einer umständlichen Beschreibung werth geachtet worden')[79], while on the other hand pitying the Paris professors for failing to note the ancient origins of some trades which Schreber retraced to Renaissance literati including Polydorius Vergilius and others. Some oeconomic propositions on certain trades and techniques may look sensible and irrefutable on paper. But when translated from French into Saxon oeconomic reality they would change shape, facing changed contexts and differing modes of production. In the French original for instance an entry on candle-making – in German translation *Lichtziehen* – featured a footnote reminding the reader that the Paris butchers were prohibited to smelt the raw tallow themselves. Justi translated the footnote, but added a lengthy explanation, to render this reference comprehensible to a German readership.[80] It was not so much of a strange thing discussing tallow-smelting within the section on candle-making rather than under 'butchery', Justi wrote, and immediately provided a rationale for this: the only sensible reason why butchers, in the German lands and everywhere else, should be permitted to sell their tallow to candle-makers in 'smelted' form (that is refined condition) the way the Paris butchers were required to was because unprocessed tallow went stale so quickly, rendering it useless to candle-making. The downside was that candle-makers receiving their tallow in refined form from the butchers had difficulties asserting its quality.[81]

Thus certain processes that looked straightforward on paper had hidden lives requiring further elaboration and modification lest objects and manufactures would be rendered useless by incomprehensible, careless or badly translated instructions of how to produce and transform them.[82] Chapter 8 will now look at representative aspects of premodern industrial policy in its wider contexts of culture and institutions. The origins of modern economic growth have often been (on top of other factors such as factor endowment, climate and geography, military politics) associated with, or attributed to the prevalence of a community of literati, a highly skilled work force, proactive states and institutions favouring a 'culture of growth'.[83] By all these measures the early modern Holy Roman Empire would have ticked most of these boxes. It was in the early modern Holy Roman Empire, where scientists like Otto von Guericke first experimented with the key gadgets (vacuum) that later on empowered the wider application of steam engines; skill levels and technical knowledge in the German urban craft industries belonged to the highest of their class. Since the Middle Ages a complex system of artisanal apprentice and craftsmanship culture had evolved, and manufactories and large workshops were spread out across German towns and countryside literally everywhere. 'Mercantilist' policies, named as crucial for engineering Britain's transformation into the first modern economy, had been conceptualized in the German-speaking lands, and much more systematically through a formal genre known as *Kameralwissenschaften* or 'cameralist' political economy sporting a transformative drive towards 'Schumpeterian' development, creativity and a 'culture of growth'. Artisanal and technological skill levels were particularly high in urban industry. There had been a long history of manufacturing matching the Smithian *manufactory* model since the Middle Ages.[84] Timber and coal abounded. Since the Thirty Years War German princes and rulers had become ever-more aware of the virtues of 'liberal' institutions facilitating market development and simultaneously strengthening capitalism and development through proactive policies of interventionism. But wages were low, and lacking was, above all, political integration, which also had a knock-on effect on market size, market integration and economies of scale. Here Britain had a decisive advantage over most of its competitors – and turned out to become the 'first industrial nation'.

8

Manufacturing Wealth:
Industrial Policy and the Rise of
the European Economy, 1350–1850s

The little manufactory, a baron and the white gold

The little factory continued for almost 100 years, from 1736 to 1834, albeit times were not always rosy.[1] From 1815 onwards it repeatedly approached bankruptcy. However, during what for an industrial venture of these days certainly was a rather biblical lifespan – many *ancien régime* manufactories were aborted after few years – the little *Manufaktur* produced some of the finest Faience pottery of its day and age, capturing markets across the Holy Roman Empire and beyond. Erected around 1745 in the common baroque style of its age the adjacent château or manor house of Wrisbergholzen (see Figure 8.1), residence of Baron Rudolph (Rudolf) Johann von Wrisberg (1677–1764), to the present day contains a *Fliesenzimmer* (faience tile room). Furnished around 1752, this room is covered top to bottom with almost 700 fine-lined tiles featuring popular motifs according to the Spanish and Dutch style, manufactured on the nearby industrial estate of Wrisbergholzen village, in what can only be called mass production.[2] Most of the emblematic patterns found on the tiles drew on motifs depicted in Diego de Saavedra Fajardo's mirror for princes, *Empresas Políticas: Idea de un príncipe político cristiano* (1640), probably from the 1668/70 French translation,[3] a work contained within Baron Rudolph's private library, which subsequently made it to Princeton University.[4] Saavedra Fajardo had travelled the German lands during the Thirty Years War (1618–48) as plenipotentiary to several Catholic princes.[5] A hundred years later his anti-Machiavellian *Fürstenspiegel* still provided a template book for manufacturers in the remoter German lands. We do not know *why* the faience room was furnished the way it was, and what its purpose would have been, other than showing off. With his day job as a judge, Baron Rudolph spent most of his time as president of the

Oberappellationsgericht, the Supreme Court of the Electorate of Hanover at Celle, or at Hanover and London, where he served as secret councillor to the Elector Georg of Brunswick-Lüneburg (who also happened to be king of Great Britain). He also acted as the Hanoverian representative at the imperial diet of Regensburg (Ratisbon) in 1719 where he accumulated a reputation for defending the Protestant interest.[6] Rudolph personally ordered at least two muster books (for tiles) for his library at Wrisberg, so at least he showed a personal interest and obviously some pride in his industrial venture.[7]

Why should we bother? Located off the major trade routes, deep down in the remote woods of Lower Saxony, neither the manufactory nor its founders ever made it into a history book. But Wrisberg was northern Germany's first and for a long time most successful faience manufactory; its products were sold widely across the Germanies and beyond, for nearly a century after its initial foundation. It embodied the key material and managerial principles of contemporary manufacturing capitalism. Other German regions, often likewise remote, were similarly industrialized or had known heavy industry and large-scale workshop enterprises since the later Middle Ages. Even hinterlands down in the woods such as the Weiltal – an idyllic river valley up in the Taunus mountains north of the free imperial city of Frankfurt-am-Main containing no more than a few handfuls of hamlets and villages but certainly no major cities or towns – sported many industrial ventures. Since the 15th century the valley had been strewn with fulling mills, cutting mills, paper mills, smithies, nail manufactories, and iron and smelting works, as well as lead mines.[8] Many businesses continued as proper factories into the 19th century; some, such as the Sorg iron works during the 17th century sold oven plates and other heavy goods as far south as Basle in Switzerland.

Now, this should make us pause and revisit some common historians' assumptions. One has it, for instance, that early modern European industry was commonly located in cities, because cities were fortified and easier to defend. Resulting in higher real wages, this peculiar military geography is said to have encouraged, among other things, early substitutions of capital for labour, facilitating industrialization, a 'great divergence' and Europe's world-historical leap ahead.[9] Another once-fashionable theory about industry before the Industrial Revolution would locate early modern manufacturing mainly in the countryside; as a dispersed, decentralized home or 'putting-out' industry financed and managed by 'capitalist' merchants or *Verleger* who usually operated internationally (and occasionally globally) when selling the products (remember David Hume's casual remarks on Germany that we encountered in Chapter 1, and the sales fetched by German linens in the British-American plantations).[10] Even though political economy since the days of Giovanni Botero (*c.*1544–1617) to agronomist and economic geographer Johann Heinrich von Thünen (1783–1850) had emphasized the role of cities in manufacturing and economic development, with cities engineering economic synergies, clustering regional industrial power and optimizing markets; in the German lands industry was everywhere and widely spread out across the countryside, including large-scale manufactories. It did not necessarily behave in the way suggested by historians' theories including the 'proto-industrialization' hypothesis, somewhat dismissing the role played by bigger workshops and enterprises described by Smith in the first chapter of the first book of the *Wealth of Nations*, illustrating the benefits of division of labour. In fact, as a business and enterprise type the manufactory has been notably absent from many recent accounts on the making and breaking of the wealth of nations.

Large-scale capitalist manufacturing also extended far beyond the usual suspects in modern modernization stories – linen, cotton, woollens, silk and iron. The Wrisberg enterprise comprised several production rooms, firing hearths and storage rooms for clay. Faience was a substitute for higher-grade porcelain, which at the time remained a luxury good, certainly for most Germans. Wrisberg stuff on the other hand was affordable to people of lower rank. Specializing in salt- and teapots, ink stands, vases and plates, often in the shape of lions and other animals, motifs were copied from Chinese blueprints.[11] Stamped WR (for Wrisberg) as a trademark sign they subsequently attained a proverbial reputation representing faience of the highest quality. This faience moment thus represents a brief, intermittent and, seemingly, transitory period in the history of manufacturing capitalism. But during this process, artisans and entrepreneurs frenetically raced to imitate the 'real stuff' and cameralist craving: porcelain, the 'white gold'. Ever since tea-drinking had spread out from China and Japan to Europe in the age of 'industrious revolution' (1650s onwards), new materialities of consumption had emerged, accompanied by a frenzy of publications, translations and manuals containing instructions on how to make porcelain and copy all sorts of other useful things.[12] As a lower-grade substitute, faience provided a nursery for capitalism and a training ground for German entrepreneurs imitating, emulating and adapting new products and technologies that had proven useful in other contexts, thus capturing a corner in the growing market for affordable 'daily' luxuries, including second-hand stuff.[13] Some examples of prime Wrisberg faience are given in Figures 8.2 to 8.8.

Literally all rulers in the German-speaking lands, from the Prussian King Frederick II 'the Great' or the Saxon Duke and Polish King Frederick Augustus 'the Strong' of Saxony (1670–1733), as well as lesser noblemen such as our Baron Rudolph von Wrisberg engaged in this manufacturing craze, and it far extended beyond pottery; the present example is just meant to prove a wider point. Wrisberg had founded the manufactory in 1736, after a planning phase and systematic examination of local conditions, especially of the adjacent clay pits. Initially the plan had been to produce clay pipes – *the throwaway mass-produced item par excellence* during the age

Figure 8.1: Wrisberg Castle, *c.*1850

Source: Image © Volker Gehring

Figure 8.2: Wrisberg faience: depiction of an odalisque, *c.*18th century

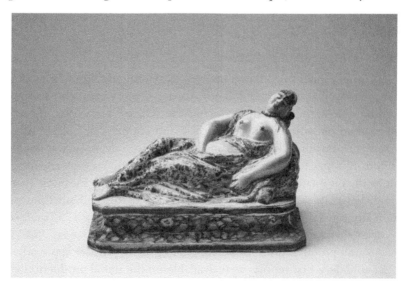

Source: Image © Volker Gehring

Figure 8.3: Wrisberg faience: roller jug, *c.*1740

Source: Image © Volker Gehring

of mercantile capitalism.[14] Based on ever-increasing supplies of Dutch and German, as well as imported Atlantic, tobacco, and a habit that had been spreading across the continent during the Thirty Years War, tobacco-smoking had become ubiquitous in city and countryside alike.[15] After a few test runs burning the clay from the local pits a decision was made to switch from pipes to faience instead. A master painter was recruited who went by the onomatopoetic last name of Vielstich (literally meaning 'many-an-engraver'). By September 1736 the firing hearths and smelting pans were ready for use. The first full production run in spring 1737 yielded a type of earthenware similar to glass in terms of quality. By May 1737 the adjacent mill producing the enamelling and glazing powder was ready for use. By mid-July first reports were available on the initial production run; the faience thus rendered wasn't perfect yet, but fetched some initial sales. In 1738 and 1739 some irregularities in the account books and ledgers were amended; by 1740 the supply of workers was large enough to allow

Figure 8.4: Wrisberg faience: vase with lid, unknown date of production

Source: Image © Volker Gehring

wage reductions, corresponding to the features of capitalist enterprise.[16] Thereafter production facilities were steadily extended and new firing ovens erected. New businesses moved into the adjacent village of Wrisbergholzen, including a paper manufactory. The steadily growing village population included a number of newly arrived Huguenot migrants.[17] Some craftsmen recruited to the factory attained European-wide fame and reputation. They included Louis Victor Gerverot, master painter at Wrisberg between 1815 and 1825, who had worked in England, France and Holland as well as many other German states. Some of the master painters acted as managing entrepreneurs, taking the factory out on lease; with cheap raw materials such as clay, timber (for construction) and firewood sourced from the baronial forests. Required to produce annual profit and loss statements, factors and

Figure 8.5: Wrisberg faience: heraldic lion presumably representing the Brunswick coat of arms

Source: Image © Volker Gehring

master smelters were entitled to an additional 4 per cent of any profits made on the venture per year.[18]

According to the classification used by Marxist historians the Wrisberg manufactory belonged to the type of private feudal-capitalist or 'noble manufactory' – an enterprise that has gained somewhat less attention from historians than state-run enterprises.[19] Rudolph, who served on the Secret Council for George II, may have seen some of the mainstream cameralist works of his age; established under George II in 1737, the University of Göttingen became a major Enlightenment university of his time sporting one of the leading faculties in *Kameralwissenschaften*.[20] Through his connections, Rudolph von Wrisberg may have learned about Walpole's industrial policy during the 1720s that had transformed British manufacturing through a series of customs reforms abolishing export duties on most manufactures, and the establishment of the Scottish Board of Trustees for the Fisheries and Manufactures in 1727 which actively contributed to a growing Scottish linen industry.[21] In 1748 we find him responsible for Hanoverian industrial policy, signing off a printed edict regarding the inspection and stamping of cloth manufactured for sale within and outside the electoral lands. This mirrored common practice in many countries of the time, not least Scotland; perhaps Rudolph even had the Scottish model in mind.[22] In any

Figure 8.6: Wrisberg faience: vase with chinoiserie motifs, *c.*1754

Source: Image © Volker Gehring

case the Wrisberg project thus represented the cameralist developmental state project writ small.

But Wrisberg was out in the woods, in the middle of nowhere: a manufactory like literally thousands of others in the late Holy Roman Empire.[23] Some manufactories did not last very long. Some of them only prospered because they were protected by licence, monopoly or other privileges. Some of them *did* write losses (many successful businesses do, sometimes for years and years). Usually their share in total employment was small. They all but vanished when factories took over. To many historians they appear like a dead end in the history of capitalism.[24] Historian Hans-Ulrich Wehler, however, cautioned his readers not to interpret business history following mechanical 'stage' assumptions: decentralized rural household handicraft (*Verlag*; 'proto-industry') coexisted and usually coincided with urban artisanal or small workshop production, manufactories and later

Figure 8.7: Wrisberg faience: roller jug, *c.*1750–60

Source: Image © Volker Gehring

factories; manufactories and workshop forms of production continued into the industrial age, as did decentralized handicraft production. It was the mix that changed over time, and certainly – when measured in its contribution to output, value-added and employment – the factory took centre stage in many parts of Europe, *c.*1830s–1970s. Thus dead ends in history are, if at all, only dead ends *ex posteriori*, and they often become so only by chance. Reading history backwards carries the risk of interpreting developments prior to the actual event as either leading *towards* that end, or *straying aside* from the chosen narratological end point about 'success', 'best practice', 'natural way of doing things' or telos. This is Hegel's *Weltgeist* on horseback, which occasionally still lurks behind modern narratives of historical economic growth and global economic change, but which is not particularly helpful when trying to understand historical economic change.[25]

The present chapter thus concludes the book with a round-up on the history of manufacturing capitalism from the Renaissance to the Industrial

Figure 8.8: Tile room (*Fliesenzimmer*) at Wrisberg Castle, Wrisbergholzen, Lower Saxony

Source: Taken on 11 September 2022 by © Karl Schünemann

Figure 8.9: Albrecht Dürer, wire manufactory (water colour, 1494)

Source: Wikimedia

Revolution, to elicit a rather basic point: *the force of the longue durée*. Industrialization was no sudden break away from a world that had previously been stuck in stagnation, hampered by cultural–economic inertia, until all of a sudden an industrial enlightenment created new cultures of growth. Nor did the industrial transformations and 'revolutions' of the 18th and 19th centuries represent first encounters with industrialization (see Figure 8.9 for a medieval example) – if we define 'industrialization' using its traditional meaning (what the German language has as *Vergewerblichung*), that is, intensification of industrial production both in terms of output growth and increasing weight in national income and occupation, often accompanied by improvements in technological efficiency and distribution. The 'industrial revolutions' of the 18th and 19th centuries represented specific variants of industrialization thus framed.[26] But the practices, cultures and political economies of industrialization had been laid in the seven or eight centuries before.

Oeconomies of failure and success: between Smithian and Schumpeterian growth

Perhaps one of the sharpest interpretations was offered by Marx (*Das Kapital*, Vol 1). For Marx the *manufactories* – the type of industrial enterprise used by Smith in the *Wealth of Nations* to illustrate the efficiency gains that accrued from the division of labour – did not represent an interim stage in the business history of capitalism (as claimed by later historians), but a *phenomenon sui generis*. Manufactories embodied modern capitalism's principles *in nuce*, including the division of labour, profit extraction and workers' alienation from the means of production.[27] Productive tasks were centralized under one roof, directed by managers and overseers, and work discipline rigidly enforced. Workers loathed them (a classical characteristic of capitalism).[28] True, neither pins (the example used by Smith) nor coaches (Marx) were pillars of later industrial capitalism.[29] But it is in niches and on the margins where innovation and economic dynamics often occur before branching out more broadly, turning into general economic development. 'Wherein consisted the *fundamental novelty of this form of organisation?*' asked Sombart, in *Der Moderne Kapitalismus*:

> Obviously in the fact that it enabled craft-based work to be informed by the arts without the artist and the craftsman being one and the same person, as had been the case before. Mind and body were torn out of their living unity, so to speak, but returned to an inner unity again in a supra-individual, ideal form. The artist climbed down once more to the spheres of commercial production, but in a different way compared to the Middle Ages. His spirit was made useful for a large area of human endeavour. The idea of individuality, of artistic distinctiveness

and character, was not realised on the primitive and sensual level of the genius who wastes his power by carving or operating with melting pots himself, but by subordinating the world of material labour to his spirit, and by turning the many who are only fit for executing work into willing tools in his hands. While in the Middle Ages the artist's means for realising his ideas had been plane, stylus or hammer, now the artist had a sophisticated system of individual labourers, living beings, at his disposal, and was able to act on the dead material in a far more perfect fashion with the help of their mediation. Thus, the fundamental idea behind the new organisation of the arts and crafts was that the notion of the differentiation of skills should now also be applied to the creative work in a much deeper sense than had been the case before.[30]

Perhaps Sombart was getting carried away here; but creativity and distinction mattered in capitalism, from the Renaissance until today.[31] Manufactories represented dynamics at the frontier, pushing the margins of the possible, potentially crossing the important threshold separating *Smithian* (preindustrial extensive economic growth) from *Schumpeterian* growth (modern economic development).[32] Manufactories thus exuded capitalism from every pore.[33] They operated outside the urban guild restrictions, that is, within the 'free market' or more liberal, competitive systems of market economy; they potentially triggered capital accumulation.

This is not to deny the role played by artisanship, craftsmanship, apprenticeship and decentralized home production in making (and apparently sometimes breaking) Europe's industrial history; historians have intensely debated the positive and negative contribution made to industrial growth by guilds and other urban industrial associations.[34] But manufactories and manufactural capitalism represented a different league, potentially upping the game. As we have seen previously, historians have posited two ways of interpreting historical economic development. One model is often known as Smithian growth (after Adam Smith); the other Schumpeterian (after the great Austro-American economist and sociologist Joseph Alois Schumpeter). The two are not always made explicit or distinguished, but can often be seen at work behind the scenes, and probably do the job explaining transitions to capitalism,[35] varieties of capitalism,[36] or even worlds of 'surprising resemblances'.[37] But Smithian growth (*Wealth of Nations,* 1776) is extensive, using known parameters of technology and efficiency, by means of optimizing production processes and work flows, or distributing final products more efficiently.[38] It means moving *alongside* a known production frontier – not pushing it out; what Schumpeter (*Theory of Economic Development*; German original 1911) labelled the 'circular flow' of an economic system that was, essentially, static.[39] But there was a different

175

paradigm – *Schumpeterian* growth – which was principally more dynamic than Smithian growth, at least in outlook; aimed at achieving economic transformation beyond the ceilings provided by the stationary nature of Smithian work flows, Schumpeterian growth is about disruption, change, creativity and the transformation – and not merely optimization – of existing process flows and the world of goods. It pushes out the potential menu of choices available to policy makers and individual economic actors. Known in its elementary form since the time of Bacon, or in its early modern form of cameralism, it was based on a principally optimistic attitude toward nature *and* the future (Chapter 2), and the transformative belief in economic synergies generated by radically redesigning markets.[40] In the cameralist model this included nation-building (or consolidation), city development, spatial ordering, infrastructure improvement, the promotion of monetary velocity and economic circulation (Chapter 6), and the promotion of useful knowledge. We encountered elements of that model in previous chapters on the open human future (Chapter 2), market regulation (Chapter 4), monetary management (Chapters 5 and 6) – tools occasionally conceptualized to break the shackles provided by antiquated feudal modes of production. While manufactories and manufacturing policies discussed in the present chapter are difficult to limit exclusively to either – because they usually combined Smithian *and* Schumpeterian features – in their vision of economic development and potentially infinite growth through manufacturing they far exceeded Smith's vison, which was theoretically much more parsimonious regarding the possibility of economic development. After using manufactories (in the first chapters of the *Wealth of Nations*) to illustrate the benefits of division of labour, Smith stopped short of explaining their wider implications potentially achieving intensive or real economic growth.

Now, lest the present story mutate into Whiggish narrative of historical change driven by telos – not all cameralist projects of transforming oeconomy were successful, and some historians have labelled them outright fakes or practical pranks.[41] Why did some *ancien régime* manufactories and *Fabriquen* fail? Contemporaries offered several reasons. In a letter to the philosopher Gottfried Wilhelm Leibniz dated 24 January 1682, Johann Daniel Crafft or Krafft, a Saxon *Projektemacher* who ran several such manufacturing businesses in Saxony and Bohemia praised the English, French and Dutch cultures of manufactory capitalism but lamented a German culture of hesitancy. In the Holy Roman Empire princes and dukes were too risk-averse to provide such promising projects with the necessary venture capital (implying that the private sector didn't produce enough liquid funds for investment).[42] The 1660s and 1670s had seen a revival of large-scale manufacturing across the continent, often supported by the state and emulating the French template set by the policies of Jean Baptiste Colbert (1619–83). Manufactories and bigger workshops were established left, right and centre, in the German-speaking lands, the Austrian hereditary monarchy, Scotland, Sweden and certainly France. Even Portugal went through a temporary manufacturing boom, as List noted in *National System of Political Economy* (orig. German 1841). During the last two decades of the 17th century, under the administration of Dom Luís de Menezes, third Count of Ericeira, Portugal successfully managed a process of import substitution, supplying 'herself and her colonies with native goods manufactured of home-grown raw material, and prospered exceedingly'. Probably influenced by Colbert's policies, during the 1660s and 1670s Portuguese 'mercantilist' economic writers such as Duarte Ribeiro de Macedo would emphasize the virtues of industrial policy in making the nation rich.[43] But after the Treaty of Methuen (on which Ricardo based his infamous argument on comparative advantage and mutually advantageous trade), 'Portugal was deluged with English manufactures, and the first result of this inundation was the sudden and complete ruin of the Portuguese manufactories'.[44] Contemporaries occasionally considered Ericeira to be 'not improperly called the *Colbert* of Portugal; for then the country stood not in need of the manufactures of foreigners'.[45]

It is no foregone conclusion that industrial policy thus conceptualized was automatically bound to fail: in the Portuguese case – a country which during the second half of the 17th century held up well in terms of average incomes with England, and possibly also in the level of industrialization[46] – it was successful; the reversal of fortune was the result of deliberate political choices. Saxon *Projektemacher* Crafft also listed intellectual inertia, traditionalism and people sticking to their accustomed practices as reasons why industrialization came off so sluggishly in the German-speaking countries of the Baroque age.[47] A 1788 analysis of the Swedish Pomeranian economy written in the *Staatenkunde* cameralist fashion found that 'manufactories and Fabriquen failed to flourish in Swedish Pomerania after the Thirty Years War. There was no general lack of entrepreneurship [...]. Some lacked the necessary knowledge and funds, others were started without the intention to deliver in the first place'.[48] Reasons for failure included substandard raw material quality (especially wool and flax); country spinners' reluctance to produce for urban enterprises, lack of workhouses and pawnbrokers that would have supported poor workers; wages being too high (an interesting variation on a common argument that claims high wages as prime reason for *Britain's* early industrialization);[49] infringements by guilds trying to interfere with competitive market processes; unwillingness of local and regional retailers to vend domestic manufactures; lack of state monitoring; and lack of support by the fisc.[50] At the time Swedish trade policy was geared towards protecting manufacturing in Sweden's heartlands, keeping Pomeranian manufactures out of the Swedish homeland markets; contemporaries identified this as the main reasons for Pomeranian lack of development.[51] Still what matters is the Schumpeterian vision that went with such large capitalist enterprises, be that in Scotland, in Austria, many German lands, Swedish Pomerania or elsewhere; and the firm belief that given the right circumstances such economic strategies would pay off (even if they didn't in some cases, they would in others). Hyperbole, risk-taking and adventurous experiments were key on the roadmap towards modern capitalism.[52]

Since the so-called 'commercial revolution' of the 12th and 13th centuries high-quality export industries had sprung out in the vicinity of trading emporia such as Venice and Florence, Augsburg, Nuremberg and Ghent, often with the help of the state or public authority.[53] By the dawn of the Industrial Revolution most cities and towns, be that Siena in Italy, Bruges in Flanders or Jönköping and Stockholm in Sweden, had built differentiated spectrums of urban industries.[54] These processes were usually supported by governments intervening with the aim to promote specifically high added-value economic activities, considered most promising in terms of dynamically raising incomes and employment.[55] Historically such dynamics most likely occurred in industry, due to economies of scale, meaning that output could be increased at decreasing average total piece cost, utilizing higher levels of technology and knowledge and a higher income elasticity of demand for manufactures compared to essentials such as foodstuffs (Engel's Law).[56] Manufacturing also exerts important backward and forward linkages, which can act as manifest stimuli to overall economic development.

How deep were the roots of Europe's industrial transitions really? And how did these processes unfold?

Manufacturing capitalism in early modern Europe

Free trade France and ancien régime *economics*

The 'grand days of French industry commenced with Colbert', claimed List.[57] Aimed at creating a national market and promoting domestic industry, Colbert's policies were admired all over Europe. France enjoyed a lead in higher-end manufacturing; during the 17th and 18th centuries French luxury manufactures came to be depicted as 'degenerate' and 'effeminate', an expression of jealousy and a profound inferiority complex. Hörnigk modelled his bestseller (*Austria Supreme*, 1684) on state-led capitalist development on the idea of France the 'Whore' who enchanted the rest of the world with her wicked charms (meaning her high-grade luxury manufactures).[58]

Colbert's promotion of manufactures as Minister of Finance since 1665 built upon his predecessor's customs reforms of 1654, which had quadrupled tariffs on Dutch and English cloth.[59] Obsessed with statistics as a tool of knowledge, Colbert increased the degree of monitoring across the French economy, but also kept an eye on knowledge and technology transfer, founding the Académie des Sciences (1666), and recruiting foreign manufacturing experts such as Josse van Robais, a Dutchman who ran one of the finest manufactories of the period for fine clothes à la *façon de Hollande*.[60] 'From all countries', noted List, Colbert:

> bought up trade secrets, and procured better machinery and tools. By a general and efficient tariff, he secured the home markets for native industry. By abolishing, or by limiting as much as possible, the provincial customs collections, by the construction of highways and canals, he promoted internal traffic. Into all branches of the administration he introduced the most stringent economy and perfect order.[61]

While List's account could be occasionally problematic (especially from a modernist point of view), his basic instincts are confirmed by modern research. Between 1662 and 1680 France managed to turn her passive trade balance of more than five million livres into an active one carrying a surplus of more than five million livres, managing a classic pattern of import substitution.[62] The commercial crisis during the last two decades of the 17th and the first of the 18th century would be gradually overcome; cotton production expanded rapidly after 1709. Between 1721 and 1731 alone the recorded cotton cloth production of Upper Normandy nearly tripled from about 61,000 to more than 160,000 pieces.[63] Contemporaries referred to fine textiles as France's 'gold mine'.[64] Other measures included the granting of privileges and bounties to specific enterprises catering to those trades considered useful for 'getting the nation into the right business'.[65] Regulation covered quality control and sometimes also enforcement of minimum standards, to ensure international marketability.

Was Colbert a 'mercantilist'?[66] The concept of mercantilism as commonly employed by scholars is problematic[67] and may perhaps be better served by the alternative 'cameralism'. During the early modern period, most writings and policies under the 'mercantilist' label were production-, not trade-centred (contrary to what the word 'mercantile' seems to imply); they were less geared towards rough zero-sum games of beggaring one's neighbour and more towards creating synergies and potentially infinite growth through transforming the productive landscape. Especially with regard to developing internal markets and the domestic natural resource base, Colbert's policies neatly match the 'cameralist' rule book. Under Colbert some import tariffs were hefty, at rates of up to 20 per cent *ad valorem*. They were easily outpaced, though, by English import tariffs on French goods only slightly later (up to 75 per cent).[68] Based on a thorough re-evaluation of archival memos and other administrative documents produced in connection with the 1664 and 1667 tariffs, one scholar has thus doubted Colbert's qualities as a protectionist defined in a traditionalist sense.[69] Rather than advocating cut-throat tariff and trade wars, Colbert advocated for a natural order of *fair* trade with principally harmonized tariffs between trading partners and mutually advantageous trade based on countries' differential natural resource endowment. The warlike terminology employed in trade memos stemmed precisely from his desire to talk Louis XIV *out* of real-life wars, and into more peaceful avenues of economic development. Protective tariffs were applied on certain industrial products, but not with the idea to generally prohibit their importation and domestic consumption (as the British tried with French goods). Rather the aim was to increase their price, which would have transformed them into items of conspicuous consumption (*luxury*) for those who could afford them either way and would thus not have cared much about any duty whatsoever. Otherwise Colbertism was based on a principle of *competition through quality*. The point was to actively encourage quality in home-made French industrial goods across the board by 'nudges', not punishment.

These policies laid the foundation for France's subsequent transition into the industrial age. A recent authoritative study concludes that the state continued 'as an active agent in the circulation and implementation of useful knowledge' beyond Colbert, into the post-1750s age of cotton and industry.[70]

Habsburg and the Hörnigk moment

The Habsburg lands were no strangers to capitalism practised in the cameralist fashion. In Spain, '[t]he government built model factories to make glassware, cabinet work and tapestry at Madrid, and elsewhere for fabrics, hats, cottons, porcelain, brass and other wares'.[71] In the Kingdom of Naples, Habsburg administrators actively supported the building up of native manufactures during the 1730s and beyond.[72] In Flanders (Austrian Netherlands), native merchants successfully lobbied the regional diets in support for domestic manufactures.[73] The main goals of Austrian economic policy under Leopold I (b 1640, r 1658–1705), Charles VI (b 1685, r 1711–40) but especially Maria Theresa (b 1717, r 1740–80) were focused on raising industrial productivity, increasing competitiveness across the board, and abolishing local privileges and guild monopolies.[74] Measures included the encouragement of technology transfer and the establishment of quality controls with special attention given to high value-added industries such as iron, cotton and silk.[75] The main obstacles on the cameralist road towards competitive capitalism included a lack of capital (investment), low incomes and limitations in the size and integration of markets. Customs barriers and cross-border tariffs cut provinces and kingdoms like Hungary off from each other. Hungarian cameralism aimed at market integration in the same way as political oeconomy in the hereditary lands, resulting in mutually irreconcilable policy goals, *the* institutional paradox of polycentric monarchies (the standard state form in *ancien régime* Europe).[76]

Some historians have argued that post-1780 policy under Emperor Joseph II (b 1741, r 1765–90) was influenced by more liberal or 'physiocrat' ideas, due to their emphasis on abolishing guild monopolies and other barriers to market entry.[77] But there was nothing specifically physiocrat about them: cameralists were on a similar page regarding market freedom and competitive forms of economy. Sandgruber's claim about cameralist-mercantilist (the two are often used in the literature interchangeably) eyes predominantly focused on the luxury industries[78] is also misleading since strategies proposed by 'Austrian' mercantilists such as Hörnigk (1684) or later on Justi and Sonnenfels generally tended to advocate a broad-scale approach to industrial policy, supporting those industries likely to capture larger markets. Justi even seems to have favoured a sort of 'balanced' approach to economic development – develop as many branches of industry as possible. A *Commerzcollegium*, that is, board tasked with monitoring and raising industrial prowess was founded in 1666, probably initiated by the polymath, alchemist and oeconomist Johann Joachim Becher, and modelled upon the French example of the *Conseil de Commerce* established by Colbert in 1664.[79] Since 1717/18 a *Hauptkommerzkollegium* existed in Vienna; a similar institution had been set up for the Bohemian lands a few years earlier. The *Hauptkommerzkollegium* acted as the superordinate agency for subsidiary regional boards and commissions catering to the component parts of the Austrian monarchy, such as Bohemia and Silesia.[80] In 1746 a *Universal-Commerzdirektorium* was created comprising members of the Vienna *Hofkammer*, the Hungarian, Bohemian and Austrian Court Chamber. But as this institution lacked staff and infrastructure, it remained more of a think tank (*Planungsbehörde*). Concerned with improving textiles, silk and iron manufacturing, commerce and transport infrastructure and reconstituted in 1749 as the Commercien-Ober-Direktorium, it continued into the 1750s, regularly coordinating with its pendants in the Austrian Netherlands, and the Italian and Hungarian branches. In 1768 a *Staatswirthschafts* Deputation was founded, with similar responsibilities.

Since the mid-1740s regional *Kommerzkonsesse* (1749 in Styria and Lower Austria; 1752: Bohemia, Moravia and Upper Austria; 1757: Inner Austria and Vorarlberg; 1763 in Tyrol) coordinated industrial policy at the local level. This entailed the award of production licences for new masters and entrepreneurs; the organization and procurement of raw materials, quality supervision, as well as statistical surveying of industrial production. The *Konsesse* usually consisted of several princely administrators (*Landesfürstliche Räte*) as well as at least two native entrepreneurs.[81] We may compare them with the Board of Trustees established in Scotland under the regency of Walpole (1727). During the 1720s, state support was increased for artisans and craftspeople who pursued business outside the guilds' umbrellas. Industrial statistics (*Manufakturtabellen*) were compiled since 1749; government and administrators used *Statistik* as a tool of economic governmentality, generating, managing and promoting useful knowledge and productivity growth across the Austrian lands. In 1753 Maria Theresa instructed the *Ungarische Hofkanzlei* and the Vienna *Hofkammer* to meet weekly in order to assess the performance of Hungary's economy. In 1762 inspectors for the manufactories were constituted in Bohemia.[82] 'National' economic statistics on select branches of output in the composite monarchy implementing a 'Hörnigkian' (or Listian) strategy commenced in the 1760s, starting with livestock censuses. From 1789 onwards, detailed statistics were compiled on grain output, with up to 24 types recorded including legumes, fruits, forage crops and vegetables used in industrial processes, mainly sugar beet, hops and tobacco. Later on, statistics were produced for the fisheries, silviculture and forestry, including game hunting.[83] Industrial output statistics were only compiled from 1841 onwards, and the first complete industrial census had to wait until 1902.[84]

How successful was Austrian industrial policy? Answers remain difficult, not least because the statistical material is so spurious. Butschek finds moderate growth in the Austrian economy until the 1770s and some economic development thereafter, with some credit given to industrial policy since the later 17th century as well as under Maria Theresa. According to Voth, three factors were particularly significant for Austrian economic development; first relaxing restrictions on the agrarian economy which:

> improved the legal position of tenants and reduced their labor obligations (Robot). … The second, which fostered the growth of the bureaucracy, allowed the data necessary for effective policy measures to be collected for the first time and censuses to be conducted at regular intervals […]. The third element promoted direct state intervention in the economy to subsidize new enterprises, limit the power of the guilds, and import skilled laborers.[85]

Market integration seems to have improved toward the last decades of the 18th century.[86] The introduction of a comprehensive schooling system promoted education and useful knowledge.[87] There is some evidence suggesting a catch-up in key branches of industry, including an eightfold increase in manufacturing employment in Lower Austria from about 20,000 (1760) to 182,000 (1790), and a rise in iron output, for the same period and for the entire monarchy by 50 per cent – at a time when population figures remained stagnant. Agricultural yields considerably expanded in Upper Austria between 1770 and 1790 (by 77 per cent) and rose in other provinces between 12 and 25 per cent (bar Vorarlberg and Tyrol, where they declined); between 1789 and the 1830s regional rates of increase ranged from 30 to 100 per cent. An increasing share of raw cotton in imports as well as iron and cloth manufactures on Austria's export balance sheet point towards a gradual industrialization of Austria's trade balance towards the later decades of the 18th century. But according to Sandgruber nominal wages remained low and real wages declined in most parts of the Austrian lands (1700–90). Only after 1790 we see a modest increase in nominal (day) wages.[88]

Still an economic transition had been set under way in sectors that proved vital for later industrial transitions. To what extent this was due to good policy must, for the reasons discussed in Chapter 3, remain ambiguous. But similar to Prussia and Saxony, Scotland and England, Austrian governments from the mid-17th century paid increasingly close attention to manufacturing and industrial policy, in line with a general capitalist spirit that unfolded in Catholic, Calvinist and Protestant countries alike.

Scotland: cradle of capitalism, or, how to bury your dead?

'From the end of the 17th century onwards, but more especially since the union with Scotland, the course of capitalist development in England was greatly influenced by the fortunes of the capitalist spirit in the Northern Kingdom', noted Sombart in his small study on Der Bourgois in 1913.[89] Dismissing Catholic Ireland ('Down to this very day there is scarcely another land which has been so little affected by the capitalist spirit'), he went on:

Nowhere else in the world did the birth of capitalism come about in so curious a fashion as in Scotland. Nothing is more surprising than the suddenness of its appearance. It is as though a pistol shot had given the signal for the capitalist spirit, fully grown, to come into the land and dominate it. You cannot help thinking of the Victoria Regia, which blooms overnight.

By the end of the 17th century, Scotland, a small country at the north-western periphery, was among Europe's poorest nations. Crippled by harvest failures and English military-economic warfare in the wake of the Darien disaster and King William III's 'Seven Ill Years' Scottish political classes in 1707 finally voted for incorporating Union, ending the Scottish parliament and independence of one of Europe's oldest nation states.[90] By the 1800s things had completely turned around. Scotland had produced three key figures in modern economic thought – David Hume, Adam Smith and Sir James Steuart; it was Europe's second-most urbanized nation (after England) and the second one to undergo an industrial revolution (after England). Capitalist modernity had set in. This was perhaps *the* fastest such transition to capitalism experienced in the western hemisphere before the 1900s, if we measure this transition using the urbanization figures by de Vries: on that count Scottish urbanization, 1600–1850 increased by a factor of six, England's only by five; and all other European areas at much lower rates.[91]

Historians have singled out the Union of 1707, Glasgow's subsequent rise in the tobacco trades, and Scotland's incorporation into the English Atlantic Empire creating the 'biggest free trade zone of the time' as main reasons for this success.[92] This, however, is only half the story. Until well into the second half of the 18th century scarcely half the Scottish population would have regarded themselves necessarily as British, nor the Hanoverian succession as legitimate. North-west of the Highland line the Hanoverian 'British' state remained a distant imaginary. Jacobite attempts to bring the Stuart dynasty back upon the Scottish (and English) throne were rehashed several times between 1709 and 1746.[93] The Union settlement was all but given.

Similar care needs to be taken with other popular explanations of Scottish economic success. Adam Smith hit a famous note when casually reflecting on Scots cattle exports to England as one of the main sources of Scotland's wealth gained from incorporating Union. But to the present day few nations have *grown rich* on primary-sector exports (apart from Denmark and a handful of oil-exporting nations),[94] and the modern evidence on less developed countries suggests exactly the opposite. With England showing early signs of industrial transformation since the 17th century, and Scotland continuing (as it had for centuries) to specialize in raw material exports and some coarse linen, which prior to the Union fetched some sales in England but not on the world market, incorporating Union, by abolishing (almost) all tariffs on cross-border trade with England, would equally probably have meant the nation's road towards underdevelopment.

No nation has *remained rich* based exclusively on trading, either. This is why we should be careful of attributing Scottish economic success post-1707 to the colonial trades exclusively. Glasgow's colonial trades were enormously dynamic after 1740, and Scots even managed to overtake English ports as main entrepôts for North American tobacco. This explains economic development around the western ports of Scotland, but not Scottish industrialization as a whole. Whatley has identified Scotland's linen industry as a main driver of capitalism, but also salt and paper making and brewing (the woollen industry was left to England within the post-Restoration political economy[95]) – while earlier work by Devine on agrarian transformations has established sound evidence of capitalist agrarian regimes in the Lowlands long before the Union. Since the mid-17th century, Scotland's Lowland agrarian economies were thriving and increasingly market-driven, contributing to long-term economic change.[96]

The role of the state has also been discussed, albeit in the Scottish case this is tricky, because Scotland ceased to exist as an independent country, and lost Parliament and Privy Council; these had been the main state bodies doing economic policy to 1707/08. A recent study of early modern British political economy consequently ignores the Scottish experience by and large, treating post-1707 Scotland as a region and examining the British state through an Anglocentric view focused on the Westminster Parliament's activity in economic legislation.[97] But with Scottish MPs under-represented in both houses, and Westminster comparatively inert in terms of numbers of economic acts specifically concerning Scotland after 1707, Parliament simply ceased to be the route for doing economic policy in Scotland. This does not mean the British state ceased to intervene in Scottish economic life, but it worked through different channels. Studying post-1707 Scottish economic policy through a parliamentary focus thus misses the point.[98]

Industrial policy after 1707 was carried out within a regional framework, through the Convention of Royal Burghs – an association of Scotland's major towns and cities which had held state functions and implemented economic policies since the Reformation, but especially the Board of Trustees for the Fisheries and Linen Manufactures established in 1727. Part of a larger bundle of economic reforms initiated under the congenial First Minister Robert Walpole who governed Scotland through his crony the Duke of Argyll (sometimes dubbed the Viceroy of Scotland), the Walpolean government had, during 1721–23, initiated a series of customs reforms, abolishing export tariffs on most manufactures and considerably reducing, or in some cases even waiving, import duties on raw materials considered vital for British industry, including flax and hemp. Very similar policies were introduced in Prussia after 1719.[99] Primarily directed at serving English, not necessarily Scottish, economic interests, such policies unfolded their full potential when the Board was set up in 1727, triggering veritable medium- to long-run changes in productivity and value-added for Scotland's productive landscape, too, but mostly focused on linen as the key sector of Scottish industry. I have argued elsewhere that Scotland's integration in 1707 into the old 1660 English Restoration's taxation schedule for the colonial trades – vis-à-vis dynamically falling prices for colonial imports 1660s–1770s, coupled with a full draw-back (tax rebate) on import duties on tobacco when re-exported – created a cutting-edge business advantage for Glasgow in the colonial re-export trades to Europe after 1740. It may have been completely unintended but was nonetheless powerful in terms of its commercial impact upon the west of Scotland.[100] And in both trade levels as well as industrial output and productivity we can see some of these state policies finally paying off after the 1740s, contributing to a gradual economic transformation of Lowland Scotland that finally led into full-blown industrialization of linen and cotton from the 1780s onwards.

The pre-Union Scottish Parliament, on the other hand, had been very proactive economically, playing a key role in state-directed economic development, with particular emphasis on industrial policy and internal market development.[101] During the 1670s and 1680s the Scottish Parliament passed numerous acts establishing new regional and weekly market centres and fairs, cloth manufactories and large workshops for all sorts of industrial goods, usually in the Lowlands.[102] If these acts of parliament, company books, sederunt books from enterprises such as the New Mills manufactory, established in the 1640s and re-founded in the 1680s, and others were in any way indicative of a Weberian spirit,[103] the Scottish nation and state had become exceedingly capitalist long before incorporating Union. Other examples of the entrepreneurial state at work include the Darien scheme, a brave attempt at founding an American trading company in central America, or the foundation of Bank of Scotland in 1696 almost simultaneous to the Bank of England, with Scotsmen played a leading role in both.[104] Vigorous debates over the terms and conditions of the Union of 1707, which caused an impressive number of cheap printed broadsheet publications, provide vivid testimony to the level of economic literacy among the Scottish *communitas regni* and public sphere, a political community consisting of an occasionally eclectic mix of hereditary noblemen, petty lords and lairds and burghal middle-class merchants, sporting a vision of a potentially positive, open and manageable future.[105]

Scotland thus partook in a European 'industrial moment' during the second half of the 17th century, which saw manufactories and similar 'big projects' become more and more *en vogue*, be that in France under Colbert, in Portugal under Ericeira, or Saxony, Prussia and the Austrian heartlands;[106] part and parcel of the 'projecting age' and a view towards overcoming the disastrous economic consequences of the Thirty Years War (1618–48), climate change and general economic depression of the 1660s. Between the 1660s and 1707 the number of manufactories established in Scotland substantially increased, far exceeding the traditional range of luxury goods and catering for the broader mass market. The same goes for rural market centres and fairs, more and more of which were established by act of parliament. Some were permanent; others remained temporary. A few never saw the light of day. For the 'spirit of capitalism' this does not matter so much, as it literally jumps out at you. Just take a random example, an *Act in favors of the laird of Carstairs for three fairs yeerlie at Carstairs* (1669):

The king's majestie and estates of parliament, takeing to consideration that the toun of Carstairs, lying within the shirreffdome of Lanerck, perteaning heretablie to William Lockhart of Carstairs, being upon the hie road and way that leids from many places of the south and west to Edinburgh, Linlithgow and other places, and ther being diverse convenient change houses and lodgeing houses in the said toun, the same is a convenient place for keeping of fairs therin, and ther would a great deall of good and proffite arise to nighbours therabout and to diverse others of his majesties' liedges if ther wer ane warrand granted for holding of fairs yeerlie in the said toun; thairfor, the king's majestie, with advice and consent of his estates of parliament, doe heirby give and grant to the said William Lockhart of Carstairs, his airs and successors, three fairs yeerlie to be keept and holden within the said toun of Carstairs, the first upon the eighteint day of July, the second upon the tuentie day of September, and the thrid upon the first day of November, yeerlie in all tymecomeing, for buying and selling of horse, nolt, sheip, fish, flesh, meill, malt and all sort of granes, cloath, lining and wollen, and all sort of merchant commodities, with full power to the said William Lockhart and his forsaids, or such as they shall appoint, to collect, uplift and intromet with the tolls, customes and dewties belonging to the saids yeerlie fairs, and to enjoy all other freedomes, liberties, priveledges and immunities siclyk and als freelie in all respects as any other in the lyke cace hes done or may doe in tyme comeing.

The language of the act reflects a dynamic perception of markets, money and capitalist improvement across Lowland Scotland. The capitalist spirit even extended into the realm of death. A 1686 *Act for Burying in Scots Linen*, directed at promoting domestic manufacturing prescribed, upon punishment with a hefty fine, that

no corps of any person or persons whatsoever shall be buried in any shirt, sheet or anything else except in plaine linen or cloath of hards made and spunn within the kingdom, without lace or poynt, dischargeing from hencefurth the makeing use of Holland or uther linen cloath made in other kingdomes, all silke hair or woollen, gold or silver, or any other stuff whatsoever.[107]

Here a cameralist view on capitalism even extended to the realm of the deceased. The act was repeated in 1695, but revoked in the 1706–07 session, in what was one of the very last actions by the old Scottish Parliament, when linens were replaced with woollens, finally adopting the English model of crossing the Styx.[108]

The post-1707 British entrepreneurial state, in Scotland rudimentarily embodied in the Board of Trustees for the Fisheries and Manufactures (1727) actively supported linen manufacturing – Scotland's main industry at the time. It did so by awarding bounties and premiums on exports and good piecework, and establishing stamp masters across the Lowlands and Highlands, officials appointed by the state who had to check and approve ('stamp') every single piece of linen made for the market. This practice would become common across western Europe, especially in the German-speaking lands, during the subsequent age of Enlightenment. The Board also helped financing overheads such as bleachfields, which were too costly for private investors to foot, encouraging foreign skilled immigrants and many more. These policies seem to have paid off. Total linen output in Scotland between the 1720s and 1770s increased by a factor of seven; but so did average prices and quality, that is, added value.[109] The dynamics spilled over into fustian (cotton mixed with linen) and cotton as a leading sector of the British Industrial Revolution. As Nisbet has argued regarding the development of Paisley as Scotland's major industrial region specializing in higher-value cotton-linen mixtures, 'the growth of fine weaving relied largely on English markets. ... Mixed cotton-linens, known as "checks", were being woven by 1702, and within a decade fine quality lawns, or "muslins", were produced to imitate Indian varieties'.[110] Thus Scottish linen and fustian manufacturers partook in the 'Great Divergence' displacing Indian cotton from world markets, creating the first industrial nation.[111]

Sweden and the Age of Greatness, 1650–1850

Sweden was a late industrializer; modern economic growth only set in during the later 19th century.[112] GDP per capita stagnated, after a golden age had run its course between the 1650s and the 1710s – Sweden's 'Age of Greatness' (*Stormaktstiden*, 1650s–1720s).[113] By 1700 Sweden had built up a flourishing manufacturing sector, managing import substitution in most branches of manufacturing until the mid-18th century, with a proverbially competitive iron industry. It operated a profitable East Asia Company as an interloper of the bigger fish in the game (the Dutch and English EICs).[114] In copper and iron, Sweden attained a near-monopoly on European markets before the industrial revolution: England's early industrial transformation was facilitated by superior Swedish, later on Russian, iron.[115] Between the 1540s and 1740s Swedish real wages compared favourably with England's.[116] Contemporary political oeconomists looked to Sweden with admiration, as Daniel Gottfried Schreber's introduction to the German preface of Uppsala cameralist professor Anders Berch's textbook bears out (see Chapter 2). As Schön has argued,

> The basis for growth in the seventeenth century ... was a reorganization of the economy, very much led by or supported by the state. Both administration and industry were modernized, with a technological transfer inter alia through skilled immigrants. Export of industrial goods was also of importance for economic growth especially in the first half of the century. Apart from bringing about the growth of industrial output, it enabled imports of various kinds and facilitated capital import. Furthermore, export prices rose more than import prices which, of course, was favourable for the Swedish economy ... As noted earlier, this was also a period of urbanization in Sweden.[117]

By 1700 Sweden may even have surpassed the Holy Roman Empire, Spain, Italy and France in terms of per capita GDP; only the Netherlands and England enjoyed decidedly higher levels of wealth.[118] As a self-proclaimed champion of Protestantism Sweden took on a quasi-hegemonic role in northern Europe. By 1700 the Baltic had all but turned into a Swedish lake; with only a few patches of territories in the eastern littoral remaining under Polish-Lithuanian or Brandenburg-Prussian rule.[119] Useful knowledge blossomed. Creativity and well-functioning institutions, especially markets, laid foundations for subsequent 19th- and 20th-century development. During the Age of Greatness, Sweden's state embarked upon a programme of economic modernization,[120] encouraging peasant liberation, institutional improvement and a growing community of scientists who considered themselves part of a wider European community of letters, cameralism and infinite natural improvement.[121] Swedish industry worked under competitive parameters, with few monopolies and other forms of market distortions. As Kellenbenz wrote, quoting Herbert Heaton,

> For the conversion of ore to metal a large workshop was built in Stiernsund, Sweden, by the entrepreneur Polhem with 'machines and appliances which will diminish the amount or intensity of heavy manual work'. A worthy precursor of Boulton and Wedgwood, Polhem used 'machines to cut bars, slit railrods, roll iron into sheets, cut cogwheels, hammer pans, shape tinware and make all kinds of household appliances, plowshares, and clock parts'.[122]

Sweden's ironworks, many run by Scotsmen,[123] produced iron of superior quality. Between the 1620s and the 1680s yearly exports of bar iron rose from around 3,000 to 27,000 tons: 'This startling escalation was a matter of policy'.[124] The government, through its extended arm of bureaucracy the *Bergscollegium* (literally: board of mining) kept mining and smelting separate, moving away from the old, decentralized and small-scale system of peasant mining and refining to larger industrial complexes working to increasingly rationalized business models. Simple small-scale smelting was carried out by the *bergsmän*, involving little capital or specialist know-how. But the more refined stages of production – where the expected increases in value-added were greatest (refining the ore, shaping it into exportable iron bars) – were now put into the hands of 'a new class of professional ironmasters (*brukspatroner*)' employing huge sums of capital, working big business units, smelting works and other manufactories. The *Bergscollegium* state capitalism was successful, as the 'number of forges at work never fell below 400 between the middle of the seventeenth century and the middle of the eighteenth'.[125] By the 1720s Sweden had become Europe's biggest producer of bar iron, and iron Sweden's 'Peruvian goldmine'. In 1760, when polymath–oeconomist Christopher Polhem called for further improvement in the bar iron sector, he discussed how much additional value would be generated within the industry (Polhem suggested up to 14 times), and how many more people could be thus put into useful employment.[126] The relative abundance of timber and its (relative) absence in Britain, coupled with the simultaneous rise in English urbanization and the quickening–up of British economic life since the Civil Wars of the 1640s proved fortuitous, creating a dynamically expanding foreign market for Sweden's prime industry.[127] The spillover effects into other branches were considerable.

The Board of Commerce put the rationale of such policies to the Diet of Estates in 1727 thus: 'All useful manufactories fail and are destroyed soon after they are started unless they are assisted in time by public funding and given the kind of benefits and privileges that could eliminate the difficulties they face'.[128] As we have seen the Board of Trustees for Fisheries and Manufactures was established in Scotland in the same year (1727) following similar lines; its minutes document a similar state-capitalistic rationale of industrial policy. As in most other countries, a considerable share of industrial production remained decentralized and rural-domestic; in the towns, guilds still enjoyed far-reaching oeconomic powers. Such old practices of staple trade or monopoly were heavily criticized by oeconomic literati like Polhem, as infringements on markets and economic development.[129] After some tariff liberalization in 1776, the customs reforms of 1799 and 1816 introduced even stricter protectionist measures; the famous 1723 *Produktplakatet*, which had laid the foundations for Swedish trade regulation, remained in force until 1857, when Sweden's industrial revolution ran its course. 'Mercantilism' thus framed was criticized by Swedish thinkers including Finnish-born Anders Chydenius (1729–1803) who alleged that such policies increased prices for vital imports (such as salt) in the same way as for Swedish iron exports, jeopardizing Sweden's wealth.[130] But overall the laws seem to have paid off; as late as the 1790s about half of Sweden's timber exports to London were carried in ships sailing under the Swedish flag, significantly augmenting Swedish service-sector income.[131]

Sweden's industrial policy during the Age of Greatness is a prime example of state-led capitalism engineering a series of economic transitions that just fell short of an industrial revolution. Sweden's peasantry had been freed by the 'Great Reduction' of the 1660s to 1680s, by which the Swedish kings purchased back lands formerly alienated from the Crown, with proprietors now turned into free peasants and potential agrarian entrepreneurs. Since the 1680s Sweden operated one of the most efficient systems of military conscription (*indelningsverk*), which remained in place until the 20th century – the last soldier enlisted through the system established by the reforms of Charles XI in 1680 died in 1969.[132] Sweden's universities were well regarded. Literacy rates were high.

When Swedes ransacked German castles and monasteries during the Thirty Years War they repatriated entire libraries to Sweden, forming the nucleus of splendid repositories such as the one assembled by Field Marshal Carl Gustav Wrangel (1613–76) at Skokloster Castle.[133] Translations of Swedish cameralist works into German were produced, many of them by the hand of our Leipzig professor Daniel Gottfried Schreber (1708–77/78) (see Chapters 2 and 7).[134] Sweden also featured, from the 1720s, one of the best economic statistical bureaus of its time, producing demographic records and other statistics of superior quality.[135]

The Swedish political economy proudly bore out this claim toward oeconomic modernity. Topics covered during *Stormaktstiden* ranged from the creation of free markets and competitive business to the panoptic discovery of Mother Nature's hidden forces, not least by the groundbreaking research of Carl Linnaeus.[136] During the later 17th century, Swedish economic discourse became increasingly attuned to notions of unlimited growth through scientific endeavour.[137] Many Swedish cameralists sported the idea of an entrepreneurial state driving such processes of Schumpeterian growth.[138] Useful knowledge was harnessed through systematic avenues including the foundation of the Royal Swedish Academy of the Sciences (established in 1739), in which Linnaeus played a fundamental role.[139] Chancellor Oxenstierna encapsulated the key aspects of laissez-faire state capitalism thus:

> public trade, which is assumed for the good of the King and of the Kingdom, is seldom profitable, not just from experience, but because all trade demands exact, accurate credit, not according to reason of state but according to reason of commerce, which is customary among private individuals, and sometimes brings profit, and sometimes loss.[140]

His Council of Commerce would be imitated by Denmark and Russia. As we have seen such councils were also known in England (Board of Trade), established at about the same time in France under Colbert, and slightly later in Habsburg Austria (*Kommerzkonsess*), Saxony and Prussia. Oxenstierna emphasized the virtues of manufacturing and capital-intensive activities to gain the nation value-added accruing from manufacturing, rather than primary production. Some branches needed state support, such as copper mining, while others were best left free from the fetters of the state.

Yet, even contemporaries lamented that 'no great kingdom, yea, even no good principality in the world has so few and worse cities than Sweden'.[141] In population terms, Sweden remained a relatively small country (geographically it was huge) with about 1.8 million people in 1750. Swedish urbanization rates lacked far behind the Netherlands or England. With less than 5 per cent of its population located in big cities (of more than 10,000 inhabitants), Sweden shared the fate of Germany, Poland and Ireland.[142] But as we have seen in the introduction (Chapter 1) scholars have cast doubt upon defining comparative historical urbanization through the number of people living in *very big* cities (of 10,000 inhabitants or more), as this measure clearly does not capture urban dynamics in the northerly nations. In fact, Sweden's economy did not perform badly at all during the 18th century. In the 1720s–1780 period, living standards, real wages and nutrition as well as population levels increased again; some historians have even seen an agrarian revolution at work.[143] Real wages and nutrition levels gained further momentum after 1800, as did enclosures in Scania and agrarian exports, turning Sweden into a net exporter of grain by the 1820s. But in terms of per capita income, which had been comparable to England's before 1700 but stood at only about half the English levels by 1800, Sweden experienced relative economic decline after 1700.[144]

During Sweden's 'golden age' regional inequality increased. The Stockholm region and the iron manufacturing districts in Västmanland, Värmland and Örebro featured higher productivity levels and profited most from government policies directed at market improvement and economic development. 'More than 60 per cent of Sweden's manufacturing workers in 1750 were located in Stockholm'.[145] The first modern factories appeared in the textile sector during the 1830s and 1840s; but historians commonly locate Sweden's 'industrial revolution' much later, in the 1870s; the industrial sector was still too small to make a notable difference to GDP.[146] Magnusson points toward a comparatively 'porous' Swedish state and regionalized political economies (which assigned specific economic activities to specific towns, or specific economic regions) as a reason why politics failed to complete economic modernization. There was also a reversal from a rather liberal order before 1760 back towards a more absolutist political economy until the 1800s, after which government became even more proactive in promoting forces of the free market, and at the same time more directly interventionist, running railways, the postal system, reforming commercial and business law, the currency and constructing a competitive market – something that had been off the table before 1800.[147] Before the industrial age, Sweden's 'modernizing' sectors of the economy were too small to make a difference; traditional modes of production sufficed to cater for a moderately expanding Swedish economy.

Still, during its Age of Greatness, 1660–1720, Sweden had laid the foundations or enjoyed natural advantages that modern institutionalists associate with good governance and modern economic growth: useful knowledge, a literate workforce and community of letters operating at the forefront of contemporary Enlightenment values and ideology, good natural factor endowment (iron, copper, timber,[148] water), relatively high levels of individual economic freedom (especially a free peasantry, which was very uncommon for Europe in those days[149]), and a proactive state supporting capitalist development with an outlook towards non-absolutist economic governance. Sweden had captured increasing shares in the world market in some of those industries that later on proved crucial for the British industrial miracle. Contemporaries in the 1750s considered Swedes to be 'at present the most free people in the world', with at least one economist (Chydenius, 1729–1803) deploying an 'invisible hand' metaphor more than ten years prior to Adam Smith.[150] Market integration was well-developed: according to Heckscher, 'Sweden was made into one single market with regard to the most important group of commodities'.[151] Sweden had one of the most efficient administrations of the age, as reflected in the remarkably complete and comparatively efficient monitoring of population censuses and other economic data.[152] 'In the 1750s, Sweden enjoyed a political system that denied all real power to the monarch and placed sovereign power squarely in the hands of the four estates (nobles, clergy, burghers, and peasants), which met at a *riksdag* every third year'.[153] During the 19th and 20th centuries, Sweden swiftly moved into the club of the richest nations, developing signature features of a much-admired modern welfare state after the Second World War.[154] In this the country built on centuries worth of 'Schumpeterian' activities.

On silver rocks, Schumpeterian states and a 'culture of growth': early modern industrial Germany, 1400s–1900s

Prior to its dissolution in 1806, the loose confederation known as the Holy Roman Empire had achieved some degree of cooperation in key political matters, but monetary and market integration were not sustained prior to the 19th century and perhaps represented key hindrances to economic development.[155] The Germanies sported a huge variety of economic regions, with considerable variations in productivity and wealth, and in the same way as Switzerland, there were some areas, for instance in Saxony and Prussia, that would have compared favourably with England, with others remaining agrarian, feudal and backward until the 20th century.[156] The empire's north-west and south tended to have higher urbanization levels and living standards and productivity far outpacing regions east of the River Elbe; this economic morphology did not vanish with industrialization.[157]

Some argue that early modern German industrial wealth built upon a silver rock;[158] but that is a simplification (with some truth in it). There was a long history of manufacturing in the German-speaking lands, and temporal authority had played a proactive role in shaping industrial policy and capitalism since the late Middle Ages. Industrial regions had emerged all across the Empire since the 14th century if not earlier, especially around bigger trading emporia such as Augsburg, Nuremberg or Frankfurt-am-Main. Merchant capital came come to control manufacturing through the decentralized putting-out system (*Verlag*) which had spread out into the adjacent countryside around such trading hubs.[159] Such *Verleger* (putting-out merchants), called since the 17th century *Kapitalisten* (capitalists), also engaged in bigger ventures, as part of consortia and firms or *Handelsgesellschaften*[160] often running large-scale mining, smelting and other enterprises of the manufactory type. This business form was known from the Middle Ages and is beautifully captured in Dürer's watercolour of a wire manufactory or mill, the type of enterprise used by Adam Smith to illustrate the wealth of nations through division of labour (Figure 8.9). Such manufactories were widely known in textile and metal working, coach making (Sombart, Marx); but some areas were especially prone to capital concentration employing more modern technology and complex sequences of production which required considerable capital investment and government attention, such as mining, metallurgy and smelting. Especially characteristic of large-scale business concentration was the *Saigerverfahren* or Saiger process, where central European argentiferous copper deposits were first mined and then separated into their components of pure silver and copper using a complex series of chemical-metallurgical processes and prodigious amounts of lead imported from as far away as Poland or England. As the areas around Nuremberg became progressively deforested and timber as a vital energy source became dearer, from the 1470s the industry moved north into the Thuringian Forest and the Saxon lands, including the County of Mansfeld, where it made a profound imprint on Luther's economic mind. This area was marked by a high degree of commercialization, marketization and integration into wider interregional, even proto-global, trade circuits and webs of exchange.[161]

It is this long history and experience with manufacturing industry, plus a peculiar form of organizing state and polity that emerged after the Peace of Westphalia (1648), which created lasting institutional foundations for economic development in the centuries after the Thirty Years War (1618–48). Until the later 18th century, the Holy Roman Empire did not as much lag behind the north–western European average in terms of real wages and urbanization; and the transition towards industrialization was smoother and happened about two or three decades earlier than previous narratives would suggest (see Chapter 1).[162] Quantifications are difficult, especially for industrial output and employment. Home industry or putting-out organized under the *Verlag* system loomed large, but we should not underestimate the contributions made by bigger enterprise, especially the manufactories. Some of the larger *Verlag* businesses combined decentralized or 'putting-out' for basic tasks, while centralizing the more delicate finishing processes within a manufactory, where production steps could be better managed and supervised. States and temporal authorities proactively supported this manufactural oeconomy.

In his classic *Capitalism, Socialism and Democracy* (1942) Schumpeter argued that it was specifically during capitalism's later stages that people would call for the state to interfere with the economic process when things went wrong, either by direct investment (for example when large industry was failing and profit rates falling), or to curb capitalism's worst excesses such as cartelization and monopoly.[163] We can see a similar rationale at work within central European silver mining, a leading sector since the Middle Ages, during its late phases when moving into diminishing marginal returns followed by absolute decline, resulting in near complete displacement from world markets. This happened in the Tyrolean industry after 1500; in Saxony after the 1530s. In the Tyrol there was a clear trend towards business concentration, measured in output per *Gewerke* (or individual small firm active in mining), which gives us a rough proxy for the industry's capital coefficient. This coefficient increased steadily, 1470–1540, especially after Hispano-American silver made itself felt on the European (and global) market. As the 15th century drew to a close, more and more shares in silver mining were concentrated within the hands of big firms of Augsburg and Nuremberg origin, notably Fugger and Welser,[164] super-companies controlling significant chunks of the global spice and silver trades, financing the imperial election of 1519 as well as Portuguese overseas expansion around Africa and the Indian Ocean basin, 1470s–1520s. By the 1550s the Tyrolean silver mines had become all but exhausted, and the number of independent *Gewerken* at Schwaz sunk to four (meaning that the rest of the silver industry was controlled by large corporations). Copper also became less profitable. By the late 1550s the state took over ownership, management and production, through the *Österreichischen Berg- und Schmelzwerkshandel*. The Archdukes were now in active competition with the Fuggers, and the state could draw on a well-trained administration. As in other mining regions witnessing similarly declining productivity levels around the time (Saxony, Erz Mountains), the state's eye was not so much on profitability and more cast upon keeping the industry alive and the local population employed.[165]

According to Tyrolean mining expert Joseph von Sperges (1725–91), the key features of the mining industry were industriousness, high levels of technology and useful knowledge, and the capacity and willingness to take risk.[166] Anyone sifting through Agricola's *De Re Metallica*, marvelling at the engravings of machines and tools, whims and windlasses, *Wasserkünste*, pumps, water wheels, lathes, rag and chain pumps, smelting ovens and other high-tech implements used in mining and smelting will immediately realize how mining not only required a high capital coefficient, but also lots of technological sophistication and expert skill.[167] The high capital coefficient in the industry was a clear marker of capitalist business, with a focus on technological efficiency and division of labour; capital and labour were clearly separated. In combination this makes for a unique economic morphology of

Table 8.1: Administrative offices and positions in mining in a typical mining district (*Montanrevier*)

	Bergamptmann	Mining prefect
Magister Metallicorum	Bergmeister	Bergmeister
Scriba Magister Metallicorum	Bergmeister's schreiber	Bergmeister's clerk
Jurati	Geschwornen	Jurates or jurors
Publicus Signator	Gemeiner sigler	Notary
Decumanus	Zehender	Tithe gatherer
Distributor	Aussteiler	Cashier
Scriba partium	Gegenschreiber	Share clerk
Scriba fodinarum	Bergschreiber	Mining clerk

Source: Reproduced from Hoover's translation of Agricola's *De Re Metallica*

any such mining region, be that the Alps, the Harz Mountains, the Vosges or the Saxon-Bohemian Erz Mountains, regions usually located within the empire.[168] Mining regions produced some of the grand socio-economic utopias; consider Michael Gaismair's *Tyrolean Constitution* (1526), or modern writings on money and exchange as manifested in the writings of the Saxon *Münzstreit* of 1530–31 which we studied in Chapter 5; it was a mining region where the first heretic who wasn't burnt at the stake but survived successfully started a millennial religious schism (Dr Luther).

The morphology of mining regions required complex social, legal and economic set-ups, specialized bureaucracies and high degrees of literacy, as shown in Tables 8.1 and 8.2.

These point towards increasingly specialized, institutionalized and formalized processes of production suggesting above-average income and productivity levels.[169] A culture of writing was especially crucial, as Agricola argued:

Indeed, in our own days, not a few miners, persuaded by old women's tales, have re-opened deserted shafts and lost their time and trouble. Therefore, to prevent future generations from being led to act in such a way, it is advisable to set down in writing the reason why the digging of each shaft or tunnel has been abandoned, just as it is agreed was once done at Freiberg [a major Saxon mining town], when the shafts were deserted on account of the great inrush of water.[170]

While mining is technically classified as an extractive industry (meaning it can potentially be booked, in national income accounting terms, to the primary rather than the secondary sector), in 16th-century Germany

Table 8.2: Further professions to be found in mining

Praefectus fodinae *Praefectus cuniculi*	*Steiger*	Manager of the mine Manager of the tunnel
Praeses fodinae *Praeses cuniculi*	*Schichtmeister*	Foreman of the mine Foreman of the tunnel
Fossores	*Berghauer*	Miners or digger
Ingestores	*Berganschlagen*	Shovellers
Vectarii	*Hespeler*	Lever workers (windlass men)
Discretores	*Ertzpucher*	Sorters
Lotores	*Wescher und seiffner*	Washers, buddlers, sifters and so on
Excoctores	*Schmeltzer*	Smelters
Purgator Argenti	*Silber brenner*	Silver refiner
Magister Monetariorum	*Müntzmeister*	Master of the Mint
Monetarius	*Müntzer*	Coiner
Area fodinarum	*Masse*	Meer
Area Capitis Fodinarum	*Fundgrube*	Head meer
Demensum	*Lehen*	Measure

Source: Reproduced from Hoover's translation of Agricola's *De Re Metallica*

it sported those transformative forwards, backwards and lateral linkages commonly known as Schumpeterian. Linkages include the demand for cutting-edge technology, iron and other high-powered industry, the coining of money, and related transport, hospitality, commerce and other service-sector activities that would relocate to mining regions during a boom period, potentially engineering transformative changes to the social and economic fabric. Mining regions were *marginal* regions in the classification suggested by Pollard,[171] geographically, climatically, economically. Soil conditions often did not allow intensive arable farming, making these regions particularly dependent upon long-distance trade. They were marked by a prevalence of wage labour and shift work; according to the Tyrolean *Schwazer Bergrecht*, eight-hour shifts were the norm in Tyrol; Agricola, in *De Re Metallica*, had the miners' working day running at seven-hour shifts separated by one hour of shift change, thus $3 \times 7 + 3 = 24$ hours). Miners secured payment for old age and sickness and other special arrangements. Mining regions resembled later post–Second World War *Sonderwirtschaftszonen* (special economic areas with special rights, privileges and freedoms).[172] The focus was on large-scale external finance, the cutting-edge technology employed, profit-oriented rentier investment, separation of capital and labour, their connection and integration into proto-global trading and payment circuits; and a generally strong connection between state and private enterprise interests and their tendency to form cartels and monopolies. These mining regions were at the heart of contemporary capitalism.[173] In 1533, working capital advanced to the *Saigerhändler* – big Nuremberg and Augsburg consortia financing the central European smelting business usually via the Leipzig and Naumburg fairs – amounted to the tune of *c.*380,000 florins, a formidable sum.[174] When the central European copper market went through crisis in 1527/ 28 – an aggregate demand shock induced by sinking prices and stagnant sales threatening the livelihood of many a big mining and smelting firm – Leipzig merchants reacted by trying to form a cartel with support by the Saxon duke.[175] All these match the definitional criteria for 'commercial capitalism'[176] in the same way as they do Schumpeter's age of decadence or late capitalism.[177]

Georg Agricola summarized the economic significance of mining (and related businesses including smelting and refining) thus:

> Without doubt, none of the arts is older than agriculture, but that of the metals is not less ancient; in fact they are at least equal […], for no mortal man ever tilled a field without implements. In truth, in all the works of agriculture, as in the other arts, implements are used which are made from metals, or which could not be made without the use of metals; for this reason the metals are of the greatest necessity to man. When an art is so poor that it lacks metals, it is not of much importance, for nothing is made without tools. Besides, of all ways whereby great wealth is acquired by good and honest means, none is more advantageous than mining; for although from fields which are well tilled (not to mention other things) we derive rich yields, yet we obtain richer products from mines; in fact, one mine is often much more beneficial to us than many fields. For this reason we learn from the history of nearly all ages that very many men have been made rich by the mines, and the fortunes of many kings have been much amplified thereby.[178]

In Saxony, master smelters were recruited under Elector Augustus of Saxony (1526–86) from Tyrol, Prague and Salzburg; cotton and fustian weavers from the Netherlands. Since the Middle Ages, many other industries shaped up across the German-speaking lands, often under the auspices of state. By the 1560s the Saxon Electors had assembled considerable amounts of useful items in their 'curiosity cabinet' or *Kunstkammer*, whose collecting principles followed the accumulation of technological knowledge.[179] In 1710 the Meissner *Porzellanmanufaktur* was founded, attaining proverbial fame for its porcelain widely beyond Saxony. Under Elector Friedrich

Augustus II (also King Augustus III of Poland, 1696–1763) and during the post-1763 *rétablissement* programme of economic recovery from the Seven Years War the number of state-run manufactories and enterprises considerably increased.[180] The entrepreneurial state, embodied in the *Landes-, Ökonomie- und Kommerziendeputation*, awarded premiums on good piecework, encouraged immigration of skilled workers and the erection of muster workshops and manufactories, where other craftsmen and entrepreneurs could pick up best practice and technological 'hacks'. After 1750 state administration also intensified its activity in road building, surveillance and other infrastructural investment.

A country without manufacturing was like a body without life, and manufactures were the true gold and silver mines of the Prussian lands, noted Friedrich Wilhelm (1688–1740), elector in Brandenburg and king in Prussia, who took a personal interest in industrial policy, adding his handwritten comments and observations to specific files, deeds and other policy documents.[181] The 1720s saw a renewed interest by the Prussian state, through a mix of protectionist measures (prohibiting, for instance, the export of raw wool) and nudges, premiums and export bounties, thorough quality controls and other encouragements specifically targeting key branches of manufacturing. Interest-free loans were given to domestic producers to the value of raw wool that had remained unsold, in order for it to be manufactured and exported at competitive prices. Prussia also lobbied the British government, in 1719–20, through its economic attaché at London, to abolish plans prohibiting the import of foreign linens. These would have dealt a painful blow to Silesian and other Prussian linen-exporting regions, whose major foreign markets included the British plantations. In 1728 the Prussian ambassador in London was asked to produce a systematic report about the revived Scottish and Irish linen industries, with special care taken in documenting the nature and quality of raw materials used (Scots imported most of their flax either through Holland or directly from Baltic ports such as Königsberg, Narva or Riga).[182] Under Frederick II 'the Great' (r 1740–86), Prussia remained an important supplier of cheap linens to the British Empire, as noted by Prussian ambassadors in London.[183] Under Frederick, Prussia experienced some moderate industrial growth. The population doubled; urbanization rates (measured using a threshold of 5,000 inhabitants) stagnated overall, but nearly doubled for the *Kurmark* – the core area around the capital Berlin (from about 7 to 12 per cent), outpacing the German average; tax revenue tripled.[184] Manufacturing substantially expanded. Manufactories were particularly dynamic. The Prussian edict of Potsdam 1685 had explicitly encouraged the immigration of Huguenot and other religious refugees.[185] Frederick III/I (1657–1713), Elector of Brandenburg and duke, later king, in Prussia, had collected first-hand experience of successful economic transformation during his visits to the Netherlands. Major commercial and industrial ventures were promoted by the Prussian state in Berlin and the western provinces, including the giant arms manufactory of Splitgerber & Daum founded in 1712. Under Frederick II 'the Great' the Prussian army doubled in size from 39,000 to nearly 80,000. Through its demand for armour, cannon, cannon balls, muskets, munitions and uniforms, the state was not only a major customer for Prussia's own industry, but also promoter of 'useful knowledge' and technology hub.[186] Cameralist political economy was established in 1727 as a university discipline at the enlightened Prussian university of Halle where Johann Peter von Ludewig delivered his programmatic inaugural lecture on the 'new oeconomic profession', a sketch of Prussia's future progress (*Von der Neuen Oeconomie Profession*, 1727).[187]

Claims that 'Cameralist theory was rarely translated into effective practice', or that 'German territorial governments had neither the will nor the power to achieve serious economic innovations',[188] are at odds with both the archival evidence *and* the history of political economy. Since the times of the Great Elector Frederick Wilhelm (1620–88) the Prussian state had proactively interfered with the economy, applying cameralist theories by the rule book. While such investments did not necessarily have to pay off immediately, their long-term consequences were more considerable. Prussia became one of the strongest industrial powers on the continent during the 19th century. Under Frederick the Great, it had been the silk and textile industries that had received particular attention,[189] but policies extended to general market development and empowering capitalism across the board. In 1662–69 the Frederick-Wilhelm Canal had been built, an attempt at connecting Silesia with the North Sea. In 1747 the second Finow Canal was opened by Frederick II, improving water-borne traffic on Prussia's natural waterways (Havel, Oder) and further opening up Silesia to the Atlantic economy. In the same year commenced the drainage of the Oderbruch, a huge swampland along the river Oder, which ultimately yielded Prussia the conquest of another 'province without war'.[190] When Frederick died in 1786, about 80 per cent of canals in the Holy Roman Empire were located in Prussia. Their locks matched state-of-the-art hydraulic engineering standards and attracted the praise of contemporaries.[191] Frederick had been acutely aware of Prussia's underdevelopment. He acknowledged the need for robust statistics and the improvement of useful knowledge to support nascent industries and put planning for the oeconomic future upon safer grounds.[192] In 1747 he ordered trade statistics to be produced for the *Kurmark*.[193] The aim was to get a sense of the inflow and outflow of capital and goods. Such trade statistics had been compiled for England since 1694/96, and Ireland from 1696; in Scotland they were first introduced in 1755.[194] Regardless of how (in)inaccurate such *Statistik* seems from a modern scientific point of view,[195] they still testify to a fundamental gestalt switch in the understanding of the management of the wealth of nations, providing the groundwork for 19th- and 20th-century processes of capitalist transformation. Under Frederick II, the chief benefactors of government attention were the woollen, cotton and silk manufactories.[196] More than any other type of productive organization, they were geared towards capturing foreign markets.[197] Technology transfer was encouraged, as was the recruitment of foreigners, including master spinsters and weavers with specialist knowledge. Industrial policy included the foundation of the University of Halle in 1694, a Prussian Academy of Sciences (1700), and enterprises that were capital-intensive and required particularly high levels of technical expertise, such as gold and silver making, French hats, silk, clock-making, high-quality textiles such as Gobelin tapestry, glass and porcelain.[198]

When Frederick II (1712–86) took to the throne in 1740, the Prussian province of Minden-Ravensberg in the west of Germany had been *importing* yarn and linen clothes to the tune of 850,000 thalers per annum. At the time of his death during the 1780s it *exported* 327,000 thalers' worth of linen manufactures per year; a classic textbook story of successful import substitution.[199] The Electoral Marche (*Kurmark*) had in the later 17th century been a net exporter of grain; towards the 1770s 14,000 *wispel*[200] of wheat, 62,000 *wispel* of rye, 21,200 *wispel* of barley and 13,600 *wispel* of oats were *imported* every year.[201] This reverse-engineered import substitution for foodstuffs is another tell-tale sign of the type of structural-economic change we commonly associate with (the early beginnings of) modern economic development. Still, most branches of the Prussian economy only grew in line with population levels between *c.*1740 and 1800; Prussian per capita GDP remained comparatively low and stagnant. On a regional level economic change was more visible. The Duchy of Minden-Ravensberg and the Grafschaft Mark, both western provinces, became leading iron and steel producers of their time. Silesia's iron industry, another leading industry, seems to have stood up well in terms of international competitivity and productivity.[202] In the western provinces of Prussia the putting-out system was more common, while large manufactories clustered in the central provinces, around the focal point and capital city of Berlin.[203] Towards the mid-1790s, three quarters of Prussian exports consisted of manufactures. Silesian linen exports increased by four fifths between 1740 and 1786.[204] Similar to Scotland's and Ireland's linen industries, Prussia's industry expanded two to three times faster than population levels. This was reflected in a gradually industrializing balance of trade.

Yet, before the 1800s Prussian urbanization figures remained flat, at 10 or 11 per cent around 1740 and 12 per cent during the 1780s, measured in terms of cities of more than 5,000 inhabitants; suggesting no major change in tack. When benchmarked using the larger de Vriesian threshold (10,000), Prussian urbanization in 1801 stood at 8 per cent, compared to 20 per cent for England, 17 per cent in Scotland and 18 per cent for Flanders, and still a staggering 28 per cent for the Netherlands, the 'first modern economy'.[205] One factor that put a decisive break upon Prussian economic development was serfdom and the demesne system (manorial economy). Extending far into east–central Europe where more restrictive feudal modes of production prevailed, the manorial system kept personal freedom, entrepreneurial drive and productivity low.[206] This had an impact on the fiscal morphology of state: Whereas the share of non-tax state revenue stood at about 4–6 per cent in the case of Sweden or France towards the end of the 18th century, and in Britain it was at an all-time low of 2 per cent, in states such as the Habsburg monarchy, Hesse and Prussia, it usually constituted about 50 per cent. In Prussia during the second half of the 18th century, indirect taxes contributed only 27 per cent to government revenue; in Britain the figure was 80 per cent.[207] In Prussia as well as many other territorial states of the empire the nobility had to be consulted for extraordinary levies and consequently blocked any princely infringements on their hereditary privileges and tax exemptions; state revenue and political wiggle-room substantially drew upon the princely chest or 'treasure' as the title of an influential economic bestseller written in the 1680s bears out: Wilhelm von Schröder's *Fürstliche Schatz- und Rentkammer* (1686).[208] Prussian state capacity thus defined remained comparatively weak.[209] This would have put limits on what industrial policy could achieve on the ground. But 'On the whole, Prussia in the 1780s was a much more developed country than it had been just a few decades before'.[210]

More important even were the foundations laid: in terms of useful knowledge, a focus on public policy promoting a conscious approach directed at transforming oeconomy, on which post-1830 processes of import substitution industrialization could comfortably rest. These had shaped up – conceptually, semantically, practically – in the five or six centuries preceding industrialization, in the German-speaking lands as well as elsewhere; contributing to an emerging body of theory and increasingly practicable and hands-on understanding of how the wealth of nations could be *managed*, even created in the first place.

State Capacity and Capitalism from Cain to Keynes: Money, Markets and Manufacturing

Rather than summarizing the argument presented in previous chapters I would like to offer a number of observations that emerge from the discussion and wider context of the book.

First of all, what we commonly take as the vanguard or mainstream elements of modern political economy (often emanating from the French physiocrats and Scottish Enlightenment) represent rather an exceptional offshoot from a larger common ground of political economy, known by its misnomers such as 'mercantilism' or, less frequently, 'cameralism'. These are unhappy labels in any case, but probably too useful to be easily got rid of. I have discussed examples of such 'cameralist' – a second-order misnomer retained in the present work mostly for convenience and clarity – viewpoints on political oeconomies of statecraft and state capacity as seen through the lens of money, markets and manufacturing capitalism; but the problems and policies analysed in the previous pages have a much broader remit transcending the narrow boundaries framed by disciplinary labels such as scholasticism, bullionism, mercantilism, cameralism, physiocracy, classical liberalism and Historical School to name but the most common schools in pre-1850 economic thought.

Some of the questions discussed in the previous chapters have also informed narratives on global historical economic development: how does a country grow rich? Why do some nations develop faster over time than others? Why did the first industrial revolution occur in the West? While certainly not suggesting that the political economies I have discussed were the *reason* why Europe – or better: some regions in Europe – forged ahead faster than other world regions, utilizing key tools of capitalism: money, markets and manufacturing – the German-speaking countries showed no radical differences in market cultures and monetary design compared to the rest of

Europe. Markets and money were principally known and organized along similar lines in other world regions, often for centuries before the Industrial Revolution.[1] Coined money had emerged independently in separate parts of the globe since the seventh century BC, without much evidence of prior deep-level commercial interaction between these regions. Markets, too, seem to have been ubiquitous in human history (for millennia), and capitalist enterprise was known in medieval and early modern India and South-East Asia, and the Arab-speaking worlds, too.[2] In the German-speaking lands and most other parts of Europe (bar England) 'medieval' monetary theories – based on a metallic or commodity standard of money – survived unscathed into the 19th century.[3] The shared culture of markets and deep history of manufacturing empowered later catch-up transitions to modern industrial capitalism swiftly after the UK had set the course. The 14th to 19th centuries witnessed key conceptualizations and reconceptualizations of markets, money and manufacturing, especially of what could be done with money to improve economic circulation and domestic capital formation, pointing towards a gradually more dynamic view of economy – the *cameralist* vision of economic development that I have tried to reconstruct in previous chapters.

The broader questions about the origins of state, its ramifications regarding rulership, oeconomic statecraft and state capacity were neither peculiarly German nor raised exclusively during the early modern age. They have appeared to us since the first grand theological narratives of the 'Axial Age' and have accompanied modern historians', sociologists', economists', anthropologists', political scientists' and many other discourses about whether and to what extent 'economics' and its rationales are in line with higher-order moral sentiments, that is, those qualities that make us human.[4] In the Old Testament, Cain, a farmer, upon killing his brother Abel (a herdsman), fell from grace, survived, was put under special protection and gave rise, in the seventh generation, to Tubal-Cain, a bronze- or blacksmith; Cain thus became the forefather of industry (Genesis 4:22) and, according to an obviously popular early modern interpretation, of kingship, tyranny and humans' will to rule and subdue others.[5] The profoundly negative ontological connection found in the story between toil (industry; labour 'by the sweat of thy brow'), violence and a fall from grace repeats a pattern known from Genesis 3:19. The same with kingship and modern statehood: According to the Old Testament (1 Samuel 8) the origins of the modern state lay in anarchy. Anarchy was the consequence of the Israelites' fall from grace (which happened quite regularly), turning away from God (as they habitually did). Samuel gets old. His sons succeed as judges. But they lack good behaviour and attitude. Instead they prove to be corrupt: 'Then all the elders of Israel gathered together and came to Samuel at Ramah, and said to him, "You are old and your sons do not follow in your ways; appoint for us, then, a king to govern us, *like other nations*"' (1 Samuel 8:4–5, my emphasis).

Samuel consults with God who is not amused. He asks Samuel to give his fellow Israelites a list of things that a king would do to them, none of which were in the least desirable, and which have, in modern narratives, become connected to the rise of the state:

> he will take your sons and appoint them to his chariots and to be his horsemen, and to run before his chariots; and he will appoint for himself commanders of thousands and commanders of fifties, and some to plough his ground and to reap his harvest, and to make his implements of war and the equipment of his chariots. He will take your daughters to be perfumers and cooks and bakers. He will take the best of your fields and vineyards and olive orchards and give them to his courtiers. He will take one-tenth of your grain and of your vineyards and give it to his officers and his courtiers. He will take your male and female slaves, and the best of your cattle and donkeys, and put them to his work. He will take one-tenth of your flocks, and you shall be his slaves. (1 Samuel 8:11–17)

This is a famous classical pessimistic view on the origins of state representing a fall from grace; a popular reading of history shared by social scientists to the present day.[6] Indeed, in early modern Europe, Old Testament passages such as Samuel, Chronicles and Kings continued to be used as templates for government, good and bad; as advice for rulers and kings.[7] The postmodern world view has adopted the negative origin myth of state and markets provided in the Old Testament (shared by Marxists and neoliberals alike): states tax and enslave people, and wage war. States 'order' societies by classifying, sorting and coercing people, plants and animals with a view towards optimizing resource extraction.[8] The same goes for capitalism.[9] State and capitalism seem almost naturally or symbiotically connected. But in a deep-history time span, states and empires appear as a fairly recent form of social organization; throughout most of human history people seemingly tried to avoid states.[10] With states came high-powered economic organization, rational management, sedentary agriculture, cities, taxation, money, exploitation and enslavement – all important for economic development, too. From a Marxist perspective, the modern (post-1400) state contributed to rising levels of inequality and exploitation. Recent non-Marxist scholarship has tended to confirm this (more tricky is, however, the proof that there was *causation* between the two).[11] Others would argue that states can be hemmed in by capitalism, commitment and counterforce, because in times 'when dynastic rulers pursued war for its own sake, the economic system based on interest, namely capitalism, might usefully constrain them'.[12] A growing literature has assumed that states, by protecting property rights, providing the 'right' or 'inclusive' political and economic institutions, may contribute to business conditions and human lives that improve over time. By this process state capacity (and credible commitment) is measured through levels of comparative taxation and public expenditure, eventually (after the 19th century) giving rise to welfare and developmental states, increased living standards and economic development – but as by-products, not intentional processes of state formation. States that don't live up to these criteria are then classed as failures.[13]

In Marx's *Capital*, European development was based on money morphing labour and physical resources into capital. From this emerged an eternal spiral of value-added and profit upon profit (*Mehrwert*) using markets. But before this spiral could be set in motion, capital had to be accumulated in the first place. In Marx's model this task was achieved by mercantilism as the ruling classes' economic ideology during the period of early bourgeois (=early modern) capitalism. In his philosophical deliberations (*Economic Possibilities for our Grandchildren*, 1930) Keynes argued that the main brake on human development for millennia had been a 'slow rate of progress', due 'to the remarkable absence of important technical improvements and to the failure of capital to accumulate'. Downplaying the role of technological change since the invention of agriculture, metallurgy and other key breakthroughs that had taken place around the eighth millennium BC,[14] Keynes continued:

> The modern age opened ... with the accumulation of capital which began in the sixteenth century. ... this was initially due to the rise of prices, and the profits to which that led, which resulted from the treasure of gold and silver which Spain brought from the New World into the Old. From that time until to-day the power of accumulation by compound interest, which seems to have been sleeping for many generations, was re-born and renewed its strength. And the power of compound interest over two hundred years is such as to stagger the imagination.[15]

The strategies of monetary, market and manufacturing regulation studied in the previous chapters supported this process of capital accumulation *cum* state formation. Spain had deindustrialized in the 16th century because of silver's overabundance.[16] Just at the time when the Hispano-American silver flood petered out around 1600, the economic metaphor of manufacturing as the true gold/silver mine of the nation appeared in European political economy. Most European states had no native silver mines and accordingly tried to develop native industries to attract money from abroad. Such 'mercantilist' policies were marked out by Marx in the first volume of *Capital*, reflecting a drive to exploit domestic workers and foreign people through rapacious policies of expropriation, colonialization and servitude, producing global misery for workers, slaves and other subalterns alike, driving capital formation through 'primitive' or original accumulation. In Chapters 4 to 8 I have tried to explain how cameralist strategies of market, monetary and velocity management helped continental states cope with potential shortfalls or ceilings on the amount of circulating money, thus widening the possibilities for capital formation and economic development through state consolidation, market development and industrial policy.

Markets were needed for money to circulate. Historically we cannot think of markets without the state, or the state without markets. Markets were not neutral, in the sense of autonomous entities working according to their own mechanisms based on individual actors making completely autonomous decisions. They were physical places closely circumscribed by spatial arrangements and specifically attuned socio-chronological rules aimed at optimizing monetary and goods flows thus empowering economic development (see Chapter 4). Nor was money neutral. It was an instrument of state, principally invented to turn self-sufficient economic actors into productive taxpayers;[17] but a by-product, again, was economic development. Money's function as a means of exchange and facilitator of transactions – an argument found in political economy writings from Aristotle to Jevons's classic textbook on money[18] – was probably secondary to its primary set-up as a tool of state. Some actors had preferential access to money and markets and coveted knowledge: information on money's values and coins' purchasing power they could use in ways potentially harmful to the 'common good'. States adopted strategies to curb these activities and use money as a dynamic tool. Circulation and velocity represented themes so common in early modern political economy that we almost lost sense of it.

Lastly: manufacturing and capitalism. Historians' debates often evolve around the question of when and where capitalism 'originated', with special reference to Marx's concept of original or 'primitive' accumulation as the early modern start-up phase for the spiral that fuelled post-1800 industrial capitalism: in agriculture, commerce or industry.[19] Apart from the fact that such 'origin debates' are not always useful and fruitful, as Sombart noted long time ago,[20] we can find capitalist forms of enterprise in practically all branches of medieval and early modern economy, from agriculture (demesne, large agrarian estates), commerce (in particular inter-oceanic and later colonial trade, which Braudel once famously called 'capitalism on home ground'[21]), finance (anyway) to industry – during practically all ages, and in most European regions. Capitalism flourished in the economic hothouses of the late medieval Italian city states, in the vicinity of Upper German finance and trading *monopoleis* such as Augsburg and Nuremberg in the age of Luther and the Peasant War, in 16th- and 17th-century Flanders or the Netherlands as the 'first modern economy'; not to speak of post-1688 England and Scotland, regions that first experienced a commercial revolution (England after 1660; Scotland after 1740) before transiting into the first industrial nations in history.[22] Industrial capitalism, which turned global during the 19th and 20th centuries, represented just one among many variants of modern capitalism; but what we see emerging from the historical record is a long legacy of experiences with industrial capitalism in Europe since the later Middle Ages. This legacy was reflected in cameralist writings discussing how the emerging princely fiscal-military states should best deal with processes of capitalist accumulation, exploitation, rent-seeking and other social and economic asymmetry in the marketplace. Their answers were models of coordinated capitalism that we have encountered by ways of case study in the preceding chapters.

Since the Middle Ages and into the 1970s the origin of the wealth of nations was most clearly manifested in manufacturing and industry. Large industrial enterprise or manufactories were not a specifically European phenomenon, but also common in early modern India and elsewhere.[23] During the early modern period these were embodied in the large proto-factory enterprises called, in contemporary German palaver, *Manufakturen*. The German-speaking lands were littered with them, and they were built in the hundreds even in smaller territories and remote woodland locations, or in the countryside. We took a closer look at them in Chapters 7 and 8. Curiously, Smith's *Wealth of Nations* commenced exactly with such an example of workshop or *Manufaktur*. Smith didn't develop the argument to full potential, for instance by explaining modern or *Schumpeterian* growth: in Smith's model, manufacturing was the source of the wealth of nations chiefly because of the efficiencies gained by the principle of division of labour (Smithian growth); but very often manufactories represented much more than that. Entailing the productive *transformation* of matter, the *creation* of value using one's (or someone else's) brains, training, creativity, ingenuity and machines, to create more value than the initial inputs that had gone into it at the beginning, manufactories became the economic embodiment of the modern spirit of capitalism.[24]

Thus the 'cameralist' package represented a formidable toolbox for potentially transforming *oeconomy*, engineering capitalism and economic development, and the modern wealth of nations.

Notes

Chapter 1

[1] Adam Smith, *Wealth of nations*, Books I–III, ed. Andrew Skinner (London: Penguin Classics, 2003), p 508.

[2] See, for example, Albert O. Hirschman, *The passion and the interests: political arguments for capitalism before its triumph* (Princeton, NJ: Princeton University Press, 1977); Milton L. Myers, *The soul of modern economic man: ideas of self-interest – Thomas Hobbes to Adam Smith* (Chicago: University of Chicago Press, 1984); Istvan Hont, *Jealousy of trade: international competition and the nation state in historical perspective* (Cambridge, MA: Belknap, 2005); more recently, Koji Yamamoto, *Taming capitalism before its triumph: public service, distrust, and 'projecting' in early modern England* (Oxford: Oxford University Press, 2018). For historical perspectives on the role and nature of economic regulation, see, for example, Steven L. Kaplan, *The stakes of regulation: perspectives on* bread, politics and political economy *forty years later* (London: Anthem, 2015), pp 116–18; and for important changes during the age of Enlightenment, Steven L. Kaplan and Sophus A. Reinert (eds), *The economic turn: recasting political economy in Enlightenment Europe* (London: Anthem, 2019). An authoritative new survey of Enlightenment thought and capitalism through the lens of a protagonist can be found in Margaret Schabas and Carl Wennerlind (eds), *David Hume's political economy* (Abingdon: Routledge, 2005); Margaret Schabas and Carl Wennerlind, *A philosopher's economist: Hume and the rise of capitalism* (Chicago: University of Chicago Press, 2020); see also Margaret Schabas, *The natural origins of economics* (Chicago: University of Chicago Press, 2007), p 18; Christopher J. Berry, *The idea of commercial society in the Scottish Enlightenment* (Edinburgh: Edinburgh University Press, 2015), Ch. 7, esp. pp 198–201. From a philosophical viewpoint, see Lisa Herzog, *Inventing the market: Smith, Hegel, and political theory* (Oxford: Oxford University Press, 2013). Regarding continental visions of Enlightenment political economy, see Ere Nokkala and Nicholas B. Miller (eds), *Cameralism and the Enlightenment: happiness, governance, and reform in transnational perspective* (Abingdon: Routledge, 2020).

[3] Quentin Skinner, 'Ambrogio Lorenzetti's *Buon Governo* frescoes: two old questions, two new answers', *Journal of the Warburg and Courtauld Institutes* 62 (1999), 1–28; Sophus A. Reinert, *Translating empire: emulation and the origins of political economy* (Cambridge, MA: Harvard University Press, 2011), Introduction (esp. pp 5–8).

[4] Schabas and Wennerlind, *A philosopher's economist*, Introduction. The concept has been applied to earlier authors, such as William Temple; see a PhD dissertation defended at the European University Institute by Juha Haavisto, *William Temple's political and economic thought: a restauration view of [the] consequences of human nature* (2022); for Italy, see Sophus A. Reinert, *The academy of fisticuffs: political economy and commercial society in Enlightenment Italy* (Cambridge, MA: Harvard University Press, 2018).

5   A common confusion reduces mercantilism to rogue economic nationalism and 'zero-sum' games; see, for example, Albert O. Hirschman, *National power and the structure of foreign trade* (Berkeley: University of California Press, 1945); or, more recently, Joel Mokyr, *The enlightened economy: an economic history of Britain 1700–1850* (New Haven, CT: Yale University Press, 2009), Ch. 4. But see Moritz Isenmann (ed), *Merkantilismus? Wiederaufnahme einer Debatte* (Stuttgart: Franz Steiner, 2014); Philip J. Stern and Carl Wennerlind (eds), *Mercantilism reimagined: political economy in early modern Britain and its empire* (New York: Oxford University Press, 2014), Introduction, pp 3–22; Lars Magnusson, *The political economy of mercantilism* (Abingdon: Routledge, 2015). Earlier classics include Gustav von Schmoller, *The mercantile system and its historical significance* (New York: Macmillan, [1884] 1902); Eli F. Heckscher, *Der Merkantilismus*, 2 vols, transl. G. Mackenroth (Jena: Fischer, 1931); Jacob Viner, *Studies in the theory of international trade* (London: Allen & Unwin, 1937); essays collected in Donald C. Coleman (ed), *Revisions in mercantilism* (London: Methuen, 1969).

6   Paul Bairoch, *Economics and world history: myths and paradoxes* (Chicago: University of Chicago Press, 1995); Donald Sassoon, *The anxious triumph: a global history of capitalism, 1860–1914* (London: Penguin, 2020); Eric Helleiner, *The neomercantilists: a global intellectual history* (Ithaca, NY: Cornell University Press, 2021); for a deeper history, see Sophus A. Reinert and Robert Fredona, 'Political economy and the Medici', *Business History Review* 94:1 (2020), 125–77, special issue on 'Italy and the origins of capitalism'.

7   Friedrich List, *Das nationale System der politischen Ökonomie* (Stuttgart: Cotta, 1841), chapter on 'The Italians'; historicizing of List's work, see Hont, *Jealousy of trade*; Alexander Hamilton, *Report on the subject of manufactures* (Philadelphia, 1791); a new collection of essays: Harald Hagemann, Stephan Seiter and E. Wendler (eds), *The economic thought of Friedrich List* (Abingdon: Routledge, 2019).

8   James Steuart, *Principles of political oeconomy* (London: Millar and Cadell, 1767), Book I, p 150; Deborah Redman, 'Sir James Steuart's statesman revisited in light of the continental influence', *Scottish Journal of Political Economy* 43:1 (1996), 48–70; Ramón Tortajada (ed), *The economics of James Steuart* (London: Routledge, 2002); Anthony Brewer, 'James Steuart (James Denham-Steuart) (1712–1780)', in Gilbert Faccarello and Heinz D. Kurz (eds), *Handbook on the history of economic analysis* (Cheltenham: Edward Elgar, 2016), Vol I, pp 54–6.

9   Keith Tribe, 'Polizei, Staat und die Staatswissenschaften bei J.H.G. von Justi', in Bertram Schefold (ed), *Vademecum zu einem Klassiker des Kameralismus: Johann Heinrich Gottlob von Justi, Grundsätze der Policey-Wissenschaft* (Düsseldorf: Verlag Wirtschaft und Finanzen, 1993), pp 107–40. Steuart also had encounters with French economic thought known as 'Physiocracy'.

10 Edinburgh University Library, CC MS 2291/2, *Memoirs of the Life of Sir James Steuart-Denham of Coltness & Westshields Baronet*, p 42.

11 There are many possible conceptualizations and definitions of capitalism, which is a fundamentally contested concept; some would even argue that it is not a helpful construct at all. The literature is massive now; major recent syntheses and surveys include Larry Neal and Jeffrey G. Williamson (eds), *The Cambridge history of capitalism*, 2 vols (Cambridge: Cambridge University Press, 2015); Jürgen Kocka, *Capitalism: a short history* (Princeton, NJ: Princeton University Press, 2016); Kaveh Yazdani and Dilip Menon (eds), *Capitalisms: towards a global history* (New Delhi: Oxford University Press, 2020); Catherine Casson and Philipp Robinson Rössner (eds), *Evolutions of capitalism: historical perspectives, 1200–2000* (Bristol: Bristol University Press, 2022).

12 Patrick O'Brien, 'The nature and historical evolution of an exceptional fiscal state and its possible significance for the precocious commercialization and industrialization of the British economy from Cromwell to Nelson', *Economic History Review* 64:2 (2011), 408–46;

Patrick O'Brien, 'The formation of states and transitions to modern economies: England, Europe, and Asia compared', in Neal and Williamson (eds), *The Cambridge history of capitalism*, I, pp 357–402, at 363–4; Steven Pincus and James A. Robinson, 'Faire la guerre et faire l'État: Nouvelles perspectives sur l'essorde l'État développementaliste', *Annales* 71:1 (2016), 5–35.

[13] Prasannan Parthasarathi, *Why Europe grew rich and Asia did not: global economic divergence, 1600–1850* (Cambridge: Cambridge University Press, 2011); William J. Ashworth, *The Industrial Revolution: the state, knowledge and global trade* (London: Bloomsbury, 2017).

[14] Georg von Schanz, *Englische Handelspolitik gegen Ende des Mittelalters, mit besonderer Berücksichtigung des Zeitalters der beiden ersten Tudors, Heinrich VII. und Heinrich VIII*, 2 vols (Leipzig: Duncker & Humblot, 1881); Reinert and Fredona, 'Political economy and the Medici'; Kent Deng, 'One-off capitalism in Song China, 960–127 CE', in Yazdani and Menon (eds) *Capitalisms: towards a global history*, pp 227–50.

[15] See, for example, Robert C. Allen, 'The spread of manufacturing', in Neal and Williamson (eds), *The Cambridge history of capitalism*, II, pp 22–46.

[16] Mariana Mazzucato, *Mission economy: a moonshot guide to changing capitalism* (New York: Harper Collins, 2021).

[17] Erik S. Reinert, 'The role of the state in economic growth', *Journal of Economic Studies* 26:4/5 (1999), 268–326; reprinted and revised as Ch. 2 in Erik S. Reinert, *The visionary realism of German economics: from the Thirty Years' War to the Cold War*, ed. Rainer Kattel (London: Anthem, 2019).

[18] List, *Das nationale System der politischen Ökonomie*. For historical applications to British industrialization, see Parthasarathi, *Why Europe grew rich*; Peer Vries, 'Governing growth: a comparative analysis of the role of the state in the rise of the West', *Journal of World History* 13:1 (2002), 67–138; Peer Vries, *State, economy and the great divergence: Great Britain and China, 1680s–1850s* (London: Bloomsbury, 2015). Intellectual histories of the infant industry argument are discussed in Reinert, *Visionary realism*; Hont, *Jealousy of trade*; Reinert, *Translating empire*; Rosario Patalano and Sophus A. Reinert (eds), *Antonio Serra and the economics of good government* (Basingstoke: Palgrave Macmillan, 2016); and essays in Philipp Robinson Rössner (ed), *Economic growth and the origins of modern political economy: economic reasons of state, 1500–2000* (Abingdon: Routledge, 2016).

[19] Skinner, 'Ambrogio Lorenzetti's *Buon Governo* frescoes'.

[20] For the German peasant wars, which also evolved around the issue of bad money and coin debasement, tax conflicts and undue rent extractions, see Philipp Robinson Rössner, *Deflation – Devaluation – Rebellion: Geld im Zeitalter der Reformation* (Stuttgart: Franz Steiner, 2012), Ch. 4. For a general overview, see Jack A. Goldstone, *Revolution and rebellion in the early modern world* (Berkeley: University of California Press, 1993).

[21] But not into Harold James, *The war of words: a glossary of globalization* (New Haven, CT: Yale University Press, 2021).

[22] Peter B. Evans, Dietrich Rueschemeyer and Theda Skocpol (eds), *Bringing the state back in* (Cambridge: Cambridge University Press, 1999).

[23] O'Brien, 'The nature and historical evolution'; Ashworth, *The Industrial Revolution*; Parthasarathi, *Why Europe grew rich*; Vries, 'Governing growth'; Vries, *State, economy and the great divergence*; Norris A. Brisco, *The economic policy of Robert Walpole* (New York: Columbia University Press, 1907), Ch. 6 ('The industrial policy'), upon which has drawn Ha-Joon Chang, *Kicking away the ladder: development strategy in historical perspective* (London: Anthem, 2003).

[24] Most recent surveys, weighing the state's role against other factors, include Peer Vries, *Escaping poverty: the origins of modern economic growth* (Vienna: Vienna University Press/ Göttingen: V&R unipress, 2013); Mark Koyama and Jared Rubin, *How the world became rich: the historical origins of economic growth* (Cambridge: Polity, 2022).

[25] For early modern Germany, see Reinert, *Visionary realism*; British, French and German debates are captured in Hont, *Jealousy of trade*; Reinert, *Translating empire*. On 17th- and 18th-century Sweden, see Carl Wennerlind, 'The political economy of Sweden's *Age of Greatness*: Johan Risingh and the Hartlib Circle', in Rössner (ed) *Economic growth and the origins of modern political economy*, pp 156–86; Carl Wennerlind, 'Atlantis restored: natural knowledge and political economy in early modern Sweden', *American Historical Review*, forthcoming.

[26] Jean-Laurent Rosenthal and Roy Bin Wong, *Before and beyond divergence: the politics of economic change in China and Europe and Wong* (Cambridge, MA: Harvard University Press, 2011); John V.C. Nye, *War, wine, and taxes: the political economy of Anglo-French trade, 1689–1900* (Princeton, NJ: Princeton University Press, 2018); Mokyr, *Enlightened economy*.

[27] Reinert, *Visionary realism*; Mazzucato, *Mission economy*; Rainer Kattel and Mariana Mazzucato, 'Mission-oriented innovation policy and dynamic capabilities in the public sector', *Industrial and Corporate Change* 27:5 (2018), 787–801.

[28] Erik S. Reinert and Arno M. Daastøl, 'The other canon: the history of Renaissance economics', in Erik S. Reinert (ed), *Globalization, economic development and inequality: an alternative perspective* (Cheltenham: Edward Elgar, 2007), pp 21–70; a paper quoted in Joel Mokyr, *A culture of growth: the origins of the modern economy* (Princeton, NJ: Princeton University Press, 2018).

[29] Jack A. Goldstone, 'Efflorescences and economic growth in world history: rethinking the "rise of the West" and the Industrial Revolution', *Journal of World History* 13:2 (2002), 323–89; Gregory Clark, *A farewell to alms: a brief economic history of the world* (Princeton, NJ: Princeton University Press, 2007).

[30] Koyama and Rubin, *How the world became rich*.

[31] For example, Kenneth Pomeranz, *The great divergence: China, Europe, and the making of the modern world economy* (Princeton, NJ: Princeton University Press, 2000); Robert C. Allen, *The British Industrial Revolution in global perspective* (Cambridge: Cambridge University Press, 2009).

[32] For example, Douglass C. North, *Understanding the process of economic change* (Princeton, NJ: Princeton University Press, 2005); Avner Greif, *Institutions and the path to the modern economy: lessons from medieval trade* (Cambridge: Cambridge University Press, 2006); Deirdre N. McCloskey, *The bourgeois virtues: ethics for an age of commerce* (Chicago: University of Chicago Press, 2006); Avner Greif and Guido Tabellini, 'Cultural and institutional bifurcation: China and Europe compared', *American Economic Review* 100:2 (2010), 135–40; Mokyr, *Enlightened economy*; Mokyr, *Culture of growth*; Deirdre N. McCloskey, *Bourgeois dignity: why economics can't explain the modern world* (Chicago: University of Chicago Press, 2010); Deirdre N. McCloskey, *Bourgeois equality: how ideas, not capital or institutions, enriched the world* (Chicago: University of Chicago Press, 2016).

[33] For example, Eric Jones, *The European miracle: environments, economies and geopolitics in the history of Europe and Asia*, 3rd edn (Cambridge: Cambridge University Press, 2003); Philip T. Hoffman, *Why did Europe conquer the world?* (Princeton, NJ: Princeton University Press, 2015); Rosenthal and Wong, *Before and beyond divergence*.

[34] Parthasarathi, *Why Europe grew rich*; Vries, 'Governing growth'; Vries, *State, economy and the great divergence*.

[35] Roy Bin Wong, *China transformed: historical change and the limits of European experience* (Ithaca, NY: Cornell University Press, 1997); Andre Gunder Frank, *ReORIENT: global economy in the Asian age* (Berkeley: University of California Press, 1998). A different scope is in Victor Lieberman, *Strange parallels: Southeast Asia in global context, c.800–1830, vol 2: mainland mirrors: Europe, Japan, China, South Asia, and the islands* (Cambridge: Cambridge University Press, 2009).

[36] Especially Wong, *China transformed*; Pomeranz, *Great divergence*; works that consider the role of the state but mainly as a provider of institutions supporting markets and economic exchange.

[37] For example, Lisbet Koerner, *Linnaeus: nature and nation* (Cambridge, MA: Harvard University Press, 2001); Fredrik Albritton Jonsson, 'Climate change and the retreat of the Atlantic: the cameralist context of Pehr Kalm's voyage to North America 1748–51', *William and Mary Quarterly* 72:1 (2015), 99–126; Carl Wennerlind, 'The magnificent spruce: Anders Kempe and anarcho-cameralism in Sweden', *History of Political Economy* 53:3 (2021), 425–41.

[38] Albion W. Small, *The cameralists: the pioneers of German social polity* (Chicago: University of Chicago Press, 1909); Kurt Zielenziger, *Die alten deutschen Kameralisten: Ein Beitrag zur Geschichte der Nationalökonomie und zum Problem des Merkantilismus* (Jena: G. Fischer, 1914); Magdalene Humpert, *Bibliographie der Kameralwissenschaften* (Cologne: Kurt Schröder, 1937).

[39] For example, Mokyr, *Enlightened economy*, Ch. 4; Agnar Sandmo, *Economics evolving: a history of economic thought* (Princeton, NJ: Princeton University Press, 2011).

[40] Paul Warde, 'Sustainability, resources and the destiny of states in German cameralist thought', in K. Forrester and S. Smith (eds), *Nature, action and the future: the environment in political thought* (Cambridge: Cambridge University Press, 2018), pp 43–69.

[41] Otto Brunner, Werner Conze and Reinhart Koselleck (eds), *Geschichtliche Grundbegriffe: Historisches Lexikon zur politisch-sozialen Sprache in Deutschland*, 8 vols (Stuttgart: Klett Cotta, 1972–97); Reinhart Koselleck, *Historische Semantik und Begriffsgeschichte* (Stuttgart: Klett-Cotta, 1979); Ernst Müller and Falko Schmieder, *Begriffsgeschichte und historische Semantik: ein kritisches Kompendium*, 2nd edn (Frankfurt-am-Main: Suhrkamp, 2019); Margrit Pernau and Dominic Sachsenmaier (eds), *Global conceptual history: a reader* (London: Bloomsbury, 2020).

[42] As *partes pro toto*: Hont, *Jealousy of trade*; Quentin Skinner, *The foundations of modern political thought*, 2 vols (Cambridge: Cambridge University Press, 1978).

[43] Joseph A. Schumpeter, *History of economic analysis* (New York: Oxford University Press, 1954).

[44] Karl Pribram, *A history of economic reasoning* (Baltimore, MD: Johns Hopkins University Press, 1986).

[45] Mark Blaug, *Economic theory in retrospect*, 5th edn (Cambridge: Cambridge University Press, 2018).

[46] For example, Brandon Dupont, *The history of economic ideas: economic thought in contemporary context* (Abingdon: Routledge, 2017), p 2.

[47] Andre Wakefield, 'Butterfield's nightmare: the history of science as Disney history', *History and Technology: An International Journal* 30:3 (2014), 232–51.

[48] For example, Alessandro Stanziani, *Rules of exchange: French capitalism in comparative perspective, eighteenth to early twentieth centuries* (Cambridge: Cambridge University Press, 2012).

[49] For example, Lars Magnusson, *Mercantilism: the shaping of an economic language* (London: Routledge, 1994); Emily Erikson, *Trade and nation: how companies and politics reshaped economic thought* (New York: Columbia University Press, 2021).

[50] For example, Michael Perelman, *The invention of capitalism: classical political economy and the secret history of primitive accumulation* (Durham, NC: Duke University Press, 2000).

[51] For example, Bernard Harcourt, *The illusion of free markets: punishment and the myth of natural order* (Cambridge, MA: Harvard University Press, 2011).

[52] Exceptions include Florian Schui, *Early debates about industry: Voltaire and his contemporaries* (London: Macmillan, 2005); Magnusson, *Mercantilism* goes a bit in that direction.

53 I have borrowed this phrase from Wong, *China transformed*, a study that pays little attention to either ideas or concepts but defines historical political economy chiefly through politics.

54 Joel Kaye, *Economy and nature in the fourteenth century: money, market exchange, and the emergence of scientific thought* (Cambridge: Cambridge University Press, 2004).

55 For example, Nokkala and Miller, *Cameralism and the Enlightenment*; Heinz-Gerhard Haupt and Jürgen Kocka (eds), *Comparative and transnational history: central European approaches and new perspectives* (New York: Berghahn, 2009); Marten Seppel and Keith Tribe (eds), *Cameralism in practice: state administration and economy in early modern Europe* (Woodbridge: Boydell & Brewer, 2017); Andrew David Edwards, Peter Hill and Juan Neves-Sarriegui, 'Capitalism in global history', *Past & Present* 249:1 (2020), e1–e32, at e9–e13, available from: https://doi.org/10.1093/pastj/gtaa044; Edmond Smith, *Merchants: the community that shaped England's trade and empire, 1550–1650* (New Haven, CT: Yale University Press, 2021).

56 Michael J. Braddick, *State formation in early modern England, c.1550–1700* (Cambridge: Cambridge University Press, 2000); Julian Hoppit, *Britain's political economies: parliament and economic life, 1660–1800* (Cambridge: Cambridge University Press, 2017).

57 Walter Eucken, *Grundsätze der Wirtschaftspolitik*, 7th edn (Tübingen: Mohr Siebeck, [1952] 2004), pp 325–50; essays in Stern and Wennerlind, *Mercantilism reimagined*.

58 Jacob M. Price, 'Multilateralism and/or bilateralism: the settlement of British trade balances with "The North", *c.*1700', *Economic History Review* 14:2 (1961), 254–74; J. Sperling, 'The international payments mechanism in the seventeenth and eighteenth centuries', *Economic History Review* 14:3 (1962), 446–68; David Ormrod, *The rise of commercial empires: England and the Netherlands in the age of mercantilism, 1650–1770* (Cambridge: Cambridge University Press, 2003).

59 See, for example, Kapil Raj, *Relocating modern science: circulation and the construction of knowledge in South Asia and Europe, 1650–1900* (Basingstoke: Palgrave Macmillan, 2010); Felicia Gottmann, *Global trade, smuggling, and the making of economic liberalism: Asian textiles in France 1680–1760* (Basingstoke: Palgrave Macmillan, 2016); Felicia Gottmann (ed), *Commercial cosmopolitanism? Cross-cultural objects, spaces, and institutions in the early modern world* (Abingdon: Routledge, 2021).

60 Helleiner, *The neomercantilists*.

61 For example, Steve Murdoch, *Network north: Scottish kin, commercial and covert associations in northern Europe 1603–1746* (Leiden: Brill, 2005), pp 242–4; Allan Macinnes, *Union and empire: the making of the United Kingdom in 1707* (Cambridge: Cambridge University Press, 2009).

62 Nikolaus Olaf Siemaszko, *Das oberschlesische Eisenhüttenwesen 1741–1860: Ein regionaler Wachstumssektor* (Stuttgart: Franz Steiner, 2011); Julian Hoppit, 'Taxing London and the British fiscal state, 1660–1815', in Julian Hoppit, Duncan Needham and Adrian Leonard (eds), *Money and markets: essays in honour of Martin Daunton* (Woodbridge: Boydell & Brewer, 2019).

63 Helleiner, *The neomercantilists*, p 4.

64 Ibid., p 16.

65 Surveys include David Blackbourn and Geoff Eley, *The peculiarities of German history: bourgeois society and politics in nineteenth-century Germany* (Oxford: Oxford University Press, 1984); William Hagen, *German history in modern times: four lives of the nation* (Cambridge: Cambridge University Press, 2012); Helmut Walser Smith, *Germany: a nation in its time – before, during, and after nationalism, 1500–2000* (New York: Liveright, 2020).

66 Joyce Appleby, *The relentless revolution: history of capitalism* (New York: W.W. Norton, 2011), p 21.

67 Ellen Meiksins Wood, *The pristine culture of capitalism: a historical essay on old regimes and modern states* (London: Verso, 1991), p 1; Joseph E. Inikori, 'The first capitalist nation: the development of capitalism'; in: Yazdani and Menon (eds), *Capitalisms: towards a global history*, pp 251–72, at p 252. See also Maurice Dobb, *Studies in the development of capitalism* (London: Routledge, 1947).

68 For example, Douglass C. North, John J. Wallis and Barry R. Weingast, *Violence and social orders: a conceptual framework for interpreting recorded human history* (Cambridge: Cambridge University Press, 2009); Pincus and Robinson, 'Faire la guerre et faire l'État'.

69 O'Brien, 'The nature and historical evolution'.

70 For instance, Neal and Williamson, *Cambridge history of capitalism*; Martha C. Howell, *Commerce before capitalism in Europe, 1300–1600* (Cambridge: Cambridge University Press, 2010). On Dutch political economy in the 'Golden Age' and its embeddings within European political economy, see Sophus A. Reinert, 'Cameralism and commercial rivalry: nationbuilding through economic autarky in Seckendorff's 1665 *Additiones*', *European Journal of Law and Economics* 19:3 (2005), 271–86; Oscar Gelderblom, *The political economy of the Dutch Republic* (Farnham: Ashgate, 2009); Arthur Weststeijn, *Commercial republicanism in the Dutch Golden Age: the political thought of Johan & Pieter de la Court* (Leiden: Brill, 2011).

71 Roger Fouquet and Stephen Broadberry, 'Seven centuries of European economic growth and decline', *Journal of Economic Perspectives* 29:4 (2015), 227–45; contributions in Joerg Baten (ed), *A history of the global economy: 1500 to the present* (Cambridge: Cambridge University Press, 2016), esp. the chapter on north-west Europe by J.L. van Zanden; Alexandra M. de Pleijt and Jan Luiten van Zanden, 'Accounting for the "little divergence": what drove economic growth in pre-industrial Europe, 1300–1800', *European Review of Economic History* 20:4 (2016), 387–409; and the most recent critical contribution to the debate: António Henriques and Nuno Palma, *Comparative European institutions and the 'little divergence' 1385–1800*, CEPR Discussion Paper 14124 (2019).

72 Summaries in Koyama and Rubin, *How the world became rich*; Vries, *Escaping poverty*.

73 Allen, *British Industrial Revolution*.

74 Daron Acemoglu, Simon Johnson and James Robinson, 'The rise of Europe: Atlantic trade, institutional change, and economic growth', *American Economic Review* 95:3 (2005), 546–79.

75 Markus Cerman, *Villagers and lords in Eastern Europe, 1300–1800* (Basingstoke: Palgrave Macmillan, 2011).

76 Wide in perspective, yet shorthand regarding pre-Smithian ideas, see José Luís Cardoso, 'The political economy of rising capitalism', in Neal and Williamson (eds), *The Cambridge history of capitalism*, I, pp 574–99. More comprehensive overviews – yet not specifically attuned to the political economy of early modern capitalism – can be found in relevant specialist works, for example, Bertram Schefold, *Beiträge zur ökonomischen Dogmengeschichte*, ed. V. Caspari (Düsseldorf: Verlag Wirtschaft und Finanzen, 2004), now made available in translation: Bertram Schefold, *Great economic thinkers from the classicals to the moderns: translations from the series Klassiker der Nationalökonomie* (Abingdon: Routledge, 2016) and Bertram Schefold, *Great economic thinkers from antiquity to the Historical School: translations from the series Klassiker der Nationalökonomie* (Abingdon: Routledge, 2011); Alessandro Roncaglia, *The wealth of ideas: a history of economic thought* (Cambridge: Cambridge University Press, 2009); Faccarello and Kurz (eds), *Handbook on the history of economic analysis*, 3 vols.

77 Ashworth, *The Industrial Revolution*, p 147.

78 Karl Acham, Knut Wolfgang Nörr and Bertram Schefold (eds), *Erkenntnisgewinne, Erkenntnisverluste: Kontinuitäten und Diskontinuitäten in den Wirtschafts-, Rechts- und Sozialwissenschaften zwischen den 20er und 50er Jahren* (Stuttgart: Franz Steiner, 1998); Reinert, *Visionary realism*; Johannes Burkhardt and Birger P. Priddat (eds), *Geschichte*

der Ökonomie (Frankfurt-am-Main: Deutscher Klassiker, 2009); Lars P. Feld, Ekkehard A. Köhler and Daniel Nientiedt, 'The German anti-Keynes? On Walter Eucken's macroeconomics', *Journal of the History of Economic Thought* 43:4 (2021), 548–63.

[79] Ephraim Gerhard, *Einleitung zur Staats-Lehre* (Jena: Meyer, 1716), p 59.

[80] Karl Marx, *Das Kapital*, I, Postscript 1873.

[81] After Jörg-Peter Findeisen, 'Zukunftsorientiertes Wirtschaftsdenken in Schwedisch-Pommern', in Haik Thomas Porada (ed) *Beiträge zur Geschichte Vorpommerns: Die Demminer Kolloquien 1985–1994* (Schwerin: Helms, 1997), pp 83–94, at 84.

[82] Friedrich A. Hayek, *The road to serfdom* (Abingdon: Routledge Classics, 2001), p 21 (first publ. Chicago: University of Chicago Press, 1944).

[83] Hayek, *The road to serfdom*; Douglas Moggach, 'Freedom and perfection: German debates on the state in the eighteenth century', *Canadian Journal of Political Science/Revue canadienne de science politique* 42:4 (2009), 1003–23, at 1006–9.

[84] On Justi, see various chapters in Reinert, *Visionary realism*; Ulrich Adam, *The political economy of J.H.G. Justi* (Oxford: Lang, 2006); Jürgen G. Backhaus (ed), *The beginnings of political economy: Johann Heinrich Gottlob von Justi* (Boston, MA: Springer, 2009); Xuan Zhao, 'Public happiness through manufacturing and innovation: the theory of industrialization of Johann Heinrich Gottlob von Justi', *History of Political Economy* 53:3 (2021), 461–78. An idiosyncratic interpretation of German cameralism is Andre Wakefield, *Disordered police state: German cameralism as science and practice* (Chicago: University of Chicago Press, 2009).

[85] For Swedish Pomeranian cameralism, see Jörg-Peter Findeisen, *Fürstendienerei oder Zukunftsweisendes unter feudalem Vorzeichen: Wirtschaftspolitische Reformpublizistik in Schwedisch-Pommern zwischen 1750 und 1806* (Sundsvall: Mitthögskolan, 1994), pp 149–56.

[86] One of the earliest uses is in Philip Wilhelm von Hornick (*Hörnigk*), *Oesterreich über alles, wann es nur will* (Nuremberg, 1684), now available in English translation (by Keith Tribe) with extended commentary: Philipp Robinson Rössner (ed), *Philipp Wilhelm von Hörnigk's Austria Supreme (if it so wishes) (1684): a strategy for European economic supremacy* (London: Anthem, 2018).

[87] Joerg Baten, 'Southern, eastern and central Europe', in Baten (ed), *A history of the global economy*, pp 42–73, at p 46.

[88] William Temple, *Observations upon the United Provinces of the Netherlands* (London: Maxwell, 1673), pp 212–13; Christopher Close, *State formation and shared sovereignty: the Holy Roman Empire and the Dutch Republic, 1488–1696* (Cambridge: Cambridge University Press, 2021).

[89] For example, Acemoglu et al, 'The rise of Europe'.

[90] Jan de Vries, *European urbanization, 1500–1800* (London: Methuen, 1984).

[91] Antoni Mączak and T. Christopher Smout (eds), *Gründung und Bedeutung kleinerer Städte im nördlichen Europa der frühen Neuzeit* (Wiesbaden: Harrassowitz, 1991); Heinz Schilling, *Die Stadt in der Frühen Neuzeit* (Berlin: De Gruyter Oldenbourg: 2015).

[92] Wolfgang Stromer von Reichenbach, *Oberdeutsche Hochfinanz 1350–1450*, 3 vols (Wiesbaden: Steiner, 1970); the flagship work of the German Democratic Republic: Adolf Laube, Max Steinmetz and Günter Vogler, *Illustrierte Geschichte der deutschen frühbürgerlichen Revolution*, 2nd edn (Berlin [East]: Dietz, 1982); Donald J. Harreld, *High Germans in the Low Countries: German merchants and commerce in golden age Antwerp* (Leiden: Brill, 2007); Thomas Max Safley, *Family firms and merchant capitalism in early modern Europe: the business, bankruptcy and resilience of the Höchstetters of Augsburg* (Abingdon: Routledge, 2021).

[93] Philipp Robinson Rössner, *Martin Luther on commerce and usury* (London: Anthem, 2015); Manfred Straube, *Geleitswesen und Warenverkehr im thüringisch-sächsischen Raum zu Beginn der Frühen Neuzeit* (Cologne: Böhlau, 2015) provides incontrovertible evidence, from land traffic volumes and frequency, on regional specialization and economic

development. A useful primer is also Tom Scott, *Society and economy in Germany, 1300–1600* (Basingstoke: Palgrave Macmillan, 2002).

[94] Rolf Kießling, 'Markets and marketing, town and country', in Robert Scribner (ed), *Germany: a new social and economic history, 1450–1630* (London: Arnold, 1996), pp 145–80.

[95] Ekkehard Westermann, *Das Eislebener Garkupfer und seine Bedeutung für den europäischen Kupfermarkt 1460–1560* (Cologne: Böhlau, 1971); Ian Blanchard, *International lead production and trade in the 'Age of the Saigerprozess' 1460–1560* (Stuttgart: Franz Steiner, 1995).

[96] Captured in the monumental studies by Gustav Schmoller, 'Zur Geschichte der national-ökonomischen Ansichten in Deutschland während der Reformations-Periode', *Zeitschrift für Gesamte Staatswissenschaft* 16:3/4 (1860), 461–716; Wilhelm Roscher, *Geschichte der Nationaloekonomik in Deutschland* (Munich: Oldenbourg, 1874), pp 54–97.

[97] Klaus Weber, *Deutsche Kaufleute im Atlantikhandel 1680–1830: Unternehmen und Familien in Hamburg, Cadiz und Bordeaux* (Munich: Beck, 2004); Christine Fertig and Ulrich Pfister, 'Coffee, mind and body: global material culture and the eighteenth century Hamburg import trade', in Anne Gerritsen and Giorgio Riello (eds), *The global lives of things: the material culture of connections in the early modern world* (Abingdon: Routledge, 2016), pp 221–40; Yuta Kikuchi, *Hamburgs Ostsee- und Mitteleuropahandel 1600–1800: Warenaustausch und Hinterlandnetzwerke* (Göttingen: Vandenhoeck & Ruprecht, 2018); Joseph E. Inikori, 'Atlantic slavery and the rise of the capitalist global economy', *Current Anthropology* 61:S22 (2020), S159–S171.

[98] Christian Kleinschmidt, 'Weltwirtschaft, Staat und Unternehmen im 18. Jahrhundert: Ein Beitrag zur Protoindustrialisierungsdebatte', *Zeitschrift für Unternehmensgeschichte/Journal of Business History* 47:1 (2002), 72–86, at 75–77; Margrit Schulte Beerbühl, *Deutsche Kaufleute in London: Welthandel und Einbürgerung, 1600–1818* (Munich: Oldenbourg, 2007); Klaus Weber, 'Germany and the early modern Atlantic world: economic involvement and historiography', in Rebekka von Mallinckrodt, Josef Köstlbauer and Sarah Lentz (eds), *Beyond exceptionalism: traces of slavery and the slave trade in early modern Germany, 1650–1850* (Berlin: De Gruyter Oldenbourg, 2021), pp 26–56.

[99] Joseph E. Inikori, *Africans and the Industrial Revolution in England: a study in international trade and economic development* (Cambridge: Cambridge University Press, 2002), p 59; Weber, 'Germany and the early modern Atlantic world', p 32.

[100] J.Y.T. Greig (ed), *The letters of David Hume* (Oxford: Clarendon Press, 1932), as quoted in Tatsuya Sakamoto and Hideo Tanaka (eds), *The rise of political economy in the Scottish Enlightenment* (London: Routledge, 2003), pp 90–1.

[101] Richard H. Tilly and Michael Kopsidis, *From old regime to industrial state: a history of German industrialization from the eighteenth century to World War I* (Chicago: University of Chicago Press, 2020).

[102] Ulrich Pfister, 'The timing and pattern of real wage divergence in pre-industrial Europe: evidence from Germany, c.1500–1850', *Economic History Review* 70:3 (2017), 701–29.

[103] Ulrich Rosseaux, *Die Kipper und Wipper als publizistisches Ereignis (1620–1626): Eine Studie zu den Strukturen öffentlicher Kommunikation im Zeitalter des Dreißigjährigen Krieges* (Berlin: Duncker und Humblot, 2001); Martha White Paas, John Roger Paas and George C. Schoolfield, *The Kipper und Wipper inflation, 1619–23: an economic history with contemporary German broadsheets* (New Haven, CT: Yale University Press, 2012).

[104] Justus Nipperdey, 'Von der Katastrophe zum Niedergang. Gewöhnung an die Inflation in der deutschen Münzpublizistik des 17. Jahrhunderts', in Rudolf Schlögl, Philip R. Hoffmann-Rehnitz and Eva Wiebel (eds), *Die Krise in der Frühen Neuzeit* (Göttingen: Vandenhoeck & Ruprecht, 2016), pp 233–63.

[105] Findeisen, 'Zukunftsorientiertes Wirtschaftsdenken in Schwedisch-Pommern'; Koerner, *Linnaeus*; Hanna Hodacs, 'Local, universal, and embodied knowledge: Anglo-Swedish

contacts and Linnaean natural history', in Patrick Manning and Daniel Rood (eds), *Global scientific practice in an age of revolutions, 1750–1850* (Pittsburgh, PA: University of Pittsburgh Press, 2016), pp 90–104, at p 91.

[106] Albeit Prussia repeatedly engaged in African and East Indian trade ventures, as did the Counts of Hanau, who developed (unsuccessfully), under the guidance of the great alchemist-economist Johann Joachim Becher, a plan to colonize Surinam; Pamela Smith, *The business of alchemy: science and culture in the Holy Roman Empire* (Princeton, NJ: Princeton University Press, 2016).

[107] Hans-Ulrich Wehler, *Deutsche Gesellschaftsgeschichte, Volume I: 1700–1815*, 4th edn (Munich: Beck, 2007), pp 53–5. Recently, a similar narrative was adopted in Daron Acemoglu, Davide Cantoni, Simon Johnson and James A. Robinson, 'The consequences of radical reform: the French Revolution', *American Economic Review* 101:7 (2011), 3286–330. Evidence contradicting such simplistic binaries is presented in Cerman, *Villagers and lords*. Further important studies include Thomas Nipperdey, *Deutsche Geschichte: Bürgerwelt und starker Staat, 1800–1866* (Munich: C.H. Beck, 1983); Hagen, *German history in modern times*; Reinhart Koselleck, *Preußen zwischen Reform und Revolution: Allgemeines Landrecht, Verwaltung und soziale Bewegung von 1791 bis 1848* (Munich: Deutscher Taschenbuch Verlag, 1989).

[108] Tilly and Kopsidis, *From old regime to industrial state*, pp 2–3, and Ch. 1 for population levels and the share of agricultureagrarian in total population. See also Pfister, 'The timing and pattern of real wage divergence in pre-industrial Europe: evidence from Germany, *c.*1500–1850'.

[109] James C. Scott, *Seeing like a state: how certain schemes to improve the human condition have failed* (New Haven, CT: Yale University Press, 1998); applied to early modern Germany, Paul Warde, 'Cameralist writing in the mirror of practice: the long development of forestry in Germany', in Seppel and Tribe (eds), *Cameralism in practice*, pp 111–32; Richard Hölzl, 'Towards ecological statehood? Cameralism and the human-nature interface in the eighteenth century', in Nokkala and Miller (eds), *Cameralism and the Enlightenment*, pp 148–70.

[110] Foundational surveys include Friedrich Lütge, *Geschichte der deutschen Agrarverfassung vom frühen Mittelalter bis zum 19. Jahrhundert* (Stuttgart: Ulmer, 1963); Cerman, *Villagers and lords*; Witold Kula, *An economic theory of the feudal system: towards a model of the Polish economy 1500–1800* (London: NLB, 1976).

[111] Most recently, Arnd Kluge, *Die Zünfte* (Stuttgart: Franz Stener, 2012); Sheilagh Ogilvie, *Institutions and European trade: merchant guilds, 1000–1800* (Cambridge: Cambridge University Press, 2014); Sheilagh Ogilvie, *The European guilds: an economic analysis* (Princeton, NJ: Princeton University Press, 2019).

[112] I have discussed this at length in Philipp Robinson Rössner, *Freedom and capitalism: mercantilism and the making of the modern economic mind* (Cham: Palgrave Macmillan, 2020).

[113] See Rössner, *Deflation – Devaluation – Rebellion*, esp. Ch. 3 on the politics and management of money and Ch. 4 on the social consequences of badly managed currency.

[114] Authoritative surveys include Heinz Schilling, *Das Reich und die Deutschen: Höfe und Allianzen – Deutschland 1648–1763* (Berlin: Siedler, 1989), pp 130–46; Peter H. Wilson, *The Holy Roman Empire: a thousand years of European history* (London: Allen Lane, 2016), Chs. 8–10, esp. pp 415–21 on imperial structures of governance.

[115] Ingomar Bog, *Der Reichsmerkantilismus: Studien zur Wirtschaftspolitik des Heiligen Römischen Reiches im 17. und 18. Jahrhundert* (Stuttgart: Fischer, 1959).

[116] Erik S. Reinert and Ken Carpenter, 'German language economic bestsellers before 1850: also introducing Giovanni Botero as a common reference point of cameralism and mercantilism', in Rössner (ed) *Economic growth and the origins of modern political economy*, pp 26–53.

[117] See new data by Nuno Palma, Adam Brzezinski, Yao Chen and Felix Ward, 'The vagaries of the sea: evidence on the real effects of money from maritime disasters in the Spanish Empire', CEPR Discussion Paper 14089 (revised 2021).

[118] Marc Raeff, *The well-ordered police state: social and institutional change through law in the Germanies and Russia, 1600–1800* (New Haven, CT: Yale University Press, 1983). A recent heterodox interpretation is Mark Neocleous, *The fabrication of social order: a critical theory of police power* (London: Pluto Press, 2000).

[119] Clemens Kaps, 'Cores and peripheries reconsidered', *The Hungarian Historical Review* 7:2 (2018), 191–221, at 211–15; Mária Hidvegi, 'Land, people, and the unused economic potential of Hungary: knowledge transfer in the context of cameralism and statistics, 1790–1848', *History of Political Economy* 53:3 (2021), 571–94.

[120] Moggach, 'Freedom and perfection', p 1006.

[121] Rössner, *Freedom and capitalism*. A rebuttal of such interpretations also known as Midas Fallacy is in Cosimo Perrotta, 'Serra and underdevelopment', in Patalano and Reinert (eds), *Antonio Serra and the economics of good government*, pp 214–33.

[122] See also Alix Cooper, ' "The possibilities of the land": the inventory of "natural riches" in the early modern German territories', in Margaret Schabas and Neil de Marchi (eds), *Oeconomies in the age of Newton* (Durham, NC: Duke University Press, 2003), pp 129–53, at 134–5.

[123] For example, José Luís Cardoso and Alexandre Mendes Cunha, 'Enlightened reforms and economic discourse in the Portuguese-Brazilian empire (1750–1808)', *History of Political Economy* 44:4 (2012), 619–42.

[124] For example, Ernest Lluch, 'Cameralism beyond the Germanic world: a note on Tribe', *History of Economic Ideas* 5:2 (1997), 85–99; Adriana Luna Fabritius, 'Cameralism in Spain. *Polizeywissenschaft* and the Bourbon reforms', in Nokkala and Miller (eds), *Cameralism and the Enlightenment*, pp 245–66.

[125] See Carl Wennerlind, 'Theatrum Œconomicum: Anders Berch and the dramatization of the Swedish improvement discourse', in Robert Freedona and Sophus Reinert (eds), *The legitimacy of power: new perspectives on the history of political economy* (Basingstoke: Palgrave Macmillan, 2018); Wennerlind, 'The political economy of Sweden's *Age of Greatness*'; Koerner, *Linnaeus*.

[126] Sophus A. Reinert, 'Northern lights: political economy and the *Terroir* of the Norwegian enlightenment', *Journal of Modern History* 92:1 (2020), 76–115.

[127] Danila E. Raskov, 'Cameralism in eighteenth-century Russia: reform, translations and academic mobility', in Nokkala and Miller (eds), *Cameralism and the Enlightenment*, pp 274–301.

[128] Most recently, Seppel and Tribe, *Cameralism in practice*; see also the special issue of 'The political economies of happiness: cameralism, capitalism, and the making of the modern economic mind', *History of Political Economy* 53:3 (2021).

[129] On cameralist population theory, see the exhaustive monograph by Justus Nipperdey, *Die Erfindung der Bevölkerungspolitik: Staat, politische Theorie und Population in der Frühen Neuzeit* (Göttingen: Vandenhoeck & Ruprecht, 2012).

[130] See the classic Reinhart Koselleck, *Vergangene Zukunft zur Semantik geschichtlicher Zeiten* (Frankfurt-am-Main: Suhrkamp, 1979), Engl. transl. Reinhart Koselleck, *Futures past: on the semantics of historical time* (New York: Columbia University Press, 2005), with a preface by the translator Keith Tribe; Laurent Baronian, 'The time-spaces of capitalism: Suzanne de Brunhoff and monetary thought after Marx', *Journal of the History of Economic Thought* 43:3 (2021), 420–32; full references in Chapter 2 of this volume.

[131] Findeisen, 'Zukunftsorientiertes Wirtschaftsdenken in Schwedisch-*Pommern*'; Lars Magnusson, 'Comparing cameralisms: the case of Sweden and Prussia', in Seppel and Tribe (eds), *Cameralism in practice*, pp 17–38.

[132] Mokyr, *Culture of growth*.

[133] Jan de Vries, *The industrious revolution: consumer behavior and the household economy, 1650 to the present* (New York: Cambridge University Press, 2009).

[134] Maxine Berg, *Consumers and luxury: consumer culture in Europe 1650–1850* (Manchester: Manchester University Press, 1999); Frank Trentmann, *Empire of things: how we became a world of consumers, from the fifteenth century to the twenty-first* (London: Penguin, 2017).

[135] Cary J. Nederman, *Lineages of European political thought: explorations along the medieval/modern divide from John of Salisbury to Hegel* (Washington, DC: Catholic University of America Press, 2009).

[136] Smith, *Wealth of Nations*, Book II, Ch. 3. On Smith's economic theory, see Thomas R. de Gregori, 'Prodigality or parsimony: the false dilemma in economic development theory', *Journal of Economic Issues* 7:2 (1973), 259–66. See Simon Werrett, *Thrifty science: making the most of materials in the history of experiment* (Chicago: University of Chicago Press, 2019), Ch. 1 for an interesting conceptual history of parsimony as thrift. 'Industry' in the times of Smith still referred to someone being industrious, not heavy-scale manufacturing. At Smith's time, however, the concept gradually morphed towards its more modern meaning; see Schui, *Early debates about industry*.

[137] See the review of recent literature on materiality and cameralist political economy, Lissa Roberts, 'Practicing oeconomy during the second half of the long eighteenth century: an introduction', *History and Technology* 30:3 (2014), 133–48; Werrett, *Thrifty science*, pp 17–19; Chapter 8 of this volume.

[138] Mokyr, *Enlightened economy*, Ch. 4 proposes such causality with regards to mercantilist political economy giving way to laissez-faire and 'enlightened' economic ideology and ideas better attuned with modern economic growth.

Chapter 2

[1] Anders Berch, *Inledning til Almänna Hushålningen, innefattande Grunden til Politie, Oeconomie och Cameralwetenskaperna* (Stockholm: Lars Salvius, 1747), Ger. transl. *Anleitung zur allgemeinen Haushaltung in sich fassend die Grundsätze der Policey-, Oeconomie-, und Cameralwissenschaften*, transl. J.G. Schreber (Halle: Curts, 1763).

[2] Sven-Eric Liedman and Mats Persson, 'The visible hand: Anders Berch and the university of Uppsala chair in economics', *The Scandinavian Journal of Economics* 94, Supplement (1992), S259–S269; Lars Magnusson, *An economic history of Sweden* (London: Routledge, 2000); Wennerlind, 'Theatrum Œconomicum'.

[3] Mokyr, *A culture of growth*.

[4] Holger Böning et al (eds), *Volksaufklärung: Eine praktische Reformbewegung des 18. und 19. Jahrhunderts*; Marcus Popplow (ed), *Landschaften agrarisch-ökonomischen Wissens: Strategien innovativer Ressourcennutzung in Zeitschriften und Sozietäten des 18. Jahrhunderts* (New York: Waxmann, 2010). On useful knowledge in a British Enlightenment context, see Mokyr, *Enlightened economy*.

[5] See Chapter 1; special issue on 'The political economy of happiness: cameralism, capitalism and the making of the modern economic mind', *History of Political Economy* 53:3 (2021). Recent English-language studies include Rössner (ed), *Economic growth and the origins of modern political economy*; Seppel and Tribe (eds), *Cameralism in practice*; Ere Nokkala, *From natural law to political economy: J.H.G. von Justi on state, commerce and international order* (Zurich: LIT, 2019); Nokkala and Miller (eds), *Cameralism and the Enlightenment*; Rössner, *Freedom and capitalism*; Xuan Zhao, *The political economy of Johann Heinrich Gottlob von Justi (1717–1771): the eighteenth-century entrepreneurial state*, unpublished University of Manchester PhD thesis (2020).

6   For example, Mark Elvin, 'A working definition of 'modernity'?', *Past & Present* 113 (1986), 209–13; Jens Beckert, *Imagined futures: fictional expectations and capitalist dynamics* (Cambridge, MA: Harvard University Press, 2016).

7   Koselleck, *Futures past*; Lucian Hölscher, *Die Entdeckung der Zukunft*, new edn (Göttingen: Wallstein, 2016).

8   A genealogy of the public vices versus virtues argument is presented in the now classic Hirschman, *The passion and the interests*; an updated version in Yamamoto, *Taming capitalism before its triumph*.

9   Leonhard Fronsperger, *Von dem Lob deß Eigen Nutzen* (Frankfurt-am-Main: Feyerabend, 1564), folio 29 recto et verso. See an English translation: Erik S. Reinert and Philipp Robinson Rössner (eds), *Fronsperger and Laffemas: 16th-century Precursors of Modern Economic Ideas* (London & New York: Anthem, 2023).

10   Bernard de Mandeville, 'The grumbling hive, or knaves turn'd honest', in *The fable of the bees: or, private vices, publick benefits* [1705/1714], ed. F.B. Kaye, vol 1 (Oxford: Clarendon Press, 1924), pp 24–5.

11   Rainer Klump and Lars Pilz, 'The formation of a "spirit of capitalism" in Upper Germany: Leonhard Fronsperger's "On the praise of self-interest"', *Journal of the History of Economic Thought* 43:3 (2021), 401–19.

12   Koselleck, *Futures past*; Reinhart Koselleck, *Zeitschichten*, 6th edn (Frankfurt-am-Main: Suhrkamp, 2021), Engl. transl. *Sediments of time: on possible histories* (Stanford: Stanford University Press, 2018). The concept of 'time-scape' has been introduced in Achim Landwehr, *Geburt der Gegenwart: eine Geschichte der Zeit im 17. Jahrhundert* (Frankfurt-am-Main: Fischer, 2014).

13   Baronian, 'The time-spaces of capitalism'.

14   Paul Slack, *The invention of improvement: information and material progress in seventeenth-century England* (Oxford: Oxford University Press, 2015), p 2.

15   Ibid., p 1.

16   Ibid., p 258.

17   A taste of such future-looking oeconomic sciences and their general impact and context is given in Carl Wennerlind, 'Money: Hartlibian political economy and the new culture of credit', in Stern and Wennerlind (eds), *Mercantilism reimagined*, pp 74–96, at p 77; see also Andrea Finkelstein, 'Nicholas Barbon and the quality of infinity', *History of Political Economy* 32:1 (2000), 83–102; Fredrik Albritton Jonsson, 'The origins of Cornucopianism: a preliminary genealogy', *Critical Historical Studies* 1:1 (2014), 151–68; Vera Keller, *Knowledge and the public interest, 1575–1725* (Cambridge: Cambridge University Press, 2015), for example, Ch. 6.

18   Wakefield, 'Butterfield's nightmare: the history of science as Disney history'.

19   Fredrik Albritton Jonsson and Carl Wennerlind, *Scarcity: economy and nature in the age of capitalism* (Cambridge, MA: Harvard University Press, 2023).

20   But see Magnusson, *Mercantilism*.

21   See, for example, Schui, *Early debates about industry*.

22   Beckert, *Imagined futures*; see also Arjun Appadurai, *The future as cultural fact: essays on the global condition* (New York: Verso, 2013); Francesco Boldizzoni, 'Capitalism's futures past: expectations in history and theory', *Critical Historical Studies* 4:2 (2017), 255–66.

23   For example, Roberts, 'Practicing oeconomy during the second half of the long eighteenth century', and further papers in said special issue; Werrett, *Thrifty science*.

24   Koselleck, *Futures past*; see also Brunner, Conze and Koselleck (eds), *Geschichtliche Grundbegriffe*; Hölscher, *Entdeckung der Zukunft*; Landwehr, *Geburt der Gegenwart*; Judith Pollmann, 'Archiving the present and chronicling for the future in early modern Europe', *Past & Present* 230:S11 (2016), 231–52.

25 Mokyr, *Enlightened economy*, Ch. 4, for a mainstream interpretation of mercantilism's contribution (and by this way, cameralism is included) to 'Enlightenment' economics; Dorinda Outram, *The Enlightenment*, 2nd edn (Cambridge: Cambridge University Press, 2012) is a welcome difference in that regard. See Erik S. Reinert and Philipp Robinson Rössner, 'Cameralism and the German tradition of development economics', in Erik S. Reinert, Jayati Ghosh and Rainer Kattel (eds), *Elgar handbook of alternative theories of economic development* (Cheltenham: Edward Elgar, 2016), pp 63–86.

26 See Chapter 1.

27 Pioneering studies include Douglass C. North, *Institutions, institutional change, and economic performance* (Cambridge: Cambridge University Press, 1990); Avner Greif, 'Cultural beliefs and the organization of society: a historical and theoretical reflection on collectivist and individualist societies', *Journal of Political Economy* 102:5 (1994), 912–50; North, *Understanding the process of economic change*; Greif, *Institutions and the path to the modern economy*; North, Wallis and Weingast, *Violence and social orders*.

28 North, *Understanding the process of economic change*.

29 Mokyr, *Culture of growth*; Jeremy Black, *The power of knowledge: how information and technology made the modern world* (New Haven, CT: Yale University Press, 2014).

30 Landwehr, *Geburt*; Hölscher, *Entdeckung*; Peter Burke, 'Introduction', in Andrea Brady and Emily Butterworth (eds), *The uses of the future in early modern Europe* (New York: Routledge, 2010); Daniel Fulda, 'Wann begann die 'offene Zukunft'? Ein Versuch, die Koselleck'sche Fixierung auf die 'Sattelzeit' zu überwinden', in Wolfgang Breul and Jan Carsten Schnurr (eds), *Geschichtsbewusstsein und Zukunftserwartung in Pietismus und Erweckungsbewegung* (Göttingen: Vandenhoeck & Ruprecht, 2013), pp 141–72; Daniel Fulda, *'Die Geschichte trägt der Aufklärung die Fackel vor': Eine deutsch-französische Bild-Geschichte* (Halle: mdv, 2016).

31 Most instructive in this regard are the recent writings by Wennerlind, 'Theatrum Œconomicum'; Wennerlind, 'The political economy of Sweden's *Age of Greatness*'.

32 Peter Wilson, *The Thirty Years War: Europe's tragedy* (Cambridge, MA: Harvard University Press, 2011).

33 For the Germanic vibe in early modern economic discourse, see Keith Tribe, *Strategies of economic order: German economic discourse, 1750–1950* (Cambridge: Cambridge University Press, 1996); Keith Tribe, *Governing economy: the reformation of German economic discourse 1750–1840* 2nd ed (Newbury: Threshold Press, 2017); on this war, see Georg Schmidt, *Die Reiter der Apokalypse: Geschichte des Dreißigjährigen Krieges* (Munich: C.H. Beck, 2018).

34 Raeff, *The well-ordered police state*; in a provocative new interpretation, Wakefield, *Disordered police state*.

35 For new interpretations, see Hagen, *German history in modern times*; Joachim Whaley, *Germany and the Holy Roman Empire 1493–1806*, 2 vols (Oxford: Oxford University Press, 2012); Wilson, *The Holy Roman Empire*.

36 Harcourt, *The illusion of free markets*.

37 Pfister, 'The timing and pattern of real wage divergence in pre-industrial Europe'.

38 Otto Walde, *Storhetstidens litterära krigsbyten: En kulturhistorisk bibliografisk studie* (Uppsala: Almqvist och Wiksell, 1916, 1920), Vol I, pp 108–11, 178; for a quote from the original *donationsbref* (certificate or letter of donation) from 1631, ibid., Appendix 2, p 338, for Prussia, Erfurt, Heiligenstadt, Würzburg and Mainz.

39 Marcus Popplow, 'Hoffnungsträger "Unächter Acacien=Baum"', in Torsten Meyer and Marcus Popplow (eds), *Technik, Arbeit und Umwelt in der Geschichte: Günter Bayerl zum 60. Geburtstag* (New York: Waxmann, 2006), pp 297–316; Vera Keller and Alexander Marr (eds), 'The nature of invention', *Intellectual History Review* 24:3 (2014); Keller, *Knowledge and the public interest*; Vera Keller and Ted McCormick, 'Science and the shape of things to come', *Early Science and Medicine*, 21:5 (2016); Smith, *The business of alchemy*.

40 Wennerlind, 'The political economy of Sweden's *Age of Greatness*'.

41 See former Harvard University/Kress Librarian Ken Carpenter's working files on early modern economics translations from and to Swedish.

42 Lars Magnusson, 'Economic thought and group interests: Adam Smith, Christopher Polhem, Lars Salvius and classical political economy', *Scandinavian Journal of History* 2:1/4 (1977), 243–64, at 257; see also Magnusson's chapter in Seppel and Tribe (eds), *Cameralism in practice* for possible connections between Anders Berch's *Inledning* and Justus Dithmar.

43 On some quibbles with grammar and translation of the ambiguous title for this work, see Tribe, *Governing economy*, Chs. 1 and 2.

44 Magnusson's chapter in Seppel and Tribe (eds), *Cameralism in practice*; Nokkala and Miller (eds), *Cameralism and the Enlightenment*.

45 Some hints on cameralism and oeconomic futures can be found in Isabel V. Hull, *Sexuality, state, and civil society in Germany, 1700–1815* (Ithaca, NY: Cornell University Press, 1996), p 155.

46 As Hölscher has argued, the German language knew the use of 'future' in the adjective long before the substantive (with a definite article), which is one of the epistemic foundations upon which the 'Hölscher' thesis of the discovery of the open future rests, including its dating to the mid-to-late 18th century; see Hölscher, *Entdeckung*; more recently, Landwehr, *Geburt*; Christopher Clark, *Time and power: visions of history in German politics, from the Thirty Years' War to the Third Reich* (Princeton, NJ: Princeton University Press, 2019), esp. Introduction and Chs. 1 and 2. Others have argued for earlier dating; see Burke, 'Introduction'; Fulda, *'Die Geschichte trägt der Aufklärung die Fackel vor'*; Fulda, 'Wann begann die "offene Zukunft"?'.

47 Rössner (ed), *Economic growth and the origins of modern political economy*; Seppel and Tribe (eds), *Cameralism in practice*; Nokkala and Miller (eds), *Cameralism and the Enlightenment*.

48 The most recent and comprehensive treatise of this matter is in William A. Deringer, *Calculated values: finance, politics, and the quantitative age* (Cambridge, MA: Harvard University Press, 2018); William A. Deringer, 'Compound interest corrected: the imaginative mathematics of the financial future in early modern England', *Osiris* 33 (2018), 109–30.

49 As a simple search of the Making of the Modern World database shows; but see *Newe gezeytung ausz Romischer Kaiserlicher Maiestat vn[d] des Konigs von Engellandt Here vor Terebona in Bickhardia: Was eererpietung der konig vo[n] Engellandt der Kaiserlichen maiestat in irer zukunfft erzaygt. Was sich auch sonst gegenn des Konig vonn Franckreich Kriegsvolck durch Krieges vbung begeben hat* (1513).

50 This does not mean there were no other uses. According to Grimm's dictionary, medieval usages of the term simply denoting movement in a geographic dimension – as in 'advent' or 'arrival', but also 'return' – continued into the 16th century and beyond. Luther and other late Renaissance writers such as Sebastian Franck occasionally seem to have used the term with a time dimension (as in 'in the future'), but with clear biblical and soteriological connotation. It is in the writings of Goethe, Herder and Schiller where we find a use and connotation of *Zukunft* that seems more or less in line with the modern sense of future as a time-scape clearly located after both present and the past. Still, even during the age of Enlightenment and Romanticism, 'future' often appeared in personified form, or slightly different connotations including 'eternity'. See Jacob and Wilhelm Grimm, *Deutsches Wörterbuch*, Vol 32, Col. 484, online edn (https://woerterbuchnetz.de/?sigle=DWB&lemma=quetschen#2, last accessed 24 May 2022); Johann Christoph Adelung, *Grammatisch-kritisches Wörterbuch der Hochdeutschen Mundart*, Vol 4 (Leipzig: Breitkopf, 1801), p 1757, (online version: https://woerterbuchnetz.de/?sigle=DWB&lemma=quetschen#5, last accessed 24 May 2022).

51 Jack Goody, *The theft of history* (Cambridge: Cambridge University Press, 2012); see contributions by Hanss and others in *Past & Present* (2020).

52 Safley's works have added a lot on early modern business ethics from the point of view of credibility, faith and honour; see, for example, Safley, *Family firms and merchant capitalism in early modern Europe*.

53 Francesco Boldizzoni, *Means and ends: the idea of capital in the West, 1500–1970* (Basingstoke: Palgrave Macmillan, 2008); Carl Wennerlind, *Casualties of credit: the English financial revolution, 1620–1720* (Cambridge, MA: Harvard University Press, 2011).

54 Jaco Zuijderduijn, *Medieval capital markets: markets for renten, state formation and private investment in Holland (1300–1550)* (Leiden: Brill, 2009).

55 Johannes Fried, *Aufstieg aus dem Untergang: Apokalyptisches Denken und die Entstehung der modernen Naturwissenschaft im Mittelalter*, 2nd edn (Munich: C. H. Beck, 2012).

56 Mokyr, *A culture of growth*.

57 Peter Spufford, *Power and profit: the merchant in medieval Europe*, new edn (London: Thames & Hudson, 2006); Roberto S. Lopez, *The commercial revolution of the middle ages, 950–1350*, new edn (Cambridge: Cambridge University Press, 2009); Gabriela Signori, 'Kontingenzbewältigung durch Zukunftshandeln: der spätmittelalterliche Leibrentenvertrag', in Markus Bernhardt, Stefan Brakensiek and Benjamin Scheller (eds), *Ermöglichen und Verhindern: vom Umgang mit Kontingenz* (Frankfurt-am-Main: Campus, 2016), pp 117–42.

58 Diana Wood, *Medieval economic thought* (Cambridge: Cambridge University Press, 2002); Markus A. Denzel, *Das System des bargeldlosen Zahlungsverkehrs europäischer Prägung vom Mittelalter bis 1914* (Stuttgart: Franz Steiner, 2008); Markus A. Denzel, *Handbook of world exchange rates* (Farnham: Ashgate, 2010), Introduction; Hans-Jörg Gilomen, 'Der Reichtum der Kirche und die Auseinandersetzungen um ihren Beitrag zum Gemeinwohl. Das Beispiel eidgenössischer Städte im Spätmittelalter', in Petra Schulze and Peter Hesse (eds), *Reichtum im späten Mittelalter: Politische Theorie – Ethische Norm – Soziale Akzeptanz* (Stuttgart: Franz Steiner, 2015), pp 203–38; Mathias Schmoeckel, 'Die Kanonistik und die Zunahme des Handels vom 13. Bis zum 15. Jahrhundert/Canon law and growing trade between the 13th and 15th century', *Vierteljahrschrift für Sozial- und Wirtschaftsgeschichte* 104:2 (2017), 237–54.

59 Rössner, *Martin Luther on commerce and usury*; Philipp Robinson Rössner, 'Burying money? Monetary origins and afterlives of Luther's Reformation', *History of Political Economy* 48:2 (2016), 225–63.

60 Landwehr, *Geburt*; Rössner, *Luther on commerce and usury*.

61 Johannes Burkhardt, *Das Reformationsjahrhundert: Deutsche Geschichte zwischen Medienrevolution und Institutionenbildung 1517–1617* (Stuttgart: Kohlhammer, 2002); Marcus Sandl, *Medialität und Ereignis: Eine Zeitgeschichte der Reformation* (Zurich: Chronos, 2011); Andrew Pettegree, *Brand Luther: how an unheralded monk turned his small town into a center of publishing, made himself the most famous man in Europe – and started the Protestant Reformation* (London: Penguin, 2015).

62 Here I am following Dieter Groh, *Göttliche Weltökonomie: Perspektiven der wissenschaftlichen Revolution vom 15. bis zum 17. Jahrhundert* (Frankfurt-am-Main: Suhrkamp, 2010), Ch. 1.

63 Wennerlind, 'The political economy of Sweden's *Age of Greatness*'.

64 For earlier elements of such future models, see Kaye, *Economy and nature in the fourteenth century*.

65 Practical examples would include Johanna Eleonora Petersen, *Anleitung zu gründlicher Verständniß, der heiligen Offenbahrung Jesu ...*, Vol 1 (1696) https://books.google.de/books?id=e8JIAAAAcAAJ&pg=PA267&dq=%22zukunft%22&hl=de&sa=X&ved=0ahUKEwjY0qWmyNvbAhUCvxQKHVriCXgQ6AEIPTAE#v=onepage&q=%22zukunft%22&f=false

66 For example, Georg Witzel, *Ecclesiasticae Demegoriae: Postill oder gemeine predig Rechter ...*, Vol 1 (1548), p LXVI; Jakob Heerbrand and Dietrich Schnepff, *Gründtlicher Bericht,*

Von zweien Schrifften der Caluinischen Predicanten (1585), p 861, https://books.google.de/
books?id=zU0rC0X_CC8C&pg=PA861&dq=%22zukunft%22&hl=de&sa=X&ved=
0ahUKEwiMpODOytvbAhVNbVAKHZ1HAE0Q6AEINzAD#v=onepage&q=
%22zukunft%22&f=false; Johann Baumgart, *Postilla* (Magdeburg: A. Gene, 1587), pp
1, 6.

67 This becomes apparent from one instance in which Hess refers to something that will
remain a problem until the end of time: 'das wird wol bis zur grossen Zukunft ein
Problem bleiben', Ludwig Freiherr von Hess, *Freymüthige Gedanken über Staatssachen*
(Hamburg: Bode, 1775), p 153.

68 Ibid., pp 377, 404.

69 Rössner, *Martin Luther on commerce and usury*.

70 Landwehr, *Geburt*.

71 I am using the definition and measuring criteria presented in Erik S. Reinert, Kenneth
Carpenter, Fernanda A. Reinert and Sophus A. Reinert, '80 economic bestsellers before
1850: a fresh look at the history of economic thought', Tallinn University of Technology
Working Paper Series in Economic Governance (2018 version), http://technologygov
ernance.eu/files/main//2017051103164242.pdf

72 Volker Leppin, *Antichrist und Jüngster Tag: Das Profil apokalyptischer Flugschriftenpublizistik im
deutschen Luthertum 1548–1618* (Gütersloh: Gütersloher Verlagshaus, 1999); Rousseaux,
Die Kipper und Wipper als publizistisches Ereignis; Nipperdey, 'Von der Katastrophe zum
Niedergang. Gewöhnung an die Inflation in der deutschen Münzpublizistik des 17.
Jahrhunderts', pp 250–1, 254, 262.

73 On Bacon, for example, Noah Millstone, 'Seeing like a statesman in early Stuart England',
Past & Present 223:1 (2014), 100–12.

74 For a historical view on the Habermas thesis, see Tim Blanning, *The pursuit of glory: Europe
1648–1815* (London: Allen Lane, 2008).

75 Landwehr, *Geburt*, p 146.

76 Cornel Zwierlein, 'Fuggerzeitungen als Ergebnis von italienisch-deutschem Kulturtransfer,
1552–1570', *Quellen und Forschungen aus italienischen Archiven und Bibliotheken* 90 (2010),
169–224.

77 Rudolf Schlögl, *Anwesende und Abwesende: Grundriss für eine Gesellschaftsgeschichte der Frühen
Neuzeit* (Constance: Konstanz University Press, 2014), pp 363–5.

78 Landwehr, *Geburt*; Hölscher, *Entdeckung*.

79 R.C. Bowler, 'Menschenbild und Wirtschaftsordnung: Der Menschenbegriff im
Kameralismus und in der Nationalökonomie', *Berichte zur Wissenschaftsgeschichte*
25:4 (2002), 283–99; Birger P. Priddat, 'Kameralismus als paradoxe Konzeption der
gleichzeitigen Stärkung von Markt und Staat. Komplexe Theorielagen im deutschen 18.
Jahrhundert', *Berichte zur Wissenschaftsgeschichte* 31 (2008), 249–63.

80 Ulrike Lötzsch, *Joachim Georg Darjes (1714–1791): Der Kameralist als Schul- und
Gesellschaftsreformer* (Cologne: Böhlau, 2016), p 247.

81 Ibid., p 24.

82 Erhard Dittrich, *Die deutschen und österreichischen Kameralisten* (Darmstadt: Wissenschaftliche
Buchgesellschaft, 1974), pp 40–9; on Klock, as well as 'early' cameralism in a wider
sense, the excellent introduction by Bertram Schefold(ed), in Kaspar Klock, *Tractatus
juridico-politico-polemico-historicus de aerario, sive censu per honesta media absque divexatione
populi licite conficiendo, libri duo* (Hildesheim: Olms-Weidmann, 2009). Older works
include Wilhelm Roscher, 'Die österreichische Nationalökonomik unter Kaiser
Leopold I', *Jahrbücher für Nationalökonomie und Statistik* 2 (1864), 25–59 and 105–22;
Small, *The cameralists*; Zielenziger, *Die alten deutschen Kameralisten*; Louise Sommer, *Die
österreichischen Kameralisten in dogmengeschichtlicher Darstellung*, 2 vols (Vienna: Konegen,
1920/25).

83 Georg Obrecht, *Fünff Vnderschiedliche Secreta Politica*. Von Anstellung/ Erhaltung vnd Vermehrung guter Policey/ vnd von billicher/ rechtmässiger vnd nothwendiger Erhöhung/ eines jeden Regenten Jährlichen Gefällen vnd Einkommmen o. V., Straßburg, 1617, 15 (facsimile in Schefold); similar in Georg Obrecht, *Politisch Bedencken und Discurs: von Verbesserung Land und Leut Anrichtung gutter Policey unnd fürnemlich von nutzlicher Erledigung großer Außgaben und billicher Vermehrung eines jeden Regenten und Oberherren jährlichen Gefähllen und Einkummen* (1606).

84 Reinert and Carpenter, 'German language economic bestsellers'.

85 Obrecht, *Politische Bedencken* [1617] 1644, p 6.

86 Peter Blickle, *Die Revolution von 1525*, new edn (Munich: Beck, 2004).

87 1752, no publisher; p 10.

88 Ibid., p 32

89 I have studied this in Philipp Robinson Rössner, 'Merchants, mercantilism, and economic development: the Scottish way, c.1700–1815', *Annales Mercaturae* 1:1 (2015), 97–126.

90 Marcus Sandl, *Ökonomie des Raumes: der kameralwissenschaftliche Entwurf der Staatswirtschaft im 18. Jahrhundert* (Cologne: Böhlau, 1999).

91 Smith, *Business of alchemy*.

92 Douglass Watt, *The price of Scotland: Darien, union and the wealth of nations* (Edinburgh: Luath, 2007).

93 The rich documentation of the pros and cons and the emerging political factions of this process have been documented richly in Whatley's meticulous studies, the most recent and definitive one being C.A. Whatley, *The Scots and the union*, new edn (Edinburgh: Edinburgh University Press, 2016); see also Karin Bowie, *Scottish public opinion and the Anglo-Scottish union, 1699–1707* (Woodbridge: Boydell & Brewer, 2011); Karin Bowie, *Public opinion in early modern Scotland, c.1560–1707* (Cambridge: Cambridge University Press, 2020).

94 Sir John Clerk, *Letter* (Edinburgh: publisher unknown, 1706), p 14.

95 Ibid., pp 15–16, 44.

96 Author unknown, *An essay for promoting of trade and increasing of the coin of the nation* (around 1706), p 5.

97 Lötzsch, *Joachim Georg Darjes*; Arthur Richter, 'Darjes, Joachim Georg', *Allgemeine Deutsche Biographie* 4 (1876), 758–9.

98 Joachim Georg Darjes, *Erste Gründe der Cameral-Wissenschaften* (2nd ed, Leipzig: Breitkopf, 1768), p 363.

99 'zum Heil der Menschheit gereichende Veränderungen', p 13.

100 Reinert et al, '80 economic bestsellers before 1850'.

101 A quote from Seckendorff: 'Harmonie, Glückseligkeit, wahren Wohlstand und Glückseligkeit ihrer höchsten und hohen Häuser, ja aller getreuen Unterthanen, allenthalben herstellen und täglich vermehren, diejenigen, so am Ruder sitzen, mit wahrer Klugheit und ungeheuchelter Tugend ausrüsten, allesamt aber zu Erlangung dieses Endzwecks mit seiner Weißheit so lange begnadigen wolle, bis dereinst alle Fürstenthümer und Herrschafften ein Ende haben warden', in Seckendorff, *Teutsche Fuersten Stat* (Jena: Meyer, 1737), Preface.

102 Johann Joachim Becher, *Politische Discurs, von den eigentlichen Ursachen, deß Auff- und Abnehmens der Städt, Länder und Republicken*, 2nd edn (Frankfurt: Zunners, 1673), pp 1–4.

103 Marcus Sandl, 'Development as possibility: risk and chance in the cameralist discourse', in Rössner (ed), *Economic reasons of state*, pp 139–55.

104 Bertram Schefold, 'Goethe's economics. Between cameralism and liberalism', in Rössner (ed), *Economic reasons of state*, pp 79–100.

105 Obrecht 1617, pp 112–13.

106 Jan Hartman and Artur Weststijn, 'An empire of trade: commercial reason of state in seventeenth-century Holland', in Sophus A. Reinert and Pernille Røge (eds), *The political*

economy of empire in the early modern world (Basingstoke: Palgrave Macmillan, 2013), pp 11–31.

[107] Von Hörnigk, *Austria supreme (if it so wishes)*.

[108] Hont, *Jealousy of trade*; Sophus A. Reinert, 'Rivalry: greatness in early modern political economy', in Stern and Wennerlind (eds), *Mercantilism reimagined*, pp 348–70.

[109] Rendered in the English translation in von Hörnigk, *Austria supreme (if it so wishes)*.

[110] Lars Behrisch, *Vermessen, Zählen, Berechnen: Die politische Ordnung des Raums im 18. Jahrhundert* (Frankfurt-am-Main: Campus, 2006); Benjamin Steiner, *Die Ordnung der Geschichte: Historische Tabellenwerke in der Frühen Neuzeit* (Vienna: Böhlau, 2008); Dirk Philipsen, *Little big number: how GDP came to rule the world and what to do about it* (Princeton, NJ: Princeton University Press, 2015); Matthias Schmelzer, *The hegemony of growth: the OECD and the making of the economic growth paradigm* (Cambridge: Cambridge University Press, 2017).

[111] Keith Tribe, *Land, labour, and economic discourse* (London: Routledge and Kegan Paul, 1978), Ch. 4; Keith Tribe, *The economy of the word: language, history, and economics* (Oxford: Oxford University Press, 2015), pp 4, 28.

[112] See, for example, Werrett, *Thrifty science*, Chs. 1 and 8.

[113] Tribe, *Land, labour, and economic discourse*, Ch. 4.

Chapter 3

[1] King James VI of Scotland (I of England), *The true lavv of free monarchy, or the reciprocall and mutuall duty betvvixt a free king and his naturall subjects: by a well affected subject of the kingdome of Scotland* ([Edinburgh 1598] London: T.P. 1642), p 4; see also p 10.

[2] Recent landmark studies on Frederician Prussia include Johannes Kunisch, *Friedrich der Große: Der König und seine Zeit*, 4th edn (Munich: C.H. Beck, 2005); relevant chapters in Christopher Clarke, *Iron Kingdom: the rise and downfall of Prussia, 1600–1947* (London: Allen Lane, 2007); Ewald Frie, *Friedrich II* (Reinbek bei Hamburg: Rowohlt, 2012); Bernd Sösemann and Gregor Vogt-Spira (eds), *Friedrich der Große in Europa: Geschichte einer wechselvollen Beziehung*, 2 vols (Stuttgart: Franz Steiner, 2012); Tim Blanning, *Frederick the Great: King of Prussia* (London: Allen Lane, 2015).

[3] Susan Richter, *Pflug und Steuerruder: Zur Verflechtung von Herrschaft und Landwirtschaft in der Aufklärung* (Cologne: Böhlau, 2014), pp 11–28.

[4] More precisely, the 'Kingdom's stock'. For example, Thomas Mun, *England's treasure by foreign trade* (London: Clark, 1664); see also Margaret Schabas and Neil de Marchi, 'Introduction', in Schabas and de Marchi (eds), *Oeconomies in the age of Newton*, pp 1–13, at pp 4–5; Tribe, *Economy of the word*, pp 23–8.

[5] Marx, *Das Kapital*; Kaveh Yazdani and Nasser Mohajer, 'Reading Marx in the divergence debate', in Benjamin Zachariah, Lutz Raphael and Brigitta Bernet (eds), *What's left of Marxism: historiography and the possibilities of thinking with Marxian themes and concepts* (Berlin: De Gruyter Oldenbourg, 2020), pp 173–240; on the concept of fiscal and fiscal-military states, for example, Patrick Bonney, *The rise of the fiscal state in Europe c.1200–1815* (Oxford: Oxford University Press, 1999); Jan Glete, *War and the state in early modern Europe: Spain, the Dutch Republic and Sweden as fiscal-military states, 1500–1660* (Abingdon: Routledge, 2006); Bartolomé Yun-Casalilla and Patrick K. O'Brien (eds), *The rise of fiscal states: a global history, 1500–1914* (Cambridge: Cambridge University Press, 2012).

[6] Comparative data in Sevket Pamuk and Kivanç Karaman, 'Different paths to the modern state in Europe: the interaction between warfare, economic structure, and political regime', *American Political Science Review* 107:3 (2013), 1–23, tables and graphs on pp 3ff.; narratives in Yun-Casalilla and O'Brien (eds), *The rise of fiscal states*.

7   Summarized in Karin Friedrich, *Brandenburg-Prussia, 1466–1806* (Basingstoke: Palgrave Macmillan, 2012), esp. Ch. 3. But see Mark Spoerer, 'The revenue structures of Brandenburg-Prussia, Saxony and Bavaria (fifteenth to nineteenth centuries): are they compatible with the Bonney-Ormrod model?', in Simonetta Cavaciocchi (ed), *La fiscalità nell'economia europea secc XIII–XVIII: atti della 'Trentanovesima Settimana di Studi', 22–26 aprile 2007/Fiscal systems in the European economy from the 13th to the 18th centuries,* Vol 2 (Florence: Firenze University Press, 2008), pp 781–92; Florian Schui, *Rebellious Prussians: urban political culture under Frederick the Great and his successors* (Oxford: Oxford University Press, 2013); Pamuk and Karaman, 'Different paths'.

8   Walter L. Dorn, 'The Prussian bureaucracy in the eighteenth century', *Political Science Quarterly* 46:3 (1931), 403–23. I am indebted to Dr Xuan Zhao for pointing me to this work. On Prussian economic administration and the myth of Friedrich as the 'omnipresent king', see Karl-Erich Born, *Wirtschaft und Gesellschaft im Denken Friedrichs des Grossen* (Wiesbaden: Steiner, 1979); literature review by Frank Göse, 'Der König und das Land', in *Friedrich300 – Colloquien, Friedrich der Große – eine perspektivische Bestandsaufnahme* on *perspectivia.net* (perspectivia.net, 2007).

9   Friedrich Lütge, *Die mitteldeutsche Grundherrschaft und ihre Auflösung,* 2nd edn (Stuttgart: Fischer, 1957); more recent surveys include Werner Rösener, *Agrarwirtschaft, Agrarverfassung und ländliche Gesellschaft im Mittelalter* (Munich: Oldenburg, 1992); Werner Troßbach and C. Zimmermann, *Die Geschichte des Dorfes: Von den Anfängen im Frankenreich zur bundesdeutschen Gegenwart* (Stuttgart: UTB, 2006); Erich Landsteiner and Ernst Langthaler (eds), *Agrosystems and labour relations in European rural societies (Middle Ages–twentieth century)* (Turnhout: Brepols, 2010); Erich Landsteiner, 'Landwirtschaft und Agrargesellschaft', in M. Cerman, F.X. Eder, P. Eigner, A. Komlosy and E. Landsteiner (eds), *Wirtschaft und Gesellschaft: Europa 1000–2000* (Innsbruck: Studienverlag, 2011), pp 178–210; Cerman, *Villagers and Lords*; Rolf Kießling, Frank Konersmann and Werner Troßbach, *Grundzüge der Agrargeschichte,* Vol 1: *Vom Spätmittelalter bis zum Dreißigjährigen Krieg (1350–1650)* (Cologne: Böhlau, 2016); Reiner Prass, *Grundzüge der Agrargeschichte,* Vol 2: *Vom Dreißigjährigen Krieg bis zum Beginn der Moderne (1650–1880)* (Cologne: Böhlau, 2016).

10   Ronald G. Asch and Heinz Duchardt (eds), *Der Absolutismus – ein Mythos? Strukturwandel monarchischer Herrschaft in West- und Mitteleuropa (ca.1550–1700)* (Cologne: Böhlau, 1996); Peter Baumgart, 'Absolutismus ein Mythos? Aufgeklärter Absolutismus ein Widerspruch? Reflexionen zu einem kontroversen Thema gegenwärtiger Frühneuzeitforschung', *Zeitschrift für Historische Forschung,* 27 (2000), 573–89; Nicholas Henshall, *The myth of absolutism: change and continuity in early modern European monarchy* (London and New York: Longman, 2001); Heinz Duchardt, *Barock und Aufklärung,* 4th edn (Munich: Oldenbourg, 2007); Dagmar Freist, *Absolutismus* (Darmstadt: Wissenschaftliche Buchgesellschaft, 2008).

11   For example, Giorgio Agamben, *Herrschaft und Herrlichkeit: Zur theologischen Genealogie von Ökonomie und Regierung: Homo sacer II.2,* pbk edn (Frankfurt-am-Main: Suhrkamp, 2010); Dotan Leshem, *The origins of neoliberalism: modeling the economy from Jesus to Foucault* (New York: Columbia University Press, 2017).

12   Erik S. Reinert and Fernanda A. Reinert, '33 economic bestsellers published before 1750', *The European Journal of the History of Economic Thought* 25:6 (2018), 1206–63.

13   Roberts, 'Practicing oeconomy during the second half of the long eighteenth century'; Werrett, *Thrifty science.*

14   On different traditions of economic thought and the underlying semantics, see, most recently, Keith Tribe, *Constructing economic science: the invention of a discipline 1850–1950* (Oxford: Oxford University Press, 2022); Tribe, *Economy of the word.* A classic late *Hausväter* or *oeconomy* piece in the German language is Wolf Helmhardt von Hohberg,

Georgica Curiosa: Das ist: Umständlicher Bericht und klarer Unterricht Von dem Adelichen Land- und Feld-Leben / Auf alle in Teutschland übliche Land- und Haus-Wirthschafften gerichtet (Nuremberg: Endter, 1682). See Otto Brunner, *Adeliges Landleben und europäischer Geist: Leben und Werk Wolf Helmhards von Hohberg* (Salzburg: Müller, 1949); Johannes Burkhardt and Birger P. Priddat (eds), *Geschichte der Ökonomie* (Frankfurt-am-Main: Deutscher Klassiker Verlag, 2000), pp 128–42, and commentary, pp 759–76. For an intellectual genealogy (*Begriffsgeschichte*) of the term 'Wirtschaft' (*economy, economics*), see Johannes Burckhardt, Otto Gerhard Oexle and Peter Spahn, 'Wirtschaft', in Brunner, Conze and Koselleck (eds), *Geschichtliche Grundbegriffe*, Vol 7; relevant passages on the entry in Zincke's economic encyclopedia (1748) in Burkhardt and Priddat (eds), *Geschichte der Ökonomie*, pp 181–215, 796–805.

[15] Mauricio Drelichman and Hans-Joachim Voth, *Lending to the borrower from hell: debt, taxes, and default in the age of Philip II* (Princeton, NJ: Princeton University Press, 2017).

[16] For example, Michel Foucault, *Security – territory – population (lectures at the College de France)* (Basingstoke: Palgrave Macmillan, 2007); German edn, Michel Foucault, *Sicherheit, Territorium, Bevölkerung: Geschichte der Gouvernementalität I. Vorlesungen am Collège de France 1977/1978* (Frankfurt-am-Main: Suhrkamp, 2014); Michel Foucault, *Die Geburt der Biopolitik: Geschichte der Gouvernementalität II* (Frankfurt-am-Main: Suhrkamp, 2014).

[17] Karl Polanyi, *The great transformation: economic origins of our time* (New York: Farrar & Rinehart,1944); Daron Acemoglu and James A. Robinson, *The narrow corridor: states, societies, and the fate of liberty* (London: Penguin, 2020). From a historian's point of view, Stephan Epstein, *Freedom and growth: markets and states in pre-modern Europe* (London: Routledge, 2000).

[18] From a modern economists' point of view, for example, Douglass C. North and Robert Paul Thomas, *The rise of the Western world: a new economic history*, new edn (Cambridge: Cambridge University Press, 2009); Daron Acemoglu and James A. Robinson, *Why nations fail: the origins of power, prosperity, and poverty* (New York: Crown, 2012); Timothy Besley and Torsten Persson, *Pillars of prosperity: the political economics of development clusters* (Princeton, NJ: Princeton University Press, 2013); North, Wallis and Weingast, *Violence and social orders*; David Stasavage, *States of credit: size, power, and the development of European polities* (Princeton, NJ: Princeton University Press, 2017); M. Malinowski, 'Economic consequences of state failure; legal capacity, regulatory activity, and market integration in Poland, 1505–1772', *Journal of Economic History* 79:3 (2019), 862–96. For diverging viewpoints, Gregory Clark, 'The political foundations of modern economic growth: England, 1540–1800', *Journal of Interdisciplinary History* 26:4 (1996), 563–88; Henriques and Palma, *Comparative European institutions and the little divergence, 1385–1800*.

[19] Further to the works listed previously: Mark Dincecco, *Political transformations and public finances: Europe, 1650–1913* (Cambridge: Cambridge University Press, 2011); Mark Dincecco with Massimiliano Onorato, *From warfare to wealth: the military origins of urban prosperity in Europe* (Cambridge: Cambridge University Press, 2017); Mark Dincecco, *State capacity and economic development: present and past* (Cambridge: Cambridge University Press, 2017).

[20] Key works include Paul M. Kennedy, *The rise and fall of the great powers: economic changes and military conflict from 1500 to 2000* (London: Vintage, 1989); Geoffrey Parker, *The military revolution, 1500–1800: military innovation and the rise of the West*, 2nd edn (Cambridge: Cambridge University Press, 1996); Frank Tallett, *War and society in early modern Europe: 1495–1715*, new edn (Abingdon: Routledge, 2016).

[21] Apart from works already mentioned, see the survey in Marjolein 't Hart, 'Warfare and capitalism: the impact of the economy on state making in northwestern Europe,

seventeenth and eighteenth centuries', *Review (Fernand Braudel Center)* 23:2 (2000), 209–28; O'Brien, 'The nature and historical evolution'.

[22] For example, Mark Dincecco, 'The rise of effective states in Europe', *The Journal of Economic History* 75:3 (2015), 901–18, with a good literature overview.

[23] Acemoglu and Robinson, *Why nations fail*; Acemoglu and Robinson, *Narrow corridor*. For a critique of Acemoglu and Robinson, see, inter alia, Henriques and Palma, *Comparative European institutions and the little divergence, 1385–1800*; Peer Vries, 'Does wealth entirely depend on inclusive institutions and pluralist politics? A review of Daron Acemoglu and James A. Robinson, "Why nations fail. The origins of power, prosperity and poverty"', *Tijdschrift voor Sociale en Economische Geschiedenis* 9:3 (2012), 74–93; Francesco Boldizzoni, 'On history and policy: time in the age of neoliberalism', *Journal of the Philosophy of History* 9:1 (2015), 4-17.

[24] In global history, such a model of the European state is implied in, for example, Wong, *China transformed*; Keith Tribe, '"Das Adam Smith Problem" and the origins of modern Smith scholarship', *History of European Ideas* 34 (2008), 514–25; Rosenthal and Wong, *Before and beyond divergence*; Moritz Isenmann, 'Die langsame Entstehung eines ökonomischen Systems. Konkurrenz und freier Markt im Werk von Adam Smith', *Historische Zeitschrift* 307:3 (2018), 655–91.

[25] For example, Evans, Rueschemeyer and Skocpol (eds), *Bringing the state back in*; Chang, *Kicking away the ladder*; Erik Reinert, *How rich countries got rich … and why poor countries stay poor* (London: Constable, 2007); Kattel and Mazzucato, 'Mission-oriented innovation policy'; Mariana Mazzucato, *The entrepreneurial state: debunking public vs. private sector myths*, new edn (London: Allen Lane, 2018); Reinert, Ghosh and Kattel (eds), *Handbook of alternative theories of economic development*; Reinert, *Visionary realism*; Arkebe Oqubay, Christopher Cramer, Ha-Joon Chang and Richard Kozul-Wright (eds), *Oxford handbook of industrial policy* (Oxford: Oxford University Press, 2020); Mazzucato, *Mission economy*. Historical perspectives offered in Vries, 'Governing growth'; Prasannan Parthasarathi, *Why Europe grew rich*; further foundational studies include Vries, *State, economy and the great divergence*; Ashworth, *The Industrial Revolution*; Peer Vries, *Averting a great divergence: state and economy in Japan, 1868–1937* (London: Bloomsbury, 2019).

[26] For example, Dincecco, 'The rise of effective states in Europe'; Stasavage, *States of credit*, Introduction; Malinowski, 'Economic consequences of state failure'.

[27] Charles Tilly, *Coercion, capital, and European states, AD 990–1990*, 2nd edn (Cambridge, MA: Blackwell, 1992); Johannes Burkhardt, 'Die Friedlosigkeit der Frühen Neuzeit. Grundlegung einer Theorie der Bellizität Europas', *Zeitschrift für historische Forschung* 24:4 (1997), 509–74; Acemoglu and Robinson, *Narrow corridor*; Stasavage, *States of credit*; Hoffman, *Why did Europe conquer the world?*. See Merry Wiesner Hanks, *Early modern Europe 1450–1789*, 2nd edn (Cambridge: Cambridge University Press, 2013), p 88; and many more.

[28] Koyama and Rubin, *How the world became rich*, p 61.

[29] Most recently, Noel D. Johnson and Mark Koyama, 'States and economic growth: capacity and constraints', *Explorations in Economic History* 64 (2017), 1–20, at 3. The reference to Chang is Chang, *Kicking away the ladder*.

[30] Henry Kamen, *Early modern European society*, 3rd edn (New Haven, CT: Yale University Press, 2021), p 352.

[31] Jared Rubin, *Rulers, religion, and riches: why the west got rich and the middle east did not* (Cambridge: Cambridge University Press, 2017), p 31.

[32] Joel Mokyr, 'The past and the future of innovation: some lessons from economic history', *Explorations in Economic History* 69 (2018), 13–26, at 15.

[33] For example, Wong, *China transformed*; Rosenthal and Wong, *Before and beyond divergence*.

[34] Macchiavelli, *The Prince*, Ch. 14.

35 Helmut Walser Smith, *Germany: a nation in its time: before, during, and after nationalism, 1500–2000* (New York: Norton, 2022).

36 *Pace* psychologist Steven Pinker, *The better angels of our nature: why violence has declined* (New York: Penguin, 2012), who argues the opposite.

37 Julius Bernhards von Rohr, *Einleitung zur Staats-Klugheit* (Leipzig: Martini, 1718), p 550.

38 See Quentin Skinner, *Machiavelli: a very short introduction*, new edn (Oxford: Oxford University Press, 2000).

39 Skinner, 'Ambrogio Lorenzetti's Buon Governo frescoes'; Sophus A. Reinert, 'Achtung! Banditi! An alternate genealogy of the market', in Rössner (ed), *Economic growth and the origins of modern political economy*, pp 239–95, reprinted in Reinert, *The academy of fisticuffs*.

40 Quentin Skinner, 'Lorenzetti and the portrayal of virtuous government', reprinted in Quentin Skinner, *Visions of politics, Volume 2: Renaissance virtues* (Cambridge: Cambridge University Press, 2004), p 47. On Cicero reception and Republicanism in early modern political economy, see Reinert, *Translating empire*, Ch. 1; Steve Pincus, 'Revolution in political economy', in *1688: the first modern revolution* (New Haven, CT: Yale University Press, 2009).

41 Reinert and Carpenter, 'German language economic bestsellers', pp 26–54, at 44; most recently on Schröder, see Vera Keller, 'Happiness and projects between London and Vienna: Wilhelm von Schröder on the London Weavers' Riot of 1675, workhouses, and technological unemployment', *History of Political Economy* 53:2 (2021), 407–23.

42 As noted in List, *Das nationale System der politischen Ökonomie*, Book I (*Die Geschichte*), Ch. 1 ('Die Italiener'), 1925 edn (Stuttgart: Cotta, 1925), pp 21–8; Franco Franceschi, 'Big business for firms and states: silk manufacturing in Renaissance Italy', *Business History Review* 94:1 (2020), special issue on 'Italy and the origins of capitalism', 95–123; Reinert and Fredona, 'Political economy and the Medici', 125–77.

43 Quoted in Franceschi, 'Big business for firms and states', 112.

44 Ibid., 114–20.

45 For a deeper historical viewpoint, see, for example, Sophus A. Reinert, 'The Italian tradition of political economy: theories and policies of development in the semi-periphery of the enlightenment', in *The origins of development economics: how schools of economic thought have addressed development*, eds. Jomo K. Sundaram and Erik S. Reinert (London: Zed Books, 2005), pp 24–47.

46 List, *Das nationale System der politischen Ökonomie*. On List in a longer intellectual context, see Hont, *Jealousy of trade*, Introduction; essays in Hagemann, Seiter and Wendler (eds), *The economic thought of Friedrich List*. General historical works on economic state craft, especially before the Industrial Revolution, include: Edward Miller, 'Government economic policies', in Carlo M. Cipolla (ed), *The Fontana economic history of Europe, Vol 1: the middle ages* (London: Collins, 1992), pp 339–70; Vries, *State, economy and the great divergence*; Parthasarathi, *Why Europe grew rich*. On Germany in the early modern period, see, for example, Karl Weidner, *Die Anfänge einer staatlichen Wirtschaftspolitik in Württemberg* (Stuttgart: Kohlhammer, 1931); Fritz Blaich, *Die Wirtschaftspolitik des Reichstags im Heiligen Römischen Reich: ein Beitrag zur Problemgeschichte wirtschaftlichen Gestaltens* (Stuttgart: Fischer, 1970); Fritz Blaich, *Die Epoche des Merkantilismus* (Wiesbaden: Franz Steiner, 1973); Fritz Blaich, 'Die Bedeutung der Reichstage auf dem Gebiet der öffentlichen Finanzen im Spannungsfeld zwischen Kaiser, Territorialstaaten und Reichsstädten (1495–1679)', in Aldo De Maddalena and Hermann Kellenbenz (eds), *Finanzen und Staatsräson in Italien und Deutschland in der Frühen Neuzeit* (Berlin: Duncker & Humblot, 1992), pp 79–112. For early modern Britain, see Anna Gambles, 'Free trade and state formation: the political economy of fisheries policy in Britain and the United Kingdom, circa 1780–1850', *Journal of British Studies* 39:3 (2000), 288–316; Raymond L. Sickinger,

231

'Regulation or ruination: parliament's consistent pattern of mercantilist regulation of the English textile trade, 1660–1800', *Parliamentary History* 19:2 (2000), 211–32; William J. Ashworth, *Customs and excise: trade, production, and consumption in England, 1640–1845* (Oxford: Oxford University Press, 2003); William J. Ashworth, 'Bounties, the economy and the state in Britain, 1689–1800', in Perry Gauci (ed), *Regulating the British economy, 1660–1850* (Farnham: Ashgate, 2011); Julian Hoppit, 'The nation, the state, and the first industrial revolution', *The Journal of British Studies* 50:2 (2011), 307–31; C. Dudley, 'Party politics, political economy, and economic development in early eighteenth-century Britain', *Economic History Review*, second series 66:4 (2013), 1084–100; Steve Pincus and James A. Robinson, 'Wars and state-making reconsidered – the rise of the developmental state', *Annales: Histoire, Sciences Sociales*, English edn 71:1 (2016), 9–34; Hoppit, *Britain's political economies*. In a wider context, see Vries, 'Governing growth'; Silvia Conca Messina, *A history of states and economic policies in early modern Europe* (Abingdon: Routledge, 2019); Ann Coenen, 'Infant industry protectionism and early modern growth? Evidence from eighteenth-century entrepreneurial petitions in the Austrian Netherlands', in Rössner (ed), *Economic reasons of state*, pp 220–38; Peer Vries, 'Economic reason of state in Qing China. A brief comparative overview', ibid., pp 204–20; Prasannan Parthasarathi, 'State formation and economic growth in South Asia, 1600–1800', ibid., pp 189–203; William J. Ashworth, 'The demise of regulation and rise of political economy: taxation, industry and fiscal pressure in Britain 1763–1815', ibid., pp 122–36. Furthermore: Francesca Schinzinger, 'Wirtschaftspolitik der Habsburger in Neapel 1707–1734', in Fritz Blaich et al (eds), *Die Rolle des Staates für die wirtschaftliche Entwicklung* (Berlin: Duncker & Humblot, 1982), pp 143–67; from a history of economic thought perspective, Reinert, *Visionary realism*; Reinert, *How rich countries got rich*.

[47] For example, Acemoglu and Robinson, *Why nations fail*; North and Thomas, *The rise of the Western world*; North, Wallis and Weingast, *Violence and social orders*; Stasavage, *States of credit*. In a more historically nuanced way, see the excellent study by Alejandra Irigoin and Regina Grafe, 'Bounded Leviathan. Fiscal constraints and financial development in the early modern Hispanic world', in *Questioning credible commitment: perspectives on the rise of financial capitalism*, eds. D'Maris Coffman, Adrian Leonard and Larry Neal (Cambridge: Cambridge University Press, 2013), pp 199–227; António Henriques and Nuno Palma, *Comparative European institutions and the 'little divergence' 1385–1800*, CEPR Discussion Paper 14124 (2019).

[48] An oft-quoted study is Drelichman and Voth, *Lending to the borrower from hell*.

[49] For 20th-century European capitalisms, see Peter Hall, *Governing the economy: the politics of state intervention in Britain and France* (Oxford: Oxford University Press, 1986); and for a narratological approach, Jim Tomlinson, *Managing the economy, managing the people: narratives of economic life in Britain from Beveridge to Brexit* (Oxford: Oxford University Press, 2017).

[50] Eucken, *Grundsätze*.

[51] Rolf Sprandel, *Verfassung und Gesellschaft im Mittelalter* (Paderborn: F. Schöningh, 1978); Wolfgang Reinhard, *Geschichte der Staatsgewalt: Eine vergleichende Verfassungsgeschichte Europas von den Anfängen bis zur Gegenwart* (Munich: C.H. Beck, 1999), pp 52–80, 100–9, 122–4; Martin van Creveld, *The rise and decline of the state* (Cambridge: Cambridge University Press, 1999), Chs. 2 and 3; Joseph Strayer, *On the medieval origins of the modern state*, new edn (Princeton, NJ: Princeton University Press, 2005); Michael Mann, *The sources of social power, vol 1: a history of power from the beginning to AD 1760, vol 2: the rise of classes and nation-states, 1760–1914* (Cambridge: Cambridge University Press, 2012). A useful survey on the recent and less recent literature on early modern European statehood is Michael Gal, 'Der Staat in historischer Sicht. Zum Problem der Staatlichkeit in der Frühen Neuzeit', *Der Staat* 54:2 (2015), 241–66; and on political theory of the early modern state, apart

from works by Quentin Skinner to be discussed later, Cornel Zwierlein, *Politische Theorie und Herrschaft in der Frühen Neuzeit* (Göttingen: Vandenhoeck & Ruprecht, 2020).

52 Acemoglu and Robinson, *Why nations fail*. Further to the literature already quoted, see Greg Anderson, 'Was there any such thing as a non-modern state?', in John L. Brooke, Julia C. Strauss and Greg Anderson (eds), *State formations: global histories and cultures of statehood* (Cambridge: Cambridge University Press, 2018), pp 58–72; Quentin Skinner, 'On the person of the state', ibid., pp 23–44.

53 Von Schmoller, *The mercantile system and its historical significance*; Karl Bücher, *Die Entstehung der Volkswirtschaft*, 4th edn (Tübingen: Laupp, 1904), pp 101–74; Schabas, *The natural origins of economics*; Sophus A. Reinert, ' "One will make of political economy … what the Scholastics did with Philosophy": Henry Lloyd and the mathematization of economics', *History of Political Economy* 34:4 (2007), 643–77; Alexandra Gittermann, *Die Ökonomisierung des politischen Denkens: Neapel und Spanien im Zeichen der Reformbewegungen des 18. Jahrhunderts unter der Herrschaft Karls III* (Stuttgart: Franz Steiner, 2008); Magnusson, *The political economy of mercantilism*; Kaplan and Reinert (eds), *The economic turn*.

54 Tom Scott, *The city-state in Europe, 1000–1600: hinterland, territory, region* (Oxford: Oxford University Press, 2014); Patrick Lantschner, 'City states in the later medieval Mediterranean world', *Past & Present* 254:1 (2022), 3–49.

55 Peter Blickle, *Deutsche Untertanen: ein Widerspruch* (Munich: Beck, 1981).

56 Wieland Held, *Zwischen Marktplatz und Anger: Stadt-Land-Beziehungen im 16. Jahrhundert in Thüringen* (Weimar: Böhlau, 1988); Scott, *Society and economy in Germany*, pp 132–37, 142–53.

57 Luca Scholz, *Borders and freedom of movement in the Holy Roman Empire* (Oxford: Oxford University Press, 2020).

58 Stephan R. Epstein and Maarten Prak (eds), *Guilds, innovation and the European economy, 1400–1800* (Cambridge: Cambridge University Press, 2010); Ogilvie, *European guilds: an economic analysis*.

59 Scott, *The city-state in Europe*. Outside Germany there were a few proverbial exceptions: republics that attracted the attention of contemporaries and posterity alike included the United Provinces (the Netherlands, which formally remained part of the Empire until 1648/50), the Cromwellian interregnum during the British Civil Wars or the Swiss Confederation. Their political economies emphasized individual and corporate liberties, often with productivity and income levels far exceeding the European average. Both the Swiss Republic as well as the United Provinces remained formally part of the Holy Roman Empire until 1648/50. See André Holenstein, Thomas Maissen and Maarten Prak (eds), *The Republican alternative: the Netherlands and Switzerland compared* (Amsterdam: Amsterdam University Press, 2008); Weststijn, *Commercial republicanism in the Dutch golden age*; Thomas Maissen, *Die Geburt der Republic: Staatsverständnis und Repräsentation in der frühneuzeitlichen Eidgenossenschaft* (Göttingen: Vandenhoeck & Ruprecht, 2014); John Pocock, *The Machiavellian moment: Florentine political thought and the Atlantic republican tradition* (Princeton, NJ: Princeton University Press, 2016).

60 Heinz Schilling, *Höfe und Allianzen: Deutschland 1648–1763* (Berlin: Siedler, 1989), pp 140–4; Rubin, *Rulers, religion, and riches*.

61 Helmut Neuhaus, *Das Reich in der Frühen Neuzeit*, 2nd edn (Munich: Oldenbourg, 2003).

62 Gerhard Köbler, *Historisches Lexikon der deutschen Länder: Die deutschen Territorien vom Mittelalter bis zur Gegenwart*, 8th edn (Munich: Beck, 2019); for comparison: Thomas Ertman, *Birth of the Leviathan: building states and regimes in medieval and early modern Europe* (Cambridge: Cambridge University Press, 2011). Major recent English-language surveys on the Holy Roman Empire include Hagen, *German history in modern times*; Whaley, *Germany and the Holy Roman Empire*; Wilson, *The Holy Roman Empire*.

[63] Neuhaus, *Das Reich in der Frühen Neuzeit*, pp 91–5. With some remarks on currency and economic policy on imperial circle basis, Winfried Dotzauer, *Die deutschen Reichskreise in der Verfassung des alten Reiches und ihr Eigenleben (1500–1806)* (Darmstadt: Wissenschaftliche Buchgesellschaft, 1989); Konrad Schneider, 'Zur Tätigkeit der Generalwardeine des Oberrheinischen Reichskreises, vornehmlich im 18. Jahrhundert', *Jahrbuch für westdeutsche Landesgeschichte* 17 (1991), 95–128. Winfried Dotzauer, *Die deutschen Reichskreise (1383–1806): Geschichte und Aktenedition* (Stuttgart: Franz Steiner, 1998); Peter Claus Hartmann, 'Rolle, Funktion und Bedeutung der Reichskreise im Heiligen Römischen Reich deutscher Nation', in Wolfgang Wüst (ed), *Reichskreis und Territorium: Die Herrschaft über der Herrschaft? Supraterritoriale Tendenzen in Politik, Kultur, Wirtschaft und Gesellschaft: Ein Vergleich süddeutscher Reichskreise* (Stuttgart: Thorbecke, 2000), pp 27–37; Thomas Nicklas, *Macht oder Recht: frühneuzeitliche Politik im Obersächsischen Reichskreis* (Stuttgart: Franz Steiner, 2002); Lars Boerner and Oliver Volckart, 'The utility of a common coinage: currency unions and the integration of money markets in late Medieval Central Europe', *Explorations in Economic History* 48:1 (2011), 53–65.

[64] Schilling, *Höfe und Allianzen*, p 118–19; Blaich, *Die Wirtschaftspolitik des Reichstags*. On monetary policy, see Oliver Volckart, *Eine Währung für das Reich: Die Akten der Münztage zu Speyer 1549 und 1557* (Stuttgart: Franz Steiner, 2017).

[65] Bog, *Der Reichsmerkantilismus*.

[66] On monetary issues as an integrating factor in imperial politics, see Oliver Volckart, 'The dear old Holy Roman Realm: how does it hold together? Monetary policies, cross-cutting cleavages and political cohesion in the age of Reformation', *German History* 38:4 (2020), 365–86.

[67] See J. Törzsök, *Friendly advice by Nārāyaṇa & 'King Vikrama's adventures* (New York: NYU Press, 2007), p 323. I am indebted to Harald Wiese (Leipzig) for providing this reference.

[68] Both quotes from an unpublished working paper courtesy of Prof Harald Wiese, Universität Leipzig.

[69] Aquinas, *On Kingship, to the King of Cyprus (De regno [De regimine principum), ad regem Cypri),*(1267) Ch. 15: 'Est tamen praeconsiderandum quod gubernare est, id quod gubernatur, convenienter ad debitum finem perducere. Sic etiam navis gubernari dicitur dum per nautae industriam recto itinere ad portum illaesa perducitur. Si igitur aliquid ad finem extra se ordinetur, ut navis ad portum, ad gubernatoris officium pertinebit non solum ut rem in se conservet illaesam, sed quod ulterius ad finem perducat. Si vero aliquid esset, cuius finis non esset extra ipsum, ad hoc solum intenderet gubernatoris intentio ut rem illam in sua perfectione conservaret illaesam'. https://www.corpusthomisticum. org/orp.html

[70] Aquinas, *De Regno*, Ch. 16.

[71] From a development perspective, see Reinert and Carpenter, 'German language economic bestsellers'; Erik S. Reinert, 'Italy and the birth of development economics', in Erik S. Reinert, Jayati Ghosh and Rainer Kattel (eds), *Elgar handbook of alternative theories of development* (Cheltenham: Edward Elgar, 2016), pp 3–42, at p 15. See also brief remarks on *Fürstenspiegel* and later economic policies, John McGovern, 'The rise of new economic attitudes – economic humanism, economic nationalism – during the later middle ages and the Renaissance, AD 1200–1550', *Traditio* 26 (1970), 217–53; Cary C. Nederman, 'The monarch and the marketplace: economic policy and royal finance in William of Pagula's Speculum regis Edwardi III', *History of Political Economy* 33:1 (2001), 51–69; Lars Magnusson, *Nation, state and the industrial revolution: the visible hand* (Abingdon: Routledge, 2009).

[72] 'Gegen die Armen seidt freigebig es ist auch Christi befell, dadurch Samlet Ihr Euch einen vnuergencklichen Schatz im himmell, welchen keine motten oder Rust fressen, oder diebe

nach graben werden', *Politisches Testament des Großen Kurfürsten* (19 Mai 1667), printed in Richard Dietrich (ed), *Die politischen Testamente der Hohenzollern* (Cologne: Böhlau, 1986), pp 179–204.

[73] *Deuteronomy* 17:17 (Old Testament, 5 Moses). On Deuteronomy as one of the earliest 'princes mirrors', see Stuart Lasine, 'Samuel-Kings as a mirror for princes: parental education and Judean royal families', *Scandinavian Journal of the Old Testament: An International Journal of Nordic Theology* 34:1 (2020), 74–88, at 76.

[74] As I have argued in Rössner, 'Burying money'.

[75] See, for example, Sascha O. Becker, Steven Pfaff and Jared Rubin, 'Causes and consequences of the Protestant Reformation', *Explorations in Economic History* 62 (2016), 1–25; Davide Cantoni, Jeremiah Dittmar and Noam Yuchtman, 'Religious competition and reallocation: the political economy of secularization in the Protestant Reformation', *Quarterly Journal of Economics* 133:4 (2018), 2036–96; Jeremiah E. Dittmar and Ralf R. Meisenzahl, 'Public goods institutions, human capital, and growth: evidence from German history', *The Review of Economic Studies* 87:2 (2020), 959–96.

[76] On primitive or original accumulation, see Marx, *Kapital*, Vol I; Yazdani and Mohajer, 'Reading Marx in the divergence debate'; for a Foucauldian reading of 18th-century market governmentality, see Harcourt, *The illusion of free markets*.

[77] A concise synopsis can be found in Jonsson, 'The origins of cornucopianism'; and in a forthcoming book which I have had the pleasure reading in draft: Jonsson and Wennerlind, *Scarcity*.

[78] James VI, *Basilikon Doron or His Majesties Instrvctions To His Dearest Sonne, Henry the Prince* (Edinburgh, 1599). I have used the online edition on: www.stoics.com/basilikon_do ron.html#'Merchants1 (last accessed 17 January 2022). On the *Basilikon Doron*, its use in politics and public discourse and intended authorship, see James Doelman, ' "A King of Thine Own Heart": the English reception of King James VI and I's Basilikon Doron, *The Seventeenth Century* 9:1 (1994), 1–9.

[79] Ibid.

[80] https://digi20.digitalesammlungen.de/de/fs1/object/display/bsb00046070_00140.html, p 142 (Latin), p 143 (German translation).

[81] Erasmus, *Institutio Principis Christiani*, Ch 4. On money in the age of Erasmus, see, for example, John Munro, 'The coinages and monetary policies of Henry VIII', in *The collected works of Erasmus: Correspondence*, Vol 14: *Letters 1926 to 2081* (1528), eds. Charles Fantazzi and James Estes (Toronto: University of Toronto Press, 2011), pp 423–76, at p 441, for Erasmus's transactions and correspondence with his banker, Erasmus Schetz.

[82] Rössner, *Deflation – Devaluation – Rebellion*, Ch. 4.

[83] Monetary data in Thomas J. Sargent and François R. Velde, *The big problem of small change* (Princeton, NJ: Princeton University Press, 2002).

[84] Johann Heinrich Gottlob Justi, *Grundfeste zur Macht und Glückseligkeit der Staaten* Vol 1 (Königsberg: Hartungs Erben, 1760), p 602.

[85] On England, see Early Modern Research Group, 'Commonwealth: the social, cultural, and conceptual contexts of an early modern keyword', *The Historical Journal* 54:3 (2011), 659–87, at 663–6.

[86] Martha Howell, 'Whose "common good"? Parisian market regulation, *c.*1300–1800', in Simon Middleton and James E. Shaw (eds), *Market ethics and practices, c.1300–1850* (Abingdon: Routledge, 2017), pp 46–62, at p 47.

[87] Peter Blickle, 'Der Gemeine Nutzen. Ein kommunaler Wert und seine politische Karriere', in Herfried Münkler and Harald Bluhm (eds), *Forschungsberichte der interdisziplinären Arbeitsgruppe 'Gemeinwohl und Gemeinsinn' der Berlin-Brandenburgischen Akademie der Wissenschaften, Vol 1: Gemeinwohl und Gemeinsinn: Historische Semantiken politischer Leitbegriffe* (Berlin: Akademie, 2001), pp 85–107.

88 Peter Hibst, 'Begriffsgeschichtliche Untersuchungen zur politischen Theorie vom 5. vorchristlichen bis zum 15. nachchristlichen Jahrhundert', *Archiv für Begriffsgeschichte* 33 (1990), 60–95; Blickle, 'Der Gemeine Nutzen'.

89 Gaismair's revolutionary reform programme is printed in Günther Franz (ed), *Quellen zur Geschichte des Bauernkrieges* (Darmstadt: Wissenschaftliche Buchgesellschaft, 1963), no. 92. Interpretation in Siegfried Hoyer, 'Die Tiroler Landesordnung des Michael Gaismair. Überlieferung und zeitgenössische Einflüsse', in Fridolin Dörrer (ed), *Die Bauernkriege und Michael Gaismair* (Innsbruck: Tiroler Landesarchiv, 1982), pp 67–78; Tom Scott, 'The Reformation and modern political economy: Luther and Gaismair compared', in Thomas A. Brady (ed), *Die deutsche Reformation zwischen Spätmittelalter und Früher Neuzeit* (Munich: Oldenbourg, 2001), pp 173–202; Blickle, *Die Revolution von 1525*, for example, pp 199, 215, 223–5, 289–90.

90 Thomas Simon, 'Gemeinwohltopik in der mittelalterlichen und frühneuzeitlichen Politiktheorie', in Münkler and Bluhm (eds), *Forschungsberichte*, pp 129–46, at p 129; Blickle, 'Der Gemeine Nutzen', p 102.

91 Early Modern Research Group, 'Commonwealth', 666; Phil Withington, *The politics of commonwealth: citizens and freemen in early modern England* (Cambridge: Cambridge University Press, 2005); M.S. Kempshall, *The common good in late medieval political thought* (Oxford: Clarendon Press, 2006).

92 Reinert, 'Economic bestsellers', pp 44–9; Raskov, 'Cameralism in eighteenth-century Russia'.

93 See Adam, *The political economy of J.H.G. Justi*; Jürgen Backhaus, Ulrich Adam and Erik S. Reinert, 'Introduction', in Backhaus (ed), *The beginnings of political economy*; a bio-bibliography of Justi in Reinert, *Visionary realism*, Ch. 5. Most recently, see an unpublished PhD thesis by Zhao, *The political economy of Johann Heinrich Gottlob von Justi (1717–1771)*. See further works and references in Chs. 1 and 2.

94 List, *Das nationale System*, p 9; Ulrich Engelhardt, 'Zum Begriff der Glückseligkeit in der kameralistischen Staatslehre des 18. Jahrhunderts (J.H.G. von Justi)', *Zeitschrift für historische Forschung* 8 (1981), 37–79; Adriana Luna Fabritius, 'The secularization of happiness in early eighteenth-century Italian political thought: revisiting the foundations of civil society', in László Kontler and Mark Somos (eds), *Trust and happiness in the history of European political thought* (Leiden: Brill, 2017), pp 169–95; on an Italian context, Federico D'Onofrio, 'On the concept of "felicitas publica" in eighteenth-century political economy', *Journal of the History of Economic Thought* 37:3 (2015), 449–71; Darrin McMahon, *Happiness: a history* (New York: Grove Press, 2006), for a broader conceptual history of 'happiness'.

95 On cameralism and *Medicinalpolicey*, see Torsten Grumbach, *Kurmainzer Medicinalpolicey 1650–1803: Eine Darstellung entlang der landesherrlichen Verordnungen* (Frankfurt-am-Main: Klostermann, 2006).

96 Johann Heinrich (von) Justi, *Kurzer systematischer Grundriß aller ökonomischen und Kameralwissenschaften* (1761), reprinted in Burkhardt and Priddat (eds), *Geschichte der Ökonomie*, pp 216–324.

97 See Backhaus (ed), *Beginnings*, 'Introduction', pp 1–18; Reinert and Carpenter, 'German language economic bestsellers', pp 44–50; Seppel and Tribe (eds), *Cameralism in practice*.

98 Fabritius, 'The secularization of happiness'; Engelhardt, 'Zum Begriff der Glückseligkeit'.

99 Sandl, 'Development as possibility'; Engelhardt, 'Zum Begriff der Glückseligkeit', 41–2; Mary Lindemann, '"A political *fiat lux*": Wilhem von Schroeder (1640–1688) and the co-production of chymical and political oeconomy', in Sandra Richter and Guillaume Garner (eds), *'Eigennutz' und 'gute Ordnung': Ökonomisierungen der Welt im 17. Jahrhundert* (Wiesbaden: Harrassowitz, 2016), pp 353–78; Vera Keller, 'Perfecting the state: alchemy and *oeconomy* as academic forms of knowledge in early modern German-speaking

lands', in Mary Lindemann and Jared Poley (eds), *Money in the German-speaking lands* (New York: Berghahn, 2017).

[100] Justi, *Grundsätze* (1782, 3rd edn [1756]), pp 219, 222.

[101] Friedrich-Christoph Förster, *Ausführliches Handbuch der Geschichte, Geographie und Statistik der Mark Brandenburg und der dazu gehoerenden Marken* Pt. II (Berlin: Christiani, 1824), p123–4.

[102] *Politisches Testament des Großen Kurfürsten* (19 May 1667), reprinted in Dietrich (ed), *Die politischen*, pp 179–204.

[103] A German translation of the *Antimachiavell* is to be found on http://friedrich.uni-trier.de/de/volz/7/text/. On luxury and Smith, see, for example, Terry Peach, 'Adam Smith's "optimistic deism", the invisible hand of providence, and the unhappiness of nations', *History of Political Economy* 46:1 (2014), 55–83; Herzog, *Inventing the market*, Ch. 2.

[104] Frederick the Great, *Political Testament* (1752), (Berlin: Reclam, 1986) section on *Die Einnahmen der Kriegskasse und ihre Verwaltung*.

[105] See Introduction. I have extended the argument in Philipp Robinson Rössner, 'Marx, mercantilism and the Cameralist path to wealth', *Vierteljahrschrift für Sozial- und Wirtschaftsgeschichte* 108:2 (2021), 224–54.

[106] This is the argument in Reinert, *Visionary realism*; Reinert, *How rich countries got rich*.

[107] See, for example, Mary Rose, 'The politics of protection: an institutional approach to government – industry relations in the British and United States cotton industries, 1945–73', *Business History* 3 (1997), 128–50; Barry Eichengreen, *The European economy since 1945: coordinated capitalism and beyond* (Princeton, NJ: Princeton University Press, 2008); Jim Tomlinson, 'Managing decline: the case of Jute', *Scottish Historical Review* 90:230 (2011), 57–79; Carlo Joseph Morelli, Jim Tomlinson and Valerie Wright, 'The managing of competition: government and industry relationships in the jute industry 1957–63', *Business History* 54:5 (2012), 765–82, esp. 766–7.

[108] Sverre A. Christensen, 'Capitalism and state ownership models', in Casson and Rössner (eds), *Evolutions of capitalism: historical perspectives 1200–2000*, pp 127–56.

[109] Wilhelm Röpke, *Jenseits von Angebot und Nachfrage* (Erlenbach/Zürich/Stuttgart: Eugen Rentsch Verlag, 1958); Wilhelm Röpke, *Die Lehre von der Wirtschaft*, 13th edn (Berne: Haupt, 1994), Ch. 1. On German ordoliberalism, see Keith Tribe, *Governing economy: the reformation of German economic discourse, 1750–1840* (Cambridge: Cambridge University Press, 1988); Stefan Kolev, *Neoliberale Staatsverständnisse im Vergleich*, 2nd edn (Berlin: De Gruyter Oldenbourg, 2017); Stefan Schwarzkopf (ed), *Handbook of economic theology* (Abingdon: Routledge, 2019); on ordoliberalism's grounding in Lutheran theology and social theory, Philipp Manow, 'Ordoliberalismus als ökonomische Ordnungstheologie', *Leviathan*, 29:2 (2001), 179–98; Troels Krarup, ' "Ordo" versus "Ordnung": Catholic or Lutheran roots of German ordoliberal economic theory?' *International Review of Economics* 66 (2010), 305–23.

[110] Henriques and Palma, *Comparative European institutions and the little divergence, 1385–1800*. For bigger surveys, see Vries, 'Governing growth'; Vries, *State, economy and the great divergence*; Messina, *History of states and economic policies*. For medieval and early modern Europe, also Epstein, *Freedom and growth*.

[111] Angus Maddison, *The world economy: a millennial perspective* (OECD, 2000); 'Maddison Database', see www.rug.nl/ggdc/historicaldevelopment/maddison/?lang=en. Recent developments are laid out in Jutta Bolt and Jan Luiten van Zanden, 'Maddison style estimates of the evolution of the world economy. A new 2020 update', Maddison-Project Working Paper WP-15 (October 2020). On English/British GDP growth since the late Middle Ages, see the collective Stephen Broadberry, Bruce M.S. Campbell et al, *British economic growth, 1270–1870* (Cambridge: Cambridge University Press, 2015). Approaches that revolutionized the study of historical national income included Nick F.R. Crafts, *British economic growth during the industrial revolution* (Oxford: Oxford University Press, 1985),

revising an earlier method presented in Phyllis Deane and W.A. Cole, *British economic growth 1688–1959: trends and structure*, 2nd edn (Cambridge: Cambridge University Press, 1967). Relatively up-to-date figures can be found in Stephen Broadberry and Kevin H. O'Rourke (eds), *The Cambridge economic history of modern Europe*, 2 vols (Cambridge: Cambridge University Press, 2010); Roderick Floud, Jane Humphries and Paul Johnson (eds), *The Cambridge economic history of modern Britain*, 3 vols (Cambridge: Cambridge University Press, 2014). Methodological approaches and problems have been discussed, inter alia, in Herman J. Jong and Nuno Palma, 'Historical national accounting', in Matthias Blum and Christopher L. Colvin (eds), *An economist's guide to economic history* (Cham: Palgrave Macmillan, 2018), pp 395–403; Georg Christ and Philipp Robinson Rössner (eds), *History and economic life: a student's guide to approaching economic and social history sources* (Abingdon: Routledge, 2020). See especially Nuno Palma, 'Historical account books as a source for quantitative history', in ibid. On the related problem of wages, see the critical account in John Hatcher and Judy Z. Stephenson (eds), *Seven centuries of unreal wages: the unreliable data, sources and methods that have been used for measuring standards of living in the past* (Cham: Palgrave Macmillan, 2018).

[112] Thomas Piketty, *Capital in the twenty-first century* (Cambridge, MA: Belknap, 2014).

[113] Kattel and Mazzucato, 'Mission-oriented innovation policy'; Reinert, *How rich countries got rich*.

[114] Pat Hudson, *The Industrial Revolution*, 2nd edn (London: Hodder Arnold, 2005).

[115] For late medieval Germany, Sidney Pollard, *Peaceful conquest: the industrialization of Europe, 1760–1970* (Oxford: Oxford University Press, 1981); Wolfgang von Stromer, 'Gewerbereviere und Protoindustrien in Spätmittelalter und Frühneuzeit', in Hans Pohl (ed), *Gewerbe- und Industrielandschaften vom Spätmittelalter bis ins 20. Jahrhundert* (Stuttgart: Franz Steiner, 1986), pp 39–111; Karl Heinrich Kaufhold, 'Gewerbelandschaften in der Frühen Neuzeit (1650–1800)', in ibid., pp 112–202.

[116] Paul Krugman, *Geography and trade* (Cambridge, MA: Leuven University Press & MIT Press, 1991); Marcus Sandl, *Ökonomie des Raumes: Der kameralwissenschaftliche Entwurf der Staatswirtschaft im 18. Jahrhundert* (Cologne: Böhlau, 1999).

[117] Karl Gunnar Persson, *Grain markets in Europe, 1500–1900: integration and deregulation* (Cambridge: Cambridge University Press, 2005); Victoria Bateman, *Markets and growth in early modern Europe* (London: Pickering & Chatto, 2012).

[118] Kula, *An economic theory of the feudal system*. An excellent recent survey is Cerman, *Villagers and lords*; for a critical essay on method, Francesco Boldizzoni, *The poverty of Clio: resurrecting economic history* (Princeton, NJ: Princeton University Press, 2011).

[119] Joseph E. Stiglitz and Justin Lin Yifu (eds), *The industrial policy revolution 1: the role of government beyond ideology* (Basingstoke: Palgrave Macmillan, 2013), Foreword and Introduction.

[120] A case study is Regina Grafe, *Distant tyranny: markets, power and backwardness in Spain, 1650–1800* (Princeton, NJ: Princeton University Press, 2012); Regina Grafe, 'Polycentric states: the Spanish reigns and the "failures" of mercantilism', in Stern and Wennerlind (eds), *Mercantilism reimagined*, pp 241–62.

[121] Schilling, *Höfe und Allianzen*, p 90.

[122] Moritz Isenmann, 'From privilege to economic law: vested interests and the origins of free trade theory in France (1687–1701)', in Rössner (ed), *Economic reasons of state*.

[123] Grafe, *Distant tyranny*.

[124] Robert B. Ekelund, Jr and Robert D. Tollison, *Mercantilism as a rent-seeking society: economic regulation in historical perspective* (Texas: A&M University Press, 1981); Nuala Zahedieh, 'Regulation, rent-seeking, and the Glorious Revolution in the English Atlantic economy', *Economic History Review* 63:4 (2010), 865–90.

[125] Barbara L. Solow and Stanley L. Engerman (eds), *British capitalism and Caribbean slavery: the legacy of Eric Williams* (Cambridge: Cambridge University Press, 1987); Inikori, *Africans and the industrial revolution in England*.

[126] On modern railways, the problem of spillover effects and linkages has been discussed inter alia by Robert Fogel, *Railroads and American economic growth* (Baltimore, MD: Johns Hopkins University Press, 1970); Rainer Fremdling, *Eisenbahnen und deutsches Wirtschaftswachstum 1840–1879: Ein Beitrag zur Entwicklungstheorie*, 2nd edn (Dortmund: Gesellschaft für Westfälische Wirtschaftsgeschichte e.V., 1985).

[127] Markus Friedrich, *Die Geburt des Archivs* (Munich: Oldenbourg, 2013); Philipp Müller, 'Archives and history: towards a history of 'the use of state archives' in the 19th century', *History of the Human Sciences* 26:4 (2013), 27–49; Alexandra Walsham, 'The social history of the archive: record-keeping in early modern Europe', *Past & Present* 230:S11 (2016), 9–48; Arlette Farge, *The allure of the archives* (Princeton, NJ: Princeton University Press, 2017).

[128] Eucken, *Grundsätze*, pp 334–7.

[129] Frederick Chapin Lane, 'The role of governments in economic growth in early modern times', *Journal of Economic History* 35 (1975), 8–17, at 10–11.

[130] Frederick Chapin Lane, *Venice and history: the collected papers of Frederic C. Lane*, new edn (Baltimore, MD: Johns Hopkins University Press, 2020), nos. 22–4; Acemoglu and Robinson, *Why nations fail*; Acemoglu and Robinson, *Narrow corridor*.

[131] For 17th-century fairs and economic planning by the Scottish Parliament, see Ian D. Whyte, 'The growth of periodic market centres in Scotland, 1600–1707', *Scottish Geographical Magazine* 95 (1979), 13–26; Gordon Marshall, *Presbyteries and profits: Calvinism and the development of capitalism in Scotland, 1560–1707* (Edinburgh: Edinburgh University Press, 1992).

[132] Oscar Gelderblom, *Cities of commerce: the institutional foundations of international trade in the Low Countries, 1250–1650* (Princeton, NJ: Princeton University Press, 2017).

[133] Nipperdey, *Die Erfindung der Bevölkerungspolitik*. See also Paul Münch, 'The growth of the modern state', in Sheilagh Ogilvie (ed), *Germany: a new social and economic history*, Vol II (London and New York: Arnold, 1996), p 215–16.

[134] Dominik Collet, 'Storage and starvation: public granaries as agents of food security in early modern Europe', *Historical Social Research* 35 (2010), 234–52; Wong, *China transformed*.

[135] For the German-speaking lands, the fundamental survey is Eberhard Isenmann, *Die deutsche Stadt im Mittelalter 1150–1550*, new edn (Cologne: Böhlau, 2014). For broader context and interlinkages with medieval social theory and thought, see Joel Kaye, *Economy and nature in the fourteenth century: money, market exchange, and the emergence of scientific thought* (Cambridge: Cambridge University Press, 1998); Wood, *Medieval economic thought*; James Davis, *Medieval market morality: life, law and ethics in the English marketplace, 1200–1500* (Cambridge: Cambridge University Press, 2011).

[136] Methodological sections and chapters in Hans-Jürgen Gerhard and Alexander Engel, *Preisgeschichte der vorindustriellen Zeit: Ein Kompendium auf Basis ausgewählter Hamburger Materialien* (Stuttgart: Franz Steiner, 2006); Hans-Jürgen Gerhard, *Wesen und Wirkung vorindustrieller Taxen: Preishistorische Würdigung einer wichtigen Quellengattung* (Stuttgart: Franz Steiner, 2012); Jan de Vries, *The price of bread: regulating the market in the Dutch Republic* (Cambridge: Cambridge University Press, 2019).

[137] Pomeranz, *Great divergence*, Chs. 2, 4; Wong, *China transformed*; discussion in Vries, *State, economy and the great divergence*, pp 347–50.

[138] Schumpeter, *History of economic analysis*.

[139] Becher, *Politischer*. On Becher, see respective sections in Burkhardt and Priddat, *Geschichte der Ökonomie*; Herbert Hassinger, *Johann Joachim Becher, 1635–1682: Ein Beitrag zur Geschichte des Merkantilismus* (Vienna: Holzhausen, 1951); Smith, *The business of alchemy*.

[140] Nina Ellinger Bang and Knud Korst (eds), *Tabeller over Skibsfart og Varetransport gennem Øresund 1661–1783 og gennem Storebælt 1701–1748*, Vol 1.1 (Copenhagen: Gyldendal, 1939), Vol 1.2 (Copenhagen: Gyldendal, 1945); Ralph Davis, 'English foreign trade, 1700–1774', *Economic History Review*, 2nd series, XV (1962), 285–303; Ralph Davis, *British overseas trade: from 1700 to the 1930s* (Oxford: Blackwell, 1952); Ralph Davis, 'English foreign trade, 1660–1700', *Economic History Review*, 2nd series, VI (1954), 150–66; E.M. Carus Wilson and Olive Coleman, *England's export trade, 1275–1547* (Oxford: Clarendon Press, 1963); Sven Erik Åström, *From cloth to iron: the Anglo-Baltic trade in the late seventeenth century, pt. II: the customs accounts as sources for the study of the trade* (Helsingfors: Societas Scientiarum Fennica, 1965); Jürgen Schneider, Otto-Ernst Krawehl and Markus A. Denzel (eds), *Statistik des Hamburger seewärtigen Einfuhrhandels im 18. Jahrhundert: Nach den Admiralitätszoll- und Convoygeld-Einnahmebüchern* (St Katharinen: Scripta Mercaturae Verlag, 2001); Martin Rorke, 'English and Scottish overseas trade, 1300–1600', *Economic History Review*, 2nd series, 59:2 (2006), 265–88; Philipp Robinson Rössner, *Scottish trade in the wake of union (1700–1760): the rise of a warehouse economy* (Stuttgart: Franz Steiner, 2008), Ch. 2; Werner Scheltjens, *North Eurasian trade in world history, 1660–1860: the economic and political importance of the Baltic Sea* (Abingdon: Routledge, 2021); more recent research with Dutch and Danish (digitized) Sound Toll records, see Jan Willem Veluwenkamp and Werner Scheltjens (eds), *Early modern shipping and trade: novel approaches using sound toll registers online* (Leiden: Brill, 2018).

[141] A.J. Durie, *The Scottish linen industry in the eighteenth century* (Edinburgh: John Donald, 1979).

[142] Lars Behrisch, *Die Berechnung der Glückseligkeit: Statistik und Politik in Deutschland und Frankreich im späten Ancien Régime* (Ostfildern: Thorbecke, 2016); Deringer, *Calculated values*.

[143] Christopher Hill, *The century of revolution* (London: Routledge Classics, 2001).

[144] For the Scottish linen industry, see Durie, *Scottish linen industry*. For post-1763 Saxony, Karin Zachmann, 'Kursächsischer Merkantilismus', in Günter Bayerl and Ulrich Troitzsch (eds), *Sozialgeschichte der Technik: Ulrich Troitzsch zum 60. Geburtstag* (Münster: Waxmann, 1998), pp 121–30, at p 127.

[145] Reinert, 'Role of the state'; Reinert, *Visionary realism*.

[146] Ibid.; Barry Supple, 'The state and the industrial revolution', in C.M. Cipolla (ed), *The Fontana economic history of Europe*, Vol 3 (London: Collins, 1973), pp 305–13.

[147] For 18th-century Flanders (Austrian Netherlands), see Coenen, 'Infant industry protectionism and early modern growth?'; for the Kingdom of Naples, also under Habsburg rule, Schinzinger, 'Wirtschaftspolitik der Habsburger'; for the Austrian Empire, Kaps, 'Cores and peripheries reconsidered'; Mária Hidvégi, 'Land, people and the unused economic potential of Hungary: knowledge transfer in the context of cameralism and statistics, 1790–1848', *History of Political Economy* 53:3 (2021), 571–94.

[148] Miller in Cipolla (ed), *Fontana economic history of Europe* 1, pp 362, 365. See also Peter Spufford, *Monetary problems and policies in the Burgundian Netherlands 1433–1497* (Leiden: Brill, 1970); John H. Munro, *Wool, cloth and gold: the struggle for bullion in Anglo-Burgundian trade, 1340–1478* (Bruxelles: University of Toronto Press, 2020).

[149] Bog, *Reichsmerkantilismus*.

[150] A fresh interpretation of Justi's system can be found in Zhao, 'Public happiness through manufacturing and innovation'.

[151] Brisco, *The economic policy of Robert Walpole*; Rössner, *Scottish trade in the wake of Union*, Ch. 2, Appendix; Parthasarathi, *Why Europe grew rich*.

[152] Werner Sombart, *Der moderne Kapitalismus*, 4th edn, Vols I and II (Munich: Duncker & Humblot, 1927).

[153] For example, Gunner Lind, 'Early military industry in Denmark-Norway, 1500–1814', *Scandinavian Journal of History* 38:4 (2013), 405–42.

[154] Stadtarchiv Leipzig, *Titularakten*, XLIV; Grumbach, *Kurmainzer Medicinalpolicey.*

[155] On brokers, see Gelderblom, *Cities of commerce*; on the early modern fairs of Bolzano/ Bozen, Markus A. Denzel, 'Das Maklerwesen auf den Bozner Messen im 18. Jahrhundert', *Vierteljahrschrift für Sozial- und Wirtschaftsgeschichte* 96:3 (2009), 297–319.

[156] STA Leipzig *Titularakten*, XLV/7.

[157] Beater Berger, Bodo Gronemann and Jakuf Pacer (eds), *Vom Aderlass zum Gesundheitspass: Zeittafel zur Geschichte des öffentlichen Gesundheitswesens in Leipzig, Leipziger Kalender Sonderband* 2000/4 (Leipzig: Leipziger Universitaetsverlag, 2000), pp 6–7, 88–9.

Chapter 4

[1] *Stenographischer Bericht über die Verhandlungen der bayerischen Kammer der Abgeordneten, 80. Sitzung vom 10. April 1888*, 174–5 in STA Leipzig, *Acta die Marktordnung betreffend*, Vol III, fol. 12ff.

[2] After Sombart, *Der moderne Kapitalismus*, 3rd edn, Vol I/II, (Munich & Leipzig: Duncker & Humblot, 1919), p 446.

[3] For example, Fernand Braudel, *Civilization & capitalism, 15th to 18th century*, transl. S. Reynolds, new edn (London: Phoenix, 2002), Vol 2, pp 75–80; Laurence Fontaine, *The moral economy: poverty, credit, and trust in early modern Europe* (Cambridge: Cambridge University Press, 2014). On retailing, see Jon Stobart and Vicki Howard (eds), *The Routledge companion to the history of retailing* (Abingdon: Routledge, 2020).

[4] Wood, *Medieval economic thought*, p 140.

[5] See note 1.

[6] Johann Gottlob Heinrich von Justi, *Die Grundfeste zu der Macht und Glückseeligkeit der Staaten* (Leipzig & Königsberg: Hartungs Erben, 1760), Vol 1, p 591, referring to antiquity and the proverbial riches of the Phoenicians.

[7] Justi, *Grundfeste*, I, pp 591–4.

[8] Laurence Fontaine, *History of pedlars in Europe* (Durham, NC: Duke University Press, 1996).

[9] Sombart, *Der moderne Kapitalismus*, Vol II/III, 3rd edn, 1919.

[10] Sombart, *Der moderne Kapitalismus*, Vol I/II, 3rd edn (Munich: Duncker & Humblot, 1919), pp 444–51.

[11] Thomas Nipperdey, *Deutsche Geschichte 1866–1918*, Vol 2: *Machtstaat vor der Demokratie* (Munich: Beck, 1992); Dieter Ziegler, 'Das Zeitalter der Industrialisierung 1815–1914', in Michael North (ed), *Deutsche Wirtschaftsgeschichte: Ein Jahrtausend im Überblick*, 2nd edn (Munich: Beck, 2014); Richard H. Tilly and Michael Kopsidis, *A history of German industrialisation from the eighteenth century to World War I* (Chicago: Chicago University Press, 2020); Wehler, *Deutsche Gesellschaftsgeschichte*, Vol 3: *Von der 'Deutschen Doppelrevolution' bis zum Beginn des Ersten Weltkrieges 1849–1914.*

[12] Sidney Pollard, *Region und Industrialisierung: Studien zur Rolle in der Wirtschaftsgeschichte der letzten zwei Jahrhunderte* (Göttingen: Vandenhoeck & Ruprecht, 1980); Hubert Kiesewetter, *Region und Industrie in Europa 1815–1995* (Stuttgart: Franz Steiner, 2009); Siemaszko, *Das oberschlesische Eisenhüttenwesen.*

[13] Frank Trentmann, *Free trade nation: commerce, consumption, and civil society in modern Britain* (Oxford: Oxford University Press, 2009).

[14] Fontaine, *History of pedlars.*

[15] *Stenographischer Bericht über die Verhandlungen der bayerischen Kammer der Abgeordneten, 80. Sitzung vom 10. April 1888*, p 178.

[16] *Stenographischer Bericht über die Verhandlungen der bayerischen Kammer der Abgeordneten*, 263. Sitzung vom 29 April 1892, p 509.

[17] Ibid., p 508.

[18] *Stenographischer Bereicht über die Verhandlungen der bayerischen Kammer der Abgeordneten*, 201. Sitzung vom 17. Dezember 1891, p 578–9.

[19] *Stenographischer Bericht über die Verhandlungen der bayerischen Kammer der Abgeordneten*, 110. Sitzung vom 4. Dezember 1889, pp 408–9, 412–15.

[20] In 1879, taxes on peddling had been increased, with the aim of pricing this activity out of the market.

[21] Report of the Bavarian state minister for domestic affairs Freiherr von Feilitzsch, see *Stenographischer Bericht über die Verhandlungen der bayerischen Kammer der Abgeordneten*, 80. Sitzung vom 10. April 1888, pp 182–3.

[22] *Stenographischer Bereicht über die Verhandlungen der bayerischen Kammer der Abgeordneten*, 110. Sitzung vom 4. Dezember 1889, p 414–15.

[23] Richard Britnell, 'The proliferation of markets in England, 1200–1349', *Economic History Review*, 2nd series, 33 (1981), 209–21; Richard Britnell, 'Local trade, remote trade: institutions, information and market integration 1050–1330', in *Fiere e mercati nella integrazione delle economie europee, sec. XIII–XVIII*, ed. S. Cavaciocchi, Atti delle Settimane di Studi e altri Convegni 32 (Florence: Le Monnier, 2001), pp 185–203; with a systematic list and charts, Samantha Letters et al, *Gazetteer of markets and fairs in England and Wales to 1516* (Kew: List and Index Society, 2003), Vol I. The classic story is in Fernand Braudel, *Civilisation and capitalism*, (London: Phoenix 1984), Vol 1 (system of markets) and Vol 3 (discussion of capitalist world systems).

[24] See, for example, Reinhart Koselleck, *Preussen zwischen Reform und Revolution: Allgemeines Landrecht, Verwaltung und soziale Bewegung von 1791 bis 1848* (Stuttgart: Klett, 1967); Wolfgang von Hippel, *Die Bauernbefreiung im Königreich Württemberg* (Boppard: Boldt, 1977); Jerome Blum, *The end of the old order in rural Europe* (Princeton, NJ: Princeton University Press, 1978); Christof Dipper, *Die Bauernbefreiung in Deutschland, 1790–1850* (Stuttgart: Kohlhammer, 1980); Thomas Nipperdey, *Deutsche Geschichte 1800–1866: Bürgerwelt und starker Staat* (Munich: Beck, 1998).

[25] The literature on guilds is large, but good overviews – with occasional controversies – can be found in Sheilagh Ogilvie, 'Whatever is, is right'? Economic institutions in pre-industrial Europe', *Economic History Review*, 2nd series, 60:4 (2007), 649–84; Kluge, *Die Zünfte*; Epstein and Prak (eds), *Guilds, innovation and the European economy*; Ogilvie, *Institutions and European trade: merchant guilds, 1000–1800*; Ogilvie, *The European guilds: an economic analysis*.

[26] *Stenographischer Bericht über die Verhandlungen der bayerischen Kammer der Abgeordneten*, 80. Sitzung vom 10. April 1888, p 178.

[27] Hermann Wopfner (ed), *Acta Tirolensia: Urkundliche Quellen zur Geschichte Tirols, Vol 3 – Quellen zur Geschichte des Bauernkriegs in Deutschtirol 1525*, (Innsbruck: Scientia, 1908).

[28] James Davis, *Medieval market morality: life, law and ethics in the English marketplace, 1200–1500* (Cambridge: Cambridge University Press, 2014), p 8.

[29] STA Leipzig, Tit. LIV.7, *S.E. Hochw: Raths der Stadt Leipzig Ordnung Wie sich auf dem öffentlichen Marckte …* (1726), printed, pp 5–6, and a lengthy section, *Vom Aufkauff und Höckerey*, pp 39–44.

[30] STA Leipzig, Tit. LIV.17, f. 50 (new pagination), *Specification* (1654).

[31] STA Leipzig, Tit. LIV.7, *S.E. Hochw: Raths der Stadt Leipzig Ordnung Wie sich auf dem öffentlichen Marckte …* (1726), printed, pp 5–6, and a lengthy section, *Vom Aufkauff und Höckerey*, pp 21, 30, 44.

[32] On modern market design theory, see Alvin E. Roth, *Who gets what – and why: understand the choices you have, improve the choices you make* (New York: Harper Collins, 2016).

[33] For example, Howell, *Commerce before capitalism*.

[34] Stanziani, *Rules of exchange*, p 21.

[35] Popularized in writings such as Wilhelm Röpke, *Jenseits von Angebot und Nachfrage*, 4th edn (Erlenbach-Zürich: Rentsch, 1966), but also his textbooks such as *Die Lehre von der Wirtschaft*, 13th edn (Bern: Haupt, 1994), Ch. 1, where the market is portrayed as an enigma of controlled anarchy – similar to the providential argument of 'invisible hand'. On German Ordoliberalism and its wider place in 20th-century neoliberalism and mainstream economics and Hayek, see the excellent account in Kolev, *Neoliberale Staatsverständnisse im Vergleich*. On providence, Ordoliberals, neoliberalism and economic theology, see various contributions to Schwarzkopf (ed), *Routledge handbook of economic theology*, and, recently, James, *The war of words*, Ch. 12 on 'neoliberalism'.

[36] Persson, *Grain markets in Europe*; Michaela Fenske, *Marktkultur in der Frühen Neuzeit: Wirtschaft, Macht und Unterhaltung auf einem städtischen Jahr- und Viehmarkt* (Cologne/Vienna/Weimar: Böhlau, 2006); Gary M. Feinman and Christopher P. Garatty, 'Preindustrial markets and marketing: archaeological perspectives', *Annual Review of Anthropology* 39 (2010), 167–91; Mark Casson and John S. Lee, 'The origin and development of markets: a business history perspective', *Business History Review* 85:1 (2011), 9–37; R.J. van der Spek, Bas van Leeuwen and Jan Luiten van Zanden (eds), *A history of market performance: from ancient Babylonia to the modern world* (Abingdon: Routledge, 2015), Introduction; Victoria N. Bateman, *Markets and growth in early modern Europe* (Abingdon: Routledge, 2016); Bas van Bavel, *The invisible hand? How market economies have emerged and declined since AD 500* (Oxford: Oxford University Press, 2016); Tanja Skambraks, Julia Bruch and Ulla Kypta (eds), *Markets and their actors in the late middle ages* (Berlin: De Gruyter, 2021).

[37] Paul Johnson, *Making the market: Victorian origins of corporate capitalism* (Cambridge: Cambridge University Press, 2013), p 18.

[38] Mark Casson, 'The market as an institution', in Casson and Rössner (eds), *Evolutions of capitalism: historical perspectives: 1200–2000*, pp 29–53. For an historical application, Epstein, *Freedom and growth*.

[39] Piketty, *Capital in the twenty-first century*; for preindustrial inequality, see, for example, Jan Luiten van Zanden, 'Tracing the beginning of the Kuznets curve: Western Europe during the early modern period', *Economic History Review*, New series, 48:4 (1995), 643–64; Guido Alfani and Matteo di Tullio, *The lion's share: inequality and the rise of the fiscal state in preindustrial Europe* (Cambridge: Cambridge University Press, 2019).

[40] See Chapter 1.

[41] Eugene McCarraher, *The enchantments of Mammon: how capitalism became the religion of modernity* (Cambridge, MA: Belknap, 2019).

[42] A 'substantivist' interpretation was offered in Polanyi, *The great transformation*; in a recent historian's view: Fontaine, *Moral economy*; a classic remains E.P. Thompson, 'The moral economy of the English crowd in the eighteenth century', *Past & Present* 50 (1971), 76–136; Howell, *Commerce before capitalism*; a recent summary of substantivist and alternative models is provided in Chris Hann and Keith Hart, *Economic anthropology* (Cambridge: Polity Press, 2011); Keith Hart, Jean-Louis Laville and Antonio David Cattani (eds), *The human economy: a citizen's guide* (Cambridge: Polity Press, 2011).

[43] Davis, *Medieval market morality*, p 140; Fenske, *Marktkultur in der Frühen Neuzeit*.

[44] Witold Kula, *Economic theory of the feudal system*, new edn (London: Verso, 1986).

[45] Francesca Trivellato, 'The moral economies of early modern Europe', *Humanity: An International Journal of Human Rights, Humanitarianism, and Development* 11:2 (2020), 193–201, at 199.

[46] Catherine Casson, Mark Casson, John S. Lee and Katie Phillips, *Compassionate capitalism: business and community in medieval England* (Bristol: Bristol University Press,

2021). On early 16th-century German political economy and markets, see Gustav (von) Schmoller, 'Zur Geschichte der national-ökonomischen Ansichten in Deutschland während der Reformations'; Roscher, *Geschichte der Nationaloekonomik in Deutschland*; Rössner, *Martin Luther on commerce and usury*, Introduction.

[47] Arguing against that myth, for example, Harcourt, *The illusion of free markets*; Stanziani, *Rules of exchange*; Johnson, *Making the market*.

[48] Steven L. Kaplan, *Bread, politics and political economy in the reign of Louis XV*, new edn (London: Anthem, 2015); De Vries, *The price of bread*.

[49] On civic or civil economy, Luigino Bruni and Stefano Zamagni, *Civil economy: efficiency, equity, public happiness* (Bern: Peter Lang, 2007), Chs. 1, 4; and the more emotive Luigino Bruni and Stefano Zamagni, *Civil economy* (Newcastle upon Tyne: Agenda Publishing, 2016), Ch. 2.

[50] Paul Seabright, *The company of strangers: a natural history of economic life*, 2nd edn (Princeton, NJ: Princeton University Press, 2010).

[51] See Chapters 1 and 2 and Introduction.

[52] Rössner, *Luther on commerce and usury*.

[53] Maren Jonasson, Pertti Hyttinen and Lars Magnusson (eds) *Anticipating the wealth of nations: the selected works of Anders Chydenius, 1729–1803* (Abingdon: Routledge, 2012), pp 124–5.

[54] Smith, *Theory of moral sentiments* (1759); Smith, *Wealth of nations* (1776); Bruni and Zamagni, *Civil economy*, Ch. 4.

[55] Scott, *Society and economy in Germany*, pp 113–15. On capitalism taking hold in Upper Germany, based on the dynamics of such regulation – and regulatory competition between towns – see Henry Heller, *The birth of capitalism: a twenty-first-century perspective* (New York: Pluto Press, 2011), pp 61–71. The classic stadial model of city economy morphing into territorial and then nationally integrated market economies (*Volkswirtschaft*) is Karl Bücher, *Die Entstehung der Volkswirtschaft* (Tübingen: Laupp, 1893), pp 1–79, esp. pp 44ff. The literature on late medieval urban–rural market relationships and integration is considerable, not only for the German lands. A most recent survey is Werner Rösener, 'Schwerpunkte, Probleme und Forschungsaufgaben der Agrargeschichte zur Übergangsepoche vom Mittelalter zur Neuzeit', in Enno Bünz (ed), *Landwirtschaft und Dorfgesellschaft im ausgehenden Mittelalter* (Sigmaringen: Jan Thorbecke, 2020), pp 403–37, at pp 409–16. This edited volume also contains a few further indicative studies on late medieval markets and agrarian economies, reflecting the current state of the art in German-speaking academia. Notable studies further include Kießling, 'Markets and marketing, town and country'. The exhaustive study for Augsburg – a leading financial and industrial city since the late middle ages, which would also come to the forefront of German capitalism around 1500 – is Rolf Kießling, *Die Stadt und ihr Land: Umlandpolitik, Bürgerbesitz und Wirtschaftsgefüge in Ostschwaben vom 14. bis ins 16. Jahrhundert* (Cologne: Böhlau, 1989). Further indicative works include Tom Scott, *Freiburg and the Breisgau: town–country relations in the age of Reformation and peasants' war* (Oxford: Clarendon, 1987); Tom Scott, 'Economic landscapes', in Bob Scribner (ed), *Germany: a new economic and social history*, Vol 1, pp 1–31; for central Germany, see Held, *Zwischen Marktplatz und Anger*; Franz Mathis, *Die deutsche Wirtschaft im 16. Jahrhundert* (Munich: Oldenbourg, 1991), pp 34–47.

[56] Epstein, *Freedom and growth*. For a recent survey of early modern Europe, see Lütge, *Die mitteldeutsche Grundherrschaft und ihre Auflösung*; Cerman, *Villagers and lords*; essays in Guillaume Garner, *Die Ökonomie des Privilegs, Westeuropa 16.–19. Jahrhundert. L'économie du privilège, Europe occidentale XVIe–XIXe siècles* (Frankfurt-am-Main: Klostermann, 2016).

[57] For example, Richard Britnell, 'The proliferation of markets in England, 1200–1349', *Economic History Review*, 2nd series, 33 (1981), 209–21; Letters, *Gazetteer of markets and*

fairs, Vol I. For early modern Scotland, Whyte, 'The growth of periodic market centres in Scotland, 1600–1707'.

58 Bruce M.S. Campbell, 'Measuring the commercialisation of seigneurial agriculture c. 1300', in Richard H. Britnell and Bruce M. S. Campbell (eds), *A commercialising economy: England 1086 to c.1300* (Manchester: Manchester University Press, 1995), pp 132–93, at p 133.

59 Robert P. Wheelersburg, 'Uma Saami native harvest data derived from Royal Swedish taxation records 1557–1614', *Arctic* 44:4 (1991), 337–45, at 339, 344–5.

60 Epstein, *Freedom and growth*; Werner Sombart, *Der moderne Kapitalismus*, 3 vols, 4th edn (Munich: Duncker & Humblot, 1921–27); Heller, *Birth of capitalism*; Grafe, *Distant tyranny*.

61 William D. Grampp, 'An appreciation of mercantilism', in Lars Magnusson (ed), *Mercantilist economics* (Boston, MA: Kluwer, 1993), pp 59–85; Bruce Elmslie, 'Early English mercantilists and the support of liberal institutions', *History of Political Economy* 47:3 (2015), 419–48; Philipp Robinson Rössner, 'Monetary theory and cameralist economic management, c.1500–1900 AD', *Journal for the History of Economic Thought* 40:1 (2018), 99–134. An overview on historians' models of preindustrial markets can be found in Kaplan, *The stakes of regulation*.

62 Keith Tribe, *Strategies of economic order: German economic discourse, 1750–1950*, new edn (Cambridge: Cambridge University Press, 2007); Mark Casson, *Markets and market institutions: their origin and evolution* (Cheltenham: Edward Elgar, 2011); Dennis Romano, *Markets and marketplaces in medieval Italy, c.1100 to c.1440* (New Haven, CT: Yale University Press, 2015); Keith Tribe, *Governing economy: the reformation of German economic discourse 1750–1840*, new edn (Newbury: Threshold Press, 2017); Davis, *Medieval market morality*; Stanziani, *Rules of exchange*; M. Casson and Lee, 'Origin and development of markets'; see also Herzog, *Inventing the market*.

63 Klaus von Beyme, 'Historical forerunners of policy analysis in Germany', in Sonja Blum and Klaus Schubert (eds), *Policy analysis in Germany* (Bristol: Policy Press, 2013), pp 19–27, at p 22.

64 Karl Härter and Michael Stolleis (eds), *Repertorium der Policeyordnungen der Frühen Neuzeit, Vol 1, Deutsches Reich und geistliche Kurfürstentümer (Kurmainz, Kurköln, Kurtrier)* (Frankfurt-am-Main: Klostermann, 1996), pp 1–36, at p 3; Karl Härter, *Policey und frühneuzeitliche Gesellschaft* (Frankfurt-am-Main: Klostermann, 2000); Karl Härter (ed), *Policey und frühneuzeitliche Gesellschaft* (Frankfurt-am-Main: Klostermann, 2000); therein on the social normation hypothesis by Gerd Oestreich, Kersten Krüger, 'Policey zwischen Sozialregulierung und Sozialdisziplinierung, Reaktion und Aktion – Begriffsbildung durch Gerhard Oestreich 1972–1974', ibid., pp 107–20; Achim Landwehr, *Policey im Alltag: die Implementation frühneuzeitlicher Policeyordnungen in Leonberg* (Frankfurt-am-Main: Klostermann, 2000); Neocleous, *The fabrication of social order*; Peter Blickle, *Gute Policey als Politik im 16. Jahrhundert: Die Entstehung des öffentlichen Raumes in Oberdeutschland* (Frankfurt-am-Main: Klostermann, 2003); Andrea Iseli, *Gute Policey: Öffentliche Ordnung in der frühen Neuzeit* (Stuttgart: Ulmer, 2009).

65 Seppel and Tribe (eds), *Cameralism in practice*; Nokkala and Miller (eds), *Cameralism and the Enlightenment*.

66 On the general concept of space and spatial geography of development in German cameralism, see Sandl, *Ökonomie des Raumes*.

67 Johann Heinrich Gottlob von Justi, *Grundsätze der Policeywissenschaft*, 3rd edn (Göttingen: Vandenhoeck, 1782), §50, pp 260ff.

68 See, for example, STA Leipzig, Tit. LIV.16, f. 3r (1654).

69 STA Leipzig, Tit. LIV.17, f. 12v, *Specification* (1656).

70 STA Leipzig, Tit. LIV.16, f.3v (1654).

[71] Bernd Rüdiger, 'Aussenseiter, Randgruppenangehörige und Fremde in der frühneuzeitlichen Gesellschaft Leipzigs', in Bernd Rüdiger and Karsten Hommel (eds), *Kriminalität und Kriminalitätsbekämpfung in Leipzig in der frühen Neuzeit: Der Bestand 'Richterstube' im Stadtarchiv Leipzig / Leipziger Kalender Sonderband 2007/2* (Leipzig: Leipziger Universitätsverlag, 2007), pp 261, 276–7.

[72] STA Leipzig, Tit. LIV.17, f. 11r, *Specification* (1654).

[73] STA Leipzig, Tit. LIV.17, f. 11r, *Specification* (1654).

[74] STA Leipzig, Tit. LIV.17, f. 107r-108v, *Specification* (between 1728 and 1731) of retailers in butter and cheese (24 in number), cabbage (eight domestic, 13 *frembde*), fruit (30 in number) and chickens (11).

[75] Heidrun Homburg, 'Der ortsansässige Handel in der Stadt Leipzig 1771–1835', *Leipziger Kalender* (2000), 162–81, at tab. 2, 180.

[76] STA Leipzig, Tit. LIV.17, f. 116r (1739).

[77] The crisis has been reconstructed for Scotland in Philipp Robinson Rössner, 'The 1738–41 harvest crisis', *The Scottish Historical Review* XC/1 (2011), 27–63; for other European countries, Arthur E. Imhof, *Aspekte der Bevölkerungsentwicklung in den nordischen Ländern 1720–1750*, 2 vols (Bern: Francke, 1976); John D. Post, 'Climatic variability and the European mortality wave of the early 1740s', *Journal of Interdisciplinary History*, XV:1 (1984), 1–30; John D. Post, *Food shortage, climatic variability, and epidemic disease in pre-industrial Europe: the mortality peak in the early 1740s* (Ithaca, NY: Cornell University Press, 1985).

[78] STA Leipzig, Tit. LIV.17, f. 11v (1739).

[79] STA Leipzig, Tit. LIV.17, f. 116r (1739).

[80] Enno Bünz, 'Kaufleute und Krämer', in Enno Bünz (ed), *Geschichte der Stadt Leipzig, vol I: Von den Anfängen bis zur Reformation* (Leipzig: Leipziger Universitätsverlag, 2015), pp 299–318, at pp 317–18. See also Uwe Schirmer, 'Handel, Handwerk und Gewerbe in Leipzig (1250–1650)', in *Leipzigs Wirtschaft in Vergangenheit und Gegenwart*, pp 13–50.

[81] More on aspects of monetary policy in Chapter 5. On Saxon currency matters, see Wilhelm Pückert, *Das Münzwesen Sachsens 1518–1545 nach handschriftlichen Quellen. Erste Abtheilung: die Zeit von 1518–1525 umfassend* (Leipzig: Giesecke & Devrient, 1862); Walter Schwinkowski, *Das Geld- und Münzwesen Sachsens: Beiträge zu seiner Geschichte* (Dresden: Baensch, 1918); the discussion with sources in Woldemar Goerlitz, *Staat und Stände unter den Herzögen Albrecht und Georg 1485–1539* (Berlin: Teubner, 1928); Gerhard Krug, *Die meißnisch-sächsischen Groschen 1338 bis 1500* (Berlin: Deutscher Verlag der Wissenschaften, 1974); Walther Haupt, *Sächsische Münzkunde*, Vol I: Text (Berlin: Deutscher Verlag der Wissenschaften, 1978); Rössner, *Deflation – Devaluation – Rebellion*, Ch. 3.

[82] Thompson, 'Moral economy', p 83.

[83] Eberhard Isenmann, *Die deutsche Stadt im Mittelalter 1150–1550* (Cologne: Böhlau, 2014) represents the authoritative survey in the German language.

[84] On the history of stock exchanges in Germany since the 17th century, see Rainer Gömmel, Hans Pohl, Gabriele Jachmich et al (eds), *Deutsche Börsengeschichte* (Frankfurt-am-Main: Fritz Knapp, 1992). On the rise of financial capitalism since antiquity, for example, Larry Neal, *A concise history of international finance: from Babylon to Bernanke* (Cambridge: Cambridge University Press, 2015); William N. Goetzmann, *Money changes everything: how finance made civilization possible* (Princeton, NJ: Princeton University Press, 2016).

[85] Braudel, *Civilization and capitalism*, Vol 2; Peter Johanek and Heinz Stoob (eds), *Europäische Messen und Märktesysteme in Mittelalter und Neuzeit* (Cologne: Böhlau, 1996); Franz Irsigler and Michael Pauly (eds), *Messen, Jahrmärkte und Stadtentwicklung in Europa = Foires, marchés*

annuels et développement urbain en Europe (Trier: Porta Alba, 2007); Markus A. Denzel (ed), *Europäische Messegeschichte 9.–19. Jahrhundert* (Göttingen: Vandenhoeck & Ruprecht, 2019).

86 STA Leipzig, Tit. LIV.17, f. 84r–v (1721).

87 See relevant sections in Isenmann, *Stadt*.

88 Govind P. Sreenivasan, *The peasants of Ottobeuren, 1487–1726: a rural society in early modern Europe* (Cambridge: Cambridge University Press, 2004); Paul Warde, *Ecology, economy and state formation in early modern Germany* (Cambridge: Cambridge University Press, 2010).

89 But see, on credit in the medieval countryside, Jan Peters (ed), *Mit Pflug und Gänsekiel: Selbstzeugnisse schreibender Bauern, Eine Anthologie* (Cologne: Böhlau, 2003); Kurt Andermann and Gerhard Fouquet (eds), *Zins und Gült: Strukturen des ländlichen Kreditwesens in Spätmittelalter und Frühneuzeit* (Epfendorf: Bibliotheca Academica, 2016).

90 Foucault, *Security – territory – population*, lecture 11 (5 April 1978), pp 346, 341.

91 Bücher, *Die Entstehung der Volkswirtschaft*.

92 Ibid., p 356. See also lecture 12 (29 March 1978).

93 Adam Kotsko, *Neoliberalism's demons: on the political theology of late capital* (Stanford, CA: Stanford University Press, 2018); Rössner, *Freedom and capitalism*.

94 See the website of the Max Planck Institute for Legal History at the University of Frankfurt-am-Main, www.lhlt.mpg.de/forschungsprojekt/repertorium-der-policeyordnungen. The latest volume contains ordinances in Swedish Pomerania: Karl Härter, Jörg Zapnik and Pär Frohnert (eds), *Kungariket Sverige och hertigdömena Pommern och Mecklenburg / Königreich Schweden und Herzogtümer Pommern und Mecklenburg (=Repertorium der Policeyordnungen der Frühen Neuzeit 12)*, 2 vols (Frankfurt-am-Main: Klostermann, 2017).

95 Adam Smith, *Lectures on justice, police revenue and arms*, ed. Edwin Cannan (Oxford: Clarendon, 1896), Part II, 'Of police'.

96 The literature is considerable; a concise and accessible overview is presented in Iseli, *Gute Policey*.

97 For early modern Britain, Hoppit, *Britain's political economies*, esp. Chs. 2 and 3.

98 For example, James Davis, 'The ethics of arbitrage and forestalling across the late medieval world', in Simon Middleton and James E. Shaw (eds), *Market ethics and practices, c.1300–1850* (Abingdon: Routledge, 2017), pp 23–45.

99 Developed at length in Philipp Robinson Rössner, 'Freie Märkte? Zur Konzeption von Konnektivität, Wettbewerb und Markt im vorklassischen Wirtschaftsdenken und die Lektionen aus der Geschichte', *Historische Zeitschrift* 303 (2016), 349–92. See also Rössner, *Martin Luther on commerce and usury*, pp 1–178.

100 On German market integration in the early modern period, see Ulrich Pfister and Hakon Albers, 'Climate change, weather shocks and price convergence in pre-industrial Germany', *European Review of Economic History* 25:3 (2021), 467–89.

101 Hall, *Governing the economy*; Tomlinson, *Managing the economy*; Sassoon, *The anxious triumph*.

102 A classic article is Gerhard Oestreich, 'Strukturprobleme des europäischen Absolutismus', in Gerhard Oestreich, *Geist und Gestalt des frühmodernen Staates: Ausgewählte Aufsätze* (Berlin: Duncker & Humblot, 1969), pp 179–97.

103 On grain markets, Kaplan, *Bread, politics and political economy*; Kaplan, *The stakes of regulation*.

104 For example, Eric MacGilvray, *The invention of market freedom* (Cambridge: Cambridge University Press, 2011); Stanziani, *Rules of exchange*.

105 See, for example, Emma Rothschild, *Economic sentiments: Adam Smith, Condorcet and the Enlightenment* (Cambridge, MA: Harvard University Press, 2002); Kaplan and Reinert (eds), *The economic turn*; Elisabeth Wallmann, 'All production is reproduction: physiocracy and natural history in eighteenth-century France', *History of Political Economy* 54:1 (2022), 75–108.

106 A modern popular account is Ha-Joon Chang, *23 things they don't tell you about capitalism* (London: Penguin, 2011).

[107] See, most recently, the chapter on Walras in Tribe, *Economy of the word*; Reinert, ' "One will make of political economy … what the scholastics have done with philosophy"'; Schabas, *The natural origins of economics.*

[108] Bruno Ingrao, 'Free market', in Richard Arena and Christian Longhi (eds), *Markets and organization* (Berlin: Springer, 1998), pp 61–94.

[109] After Walter Eucken, *Die Grundlagen der Nationalökonomie*, 6th edn (Berlin: Springer, 1950); Helmut Woll, *Kontroversen der Ordnungspolitik* (Munich: Oldenbourg, 1999), pp 8–17. See also Gerold Ambrosius, *Staat und Wirtschaftsordnung: Eine Einführung in Theorie und Geschichte* (Stuttgart: Franz Steiner, 2001), pp 22–7; Kolev, *Neoliberale Staatsverständnisse im Vergleich.*

[110] But see Manow, 'Ordoliberalismus als ökonomische Ordnungstheologie'; or from a philosophy point of view, Krarup, ' "Ordo" versus "Ordnung"'; Giorgio Agamben, *Herrschaft und Herrlichkeit: Zur theologischen Genealogie von Ökonomie und Regierung (Homo Sacer I.2)*, 3rd edn (Frankfurt-am-Main: Suhrkamp, 2016); I am indebted to Troels Krarup for pointing me in this direction.

[111] Raymond de Roover, 'Scholastic economics: survival and lasting influence from the sixteenth century to Adam Smith', *The Quarterly Journal of Economics* 69 (1955), 161–90. In a recent survey, legal historian Schmoeckel, 'Die Kanonistik', comes to strikingly similar conclusions. Schmoeckel argues: 'For a long time, Canon law has been regarded as a reason for a traditional outlook on commerce and as a barrier against market innovations. The contrary is more convincing. In the 14th century representatives of the Church, theologians, Canonists, authors of penitentiary sums, and high representatives of the Church, particularly in Italy, developed a sense for the necessary freedom of the market and were ready to defend economic necessities. But at the same time they preserved their old principles. This twofold approach provided for flexibility and for clear, predictable rules. Both were essential for the development of a new European market' (Abstract, p 236).

[112] Before the 19th century, peasants didn't leave records generally, and the handful that did (for England and Italy some can be traced) weren't peasants in the traditional sense.

[113] Philipp Robinson Rössner, Catherine Casson, Georg Christ, Christopher Godden, John S. Lee, Sarah Roddy and Edmond Smith, 'What do we analyse – type of sources', in Christ and Rössner (eds), *History and economic life*; James C. Scott, *Seeing like a state: how certain schemes to improve the human condition have failed*, new edn (New Haven, CT: Yale University Press, 2020).

[114] Scott, *Seeing like a state.*

[115] Isenmann, *Die deutsche Stadt.*

[116] Kaye, *Economy and nature in the fourteenth century*, pp 25–6; Isenmann, *Die deutsche Stadt*; Gerhard, *Wesen und Wirkung vorindustrieller Taxen.*

[117] Karl Gunnar Persson, 'The Seven Lean Years, elasticity traps, and intervention in grain markets in pre-industrial Europe', *Economic History Review*, 2nd series, 49:4 (1996), 692–714, esp. 704ff.

[118] For the Netherlands, see de Vries, *The price of bread.*

[119] Isenmann, *Die deutsche Stadt*, pp 982–5.

[120] De Vries, *The price of bread*; Isenmann, *Die deutsche Stadt*; Hans-Jürgen Gerhard, *Wesen und Wirkung*; methodological sections and chapters in Gerhard and Engel, *Preisgeschichte der vorindustriellen Zeit.*

[121] For Germany, recent figures in Ulrich Pfister, and internationally by Robert Allen, Victoria Bateman, Karl Gunnar Persson, Greg Clark and many more. The pioneering work was Wilhelm Abel, *Agrarkrisen und Agrarkonjunktur in Mitteleuropa vom 13. bis zum 19. Jahrhundert*, 3rd edn (Berlin, 1935) (Hamburg: Parey, 1978), transl. *Agricultural fluctuations in Europe from the thirteenth to the twentieth centuries* (London: Methuen, 1980). Abel and

his disciples produced a host of further regional studies on the basis of new locally traced archival price data. International and global historians drew on earlier work by an international research group around Moritz Elsas, William Beveridge and Edwin Gay, *Internationales wissenschaftliches Komitee für die Geschichte der Preise*, whose price figures – initially often combed together from the archives quite haphazardly – to the present day mark the foundations of most global studies on prices and real wages; for German prices, see Moritz J. Elsas, *Umriß einer Geschichte der Preise und Löhne in Deutschland vom ausgehenden Mittelalter bis zum Beginn des 19. Jahrhunderts*, 3 vols (Leiden: Sijthoff, 1936–49). The 'Allen-Unger-Database' is a prime location for the material: www.gcpdb.info. Some of the Elsas material was subsequently transferred from Göttingen, where Abel had his chair, to the University of Leipzig, where it is now stored as the '*Wirtschafts- und Währungsgeschichtliche Sammlungen*'; see Markus A. Denzel (ed), *Wirtschaft – Politik – Geschichte: Beiträge zum Gedenkkolloquium anläßlich des 100. Geburtstages von Wilhelm Abel am 16. Oktober 2004 in Leipzig* (Stuttgart: Franz Steiner, 2004). On the international committee, see Arthur H. Cole and Ruth Crandall, 'The international scientific committee on price history', *The Journal of Economic History* 24:3 (1964), 381–8. Recent global studies drew inspiration (and criticism) from Robert C. Allen, 'The great divergence in European wages and prices from the middle ages to the First World War', *Explorations in Economic History* 38 (2001), 411–47; Robert C. Allen, 'Progress and poverty in early modern Europe', *Economic History Review*, 2nd series, 56 (2003), 403–43. A new critical compendium is in Hatcher and Stephenson (eds), *Seven centuries of unreal wages*. See also Chapter 3.

122 One example is Achim Landwehr, *Policey im Alltag: Die Implementation frühneuzeitlicher Policeyordnungen in Leonberg* (Frankfurt-am-Main: Klostermann, 2000).

123 STA Leipzig, Tit. LIV.7a, printed (Leipzig: Solvien, 1726), pp 32–4.

124 Ibid., p 15.

125 STA Leipzig, Tit. LIV.17, f. 18v.

126 Justi, *Grundfeste* (1760–61), Vol 1, p 761.

127 STA Leipzig, Tit. LIV.7a, printed (Leipzig: Solvien, 1726), pp 28–9.

128 Trentmann, *Empire of things*.

129 For a market ordinance in similar tune, issued in Düsseldorf 1772, (http://digital. ub.uni-duesseldorf.de/ihd/periodical/pageview/4497427?query=markt) (last accessed 7 April 2022).

130 Iseli, *Gute Policey*, pp 62–5; Kaplan, *Bread, politics and political economy*; Hans-Jürgen Gerhard and Karl Heinrich Kaufhold, *Preise im Vor- und Frühindustriellen Deutschland: Nahrungsmittel – Getränke – Gewürze, Rohstoffe und Gewerbeprodukte* (Stuttgart: Franz Steiner, 2001), Introduction and tables; Hans-Jürgen Gerhard, 'Preise als wirtschaftshistorische Indikatoren. Wilhelm Abels preishistorische Untersuchungen aus heutiger Sicht', in Denzel (ed), *Wirtschaft – Politik – Geschichte*, pp 37–58; Gerhard and Engel, *Preisgeschichte der vorindustriellen Zeit*; Gerhard, *Wesen und Wirkung vorindustrieller Taxen*.

131 Elisabeth Décultot and Daniel Fulda (eds), *Sattelzeit: Historiographiegeschichtliche Revisionen* (= Hallesche Beiträge zur Europäischen Aufklärung 52) (Berlin: Oldenbourg, 2016).

132 Epstein and Prak (eds), *Guilds, innovation and the European economy*; Kluge, *Die Zünfte*.

133 Adam Heinrich Müller, *Versuche einer neuen Theorie des Geldes mit besonderer Rücksicht auf Großbritannien* (Leipzig: Brockhaus, 1816), p 36, my translation.

134 Norbert Waszek, 'Adam Smith in Germany, 1776–1832', in Hiroshi Mizuta and Chuhei Sugiyama (eds), *Adam Smith: international perspectives* (Basingstoke: Palgrave Macmillan, 1993), pp 163–80; Bertram Schefold, *Great economic thinkers from Antiquity to the Historical School: translations from the series Klassiker der Nationalökonomie* (Abingdon: Routledge, 2011); Bertram Schefold, *Great economic thinkers from the classicals to the moderns: translations from the series Klassiker der Nationalökonomie* (Abingdon: Routledge, 2016).

135 Wehler, *Deutsche Gesellschaftsgeschichte Vol I: Vom Feudalismus des Alten Reiches bis zur defensiven Modernisierung der Reformära 1700–1815*, pp 397–486; Hagen, *German history in modern times.*

136 Christopher A. Bayly, *The birth of the modern world, 1780–1914: global connections and comparisons* (Malden: Blackwell, 2004).

137 STA Leipzig, Tit. LIV.1a, f. 13v. (1824). The 1659 document is in ibid., f. 5r-8v.

138 See earlier.

139 Tilly and Kopsidis, *A history of German industrialisation.*

140 STA Leipzig, Tit. LIV.30, f. 91r, *City Council Leipzig decree anent a petition*, 25 May 1882.

141 STA Leipzig, Tit. LIV.30, f. 97r-v, *City Council Leipzig*, protocol 26 August 1882.

142 STA Leipzig, Tit. LIV.30, f. 98v, protocol 26 August 1882.

143 STA Leipzig, Tit. LIV.30, f. 101r, *Öffentliche Plenarsitzung der Gewerbekammer zu Leipzig*, 28 September 1882. 'Das gedachte Collegium sei von der Thatsache ausgegangen, daß unser Marktwesen insofern einen völlig veränderten Charakter angenommen, als der Vertrieb der Produkte auf den Wochenmärkten nur noch in ganz vereinzelten Fällen von den Landwirthen selbst, im Uebrigen fast ausschließlich von Mittelspersonen besorgt werde'.

144 STA Leipzig, Tit. LIV.30, f. 101r, *Öffentliche Plenarsitzung der Gewerbekammer zu Leipzig*, 28 September 1882.

145 STA Leipzig, Tit. LIV.30, f. 101v, *Öffentliche Plenarsitzung der Gewerbekammer zu Leipzig*, 28 September 1882. See also *City Council*, protocol 5 October 1882, ibid., f. 103v.

146 STA Leipzig, Tit. LIV.30, f. 101v, *Öffentliche Plenarsitzung der Gewerbekammer zu Leipzig*, 28 September 1882.

147 STA Leipzig, Tit. LIV.30, f. 101v.; f. 106r-v.

148 STA Leipzig, Tit. LIV.30, f. 105r.

149 *Leipziger Nachrichten/Amtsblatt*, Nr.302, 30 October 1882.

150 *Leipziger Tageblatt und Anzeiger 104*, Saturday, 14 April 1883.

151 Amleto Spicciani, 'Pietro di Giovanni Olivi indagatore della razionalità economica medioevale', in *Usure, compere e vendite: la scienza economica del XIII secolo*, eds. Amleto Spicciani and Paolo Vian (Novara: Europia, 1998), pp 21–72, at pp 36–8; Barry Gordon, *Economic analysis before Adam Smith: Hesiod to Lessius* (London: Palgrave Macmillan, 1975), pp 222–3; Oreste Bazzichi, *Dall'economia civile francescana all'economia capitalistica moderna: Una via all'umano e al civile dell'economia* (Rome: Armando, 2015), pp 98–9, 39;.

152 Hugo Ott, 'Zur Wirtschaftsethik des Konrad Summenhart *ca.*1455–1502', *Vierteljahrschrift für Sozial- und Wirtschaftsgeschichte* 53:1 (1966), 1–2; Wolf-Hagen Krauth, *Wirtschaftsstruktur und Semantik: wissenssoziologische Studien zum wirtschaftlichen Denken in Deutschland zwischen dem 13. und 17. Jahrhundert* (Berlin: Duncker & Humblot, 1984), p 46, quoting cardinal Joseph Höffner, *Wirtschaftsethik und Monopole im fünfzehnten und sechzehnten Jahrhundert* (Jena: Fischer, 1941), pp 86ff. On Scottish price formation, the so-called *fiars prices*, see A.J.S. Gibson and T.C. Smout, *Prices, food, and wages in Scotland, 1550–1780* (Cambridge: Cambridge University Press, 1997).

153 Schmoeckel, 'Die Kanonistik', 246–7.

154 All examples taken from Otto Gerhard Oexle, 'Wirtschaft. III: Mittelalter', in Brunner, Conze and Koselleck (eds), *Geschichtliche Grundbegriffe*, Vol 7, pp 526–50, at p 547.

155 Odd Langholm, *The legacy of scholasticism in economic thought: antecedents of choice and power* (Cambridge: Cambridge University Press, 1998), p 80.

156 Schmoeckel, 'Die Kanonistik', 250–4. In an occasionally pointed and polemic manner, Jacques Le Goff, *Your money or your life: economy and religion in the middle ages* (New York: Zone Books, 1988); Lester K. Little, *Religious poverty and the profit economy in medieval Europe* (Ithaca, NY: Cornell University Press, 1994); Rodney Stark, *The victory of reason: how Christianity led to freedom, capitalism, and Western success* (New York: Random House, 2006); Thomas Barnebeck Andersen, Jeanet Bentzen, Carl-Johan Dalgaard and

Paul Sharp, 'Pre-Reformation roots of the protestant ethic', *The Economic Journal* 127 (2017), 1756–93.

157 Wolfgang Drechsler, 'The reality and diversity of Buddhist economics', *American Journal of Economics and Sociology* 78:2 (2019), 523–60, at 527.

158 Rössner, *Martin Luther on commerce and usury*.

159 Ibid., Ch. 5.

160 Thomas Max Safley, 'Bankruptcy: family and finance in early modern Augsburg', *Journal of European Economic History* 29:1 (2000), 53–75; Thomas Max Safley, 'Business failure and civil scandal in early modern Europe', *Business History Review* 83:1 (2011), 35–60; Thomas Max Safley (ed), *The history of bankruptcy: economic, social and cultural implications in early modern Europe* (New York: Routledge, 2013), esp. introductory chapter.

161 Becher, *Politischer Discurs*, 1673 edn, pp 83–5.

162 '*damit die Statt an unterschiedlichen Orten bewohnet und volckreich werde*', ibid., p 83. We encountered such regulations in the previous sections.

163 Robert von Erdberg-Krczenciewski, *Johann Joachim Becher: Ein Beitrag zur Geschichte der Nationalökonomik* (Halle/S.: Lippert, 1896), pp 33–7.

164 Ronald Edward Zupko, *A dictionary of English weights and measures from Anglo-Saxon times to the nineteenth century* (Madison: University of Wisconsin Press, 1968); Harald Witthöft and Gerhard Göbel, *Handbuch der historischen Metrologie* (St Katharinen: Scripta-Mercaturae-Verlag, 1994); Aashish Velkar, *Markets and measurements in nineteenth-century Britain* (Cambridge: Cambridge University Press, 2012); Peter Rauscher and Andrea Serles (eds), *Wiegen – Zählen – Registrieren: Handelsgeschichtliche Massenquellen und die Erforschung mitteleuropäischer Märkte (13.–18. Jahrhundert)* (Innsbruck: Studienverlag, 2015); Witold Kula, *Measures and men*, new edn (Princeton, NJ: Princeton University Press, 2016).

165 Berch, 1747; German transl. 1763 (Pt II/4, Ch. 9, §3).

166 Zedler, *Grosses vollständiges Universal-Lexicon Aller Wissenschafften und Künste* (1732–54), Vol 19 (1739), col. 1279–80.

167 Georg Heinrich Zincke, *Allgemeines Oeconomisches Lexicon*, Vol 2: M–Z (Leipzig: Gleditsch, 1780), col. 1889–91.

168 Johann Georg Krünitz et al (eds), *Oekonomische Encyklopädie oder allgemeines System der Staats- Stadt- Haus- und Landwirthschaft*, Vol 84: Mantel – Marmorwaaren, 1st edn (Berlin: Pauli 1801), pp 574ff.

169 Johann H.G. Justi, *Grundsätze der Policeywissenschaft*, 3rd edn (Göttingen: Vandenhoeck: 1782).

170 Epstein, *Freedom and growth*.

Chapter 5

1 Jean Bodin, *Les six livres de la republique*, 1.10 (Paris: du Puys, 1583), English transl. Bodin, *On Sovereignty*, trans. Julian H. Franklin (Cambridge, UK: Cambridge University Press, 1992), p 78; cited after Adam Woodhouse, '"Who owns the money?" Currency, property, and popular sovereignty in Nicole Oresme's *De moneta*', *Speculum* 92:1 (2017), 85–116.

2 Georg Agricola, *De re metallica*, transl. Herbert Clark Hoover and Lou Henry Hoover (New York: Dover Publications, 1950), p 6.

3 R.H. Tawney, *Religion and the rise of capitalism: a historical study* (New York: Harcourt Brace, 1926); Rössner, *Martin Luther on commerce and usury*, Introduction, Ch. 2 for contextualization and Ch. 3 for extended discussion of Luther's economics; for a heterodox account on Germany and commercial capitalism around 1500, see Heller, *Birth of capitalism*, pp 61–70.

4 Reinhold Reith, *Umweltgeschichte der Frühen Neuzeit* (Munich: Oldenbourg, 2011), pp 51–5. For 16th-century Tyrol, see Elisabeth Breitenlechner, Marina Hilber, Joachim Lutz, Yvonne Kathrein, Alois Unterkircher and Klaus Oeggl, 'Reconstructing the history of

copper and silver mining in Schwaz, Tirol (sic)', *RCC Perspectives* 10, Mining in Central Europe: Perspectives from Environmental History (2012), 7–20.

[5] Controversies abound among historians as to what extent coins, at different times and ages, could have been substituted by alternatives, such as book money and credit. For late medieval England, see Ian Blanchard, *Mining, metallurgy and minting in the middle ages: Vol 3: Continuing Afro-European supremacy: 1250–1450* (Stuttgart: Franz Steiner, 2005), pp 1189–07; and for an alternative viewpoint, Phillipp R. Schofield, 'Credit and its record in the later medieval English countryside', in Philipp Robinson Rössner (ed), *Cities – coins – commerce: essays in honour of Ian Blanchard on the occasion of his seventieth birthday* (Stuttgart: Franz Steiner, 2012), pp 77–88. On money and credit in the late medieval towns and countryside, see Kurt Andermann and Gerhard Fouquet (eds), *Zins und Gült Strukturen des ländlichen Kreditwesens in Spätmittelalter und Frühneuzeit* (Epfendorf: Bibliotheca Academica, 2015); Gerhard Fouquet and Sven Rabeler (eds), *Ökonomische Glaubensfragen: Strukturen und Praktiken jüdischen und christlichen Kleinkredits im Spätmittelalter* (Stuttgart: Franz Steiner, 2018). General histories of money include Peter Spufford, *Money and its use in medieval Europe* (Cambridge: Cambridge University Press, 1988); Glyn Davis, *A history of money: from ancient times to the present day*, 3rd edn (Cardiff: University of Wales Press, 1994); Jim L. Bolton, *Money in the medieval English economy 973–1489* (Manchester: Manchester University Press, 2012). From a cultural anthropology viewpoint, Jack Weatherford, *The history of money* (New York: Three Rivers Press, 1997); Jacques LeGoff, *Money and the middle ages: an essay in historical anthropology* (Cambridge: Polity Press, 2016); a cultural history of money in the early modern age is presented in Deborah Valenze, *The social life of money in the English past* (Cambridge: Cambridge University Press, 2006); Catherine Eagleton and Jonathan Williams, *Money: a history*, 2nd edn (London: British Museum Press, 2007); Diane Wolfthal and Juliann Vittulo (eds), *Money, morality, and culture in late medieval and early modern Europe* (Abingdon: Routledge, 2016). From a numismatic viewpoint, Philip Grierson, *Numismatics* (Oxford: Oxford University Press, 1975); Rory Naismith (ed), *Money and coinage in the Middle Ages* (Boston: Brill, 2018). For money in the German-speaking lands, Herbert Rittmann, *Deutsche Geldgeschichte 1484–1914* (Munich: Battenberg, 1975); Arthur Suhle, *Deutsche Münz- und Geldgeschichte von den Anfängen bis zum 15. Jahrhundert* 8th edn (Berlin: VEB Deutscher Verlag der Wissenschaften, 1975); Hans-Jürgen Gerhard, 'Ursachen und Folgen der Wandlungen im Währungssystem des Deutschen Reiches 1500–1625. Eine Studie zu den Hintergründen der sogenannten Preisrevolution', in Eckart Schremmer (ed), *Geld und Währung vom 16. Jahrhundert bis zur Gegenwart* (Stuttgart: Franz Steiner, 1993), pp 69–84; Hans-Jürgen Gerhard, 'Ein schöner Garten ohne Zaun. Die währungspolitische Situation des Deutschen Reiches um 1600', *Vierteljahrschrift für Sozial- und Wirtschaftsgeschichte* 81 (1994), 156–77; Michael North, *Das Geld und seine Geschichte: Vom Mittelalter bis zur Gegenwart* (Munich: C.H. Beck, 1994); Hans-Jürgen Gerhard, 'Miszelle: Neuere deutsche Forschungen zur Geld- und Währungsgeschichte der Frühen Neuzeit. Fragen – Ansätze – Erkenntnisse', *Vierteljahrschrift für Sozial- und Wirtschaftsgeschichte*, 83 (1996), 216–30; Bernd Sprenger, *Das Geld der Deutschen: Geldgeschichte Deutschlands von den Anfängen bis zur Gegenwart*, 3rd edn (Paderborn: Schöningh, 2002); Niklot Klüßendorf, *Münzkunde – Basiswissen* (Hanover: Hahn, 2009); Michael North, *Kleine Geschichte des Geldes: Vom Mittelalter bis heute*, new edn (Munich: C.H. Beck, 2009). Older numismatic works include Ferdinand Friedensburg, *Münzkunde und Geldgeschichte der Einzelstaaten des Mittelalters und der Neueren Zeit* (Munich: Oldenbourg, 1926); Arnold Luschin von Ebengreuth, *Allgemeine Münzkunde und Geldgeschichte des Mittelalters und der Neueren Zeit*, 2nd edn (Munich: Oldenbourg, 1926); as well as Friedrich Freiherr von Schrötter, 'Das Münzwesen des Deutschen Reichs von 1500 bis 1566', *Jahrbuch für Gesetzgebung, Verwaltung und*

Volkswirtschaft 35 (1911) 129–72 and 36 (1912), reprinted in Friedrich von Schrötter, *Aufsätze zur deutschen Münz- und Geldgeschichte des 16. bis 19. Jahrhunderts (1902–1938)*, ed. Bernd Kluge (Leipzig: Reprintverlag Leipzig im Zentralantiquariat, 1991), pp 3–76. Authoritative histories of cashless payments and bills of exchanges have been presented in Denzel, *Das System des bargeldlosen Zahlungsverkehrs europäischer Prägung vom Mittelalter bis 1914*; Denzel, *Handbook of world exchange rates*, Introduction. Cashless payment will be largely disregarded here.

6 On late medieval and early modern Saxony, see Rössner, *Deflation*, Ch. 3. On France, Christine Desan, *Making money: coin, currency, and the coming of capitalism* (Oxford: Oxford University Press, 2014); Jotham Parsons, *Making money in sixteenth-century France: currency, culture, and the state* (Ithaca, NY: Cornell University Press, 2016); and for a comparative survey, K. Kıvanç Karaman, Sevket Pamuk and Seçil Yıldırım-Karaman, 'Money and monetary stability in Europe, 1300–1914', *Journal of Monetary Economics* 115 (2020), 279–300.

7 A state theory of money was presented in Georg Friedrich Knapp, *Staatliche Theorie des Geldes* (Leipzig: Duncker & Humblot, 1891); see Mark Peacock, *Introducing money* (Abingdon: Routledge, 2013).

8 Agricola, *De re metallica*, transl. Hoover, p 17.

9 An Aristotelian framing of money and its functions in the economic process was laid out in W. Stanley Jevons, *Money and the mechanism of exchange* (New York: Appleton, 1875); to the present day, many introductory textbooks in economics will implicitly refer to Jevons. See also Josef Soudek, 'Aristotle's theory of exchange: an inquiry into the origin of economic analysis', *Proceedings of the American Philosophical Society* 96:1 (1952), 45–75; Hendrik Mäkeler, 'Nicolas Oresme und Gabriel Biel. Zur Geldtheorie im Spätmittelalter', *Scripta Mercaturae* XXXVII:1 (2003), 56–94.

10 Philipp Robinson Rössner, 'The crisis of the reformation (1517): monetary and economic dimensions of a change in paradigm', in the Istituto internazionale di storia economica F. Datini (ed), *Le crisi finanziarie: gestione, implicazioni sociali e consequenze nell'età preindustriale: selezione di ricerche / The financial crises: their management, their social implications and their consequences in pre-industrial times: selection of essays* (Florence: Firenze University Press, 2016), pp 19–47.

11 Christina von Braun, *Der Preis des Geldes: Eine Kulturgeschichte* (Berlin: Aufbau, 2012).

12 Carl Wennerlind, 'Money talks, but what is it saying? Semiotics of money and social control', *Journal of Economic Issues* 35:3 (2001), 557–74.

13 See, for instance, discussion and figures in Dennis O. Flynn, 'The microeconomics of silver and east–west trade in the early modern period', in Wolfram Fischer, R. Marvin McInnis and Jürgen Schneider (eds), *The emergence of a world economy, part I: 1500–1850* (Stuttgart: Franz Steiner, 1986), pp 37–60.

14 Nuno Palma, 'Money and modernization in early modern England', *Financial History Review* 25:3 (2018), 231–61, at 232.

15 Recent surveys on preindustrial village society include Kießling, Konersmann and Troßbach, *Grundzüge der Agrargeschichte*; Prass, *Grundzüge der Agrargeschichte*; Enno Bünz (ed), *Landwirtschaft und Dorfgesellschaft im ausgehenden Mittelalter* (Sigmaringen: Jan Thorbecke, 2020). On different moneys and spheres of payment on the countryside, see Rössner, *Deflation*, esp. Ch. 4.

16 Rössner, *Deflation*, Ch. 4.

17 For concrete examples relating to 16th-century court cases and complaints brought before territorial diets and princely administrations, see Mark Häberlein, 'Wirtschaftskriminalität und städtische Ordnungspolitik in der Frühen Neuzeit. Augsburger Kaufleute als Münzhändler und Falschmünzer', *Zeitschrift für bayerische Landesgeschichte* 61 (1998), 699–740; Rössner, *Deflation*, Ch. 4.

[18] For the Germanies in late medieval and early modern times, see extended introduction in Volckart (ed), *Eine Währung für das Reich*; Volckart, 'The dear old Holy Roman realm: how does it hold together?'; Rössner, *Deflation*, Chs. 3 and 4. See also Desan, *Making money*; Parsons, *Making money*.

[19] For the early 1500s, see Rössner, *Deflation*, Ch. 4, with detailed regional case studies for the German lands, 1460s–1520s.

[20] Sargent and Velde, *The big problem of small change*; Angela Redish, *Bimetallism: an economic and historical analysis* (Cambridge: Cambridge University Press, 2006).

[21] Rössner, *Deflation*, Ch. 4.

[22] I use this expression in a gender-neutral form. The contemporary legal and socio-economic German language terminus technicus *der Gemeine Mann* also covered women.

[23] I have reconstructed the full story and details of the first full-blown Thaler currency in its economic, social and political settings in Rössner, *Deflation*, Ch. 3. On the *Joachimsthaler* – from which the 'Dollar' ultimately (through many detours) got its name, see Karel Castelin, 'Zur Entstehung der ältesten 'Joachimsthaler', *Numismatische Zeitschrift* 80 (1963), 72–7.

[24] The two foundational studies are Westermann, *Das Eislebener Garkupfer und seine Bedeutung für den europäischen Kupfermarkt*; Blanchard, *International lead production and trade*.

[25] Rössner, *Martin Luther on commerce and usury*, Ch. 2.

[26] On the political, administrative, social and economic management of early modern mining regions, see Ekkehard Westermann (ed), *Bergbaureviere als Verbrauchszentren im vorindustriellen Europa: Fallstudien zu Beschaffung und Verbrauch von Lebensmitteln sowie Roh- und Hilfsstoffen (13.–18. Jahrhundert)* (Stuttgart: Franz Steiner, 1997); Ekkehard Westermann, 'Der wirtschaftliche Konzentrationsprozeß im Mansfelder Revier und seine Auswirkungen auf Martin Luther, seine Verwandte und Freunde', in Rosemarie Knape (ed), *Martin Luther und der Bergbau im Mansfelder Land: Aufsätze* (Lutherstadt Eisleben: Stiftung Luthergedenkstätten in Sachsen-Anhalt, 2000), pp 63–92; Angelika Westermann, *Die vorderösterreichischen Montanregionen in der Frühen Neuzeit* (Stuttgart: Franz Steiner, 2009); Franziska Neumann, 'Vormoderne Organisationen. Mitgliedschaft und 'formale Organisation' in der sächsischen Bergverwaltung des 16. Jahrhunderts', *Zeitschrift für Historische Forschung* 47:4 (2020), 591–628. Mining and administration in 15th- and 16th-century Saxony are covered in Woldemar Goerlitz, *Staat und Stände unter den Herzögen Albrecht und Georg 1485–1539* (Berlin: Teubner, 1928).

[27] Rössner, *Martin Luther on commerce and usury*, Ch. 2, for full discussion and further literature.

[28] The English language knows only one word for 'industrialization'. In the German language, 'industrialization' can be translated as either *Vergewerblichung* (referring to pre-factory manufacturing growth) or *Industrialisierung* ('industrialization' in the post-1800 sense, based on factories and machines using coal and steam). I am here referring to the former.

[29] Extended discussion in Rössner, *Deflation*, Ch. 3.

[30] Benjamin J. Cohen, *The geography of money* (Ithaca, NY: Cornell University Press, 1998).

[31] Bart D. Ehrman, *The lost gospel of Judas Iscariot: a new look at betrayer and betrayed* (Oxford: Oxford University Press, 2008).

[32] An example relating to the 15th century, see Harry Miskimin, 'Monetary movements and market structure – forces for contraction in fourteenth- and fifteenth-century England', *The Journal of Economic History* 24 (1964), 470–90; John Day, 'The great bullion famine of the fifteenth century', *Past & Present* 79 (1978), 3–54; John H. Munro, 'Bullion flows and monetary contraction in late-medieval England and the Low Countries', in John F. Richards (ed), *Precious metals in the later medieval and early modern worlds* (Durham, NC: Carolina Academic Press, 1983), pp 97–158; for northern Germany between the middle ages and the early modern period, see Michael North, *Geldumlauf und Wirtschaftskonjunktur im südlichen*

Ostseeraum an der Wende zur Neuzeit (1440–1570): Untersuchungen zur Wirtschaftsgeschichte am Beispiel des Großen Lübecker Münzschatzes, der norddeutschen Münzfunde und der schriftlichen Überlieferung (Sigmaringen: Thorbecke, 1990).

[33] Nathan Sussman, 'Debasements, royal revenues, and inflation in France during the Hundred Years' War, 1415–1422', *The Journal of Economic History* 53:1 (1993), 44–70.

[34] See graphs in Karaman, Pamuk and Yıldırım-Karaman, 'Money and monetary stability'; Eckart Schremmer and Jochen Streb, 'Revolution oder Evolution? Der Übergang von den feudalen Münzgeldsystemen zu den Papiergeldsystemen des 20. Jahrhunderts', *Vierteljahrschrift für Sozial- und Wirtschaftsgeschichte* 86 (1999), 457–76.

[35] Philipp Robinson Rössner, 'Monetary instability, lack of integration and the curse of a commodity money standard: the German lands, *c.*1400–1900 AD', *Credit and Capital Markets* 47:2 (2014), 297–340.

[36] Ibid.

[37] The economics of minting are concisely explained in John H. Munro, 'Münzkosten', in Michael North (ed), *Von Aktie bis Zoll: Ein historisches Lexikon des Geldes* (Munich: Beck, 1995), p 263; Oliver Volckart, 'Premodern debasement: a messy affair', *LSE Working Papers* 270:70 (2018), 4–5.

[38] Rössner, *Deflation*, Ch. 4.

[39] Sargent and Velde, *The big problem of small change*.

[40] Ibid., Ch. 3, esp. pp 381–6, Tab. 4.

[41] Ibid., Ch. 3.

[42] See later, and Rössner, *Deflation*, Ch. 4, for a fuller elaboration.

[43] Ibid., Ch. 3, for Saxon monetary policy between the 1450s and 1550s.

[44] This straight debasement did not work for gold currencies, as gold involved different nominals, transaction types and spheres and ranges of people.

[45] Sargent and Velde, *Big problem*, Ch. 4.

[46] Spufford, *Money and its use*; Sussman, 'Debasements'.

[47] Hans-Jürgen Gerhard, ' "Ein Adler fängt keine Mücken!": Eine Währungsreform mit Weitblick und Langzeitwirkung. Johann Philip Grauman als Gernaralmünzdirektor Friedrichs des Großen', in Angelika Westermann, Ekkehard Westermann and Josef Pahl (eds), *Wirtschaftslenkende Montanverwaltung – Fürstlicher Unternehmer – Merkantilismus* (Husum: Matthiesen, 2009); Jan Greitens, 'Geldtheorie und -politik in Preußen Mitte des 18. Jahrhunderts', *Jahrbuch für Wirtschaftsgeschichte / Economic History Yearbook* 61:1 (2020), 217–57.

[48] Sussman, 'Debasements'.

[49] Spufford, *Money and its use*, p 287.

[50] Michel Mollat, *Der königliche Kaufmann Jacques Coeur oder der Geist des Unternehmertums* (Munich: Beck, 1991).

[51] North, *Geldumlauf*.

[52] Spufford, *Money and its use*, pp 296–300.

[53] Munro, 'Münzkosten'.

[54] Bertram Schefold, 'Goethe's economics: between cameralism and liberalism', in Rössner (ed), *Economic growth and the origins of modern political economy*, pp 79–100.

[55] Rössner, *Deflation*, Introduction. See also Martin Treu (ed), *Martin Luther und das Geld: Aus Luthers Schriften, Briefen und Tischreden* (Lutherstadt Wittenberg: Stiftung Luthergedenkstätte, 2000).

[56] Rössner, *Deflation*, Ch. 4.

[57] Volckart, 'The dear old Holy Roman Realm'; Volckart (ed), *Eine Währung für das Reich*, Introduction.

[58] David Landes, *Wealth and poverty of nations* (New York: Norton, 1998); Eric L. Jones, *The European miracle: environments, economies and geopolitics in the history of Europe and Asia*,

new edn (Cambridge: Cambridge University Press, 2008); Rosenthal and Wong, *Before and beyond divergence*.

59 For modern reminiscences, see Walter Eucken, *Die Grundlagen der Nationalökonomie*, 6th edn (Berlin: Springer, 1950); Helmut Woll, *Kontroversen der Ordnungspolitik* (Munich: Oldenbourg, 1999), pp 8–17.

60 Nederman, *Lineages of European political thought*, pp 222–47.

61 Ibid. See also Kaye, *Economy and nature in the fourteenth century*.

62 Mäkeler, 'Nicolas Oresme', 58–60, 81–2; Erwin Iserloh, 'Biel, Gabriel', in *Neue Deutsche Bibliographie*, Vol 2 (Berlin: Duncker & Humblot, 1955), pp 225–6; Werner Detloff, 'Gabriel Biel', in Horst Robert Balz et al (eds), *Theologische Realenzyklopädie*, Vol 6 (Berlin: De Gruyter, 1980), pp 489–91; Stefan Kötz, 'The last Scholastic on money: Gabriel Biel's monetary theory', in David Fox and Wolfgang Ernst (eds), *Money in the Western legal tradition: Middle Ages to Bretton Woods* (Oxford: Oxford University Press, 2016), pp 71–92.

63 Spufford, *Money and its use*.

64 Nederman, *Lineages*, pp 245, 247.

65 Schefold, *Beiträge*, p 98. See contributions in Rössner (ed), *Economic reasons of state*.

66 Schefold, *Beiträge*, p 84.

67 Schefold, *Beiträge*, p 98.

68 Dittrich, *Die deutschen und österreichischen Kameralisten*; Schefold (ed), *Tractatus juridico-politico-polemico-historicus de aerario*, Introduction.

69 Heckscher, *Der Merkantilismus*, Vol 2, pp 197–216; Wilga Föste, *Das Geld im ökonomischen Denken des Merkantilismus* (Weimar (Lahn): Metropolis, 2015), pp 14–15. But see Johannes Kasnacich-Schmid, 'Grundsätze kameralistischer Geldpolitik', *Weltwirtschaftliches Archiv* 80 (1958), 90–130, for a more nuanced interpretation of cameralist monetary views.

70 Karl Pribram, *Geschichte des ökonomischen Denkens*, 2 vols (Frankfurt-am-Main: Suhrkamp, 1992); on the medieval period, see Wood, *Medieval economic thought*.

71 Heckscher, *Der Merkantilismus*.

72 John M. Keynes, *General theory of employment, interest and money* (New York: Harcourt Brace, 1936); Cilly Böhle, *Die Idee der Wirtschaftsverfassung im deutschen Merkantilismus* (Jena: Fischer, 1940); Hans-Joachim Röpke, *Die Wachstumstheorie der deutschen Merkantilisten* (PhD dissertation, Marburg University, 1971).

73 M. Tilemann[us], 'Tractat M. Cyriaci Spangenberg vom rechten Brauch und Mißbrauch der Muentze', in *Muentz Spiegel* … (Frankfurt-am-Main: Feyrabendt, 1592), p 240. Full analysis of the social and economic consequences of coin debasement in Rössner, *Deflation – Devaluation – Rebellion*, Ch. 4.

74 This was not limited to any specific set of prices, say grain or bread prices; but most works spoke of rising or falling prices in generic terms, referring roughly to what we may call the 'price level'.

75 Wilhelmine Dreissig, *Die Geld- und Kreditlehre des deutschen Merkantilismus* (Berlin: Dr. Emil Ebering, 1939), pp 31–40.

76 Rössner, *Deflation*, Ch. 2; John H. Munro, 'The monetary origins of the "Price Revolution"', in Dennis O. Flynn, Arturo Giráldez and Richard von Glahn (eds), *Global connections and monetary history, 1470–1800* (Aldershot: Ashgate, 2003), pp 1–34, tables.

77 Dennis O. Flynn and Arturo Giráldez, 'Cycles of silver: global economic unity through the mid-18th century', in Markus A. Denzel (ed), *From commercial communication to commercial integration: Middle Ages to 19th century* (Stuttgart: Franz Steiner, 2004), pp 81–111, at p 83. See also Dennis O. Flynn and Arturo Giráldez, 'Arbitrage, China and world trade in the early modern period', *Journal of the Economic and Social History of the Orient* 38 (1995),

429–48; Dennis O. Flynn and Arturo Giráldez, 'Born with a "silver spoon": the origin of world trade in 1571', *Journal of World History* 6 (1995), 201–21.

78 Rössner, *Deflation*, pp 166–250.

79 Rössner, *Martin Luther on commerce and usury*, p 176.

80 Full discussion in editor's introduction, ibid., Chs. 2–4.

81 Rudolf Bentzinger (ed), *Die Wahrheit muß ans Licht! Dialoge aus der Zeit der Reformation* (Leipzig: Reclam, 1983), pp 46, 52, 72–4.

82 Sargent and Velde, *Big problem*.

83 Gustav von Schmoller, 'Zur Geschichte der national-ökonomischen Ansichten in Deutschland während der Reformations-Periode', *Zeitschrift für Gesamte Staatswissenschaft* 16 (1860), 635–8.

84 Ibid., pp 650–1; Fritz Blaich, *Die Wirtschaftspolitik des Reichstags im Heiligen Römischen Reich: ein Beitrag zur Problemgeschichte wirtschaftlichen Gestaltens* (Stuttgart: Fischer, 1970), pp 135–53.

85 I have used the 8th edn, www.ludwig-erhard.de/wp-content/uploads/wohlstand_fuer_alle.pdf, pp 15–16.

86 A definitive biography is Volker Hentschel, *Ludwig Erhard: Ein Politikerleben* (Berlin: Ullstein, 1998); see also Volker R. Berghahn, 'Ordoliberalism, Ludwig Erhard, and West Germany's "economic basic law"', *European Review of International Studies* 2:3 (2015), 37–4.

87 I am following the text given in Wolfram Burckhardt (ed), *Nicolas von Oresme De mutatione monetarum: tractatus = Traktat über Geldabwertungen* (Berlin: Kulturverlag Kadmos, 1999).

88 See Rössner, *Deflation*, Ch. 4, for detailed examples and full empirical discussion of the social consequences of debased currency.

89 I am following the Latin text as printed in Renate Steiger et al (eds), *Gabrielis Biel collectorium circa quattuor libros Sententiarum. 4, 2, Libri quarti pars secunda: dist. 15–22* (Tübingen: J.C.B. Mohr-P. Siebeck, 1977). On Biel, most recently, Kötz, 'The last Scholastic on money'.

90 Erich Sommerfeld (ed), *Die Geldlehre des Nicolaus Copernicus: Texte – Übersetzungen – Kommentare* (Berlin: Neunplus [1978] 2003), p 1; see also Oliver Volckart, *Die Münzpolitik im Ordensland und Herzogtum Preußen von 1370 bis 1550* (Wiesbaden: Harrassowitz, 1996); Oliver Volckart, 'Early beginnings of the quantity theory of money and their context in Polish and Prussian monetary policies, *c.*1520–1550', *Economic History Review*, 2nd series, 50:3 (1997), 430–49; Groh, *Göttliche Weltökonomie*, Ch. 2.

91 Copernicus, *Denkschrift A*, printed in Sommerfeld, *Die Geldlehre des Nicolaus Copernicus*.

92 Copernicus, *Denkschrift A*, p 24, Latin; p 25, German translation.

93 Raymond de Roover, *Gresham on foreign exchange: an essay on early English mercantilism with the text of Sir Thomas Gresham's memorandum: for the understanding of the exchange* (Cambridge, MA: Harvard University Press, 1949), p 291.

94 Ibid.

95 Copernicus 1517, *Denkschrift A*, pp 24–5.

96 *Monete vilitas*; Copernicus 1526, *Denkschrift A*, pp 48–9.

97 Ibid.

98 Copernicus 1526, *Denkschrift A*, pp 54–5.

99 Ibid.

100 Ibid.

101 Ibid.

102 Bernd Sprenger, 'Preisindizes unter Berücksichtigung verschiedener Münzsorten als Bezugsgrößen für das 16. und 17. Jahrhundert – dargestellt anhand von Getreidepreisen in Frankfurt/Main', *Scripta Mercaturae* 1 (1977), 57–69.

103 Rössner, 'Monetary instability', 327–8.

[104] Copernicus 1526, *Denkschrift A*, p 56.

[105] Facsimile in Bertram Schefold (ed), *Die drei Flugschriften über den Münzstreit der sächsischen Albertiner und Ernestiner* (Düsseldorf: Verlag Wirtschaft und Finanzen, 2000); discussion in Bertram Schefold (ed), 'Wirtschaft und Geld im Zeitalter der Reformation', in Schefold (ed), *Vademecum zu drei klassischen Schriften frühneuzeitlicher Münzpolitik*, pp 5–58.

[106] *Gemeyne stimmen von der Muntz* [Dresden 1530] facsimile in Schefold (ed), *Die drei Flugschriften*, p 6.

[107] Rössner, *Deflation*, Ch. 4.

[108] *Gemeyne stimmen von der Muntz* [Dresden 1530], pp 7–10.

[109] See the original text in Osse 1557, as printed in Oswald Artur Hecker (ed), *Schriften Dr. Melchiors von Osse: mit einem Lebensabriss und einem Anhange von Briefen und Akten* (Leipzig: Teubner, 1922); discussion in Dittrich, *Kameralisten*, pp 40–2, 382. Original: *Dan wo gute montz ist, do ist viel handels; wo vil hendel und leut seind, do hat man den vortreib aller fruchte und war, und genissen des also nicht allein die hauswirte und hendeler sondern alle handwerksleute und kommen dordurch die land ingemein in besserung und aufnemen.*

[110] Georg Agricola, *De precio metallorum et monetis libri III (Der Preis der Metalle und die Münzen, 1550)*, transl. in Hans Prescher (ed), *Georgius Agricola: Schriften über Maße und Gewichte (Metrologie)* (Berlin: Deutscher Verlag der Wissenschaften, 1959), p 352. Cf. with the classic argument in Jevons, *Money*.

[111] Agricola, *De precio metallorum et monetis libri III*, p 352.

[112] Ibid.

[113] Ibid., p 258.

[114] Georg Obrecht, *Fünff Vnderschiedliche Secreta Politica*, ed. Bertram Schefold ([Straßburg, 1617] Hildesheim: Olms-Weidemann, 2003), pp 107–9.

[115] Small, *The cameralists*.

[116] See discussion in Erik S. Reinert, 'A brief introduction to Veit Ludwig von Seckendorff (1626–1692)', *European Journal of Law and Economics* 19 (2005), 221–30.

[117] *Denn man zu dem tausch nicht allerley so weit bringen, noch an jedem ort so wohl, als an dem andern, verhandeln oder angenehm machen koennen*, Seckendorff [1656] 1720, pp 406–7.

[118] For example, David Graeber, *Debt: the first 5,000 years* (New York: Melville House, 2011); Sitta von Reden, *Money in classical antiquity* (Cambridge: Cambridge University Press, 2011); Peacock, *Introducing money*.

[119] Seckendorff 1720 [1655], pp 410–11.

[120] Ibid., pp 412–13.

[121] Munro, 'Münzkosten'.

[122] Seckendorff 1720 [1655], p 416.

[123] Johann Heinrich von Justi, *Staatswirthschaft*, 1755; Johann Heinrich von Justi, *Grundsätze der Policey-Wissenschaft*, 2 vols, 1756.

[124] Johann Heinrich von Justi, *Grundsätze der Policeywissenschaft* [1756] 1782, I, p 198. On Justi, see Adam, *The political economy of J.H.G. Justi*; Erik S. Reinert, 'Johann Heinrich Gottlob von Justi (1717–1771) – the life and times of an economist adventurer', in Backhaus (ed), *The beginnings of political economy*, pp 33–74; and, more recently, Zhao, 'Public happiness through manufacturing and innovation'.

[125] Text (facsimile) in Schefold (ed), *Die drei Flugschriften*; discussion in Schefold, 'Wirtschaft und Geld im Zeitalter der Reformation'. One of the best analyses still is Roscher, *Geschichte der Nationaloekonomik in Deutschland*, pp 102–6. See also Hans-Joachim Stadermann, *Der Streit um gutes Geld in Vergangenheit und Gegenwart: Enthaltend drei Flugschriften über den Münzstreit der sächsischen Albertiner und Ernestiner um 1530 nach der Ausgabe von Walther Lotz* (Tübingen: Mohr Siebeck, [1893] 1999).

[126] At the time, the Saxon dynasty was divided between the Albertine and Ernestine line, with joint rulership over the silver mines in the Erz Mountains.

127 *Die Muentz Belangende Antwort vnd bericht* [1530] 2000, p 41). My translation based on the facsimile in Schefold (ed), *Die drei Flugschriften*. Original not paginated.

128 Munro, 'Monetary origins', tables.

129 Rössner, *Deflation*, Ch. 3.

130 See earlier.

131 See the essays in Magnusson (ed), *Mercantilist economics*.

132 Smith, *The business of alchemy*; Yamamoto, *Taming capitalism before its triumph*.

133 Roscher, 'Die österreichische Nationalökonomik unter Kaiser Leopold I', at 40.

134 On Becher, see Roscher, 'Die österreichische Nationalökonomik', pp 38–59; Herbert Hassinger, *Johann Joachim Becher, 1635–1682: Beitrag zur Geschichte des Merkantilismus* (Vienna: Holzhausen, 1951); sections in Schumpeter, *History*.

135 Becher, *Politischer Discurs* 1688 [1668], pp 269–70.

136 Rössner, *Deflation*.

137 Becher, *Politischer Discurs* 1688 [1668], p 272.

138 Ibid.

139 Becher, *Politischer Discurs* 1688 [1668], pp 272–4.

Chapter 6

1 Karl Marx, *Contribution to the critique of political economy* (1859). Translation adopted from www.marxists.org/archive/marx/works/1859/critique-pol-economy/ch02_3.htm.

2 Frank L. Holt, *When money talks: a history of coins and numismatics* (Oxford: Oxford University Press, 2021), pp 109–11. Holt's book came out long after I completed the present chapter, but I have tried to incorporate some of its findings.

3 F. Somner Merryweather, *Lives and anecdotes of misers; or the passion of avarice displayed* (London: Simpkin & Marshall, 1850).

4 Joseph von Sonnenfels, *Grundsätze der Staatspolizey, Handlung und Finanzwissenschaft*, 2nd edn (Munich: Strobel, 1801), pp 358ff.

5 Oresme 1355/58, cap. II. For Luther's interpretation, see, for example, F.W. Lomler, G. Lucius, J. Rust and L. Sackreuter (eds), *Geist aus Luther's Schriften, oder: Concordanz der Ansichten und Urtheile des großen Reformators über die wichtigsten Gegenstände des Glaubens, der Wissenschaft und des Lebens*, Vol 2: G bis J. (Darmstadt: Leske, 1829), II, p 249.

6 Bernard Mandeville, *Fable of the bees or private vices publick benefits* (London: Roberts, 1714), ed. Phillip Hart (London: Penguin Classics, 1989), p 119.

7 Mandeville, *Fable of the bees*, p 131.

8 Steuart, *Principles of political oeconomy*, Book I, Ch. XXVII, p 375.

9 After Fernand Braudel, *Civilization and capitalism, 15th–18th century*, new pbk edn (London: Phoenix Press, 2002), Vol 1, p 463.

10 Smith, *Wealth of Nations*, Book II, Ch. 3. On Smith and parsimony, see Thomas R. de Gregori, 'Prodigality or parsimony: the false dilemma in economic development theory', *Journal of Economic Issues* 7:2 (1973), 259–66. See Werrett, *Thrifty science*, Ch. 1, for an interesting conceptual history of parsimony as thrift. 'Industry' at the times of Smith still referred to someone being industrious, not industry as the factory mode of production. At Smith's time, however, the concept had begun changing towards its more modern meaning; see Schui, *Early debates about industry*.

11 Craig Muldrew, *The economy of obligation: the culture of credit and social relations in early modern England* (Basingstoke: Palgrave, 1998); on the issue of early modern monetization, see, for example, Jan Lucassen, 'Deep monetisation: the case of the Netherlands 1200–1940', *Tijdschrift voor Sociale en Economische Geschiedenis* 11:3 (2014), 73–121; Jan Lucassen, 'Deep monetization in Eurasia in the long run 1', in R.J. van der Spek and Bas van Leeuwen (eds), *Money, currency and crisis: in search of trust, 2000 BC to AD 2000* (Abingdon: Routledge,

2018); Nick Mayhew, 'Money and the economy', in Rory Naismith (ed), *Money and coinage in the middle ages* (Boston, MA: Brill, 2018), pp 203–30.

12 Surely there were some dynamics in premodern economy, and the myth of static European economy has been dispelled. See Jan de Vries and Ad van der Woude, *The first modern economy: success, failure, and perseverance of the Dutch economy, 1500–1815* (Cambridge: Cambridge University Press, 1997); the critical review by Jan L. van Zanden, 'The "revolt of the early modernists" and the "first modern economy": an assessment', *The Economic History Review*, 2nd series, 55:4 (2002), 619–41; Maarten Prak (ed), *Early modern capitalism: economic and social change in Europe 1400–1800* (London: Routledge, 2006); Robert DuPlessis, *Transitions to capitalism in early modern Europe: economies in the era of early globalization, c.1450–c.1820*, new edn (Cambridge: Cambridge University Press, 2019).

13 Steuart, *Principles*, I, p 374.

14 Nicholas Mayhew, 'Modelling medieval monetisation', and 'Appendix 2: the calculation of GDP from Domesday Book', in Richard H. Britnell and Bruce M.S. Campbell (eds), *A commercialising economy: England 1086 to c.1300* (Manchester: Manchester University Press, 1995), pp 55–77, 195–6.

15 After Jonathan Sperber, 'Marx on money', in Mary Lindemann and Jared Poley (eds), *Money in the German-speaking lands* (New York: Berghahn, 2017), pp 173–85, at p 180.

16 Wilhelm Roscher, *System der Volkswirthschaft: Ein Hand- und Lesebuch für Geschäftsmänner und Studierende*, Vol 1 (Stuttgart: Cotta, 1854), p 213.

17 Frank Hatje, 'Status, friendship, and money in Hamburg around 1800: debit and credit in the diaries of Ferdinand Beneke (1774–1848)', in Lindemann and Poley (eds), *Money in the German-speaking lands*, pp 137–55, at 139, quoting Büsch on money, circulation and civilization.

18 I have used the German edition, Karl Pribram, *Geschichte des ökonomischen Denkens* (Frankfurt-am-Main: Suhrkamp, 1998).

19 Pribram, *Geschichte*, Vol 1, pp 147–8.

20 Schumpeter, *History of economic analysis*, p 316.

21 William Potter, *The key of wealth, or a new way for improving trade* (London: R.A., 1650), Preface, not paginated; Barry Supple, *Commercial crisis and change in England, 1600–1642* (Cambridge: Cambridge University Press, 1964).

22 Thus, MV=PT.

23 Potter, *The key of wealth*, Book I, section VII; Book II, section III.

24 Translating literally as 'cheap market', meaning a glut of commodities which kept product prices low.

25 Potter, *The key of wealth*, p 41, original in italics.

26 Schumpeter, *History*, p 318–19; cf. Anne Murphy, *The origins of English financial markets: investment and speculation before the South Sea Bubble* (Cambridge: Cambridge University Press, 2009); essays in Daniel Carey and C. Finlay (eds), *Empire of credit: the financial revolution in the British Atlantic world, 1688–1815* (Dublin: Irish Academic Press, 2011); Wennerlind, *Casualties of credit*.

27 Pribram, *Geschichte*, Vol I, p 147.

28 Charles Davenant, 'On the protection and care of trade', in Sir C. Whitworth (ed), *The political and commercial works of that celebrated writer Charles D'Avenant*, 5 vols, Vol 1 (London: Horsefield et al., 1771), p 447.

29 Heckscher, *Der Merkantilismus*, Vol II, p 198.

30 Mary S. Morgan, 'Measuring instruments in economics and the velocity of money', *LSE Working Papers on the Nature of Evidence: How Well Do 'Facts' Travel?* 13/06, 2006. http://eprints.lse.ac.uk/22535/1/1306Morgan.pdf, 14–15. See also Mary S. Morgan,

The world in the model: how economists work and think (Cambridge: Cambridge University Press, 2012).

31 Andrea Finkelstein, *Harmony and the balance: an intellectual history of seventeenth-century English economic thought* (Ann Arbour: University of Michigan Press, 2000), p 112; Morgan, 'Measuring instruments', 3.

32 Quentin Skinner, 'Meaning and understanding in the history of ideas', *History and Theory* 8:1 (1969), 3–53.

33 Marjorie Grice-Hutchinson, *The School of Salamanca: readings in Spanish monetary theory, 1544–1605* (Oxford: Clarendon Press, 1952); Marjorie Grice-Hutchinson, *Early economic thought in Spain 1177–1740* (London: Allen and Unwin, 1978).

34 Quoted in Lionel Rothkrug, *Opposition to Louis XIV* (Princeton, NJ: Princeton University Press, 1965), p 90.

35 G. Strelin, *Realwörterbuch für Kameralisten und Oekonomen: Vierter Band: von Flußarbeit bis Juwelen* (Nördlingen: Beck, 1788), entry 'Geld', p 163.

36 Ibid., p 162.

37 Ibid., p 160.

38 Dorinda Outram, *The Enlightenment* (Cambridge: Cambridge University Press, 2019); on enlightened economic thought, see, most recently, Schabas and Wennerlind, *A philosopher's economist*, esp. Ch. 5 and pp 154ff.; on Hume's views of money, manufacturing and economic development, Wennerlind and Schabas (eds), *David Hume's political economy*, and the forests' worth of literature on Adam Smith and his political and economic thought, for a discussion of which there is no space here; Wennerlind, *Casualties of credit*; Carey and Finlay (eds), *Empire of credit*; (Karl Daniel) Heinrich Bensen, *Versuch eines systematischen Grundnisses der reinen und angewandten Staatslehre für Kameralisten* (Erlangen: Palm, 1798), p 302.

39 Strelin, *Realwörterbuch*, p 160.

40 Ed. Rössner, 2018.

41 See also Reinert, *Translating empire*; Sophus A. Reinert, 'The empire of emulation: a quantitative analysis of economic translations in the European world, 1500–1849', in Sophus A. Reinert and Pernille Røge (eds), *The political economy of empire in the early modern world* (London: Palgrave Macmillan, 2013), pp 105–28; Reinert, 'Rivalry'.

42 Strelin, *Realwörterbuch*.

43 Ibid.

44 Ibid., p 162.

45 O'Brien, 'The nature and historical evolution'; and further works discussed in Chapter 3.

46 Strelin, *Realwörterbuch*, p 150.

47 Eduard Baumstark, *Kameralistische Encyclopädie: Handbuch der Kameralwissenschaften und ihrer Literatur für Rechts- und Verwaltungsbeamte, Land-Stände, Gemeinde-Räthe und Kameral-Kandidaten* (Heidelberg: Groos, 1835), p 570.

48 Johann Heinrich Gottlob Justi, *Grundsätze der Policeywissenschaft*, 3rd edn (Göttingen: Vandenhoeck, 1782), pp 201–13. On bills of exchange, see Denzel, *Das System des bargeldlosen Zahlungsverkehrs europäischer Prägung vom Mittelalter bis 1914*; Denzel, *Handbook of world exchange rates*, Introduction.

49 Krünitz, Vol 17: *Geld – Gesundheits=Versammlung*. On the 'mercantilist' dimension of such claims, see Reinert and Philipp Rössner, 'Cameralism and the German tradition of development economics'.

50 Eli F. Heckscher, *Economic history of Sweden* (Cambridge, MA: Harvard University Press, 1954), pp 183–9; Helga Schultz, *Das ehrbare Handwerk: Zunftleben im alten Berlin zur Zeit des Absolutismus* (Weimar: Böhlau, 1993), pp 18–25.

51 For example, Werrett, *Thrifty science*.

[52] 'Allein der Umlauf des Geldes ist eine so wichtige Sache für die Commercien und Gewerbe, daß eines ohne das andere unmöglich stattfinden kann', J.H.G. von Justi, *Grundsätze der Policeywissenschaft*, 2nd edn (Göttingen: Vandenhoeck, 1759), Vol I, p 161.

[53] Ibid., pp 194–204; cf. Johannes Kasnacich-Schmid, 'Grundsätze kameralistischer Geldpolitik', *Weltwirtschaftliches Archiv* 80 (1958), 90–130, at 120–7.

[54] *Süddeutsche Zeitung*, 28 July 1972, p 8: *Lieber fünf Prozent Inflation als fünf Prozent Arbeitslosigkeit.*

[55] Schabas and Wennerlind, *A philosopher's economist*, pp 154–60, and on hoarding, see pp 162–3.

[56] Pehr Nicholas Christiernin, *Utdrag af Foreldsntngar angaende den i Svea Rske upsttgne Wexel-Coursen* (Stockholm: Lars Salvius, 1761); paraphrased in and quoted from Robert V. Eagly, 'Money, employment and prices: a Swedish view, 1761', *Quarterly Journal of Economics* 77:4 (1963), 626–36, at 630.

[57] Berch, *Inledning til Almänna Hushålningen, innefattande Grunden til Politie, Oeconomie och Cameralwetenskaperna.*

[58] Ibid., pp 417–23; see Reinert and Carpenter, 'German language economic bestsellers', pp 26–53, at pp 36–9.

[59] Roscher, *System der Volkswirthschaft*, pp 209–10.

[60] See Rössner, *Martin Luther on commerce and usury*, pp 1–160, for a short biographical sketch and extended discussion of Luther's contribution to modern economic thought.

[61] Luther, *Address to the Christian Nobility of the German Nation*, 1520. On the contemporary concept of nations competing, see discussion in Tom Scott, 'The Reformation between deconstruction and reconstruction: reflections on recent writings on the German Reformation', *German History* 26:3 (2008), 406–22; Caspar Hirschi, *Wettkampf der Nationen: Konstruktionen einer deutschen Ehrgemeinschaft an der Wende vom Mittelalter zur Neuzeit* (Göttingen: Wallstein Verlag, 2013); English version, Caspar Hirschi, *The origins of nationalism: an alternative history from ancient Rome to early modern Germany* (Cambridge: Cambridge University Press, 2011).

[62] Helmut T. Lehmann and E. Theodore Bachmann (eds) *Luther's Works*, Vol 35: *Word and sacrament* (Philadelphia, PA: Fortress Press, 1960), p 81.

[63] Philipp Robinson Rössner, 'Monetary theory and cameralist economic management, c.1500–1900 AD', *Journal for the History of Economic Thought* 40:1 (2018), 99–134; Philipp Robinson Rössner, 'Kameralismus, Kapitalismus und die Ursprünge des modernen Wirtschaftswachstums – aus Sicht der Geldtheorie', *Vierteljahrschrift für Sozial- und Wirtschaftsgeschichte* 102:4 (2015), 437–71; Philipp Robinson Rössner, *Velocity! The speed of monetary circulation as an historical protagonist in European economic thought and practice, c.1350–1800, Proceedings of the 2016 Istituto Datini Settimane di Studio (Prato, IT), XLVIII Study Week ('I prezzi delle cose nell'età preindustriale/The prices of things in preindustrial times')*, ed. Francesco Ammanati (Florence: Florence University Press, 2017), pp 259–90, on which parts of the present chapter are based.

[64] Wilhelm von Schröder, *Fürstliche Schatz- und Rentkammer* (Leipzig: Gerdesius, 1686, 1705 edn), p 194. On Schröder, see, most recently, Vera Keller, '"A political *Fiat Lux*": Wilhem von Schroeder (1640–1688) and the co-production of chymical and political oeconomy', in Sandra Richter and Guillaume Garner (eds), *'Eigennutz' und 'gute Ordnung': Ökonomisierungen der Welt im 17. Jahrhundert* (Wiesbaden: Harrassowitz, 2016), pp 353–78; Keller, 'Happiness and projects between London and Vienna'; Vera Keller, 'Perfecting the state: alchemy and *oeconomy* as academic forms of knowledge in early modern German-speaking Lands', in Lindemann and Poley (eds), *Money in the German-speaking lands*, pp 26–42.

[65] Bog, *Der Reichsmerkantilismus*; Rössner (ed), *Philipp Wilhelm von Hörnigk's Austria supreme (if it so wishes)*, Introduction, esp. pp 8–18 (chapter on 'Who was Hörnigk?').

66   Exceptions from the rule include Giorgio Riello, *Cotton: the fabric that made the modern world* (Cambridge: Cambridge University Press, 2013); Kenneth Lipartito, 'Reassembling the economic: new departures in historical materialism', *American Historical Review* 121:1 (2016), 101–39; Trentmann, *Empire of things*. Much-quoted general works on materiality: Arjun Appadurai (ed), *The social life of things: commodities in cultural perspective* (Cambridge: Cambridge University Press, 1986); Neil MacGregor, *A history of the world in 100 objects* (London: Penguin, 2012). Furthermore, Matthew Johnson, *An archaeology of capitalism* (Oxford: Blackwell, 1996); Janet Hoskins (ed), *Biographical objects: how things tell the stories of people's lives* (New York: Routledge, 1998); Karen Harvey (ed), *History and material culture: a student's guide to approaching alternative sources* (Abingdon: Routledge, 2009); Tara Hamling and Catherine Richardson (eds), *Medieval and early modern material culture and its meanings* (Farnham: Ashgate, 2010); Renata Ago, *Gusto for things: a history of objects in seventeenth-century Rome* (Chicago: University of Chicago Press, 2013); Paula Findlen (ed), *Early modern things: objects and their histories, 1500–1800* (Abingdon: Routledge, 2013); on early modern political economy and its archaeological implications, Natascha Mehler, 'The archaeology of mercantilism: clay tobacco pipes in Bavaria and their contribution to an economic system', *Post-Medieval Archaeology*, 43:2 (2009), 261–28.

67   Nicholas J. Mayhew, 'Modelling medieval Monetisation', in Richard H. Britnell and Bruce M.S. Campbell (eds), *A commercialising economy: England 1086 to c.1300* (Manchester: Manchester University Press, 1995) pp 55–77; Nicholas J. Mayhew, 'Money supply, and the velocity of circulation'. Mayhew assumes considerable variation in English velocity over time. A conceptual discussion of velocity as a scientific concept of analysis can be found in Morgan, 'Measuring instruments'; Mary Morgan, 'An analytical history of measuring practices: the case of velocities of money', in M. Boumans (ed), *Measurement in economics: a handbook* (London: Academic, 2007), pp 105–32. A classic survey of this matter is M.W. Holtrop, 'Theories of the velocity of circulation of money in earlier economic literature', *Economic Journal Supplement: Economic History* 4 (1929), 503–24; but see also Milton Friedman and Anna J. Schwartz, *A monetary history of the United States 1867–1960* (Princeton, NJ: Princeton University Press, 1963); the learned discussion in G. Kulke, *Der Zusammenhang zwischen der Höhe des Volkseinkommens und der Geldmenge (Stückgeld und kurzfristige Bankeinlagen)* (Berlin: Duncker & Humblot, 1975), pp 41–50; M.D. Bordo and L. Jonung, 'The long-run behavior of velocity: the institutional approach revisited', *Journal of Policy Modeling* 12:2 (1990), 165–97; M.D. Bordo and L. Jonung, *Demand for money: an analysis of the long-run behavior of the velocity of circulation*, 3rd printing (New Brunswick, NJ: Taylor & Francis, 2009), Chs. 1 and 2, with a historical dimension, and graphs on pp 4ff. Most recently, Nuno Palma, 'Reconstruction of money supply over the long run: the case of England, 1270–1870', *Economic History Review*, 2nd series, 71:2 (2018), 373–92, Table A2, p 391. For Spain, see Yao Chen, Nuno Palma and Felix Ward, 'Reconstruction of the Spanish money supply, 1492–1810', CEPR Discussion Paper (revised version 2021), p 13 and Appendix C.1, p 28, for velocity.

68   T.M. Humphrey, 'The quantity theory of money: its historical evolution and role in policy debates', in *Federal Reserve Bank of Richmond Economic Review* 40 (1974), 2–19. Fisher believed that in the medium to long run, velocity varied with economic fluctuations and stages of economic development. See I. Fisher, *Elementary principles of economics* (New York: Macmillan, 1911), pp 79, 88; Milton Friedman, 'Die Geldnachfrage: einige theoretische und empirische Ergebnisse', in Milton Friedman, *Die optimale Geldmenge und andere Essays*, 2nd edn (Munich: Verlag Moderne Industrie, 1976), pp 157–98, at pp 157, 159–60; Roscher, *System der Volkswirthschaft*, pp 209–10.

69   Jack A. Goldstone, 'Lessons from the English price revolution of the sixteenth and seventeenth centuries', *The American Journal of Sociology* 89 (1984), 1122–60. See also Peter Lindert, 'English population, wages and prices: 1541–1913', *The Journal of Interdisciplinary*

History 15 (1985), 609–34; somewhat contrary, E.A. Nicolini and F. Ramos, 'A new method for estimating the money demand in pre-industrial economies: probate inventories and Spain in the eighteenth century', *European Review of Economic History* 14 (2010), 145–77.

[70] Nicholas J. Mayhew, 'Population, money supply, and the velocity of circulation in England, 1300–1700', *The Economic History Review*, new series, 48:2 (1995), 238–57, at 240.

[71] Frank C. Spooner, *The international economy and monetary movements in France, 1493–1725* (Cambridge, MA: Harvard University Press, 1972), Ch. 2; John H. Munro, 'Petty coinage in the economy of late-medieval Flanders: some social considerations of public minting', in Eddy H.G. Van Cauwenberghe (ed), *Precious metals, coinage and the changes of monetary structures in Latin-America, Europe and Asia (late middle ages–early modern times)* (Leuven: Leuven University Press, 1989), pp 25–56, at pp 38–9; John H. Munro, 'Precious metals and the price revolution reconsidered: the conjuncture of monetary and real forces in the European inflation of the early to mid-16th century', in Dennis O. Flynn, M. Morineau and Richard Von Glahn (eds), *Monetary history in global perspective, 1500–1808/L'histoire monétaire: une perspective globale, 1500–1808/Historia monetaria: una perspectiva global, 1500–1808* (Seville: Secretariado de Publicaciones de la Universidad de Sevilla, 1998), pp 35–51, at p 47; P. Latimer, 'The English inflation of 1180–1220 reconsidered', *Past & Present* 171 (2001), 3–29, at 25. See also discussion in Philipp Robinson Rössner, 'Monetary instability, lack of integration and the curse of a commodity money standard: the German lands, c.1400–1900 AD', *Credit and Capital Markets* 47:2 (2014), 297–340, at 327–8.

[72] This was because different social groups (economic actors) used different types or classes of money – there were several 'transaction spheres' in early modern Europe. Low-value or small change coins, sometimes called 'black money', *monneie noire* and so on, depreciated more quickly in value over time than full-bodied, high-value coins such as florins or thalers; Rössner, *Deflation – devaluation – rebellion*.

[73] I am following the terminology and interpretation suggested in Francesco Boldizzoni, 'La rivoluzione dei prezzi rivisitata: moneta ed economia reale in Alta Italia (1550–1630)', *Rivista Storica Italiana* 117 (2005), 1002–36.

[74] See figures and graphs in Blanchard, *International lead production and trade*; Ian Blanchard, *The international economy in the 'Age of the Discoveries', 1470–1570: Antwerp and the English merchants' world*, ed. P.R. Rössner (Stuttgart: Franz Steiner, 2009), discussion in Ch. 1, and production figures ibid., Fig 1.1, p 20. These were based partly upon figures presented in Westermann, *Das Eislebener Garkupfer und seine Bedeutung für den europäischen Kupfermarkt*; Ekkehard Westermann, 'Zur Silber- und Kupferproduktion Mitteleuropas vom 15. bis zum frühen 17. Jahrhundert', *Der Anschnitt* 5–6 (1986), 187–211; with critical discussion in Ekkehard Westermann, 'Über Beobachtungen und Erfahrungen bei der Vorbereitung der Edition einer vorindustriellen Produktionsstatistik. Zur Brandsilberproduktion des Falkenstein bei Schwaz/Tirol von 1470–1623', in Ekkehard Westermann (ed), *Quantifizierungsprobleme bei der Erforschung der europäischen Montanwirtschaft des 15. bis 18. Jahrhunderts* (St. Katharinen: Scripta-Mercaturae-Verlag, 1988), pp 27–42; Ekkehard Westermann (ed), *Die Listen der Brandsilberproduktion des Falkenstein bei Schwaz von 1470 bis 1623* (Vienna, 1988) (Leobener Grüne Hefte, NF, VII, 1988), pp 45–50; Ekkehard Westermann, 'Zum Umfang der Silber- und Kupferproduktion Tirols 1470–1530. Probleme bei der Ermittlung von Produktionsziffern', in W. Ingenhaeff and J. Bair (eds), *Schwazer Silber – vergeudeter Reichtum? Verschwenderische Habsburger in Abhängigkeit vom oberdeutschen Kapital an der Zeitenwende vom Mittelalter zur Neuzeit* (Innsbruck: Berenkamp, 2003), pp 271–86. A more recent survey is John H. Munro, 'The monetary origins of the "price revolution"', in Dennis O. Flynn, Arturo Giráldez and Richard von Glahn (eds), *Global connections and monetary history, 1470–1800* (Aldershot: Ashgate, 2003), pp

1–34, tables. Trade data are summarized in J. de Vries, 'Connecting Europe and Asia: a quantitative analysis of the Cape-route trade, 1497–1797', in Flynn, Giráldez and von Glahn (eds), *Global connections and monetary history*, pp 35–106.

[75] Morgan, 'Measuring instruments', pp 26–7.

[76] Rössner, *Deflation*.

[77] J. von Sonnenfels, *Grundsätze der Policey, Handlung und Finanzwissenschaft*, Pt. III (Vienna: Kurzböck, 1776), p 272.

[78] Flynn and Giráldez, 'Cycles of silver'. See also Flynn and Giráldez, 'Arbitrage, China and world trade in the early modern period'; Dennis O. Flynn and Arturo Giráldez, 'Born with a "silver spoon": the origin of world trade in 1571', *Journal of World History* 6 (1995), 201–21.

[79] A hypothesis put forth as early as Wilhelm Abel, 'Zur Entwicklung des Sozialprodukts in Deutschland im 16. Jahrhundert', *Jahrbücher für Nationalökonomie und Statistik* 173 (1961), 448–89, and developed at length in his classic *Agrarkrisen und Agrarkonjunktur: Eine Geschichte der Land- und Ernährungswirtschaft Mitteleuropas seit dem hohen Mittelalter*, 3rd edn (Hamburg: Parey, 1978). Abel's basic findings have been corroborated by Ulrich Pfister, 'Die Frühe Neuzeit als wirtschaftshistorische Epoche. Fluktuationen relativer Preise 1450–1850', in Helmut Neuhaus (ed), *Die Frühe Neuzeit als Epoche* (Munich: Oldenbourg, 2009), pp 409–34; Ulrich Pfister, 'German economic growth, 1500–1850', Contribution to the XVth World Economic History Congress, Utrecht, 3–7 August 2009.

[80] For an overview on competing monetary models, as well as a compromise approach, see Nicholas J. Mayhew, 'Prices in England, 1170–1750', *Past & Present* 219:1 (2013), 3–39.

[81] On which the classic in the field, Wilhelm Abel, *Agrarkrisen und Agrarkonjunktur* (transl. *Agricultural fluctuations in Europe: from the Thirteenth to twentieth centuries*) (London: Methuen, 1980).

[82] Abel, *Agrarkrisen und Agrarkonjunktur*.

[83] T.A. Brady, *German histories in the age of Reformations, 1400–1650* (Cambridge: Cambridge University Press, 2009).

[84] In addition to data summarized and discussed in Rössner, *Deflation*. See also Ulrich Pfister, 'Consumer prices and wages in Germany, 1500–1850', CQE Working Paper 15 (2010).

[85] Rössner, *Deflation*, pp 97–310. For a compromise model, see Munro, 'Monetary origins'; Mayhew, 'Prices in England'.

[86] On ingenious attempts at connecting numismatic method with monetary analysis, see Hansheiner Eichhorn, *Der Strukturwandel im Geldumlauf Frankens zwischen 1437 und 1610: Ein Beitrag zur Methodologie der Geldgeschichte* (Wiesbaden: Steiner, 1973); Joachim Schüttenhelm, *Der Geldumlauf im südwestdeutschen Raum vom Riedlinger Münzvertrag 1423 bis zur ersten Kipperzeit 1618: Eine statistische Münzfundanalyse unter Anwendung der elektronischen Datenverarbeitung* (Stuttgart: Kohlhammer, 1987); Michael North, *Geldumlauf und Wirtschaftskonjunktur im südlichen Ostseeraum an der Wende zur Neuzeit (1440–1570): Untersuchungen zur Wirtschaftsgeschichte am Beispiel des Großen Lübecker Münzschatzes, der norddeutschen Münzfunde und der schriftlichen Überlieferung* (Sigmaringen: Thorbecke, 1990); Joachim Schüttenhelm, 'Problems of quantifying the volume of money in early modern times: a preliminary survey', in Cauwenberghe (ed), *Precious metals*, pp 83–98.

[87] See data presented in Rössner, 'Crisis of the Reformation'.

[88] Paas, Paas and Schofield, *The Kipper und Wipper inflation*.

[89] For example, Jan de Vries, *Economy of Europe in an age of crisis, 1600–1750* (Cambridge: Cambridge University Press, 1976); Jan de Vries and L.M. Smith (eds), *The general crisis of the seventeenth century* (London: Routledge, 1978); Geoffrey Parker, *Global crisis: war, climate change and catastrophe in the seventeenth century* (New Haven, CT: Yale University Press, 2013).

[90] Hartmut T. Lehmann (ed), *To the councilmen of all cities in Germany that they establish and maintain Christian schools*, Luther's Works, xlv, ed. W.I. Brandt, *The Christian in society*, Vol II (Philadelphia, PA: Concordia, 1962), p 351.

[91] John Munro, 'Patterns of trade, money, and credit', in Thomas A. Brady, Heiko A. Oberman and James D. Tracy (eds), *Handbook of European history 1400–1600: late middle ages, Renaissance and Reformation*, Vol I: *Structures and assertions* (Leiden: Brill, 1994), pp 147–95, at pp 147–50.

[92] Ibid.; Fernand Braudel and Frank C. Spooner, 'Prices in Europe from 1450 to 1750', in *The Cambridge economic history of Europe*, Vol IV: *The economy of expanding Europe in the 16th and 17th centuries*, eds. E.E. Rich and C.H. Wilson (Cambridge: Cambridge University Press, 1967), pp 374–486, at 400–4; Rössner, *Deflation*, Ch. 2.

[93] Blanchard, *International lead production*; Ekkehard Westermann, 'Der wirtschaftliche Konzentrationsprozeß im Mansfelder Revier und seine Auswirkungen auf Martin Luther, seine Verwandte und Freunde', in Rosemarie Knape (ed), *Martin Luther und der Bergbau im Mansfelder Land: Aufsätze* (Lutherstadt Eisleben: Stiftung Luthergedenkstätten in Sachsen-Anhalt, 2000), pp 63–92; Lyndal Roper, *Martin Luther: renegade and prophet* (London: Vintage, 2017); Rössner, *Martin Luther on commerce and usury*, Ch. 2.

[94] Philipp Robinson Rössner, 'History through objects: the example of coins', in Christ and Rössner (eds), *History and economic life*, pp 198–218.

[95] Holt, *When money talks*, pp 126–37.

[96] There are very few works discussing the connections between hoarding and velocity; the up-to-date account on the possibilities of interaction between numismatics and ancient monetary and economic history is Holt, *When money talks*, Chs. 7 and 8, esp. pp 126–8 on finding and understanding hoards predominantly from classical antiquity. For the German-speaking lands in the middle ages and early modern period, see Walter Hävernick and Numismatische Kommision der Länder in der Bundesrepublik Deutschland/Diskussionsvorbereitungen fuer die Numismatische Arbeitstagung Hamburg 8.–11. Oktober 1954, 'Die deutschen Münzfunde des Mittelalters und der Neuzeit' (typescript, Landesmuseum Halle, Moritzburg collections); Niklot Klüßendorf, *Münzkunde – Basiswissen* (Hanover: Hahn, 2009); Niklot Klüßendorf, *Numismatik und Geldgeschichte: Basiswissen für Mittelalter und Neuzeit* (Hanover: Hahn, 2015).

[97] Portable Antiquities: https://finds.org.uk.

[98] I am indebted to Stefano Locatelli and Nuno Palma for reminding me of this important aspect.

[99] Klüßendorf, *Münzkunde*, pp 25–30.

[100] Christopher Dyer, 'Peasants and coins: the uses of money in the middle ages', *British Numismatic Journal* 67 (1997), 30–47; I am indebted to Nuno Palma for bringing this paper to my attention; Piotr Guzowski, 'Village court records and peasant credit in fifteenth- and sixteenth-century Poland', *Continuity and Change* 29:1 (2014), 115–42.

[101] Holt, *When money talks*, p 134.

[102] Zuijderduijn, *Medieval capital markets*; C. Jaco Zuijderduijn and Tine de Moor, 'Spending, saving, or investing? Risk management in sixteenth-century Dutch households', *Economic History Review*, 2nd series, 66:1 (2013), 38–56.

[103] Lucassen, 'Deep monetisation: the case of the Netherlands 1200–1940'.

[104] On which the present section is based.

[105] *Numismatische Kommission 1954*, p 8.

[106] *Numismatische Kommission 1954*, pp 14–15.

[107] Martin Treu (ed), *Martin Luther und das Geld: Aus Luthers Schriften, Briefen und Tischreden* (Lutherstadt Wittenberg: Stiftung Luthergedenkstätte, 2000); Harald Meller and Landesmuseum (eds), *Fundsache Luther: Archäologen auf den Spuren des Reformators*

(Stuttgart: Theiss; Halle: Landesamt für Denkmalpflege und Archäologie Sachsen-Anhalt, Landesmuseum für Vorgeschichte, 2008).

[108] *Numismatische Kommission 1954*, pp 17–19. Of a total of 79 findings containing pennies found in rural hoards, 34 finds contain hoards with less than 100 pennies, 17 were of the 100–500 penny range, ten of the 500–1000 penny range and only eight of the more than 1000 penny range. Only ten out of 79 hoards found on the countryside contained gold coins; Ibid., p 19.

[109] *Numismatische Kommission 1954*, pp 21–3.

[110] Walter Hävernick, 'Fundzahlen und wirtschaftliche Kraft der Landschaften Sachsen, Thüringen und Provinz Sachsen/Anhalt (11.–18.Jahrhundert)', in Thomas Fischer & Peter Ilisch (eds) LAGOM – Festschrift für Peter Berghaus zum 60. Geburtstag m 20. November 1979 (Münster i. W.: Numismatischer Verlag Dombrowski, 1981), pp 349–52, Figs 1 and 2.

[111] Holt, *When money talks*.

[112] Scott, *Society and economy in Germany*.

[113] C. Jaco Zuijderduijn and Roos van Osten, 'Breaking the piggy bank: what can historical and archaeological sources tell us about late-medieval saving behaviour?', Utrecht University, Centre for Global Economic History Working Paper No. 0065.

[114] I am grateful to the curator of the coin collections in the Moritzburg, Halle, Federal State of Saxony-Anhalt, Mr Ulf Dräger, who gave me access to this database in December 2010.

[115] Rössner, *Deflation*, Ch. 2.

[116] Carlo M. Cipolla, 'Economic depression of the Renaissance? I', *The Economic History Review*, new series, 16:3 (1964), 519–24; Harry Miskimin, 'Monetary movements and market structure – forces for contraction in fourteenth- and fifteenth-century England', *The Journal of Economic History* XXIV (1964), 470–90; Harry Miskimin, *The economy of later Renaissance Europe, 1460–1600* (Cambridge: Cambridge University Press, 1977), for a different viewpoint. See also Schüttenhelm, *Geldumlauf*; North, *Geldumlauf*; John Day, 'The great bullion famine of the fifteenth century', *Past & Present* LXXIX (1978), 3–54; Munro, 'Monetary origins'. On the depression in the late medieval European mining economy, see Ekkehard Westermann, 'Zur spätmittelalterlichen Depression der europäischen Montanwirtschaft. Stand und offene Fragen der Forschung', in *Der Tiroler Bergbau und die Depression der europäischen Montanwirtschaft im 14. Und 15. Jahrhundert*, eds. Rudolf Tasser and Ekkehard Westermann (Innsbruck: Studien, 2004), pp 9–18.

[117] Munro, 'Monetary origins', for a modernized monetarist explanation of late medieval and early modern inflation. For an earlier monetary explanation, see Earl J. Hamilton, *American treasure and the price revolution in Spain, 1501–1650* (Cambridge, MA: Harvard University Press, 1934). The monetarist explanation of the Price Revolution ascribes the 16th-century inflation to a combined effect of monetary expansion due to the influx of American silver, as well as an increased speed in monetary circulation due to population and urbanization growth. A neo-Malthusian approach focuses on population and per capita resources, especially the deteriorating relation between the development of productive capacity (chiefly in agriculture) and claims (demand) on these resources. This led to changes in relative prices, especially a decline in real wages and living standards as grain and foodstuffs appreciated more quickly in value than other (manufactured) goods and nominal wages; see Abel, *Agrarkrisen und Agrarkonjunktur*.

[118] Munro, 'Monetary origins'.

[119] For example, North, *Geldumlauf*; Day, 'Bullion famine'; Munro, 'Monetary origins'; Spufford, *Money and its use in medieval Europe*, pp 339–62; North, *Das Geld und seine Geschichte* (Munich: C.H. Beck, 2009), Chs. 2 and 3.

[120] Day, 'Bullion famine'.

[121] Rössner, *Deflation*, pp 453–62.

122 Rössner, 'Crisis of the Reformation', pp 21–9.

123 Gustav (von) Schmoller, 'Zur Geschichte der national-ökonomischen Ansichten in Deutschland während der Reformations'; Roscher, *Geschichte der Nationaloekonomik in Deutschland*; Rössner, *Deflation*, pp 204–35; Philipp Robinson Rössner, 'Luther – Ein tüchtiger Ökonom? Über die monetären Ursprünge der Deutschen Reformation', *Zeitschrift für Historische Forschung* 42:1 (2015), 37–74; Rössner, *Martin Luther on commerce and usury*; Rössner, 'Burying money?'.

124 For example, Scott, 'The Reformation between deconstruction and reconstruction'; Brady, *German histories*.

125 As argued in Kasnacich-Schmid, 'Grundsätze kameralistischer Geldpolitik', at 127.

126 See Marx's derogatory remarks on cameralism in *Das Kapital*, afterword to the 2nd–4th editions.

127 Goldstone, 'Lessons'.

128 Ibid.

129 G.H. Zincke, *Grund=Riß einer Einleitung zu denen Cameral=Wissenschaften* (Leipzig: Fuchs, 1742), p 278.

130 Sandl, *Ökonomie des Raumes*.

131 Anon. [Johann Daniel Crafft/Krafft], *Bedencken von Manufacturen in Deutschland* (Jena: Bauhofer 1683), pp 3–4.

132 See also Schui, *Early debates about industry*.

133 C.G. Rößig, *Lehrbuch der Policeywissenschaft* (Jena, 1786), pp 260, 265, 393–4.

134 Johann Georg Büsch, *Sämtliche Schriften, Vol 9: Abhandlung vom Geldumlauf*, Buch I–III (Vienna: Bauer, 1816), pp 409–14.

135 The literature on this concept (which many may now consider obsolete) is vast; landmark contributions include Franklin F. Mendels, 'Proto-industrialization: the first phase of the industrialization process', *The Journal of Economic History*, 32:1, The tasks of economic history (1972), 241–61; Peter Kriedte, Hans Medick and Jügen Schlumbohm, *Industrialisierung vor der Industrialisierung: gewerbliche Warenproduktion auf dem Land in der Formationsperiode d. Kapitalismus* (Göttingen: Vandenhoeck & Ruprecht, 1977); Sheilagh C. Ogilvie and Markus Cerman (eds), *European proto-industrialization* (Cambridge: Cambridge University Press, 1996).

136 Büsch, *Abhandlung vom Geldumlauf*, Buch I–III, pp 437–8.

137 J.G.H. Justi, *Vergleichungen der Europäischen mit den Asiatischen und andern vermeintlich Barbarischen Regierungen* (Berlin, Stettin and Leipzig: Johann Heinrich Rüdiger, 1762), pp 310–11.

138 Kasnacich-Schmid, 'Grundsätze kameralistischer Geldpolitik', at 110.

139 Joachim Georg Darjes, *Erste Gründe der Cameralwissenschaften*, 2nd edn (Leipzig: Breitkopf, 1768), p 209.

Chapter 7

1 On Cain and Abel and a general economic reading, see Luigino Bruni, *The economy of salvation: ethical and anthropological foundations of market relations* (Cham: Springer, 2019), Ch. 4; Tomas Sedlacek, *Economics of good and evil* (Oxford: Oxford University Press, 2011) also evokes biblical stories in economics.

2 New King James version.

3 Paul Jacob Marperger, *Das neu-eröffnete manufacturen-haus/in welchem die manufacturen insgemein/derselben verschiedene arten/die dazu benöthigte materialien und darin arbeitende künstler vorgestellet werden* (Hamburg: Schillers & Kisner, 1721), pp 7, 9.

4 Bertram Schefold, *Great economic thinkers from antiquity to the historical school: translations from the series Klassiker der Nationalökonomie* (Abingdon: Routledge, 2016), pp 35–6.

5   Johann Heinrich Justi, *Vollständige Abhandlung von denen Manufacturen und Fabriken*, Vol 1 (Copenhagen: Roth, 1758), p 55.

6   Adam Smith, *Lectures on Jurisprudence*, p 224.

7   For example, *Theatre des Arts et Metiers*; transl. and ed. Johann Justi, *Schauplatz der Künste und Handwerke, oder vollständige Beschreibung derselben, verfertiget oder gebilliget von denen Herren der Academie der Wissenschaften zu Paris* (Leipzig: Johann Heinrich Rüdiger, 1762); 21 volumes appeared in total. Justi was succeeded by Daniel Gottfried Schreber as general editor (Vols 5–13).

8   Reinert, *How rich countries got rich*.

9   See Jürgen G. Backhaus (ed), *Physiocracy, antiphysiocracy and Pfeiffer* (New York: Springer, 2011); Kaplan and Reinert (eds), *The economic turn*.

10 Mokyr, *A culture of growth*, which pays little attention to manufacturing before the Industrial Revolution.

11 Jean-Louis Peaucelle, 'Adam Smith's use of multiple references for his pin making example', *The European Journal of the History of Economic Thought* 13:4 (2006), 489–512; Hiram Coten, 'The preindustrial economics of Adam Smith', *The Journal of Economic History* 45:4 (2009), 833–53.

12 This project was more than a translation. The editors of single volumes included trademark cameralists like Daniel Gottfried Schreber and even celebrities such as Johann Heinrich Justi. They often added as much text and meaning by means of comments, footnotes and annotations to turn this project into something of 'their' own. On contemporary engravings of manufacturing, see imprints in Erika Herzfeld, *Preußische Manufakturen: Großgewerbliche Fertigung von Porzellan, Seide, Gobelins, Uhren, Tapeten, Waffen, Papier u.a. im 17. und 18. Jahrhundert in und um Berlin* (Berlin: Verlag der Nationen, 1996).

13 Sven Beckert and Seth Rockman (eds), *Slavery's capitalism: a new history of American economic development* (Philadelphia: University of Pennsylvania Press, 2016), p 11, but usages of the term 'factory' and its physical manifestations as a commercial institution were much wider in the early modern period; see Wolfgang Reinhard, *Empires and encounters: 1350–1750* (Cambridge, MA: Belknap, 2015); Wolfgang Reinhard, *Die Unterwerfung der Welt: Globalgeschichte der europäischen Expansion 1415–2015* (Munich: C.H. Beck, 2018).

14 Justi, *Manufacturen*, Vol 1, 1st edn (Copenhagen: Roth, 1758), pp 5–6.

15 Wehler argued that there never was a (chrono)logical sequence or development from manufactory to factory capitalism, as there had always been a mix of industrial production types or sites, including domestic handicraft, manufactory, centralized or decentralized workshop or manufactory, quasi- or proto-factory and so on. It was the mix that changed over time. Steam engines were added after the 1700s, with some factory sites growing considerably bigger. It is difficult to place *Fabrikstadt* Krupp in Essen around 1900 alongside any quasi-factory setting of the preindustrial times, though. See Hans-Ulrich Wehler, *Deutsche Gesellschaftsgeschichte Vol 1: Vom Feudalismus des alten Reiches bis zur defensiven Modernisierung der Reformära: 1700–1815*, pp 102–12, 202ff.

16 Brunner, Conze and Koselleck (eds), *Geschichtliche Grundbegriffe*. On the project, as well as the wider remit, of *Begriffsgeschichte*, see Tribe, *Economy of the word*; Ernst Müller and Falko Schmieder, *Begriffsgeschichte und historische Semantik: Ein kritisches Kompendium* (Frankfurt-am-Main: Suhrkamp, 2016); Pernau and Sachsenmaier (eds), *Global conceptual history: a reader*. On the conceptual history of the term 'industry' in Voltaire's writings, see Schui, *Early debates about industry*.

17 Andrew Ure, *The philosophy of manufactures*, original edn (London: Charles Knight, 1835), p 1.

18 For example, Jairus Banaji, 'Globalising the history of capital: ways forward', *Historical Materialism* 26:3 (2018), 143–66, at 161–3; Jairus Banaji, *Brief history of commercial capitalism* (London: Haymarket Books, 2020).

19 Eli F. Heckscher, *Economic history of Sweden* (Cambridge, MA: Harvard University Press, 1954), pp 183–9; Barry Supple, 'The state and the industrial revolution', in C.M. Cipolla (ed), *The Fontana economic history of Europe*, Vol 3: *The industrial revolution, 1700–1914* (New York: Barnes & Noble, 1976), pp 312–13. For the German-speaking lands, Wehler, *Deutsche Gesellschaftsgeschichte 1*, pp 102–12; Karl Heinrich Kaufhold, as quoted in Sheilagh Ogilvie, 'Beginnings of industrialisation', in Sheilagh Ogilvie (ed), *Germany: a new social and economic history*, II (London: Arnold, 1996), p 291; Helga Schultz, *Handwerker, Kaufleute, Bankiers: Wirtschaftsgeschichte Europas 1500–1800* (Frankfurt-am-Main: Fischer, 1997), pp 124–32.

20 Franz von Künsberg, *Grundsätze der Fabrikpolizei besonders in Hinsicht auf Deutschland* (Weimar: Hoffmann's Witwe & Erben, 1792), p 7. On Künsberg, see Heinrich Lang, 'Das Fürstbistum Bamberg zwischen Katholischer Aufklärung und aufgeklärten Reformen', in Mark Häberlein (ed), *Bamberg im Zeitalter der Aufklärung und der Koalitionskriege* (Bamberg: University of Bamberg Press, 2014), pp 11–71, at pp 53–4.

21 Friedrich List, 'Das nationale System der politischen Ökonomie', in Ludwig Häusser (ed), *Friedrich List's gesammelte Schriften*, III (Stuttgart and Tübingen: Cotta, 1851).

22 Friedrich Lenz (ed), *Friedrich List's kleinere Schriften*, I: *Zur Staatswissenschaft und politischen Ökonomie* (Jena: Gustav Fischer, 1926), pp 367–436.

23 List called agriculture 'lifeless' or sterile (*leblos*) and thus unlikely to generate lasting economic spillover effects supporting sustained economic growth and development. This was mainly due to agriculture's limited productivity-enhancing capacities, which were much lower than in other sectors. Accordingly, List was critical of Physiocracy; see Friedrich List, 'Das nationale System der politischen Ökonomie', pp 201–36, 330–3. On the other hand, List in his *Wir wollen keine Fabriken!* (1843) called for Germany to have a balanced economy, with equal contributions of the three sectors – agriculture, manufacturing/industry and services – to national wealth; see Friedrich Lenz (ed), *Friedrich List's kleinere Schriften*, I: *Zur Staatswissenschaft und politischen Ökonomie* (Jena: Gustav Fischer, 1926), pp 594–626, at p 596. And in his *Über die Beziehungen der Landwirtschaft zur Industrie und zum Handel* (1844), ibid., pp 627–83, at p 629, he marked out agriculture as the most important and foundational sector of the economy without which neither of the other two would be able to flourish. On List, see, for example, Wilhelm Stieda, 'Friedrich List', *Berichte über die Verhandlungen der Sächsischen Akademie der Wissenschaften zu Leipzig, Philologisch-historische Klasse*, 80:1 (1928), 1–44; Hans Gehrig, *Friedrich List und Deutschlands politisch-ökonomische Einheit* (Leipzig: Koehler & Amelang, 1956); Carl Brinkmann, 'Friedrich List', in *Handwörterbuch der Sozialwissenschaften*, Vol 6 (Stuttgart: G. Fischer, 1959), pp 633–5; Walter Brauer, 'List, Friedrich', in *Neue Deutsche Biographie* (NDB), Vol 14 (Berlin: Duncker & Humblot, 1985), pp 694–7; William Otto Henderson, *Friedrich List: Der erste Visionär eines vereinten Europas: Eine historische Biographie* (Reutlingen: Verlagshaus Reutlingen, Oertel u. Spörer, 1989); David Levi-Faur, 'Friedrich List and political economy of the nation-state', *Review of International Political Economy* 4:1 (1997), 154–78; Arno Mong Daastøl, 'Friedrich List's heart, wit and will: mental capital as the productive force of progress', PhD dissertaion, Universität Erfurt, 2011; Reinert, *How rich countries got rich*.

24 William Notz (ed), *Friedrich List: Grundlinien einer politischen Ökonomie und andere Beiträge der Amerikanischen Zeit 1825–1832* (Berlin: Reimar Hobbing, 1931), p 105.

25 List, *Das nationale System der politischen Ökonomie*, after Rüdiger Gerlach, *Imperialistisches und kolonialistisches Denken in der politischen Ökonomie Friedrich Lists* (Hamburg: Kovač, 2009), p 43.

26 Erik Reinert and Arno Mong Daastøl, 'Exploring the genesis of economic innovations: the religious Gestalt-Switch and the duty to Invent as preconditions for economic growth', *European Journal of Law and Economics* 4 (1997), 233–83, a paper quoted, interestingly,

NOTES

in David S. Landes, *The wealth and poverty of nations: why some are so rich and some so poor* (New York: Norton, 1998).

[27] Joel Mokyr, *The lever of riches: technological creativity and economic progress* (Oxford: Oxford University Press, 1990); Joel Mokyr, *The gifts of Athena: historical origins of the knowledge economy* (Princeton, NJ: Princeton University Press, 2002); Mokyr, *Enlightened economy*; Mokyr, *A culture of growth*. For German popular or economic enlightenment, see, for example, Holger Böning, Hanno Schmitt and Reinhart Siegert (eds), *Volksaufklärung: eine praktische Reformbewegung des 18. und 19. Jahrhunderts* (Bremen: Ed. Lumière, 2007); Marcus Popplow, *Landschaften agrarisch-ökonomischen Wissens: Strategien innovativer Ressourcennutzung in Zeitschriften und Sozietäten des 18. Jahrhunderts* (Münster: Waxmann, 2010); Black, *The power of knowledge*.

[28] See, among other recent works, Peter Gay, *Enlightenment: the science of freedom* (New York: Norton, 1969); Roy Porter, *The Enlightenment* (London: Penguin, 2011); Georg Schmidt, *Wandel durch Vernunft: Deutschland 1715–1806* (Munich: C.H. Beck, 2009); Outram, *The Enlightenment*.

[29] Popplow, *Landschaften agrarisch-ökonomischen Wissens*; Böning, Schmitt and Siegert (eds), *Volksaufklärung*.

[30] Holger Böning, 'Das Intelligenzblatt', in Ernst Fischer, Wilhelm Haefs and York-Gothart Mix (eds), *Von Almanach bis Zeitung: Ein Handbuch der Medien in Deutschland 1700–1800* (Munich: Beck, 1999); Sabine Doering-Manteuffel, Josef Mancal and Wolfgang Wüst (eds), *Pressewesen der Aufklärung: Periodische Schriften im Alten Reich* (Berlin: Akademie-Verlag, 2001); Holger Böning, *Periodische Presse, Kommunikation und Aufklärung: Hamburg und Altona als Beispiel* (Bremen: Edition Lumière, 2002); Bob Clarke, *From grub street to fleet street: an illustrated history of English newspapers to 1899* (Aldershot: Ashgate, 2007).

[31] See also contributions in Popplow (ed), *Landschaften agrarisch-ökonomischen Wissens*.

[32] Charles W. Cole, *Colbert and a century of French mercantilism* (Hamden, MA: Archon Books, 1964). On Colbertian resonances in modern industrial policy, see Elie Cohen, 'Industrial policies in France: the old and the new', *Journal of Industry, Competition and Trade* 7 (2007), 213–27. One of the best recent reassessments of Colbert is Moritz Isenmann, 'War Colbert ein "Merkantilist"?', in Moritz Isenmann (ed), *Merkantilismus – Wiederaufnahme einer Debatte* (Stuttgart: Franz Steiner, 2014), pp 143–67. See also Günther Ammon, 'Jean-Baptiste Colbert', in Holger Janusch (ed), *Handelspolitik und Welthandel in der Internationalen Politischen Ökonomie* (Wiesbaden: Springer, 2020), pp 3–11.

[33] Modified from Weststeijn and Hartman, 'An empire of trade'.

[34] See case studies in Rössner (ed), *Economic growth and the origins of modern political economy*.

[35] This is a state at work *passim* – albeit not always explicitly acknowledged – in the surveys in Larry Neal and Jeffrey G. Williamson (eds), *The Cambridge history of capitalism, Vol 1: The rise of capitalism: from ancient origins to 1848* (Cambridge: Cambridge University Press, 2015).

[36] Rössner, *Martin Luther on commerce and usury*, Chs. 2 and 3.

[37] Elizabeth Lamond (ed), *A discourse of the common weal of this realm of England. First printed in 1581 and commonly attributed to W.S.* (Cambridge: Cambridge University Press, 1893), pp 92, 93; for criticism of Lamond's edition and regarding different claims to possible authorship, Mary Dewar, 'The authorship of the 'discourse of the commonweal', *The Economic History Review*, new series, 19:2 (1966), 388–400.

[38] Giovanni Botero, *The reason of state/Della ragione di stato*, transl. P.J. and D.P. Waley, with an introduction by D.P. Waley (London: Routledge & Kegan Paul, 1956); Giovanni Botero, *The greatness of cities*, transl. Robert Peterson 1606 (New Haven, CT: Yale University Press, 1956), pp 150–3.

[39] Ashworth, *The Industrial Revolution*, Ch. 8, pp 147–8.

[40] Von Hörnigk, *Austria Supreme (if it so wishes)*, pp 147–8.

41 Reinert and Carpenter, 'German language economic bestsellers', pp 26–53; Zac Zimmer, 'Bitcoin and Potosi silver: historical perspectives on cryptocurrency', *Technology & Culture* 58: 2 (2017), 307–34. On money, monetary policy, silver mining and global trade, see Chapter 5.

42 After Thomson in Maxine Berg, Pat Hudson and Michael Sonenscher (eds), *Manufacture in town and country before the factory* (Cambridge: Cambridge University Press, 1983), p 71.

43 Gentaro Seki, 'Policy debate on economic development in Scotland: the 1720s to the 1730s', in Sakamoto and Tanaka (eds), *The rise of political economy in the Scottish Enlightenment*, pp 22–38; Reinert and Carpenter, 'German language economic bestsellers'; Sophus Reinert, 'Giovanni Botero (1588) and Antonio Serra (1613): Italy and the birth of development economics', in Reinert, Ghosh and Kattel (eds), *Handbook of alternative theories of economic development*, Ch. 1, pp 3–41; essays in Backhaus (ed), *Physiocracy, antiphysiocracy and Pfeiffer*; Kaplan and S. Reinert (eds), *Economic turn*; Reinert and Rössner, 'Cameralism and the German tradition of development economics'.

44 Small, *The cameralists*.

45 Jan de Vries and Ad van der Woude, *The first modern economy: success, failure, and perseverance of the Dutch economy, 1500–1815* (Cambridge: Cambridge University Press, 1997).

46 Veit Ludwig von Seckendorff, *Additiones* (Leipzig: Meyer, 1703), pp 166–7. In the original: '*Diesem nach folget / daß es in FriedensZeiten an Leuten nicht ermangeln werde / wenn man dem gemeinen Mann ein erkleckliches und bestaendiges Verdienst schaffen kann: Es stehet aber eben die Kunst und difficultaet darinnen / was man vornehme und erfinde / uem solchen Verdienst / Tag= oder Jahr=Lohn zu schaffen*'. On Seckendorff, see Reinert, 'Cameralism and commercial rivalry'.

47 Developed in Reinert, *How rich countries got rich*.

48 Ibid.

49 Ibid.

50 Ibid.; Epstein, *Freedom and growth*; Stephan R. Epstein and Maarten Roy Prak (eds), *Guilds, innovation, and the European economy, 1400–1800* (Cambridge: Cambridge University Press, 2008).

51 *Zwang/monopolium*, ibid., p 169.

52 Seckendorff, *Additiones*, 1720 edn: '*Aber ein monopolium auf immer zu concediren ist ja so schaedlich und noch schlimmer als die zuenffte der handwercker*' (Jena: Johann Meyers Wittwe, 1720), p 238.

53 Seckendorff, *Additiones*, pp 172–3.

54 Ibid., pp 176–8.

55 Rudolf Forberger, *Die Manufaktur in Sachsen vom Ende des 16. bis zum Anfang des 19. Jahrhunderts* (Berlin: Deutsche Akademie der Wissenschaften zu Berlin, 1958); Ursula Forberger, 'Crafft (Kraft), Johann Daniel', in *Sächsische Biografie*, ed. Institut für Sächsische Geschichte und Volkskunde e. V./Martina Schattkowsky, Online issue: www.isgv.de/saebi/ (last accessed 20 January 2015).

56 [Johann Daniel Crafft/Krafft], *Bedencken von Manufacturen in Deutschland* (Jena: Bauhofer, 1683), pp 3–4.

57 Hörnigk, *Austria Supreme*, p 189.

58 Keller, 'Happiness and projects between London and Vienna'.

59 *Fürstliche Schatz- und Rentkammer*, Leipzig 1686.

60 1705 edn, p 344.

61 Johann Heinrich Gottlob von Justi, *Staatswirthschaft oder Systematische Abhandlung aller Oekonomischen und Cameral-Wissenschaften, die zur Regierung eines Landes erfodert [sic!] werden: In zween Theilen ausgefertiget* (Leipzig: Breitkopf, 1755), Vol I, pp 144–268.

62 Zhao, 'Public happiness through manufacturing and innovation'.

63 Justi, *Vollständige Abhandlung von den Manufacturen und Fabriquen* (1758), Vol 1, pp 49–50.

64 §187.
65 §198.
66 For example, A.J. Durie, *The Scottish linen industry in the eighteenth century* (Edinburgh: John Donald, 1979).
67 Tribe, *Land, labour, and economic discourse*; the relevant commentaries in Burkhardt and Priddat (eds), *Geschichte der Ökonomie*. On Wolf Helmhardt Hohberg, one of the 17th-century coryphées of the genre, see Brunner, *Adeliges Landleben und europäischer Geist*.
68 *Staatswirthschaft*, I, §188.
69 §185, note.
70 All §198.
71 §302.
72 Backhaus (ed), *The beginnings of political economy*; Jonsson, 'Climate change and the retreat of the Atlantic', 99–126; Seppel and Tribe (eds), *Cameralism in practice*; Nokkala and Miller (eds), *Cameralism and the Enlightenment*; Reinert, 'Northern lights'.
73 In his preface to Vol 9 on metal working and locksmithery (1769).
74 Daniel Gottfried Schreber (ed), *Schauplatz der Künste und Handwerke oder vollständige Beschreibung derselben, verfertigt oder gebilligt von den Herren der Academie der Wissenschaften zu Paris*, vol 9 (Leipzig: Johann Jacob Kanter, 1769), Preface, pp 2–4.
75 Schreber (ed), *Schauplatz*, IX, Preface, p 1.
76 Justi, *Schauplatz der Künste und Handwerke*, Vol 1 (1762), Preface, p 9.
77 Michael Stürmer (ed), *Herbst des alten Handwerks: Quellen zur Sozialgeschichte des 18. Jahrhunderts* (Munich: Deutscher Taschenbuchverlag, 1979); Peter Burke, *Popular culture in early modern Europe* (Aldershot: Scolar Press, 1994).
78 Mokyr, *A culture of growth*.
79 Schreber (ed), *Schauplatz*, Vol IX, Preface, p 4.
80 Justi (ed), *Schauplatz*, I, p 50.
81 'Es ist nur eine einzige Ursache vorhanden, warum eine gute Policey denen Fleischhauern gestatten, oder ihnen so gar gesetzlich auferlegen kann, ihren Talk nicht roh zu verkaufen, sondern denselben vorher auszuschmelzen. Diese ist, daß der Talk so leicht verdirbt, und in eine Art von Fäulung gehet, welche der Güte desselben so nachtheilig ist; dieses Verderben würde sich gar öfters ereignen, wenn die Fleischer nicht so fort Gelegenheit zum Absatz hätten, oder um einen bessern Preiß zu erhalten, denselben nicht auf das erste Geboth loßschlagen wollten. Dahingegen sind gar viele Ursachen, welche die Policey bewegen können, das Ausschmelzen des Talkes, denen Lichtziehern zu überlassen. Der Talk ist das hauptsächlichste Material der Lichtzieher; sie müssen also von dessen Güte und Aufrichtigkeit versichert seyn. Dieses können sie aber niemals, wenn sie ihn nicht selbst ausschmelzen.'
82 See also Reinert, *Translating empire*.
83 Recent global surveys include Vries, *Escaping poverty*; Koyama and Rubin, *How the world became rich*.
84 Smith, *Wealth of Nations*, 1776, Book I, Ch. 1.

Chapter 8

1 Wrisberg faiences are featured in Gordon Campbell (ed), *Grove Encyclopedia of Decorative Arts* (Oxford: Oxford University Press, 2006), Vol 2, p 563. Archival deposits and fragments of the Goertz noble family archive are stored in Landeshauptarchiv Hanover, Nebenstelle Pattensen, Dep. 63 (part of which is on microfilm). On the history of the Wrisberg estates, see Paul Graff, *Geschichte des Kreises Alfeld* (Hildesheim: A. Lax, 1928); Michael la Corte, *Emblematik als Teil der profanen Innenraumgestaltung deutscher Schlösser und Herrenhäuser: Vorkommen – Form – Funktion* (Göttingen: Cuvillier, 2019), pp 186–8; Sophie

Kaminski, *Die Idee der Nachhaltigkeit und die Landschaft des 18. und 19. Jahrhunderts am Beispiel des südlichen Raums Hildesheim* (Göttingen: Universitätsverlag Göttingen, 2020), pp 250–82. On the history of prices, wages and business economics of the Wrisberg estate, see Werner Graf von Schlitz genannt von Görtz, *Die Entwicklung der Landwirthschaft auf den Goertz-Wrisbergschen Gütern in der Provinz Hannover auf Grund archivalischen Materials* (Jena: Fischer, 1880).

2   Oskar Kiecker & Paul Graff (ed), *Kunstdenkmäler der Provinz Hannover* Vol. 2.6 (Hanover: Schulze, 1929), pp 315–16. Motifs were drawn, apart from Diego Saavedra, from artists including or Tacitus emblematicus (1584–1648), Otto van Vaen (1556–1629), or Ovidius et Horatius emblematici and Joachim Camerarius the Younger (1534–1598) called Plinius emblematicus. See Martin Boyken, *Die Spruchfliesen von Wrisbergholzen* (Hildesheim: Gerstenberg 1966); Johannes Köhler, *Angewandte Emblematik im Fliesensaal von Wrisbergholzen bei Hildesheim* (Hildesheim: A. Lax, 1988), pp 18–44, 81–2.

3   Corte, *Emblematik*, p 180, n 784.

4   J.H. Hanford, *The Princeton University Library Chronicle*, Vol 17, No. 1 (1955), pp 40–5.

5   Diego Saavedra Fajardo, *Idea de un principe politico christiano, representada en cien empresas* (Münster: Nicolao Enrico, 1640), Preface ('Al Letor'), p 1: 'En la trabaiosa ociasodad de mis continuous viajes por Alemania'. See Hugh Chisholm, 'Saavedra Fajardo, Diego de', *Encyclopædia Britannica* 23, 11th edn (Cambridge: Cambridge University Press, 1911), pp 954–5.

6   Andrew C. Thompson, *Britain, Hanover and the Protestant interest, 1688–1756* (Woodbridge: Boydell & Brewer, 2006), Ch. 3.

7   Since most 18th-century records from the private archive of the Goertz-Schlitz baronial family seem to have been lost, much of the Wrisberg business history remains conjectural; email correspondence with State Archive of Lower Saxony (Niedersächsisches Landesarchiv Abteilung Hannover), 10 January 2022, and Prof. Arndt Reitemeier, Göttingen.

8   Rudi H. Kaethner and Martha Kaethner, *Weilrod: Die Geschichte von dreizehn Taunusdörfern* (Weilrod: Geschichtsverein, 1987), pp 388–400.

9   Summarized in Allen, *British Industrial Revolution*; Vries, *Escaping poverty*; Koyama and Rubin, *How the world became rich*, pp 62–3; Rosenthal and Wong, *Before and beyond divergence*.

10   Classic accounts include Franklin F. Mendels, 'Proto-industrialization: the first phase of the industrialization process', *Journal of Economic History* 32:1 (1972), 241–26; Peter Kriedte, Hans Medick and Jürgen Schlumbohm, *Industrialisierung vor der Industrialisierung: Gewerbliche Warenproduktion auf dem Land in der Formationsperiode d. Kapitalismus* (Göttingen: Vandenhoeck und Ruprecht, 1977); D.C. Coleman, 'Proto-industrialization: a concept too many', *The Economic History Review*, new series, 36:3 (1983), 435–48; Sheilagh Ogilvie and Markus Cerman (eds), *European proto-industrialization* (Cambridge: Cambridge University Press, 1996).

11   Hela Schandelmaier, *Niedersächsische Fayencen [Pt 1]: Die niedersächsischen Manufakturen: Braunschweig I und II, Hannoversch Münden, Wrisbergholzen* (Hanover: Kestner-Museum, 1993), pp 66–7, and catalogue with images of items from Wrisbergholzen at pp 192–216.

12   For example, Daniel Gottfried Schreber, *Die Kunst Porcelain zu machen, unter Approbation der Königl: Akademie der Wissenschaften zu Paris – übersetzt und mit Anmerkungen vermehrt und den nöthigen Kupfertafeln versehen, hrsg. von dem Grafen von Milly* (Brandenburg: Bey Joh. Wendelin Halle und Joh. Samuel Halle, 1774).

13   For example, Johann Heinrich von Justi, *Vollständige Abhandlung von denen Manufacturen und Fabriken*, Vol 1 (Copenhagen: Roth, 1758), p 131; Beverly Lemire, 'Consumerism in preindustrial and early industrial England: the trade in secondhand clothes', *Journal of British Studies* 27:1 (1988), 1–24; Stuart M. Nisbet, 'The making of Scotland's first

industrial region: the early cotton industry in Renfrewshire', *Journal of Scottish Historical Studies* 29:1 (2009), 1–28; Reinert, *Translating empire*; Prasannan Parthasarathi and Giorgio Riello (eds), *The spinning world: a global history of cotton textiles, 1200–1850* (Delhi: Primus Books, 2012); Trentmann, *Empire of things*; Jon Stobart and Vicki Howard (eds), *The Routledge companion to the history of retailing* (Abingdon: Routledge, 2019).

14 Natascha Mehler, 'The archaeology of mercantilism: clay tobacco pipes in Bavaria and their contribution to an economic system', *Post-Medieval Archaeology* 43:2 (2009), 261–81; Natascha Mehler, *Tonpfeifen in Bayern (ca.1600–1745)* (Bonn: Habelt, 2010).

15 Mehler, 'Archaeology of mercantilism'; Nils Brübach, '"This precious Stinke" – Zur Wirtschaftsgeschichte des Tabaks, 1500–ca.1800', in Hans Pohl (ed), *The European discovery of the world and its economic effects on pre-industrial society 1500–1800* (Stuttgart: Franz Steiner, 1990), pp 141–52; Jordan Goodman, *Tobacco in history: the cultures of dependence* (London: Routledge, 1993); Julia A. King, 'Still life with tobacco: the archaeological uses of Dutch art', *Historical Archaeology* 41:1 (2007), 6–22. For the Ottoman Empire, see James Grehan, 'Smoking and "early modern" sociability: the great tobacco debate in the Ottoman Middle East (seventeenth to eighteenth centuries)', *American Historical Review* 111:5 (2006), 1352–77.

16 But as these years also represented, throughout Europe, years of failed harvest, crisis mortality and economic turmoil, lower wages may have reflected the economic downturn of the time; see Arthur E. Imhof, *Aspekte der Bevölkerungsentwicklung in den nordischen Ländern 1720–1750*, 2 vols (Bern: Francke, 1976); J.D. Post, *Food shortage, climatic variability, and epidemic disease in pre-industrial Europe: the mortality peak in the early 1740s* (Ithaca, NY: Cornell University Press, 1985); Philipp Robinson Rössner, 'The 1738–41 harvest crisis in Scotland', *The Scottish Historical Review* XC/1 (2011), 27–63.

17 Kaminski, *Idee der Nachhaltigkeit*, pp 275, 277–8.

18 All information from Schandelmaier, *Niedersächsische Fayencen [Pt 1]*, pp 54–8.

19 Rudolf Forberger, *Die Manufaktur in Sachsen: Vom Ende des 16. bis zum Anfang des 19. Jahrhunderts* (Berlin: Akademie Verlag, 1958), pp 8–9.

20 On cultural transfer between the Electorate and the United Kingdom, see Arnd Reitemeier (ed), *Kommunikation und Kulturtransfer im Zeitalter der Personalunion zwischen Großbritannien und Hannover* (Göttingen: Universitätsverlag, 2014), esp. the essay by Conway; Benjamin Bühring, *Die Deutsche Kanzlei in London: Kommunikation und Verwaltung in der Personalunion Großbritannien – Kurhannover 1714–1760* (Göttingen: Universitätsverlag Göttingen, 2021). On Göttingen and Justi, see Wakefield, *Disordered police state*.

21 Brisco, *The economic policy of Robert Walpole*, Ch. 3; Ashworth, *The Industrial Revolution*; Ashworth, *Customs and excise*. Underemphasized in Hoppit, *Britain's political economies*.

22 Printed broadsheet dated Hanover, 12 November 1748, http://resolver.sub.uni-goettin gen.de/purl?PPN722225261 (last accessed 25 May 2022).

23 On life and work in a late *ancien régime* porcelain manufactory, see Suzanne L. Marchand, *Porcelain: a history from the heart of Europe* (Princeton, NJ: Princeton University Press, 2020), pp 118–38.

24 Karl Heinrich Kaufhold, 'Schwerpunkte des preußischen Exportgewerbes um 1800', in Franz Mathis and Josef Riedmann (eds), *Exportgewerbe und Außenhandel vor der Industriellen Revolution: Festschrift Georg Zwanowetz* (Innsbruck: Kommissionsverlag der Österreichischen Kommissionsbuchhandlung, 1984), pp 243–60; Karl Heinrich Kaufhold, 'Aspekte einer vorindustriellen gewerblichen Betriebsform', in Meyer and Popplow (eds), *Technik, Arbeit und Umwelt in der Geschichte*, pp 41–52; Wehler, *Deutsche Gesellschaftsgeschichte, Vol I: Vom Feudalismus des Alten Reiches bis zur Defensiven Modernisierung der Reformära 1700–1815*, pp 102–12; and on subsequent transition to the factory age, ibid., pp 112–18. For a pessimistic assessment, Eli F. Heckscher, *An economic history of Sweden* (Cambridge, MA: Harvard University Press, 1954), pp 182–9; Helga Schultz, *Handwerker, Kaufleute,*

Bankiers: Wirtschaftsgeschichte Europas 1500–1800 (Frankfurt-am-Main: Fischer, 1997), pp 124–32; Kleinschmidt, 'Weltwirtschaft, Staat und Unternehmen im 18. Jahrhundert: Ein Beitrag zur Protoindustrialisierungsdebatte', at 81.

25 For example, Acemoglu and Robinson, *Why nations fail*; or, in places, Koyama and Rubin, *How the world became rich*.

26 A view promoted, inter alia, in Pomeranz, *Great divergence*.

27 Marx, *Das Kapital*, Ch. 12 on 'Teilung der Arbeit und Manufaktur'.

28 Schultz, *Handwerker*, p 128; Braudel, *Civilisation and capitalism*, Vol II, pp 329–42.

29 Schultz, *Handwerker*, p 125.

30 Sombart, *Der moderne Kapitalismus*, last edn, Vol II, pp 787–8, trans. Daniel Steur.

31 For example, Richard Sennett, *The craftsman* (London: Penguin, 2009). From a modern perspective: Mariana Mazzucato, *The value of everything: making and taking in the global economy*, 2nd edn (London: Penguin, 2019); Reinert, *Visionary realism*.

32 For early modern Scotland, this point has been defended in a sociologist's history, Gordon Marshall, *Presbyteries and profits: Calvinism and the development of capitalism in Scotland, 1560–1707* (Oxford: Clarendon Press, 1980).

33 See also Frederick W. Taylor, *The principles of scientific management* (New York: Harper, 1911), esp. pp 15–21; Morgen Witzel, *A history of management thought*, 2nd edn (Abingdon: Routledge, 2017), p 26.

34 Epstein and Prak (eds), *Guilds, innovation and the European economy*; Kluge, *Die Zünfte*; Bert De Munck, *Guilds, labour and the urban body politic: fabricating community in the southern Netherlands, 1300–1800* (New York: Routledge, 2018); Ogilvie, *The European guilds: an economic analysis*.

35 For example, Robert S. Duplessis, *Transitions to capitalism in early modern Europe: economies in the era of early globalization, c.1450–c.1820*, new edn (Cambridge: Cambridge University Press, 2019).

36 Yazdani and Menon (eds), *Capitalisms: towards a global history*; Kaveh Yazdani, '18th-century plantation slavery, capitalism and the most precious colony in the world', *Vierteljahrschrift für Sozial- und Wirtschaftsgeschichte* 108:4 (2021), 457–503.

37 Pomeranz, *Great divergence*; Wong, *China transformed*; Rosenthal and Wong, *Before and beyond divergence: the politics of economic change in China and Europe* (Cambridge, MA: Harvard University Press, 2011).

38 For an historian's application, see Martin Daunton, *Progress and poverty: an economic and social history of Britain 1700–1850* (Oxford: Oxford University Press, 1995), pp 1–19. For an economist's assessment, see, for example, Joseph J. Spengler, 'Adam Smith's theory of economic growth: Part I', *Southern Economic Journal* 25:4 (1959), 397–415; Horst Claus Recktenwald (ed), *Adam Smith: Der Wohlstand der Nationen*, 7th edn (Munich: Deutscher Taschenbuchverlag, 1996), Introduction, pp LIX–LXIII; Recktenwald was a leading German economist and editor of a modernized German translation of the *Wealth of Nations*.

39 Joseph A. Schumpeter, *Theorie der wirtschaftlichen Entwicklung. Eine Untersuchung über Unternehmergewinn, Kapital, Kredit, Zins und den Konjunkturzyklus*, 8th edn (Berlin: Duncker & Humblot, 1993), Ch. 1.

40 Reinert and Daastøl, 'The other canon: the history of Renaissance economics', Ch. 1; Mokyr, *A culture of growth*.

41 Wakefield, *Disordered police state*.

42 Krafft in a letter to Leibniz, in Leibniz, *Schriften*, Vol 3, cited in Nipperdey, *Die Erfindung der Bevölkerungspolitik*, p 326.

43 António Almodovar and José Luís Cardoso, *A history of Portuguese economic thought* (London: Routledge, 1998), pp 29–32.

44 List, *Das nationale System*, Ch. 5 on Spaniards and Portuguese. The quotations are taken from the English translation by Sampson Lloyd. On industrial policy in 17th-century

Portugal, see Jorge Borges de Macedo, *Problemas de historia da industria protuguesa no seculo XVIII* (Lisbon: Associacao Industrial Portuguesa, 1963).

45 Quoted after James Cavanah Murphy, *A general view of the state of Portugal; containing a topographical description thereof* (London: T. Cadell Jun. and W. Davies, 1798), p 57.

46 See the most recent comparative GDP figures in Henriques and Palma, *Comparative European institutions and the little divergence, 1385–1800*.

47 [Johann Daniel Crafft/Krafft], *Bedencken von Manufacturen in Deutschland* (Jena: Bauhofer, 1683), Preface.

48 Thomas Heinrich Gadebusch, *Schwedischpommersche Staatskunde* (Greifswald: Roese, 1788), Vol 2, p 45.

49 Allen, *British Industrial Revolution*.

50 Gadebusch, *Schwedischpommersche Staatskunde*.

51 Haik Thomas Porada, *Fürstendienerei oder Zukunftsweisendes unter feudalem Vorzeichen: Wirtschaftspolitische Reformpublizistik in Schwedisch-Pommern zwischen 1750 und 1806* (Sundsvall: Mitthögskolan, 1994), p 88; Jörg-Peter Findeisen, 'Zukunftsorientiertes Wirtschaftsdenken in Schwedisch-*Pommern*', pp 83–94, at p 93; Haik Thomas Porada, 'An der Schwelle einer neuen Sozialordnung. Schwedisch-Pommern nach 1750 zwischen Zunft und Konkurrenz', in *Demminer Kolloquien 1985–1994*, pp 35–76, at pp 48–9.

52 Roberts, 'Practicing oeconomy during the second half of the long eighteenth century'; Smith, *The business of alchemy*; Werrett, *Thrifty science*.

53 Karl Heinrich Kaufhold, 'Gewerbelandschaften in der frühen Neuzeit (1650–1800)', in Hans Pohl (ed), *Gewerbe und Industrielandschaften vom Spätmittelalter bis ins 20. Jahrhundert* (Stuttgart: Franz Steiner, 1986), pp 112–202; Stromer, 'Gewerbereviere und Protoindustrien in Spätmittelalter und Frühneuzeit', ibid.

54 Lars Magnusson, *Sveriges Ekonomisk Historia* (Lund: Studentlitteratur, 2016), pp 102–40.

55 From a heterodox economists' perspective, Chang, *Kicking away the ladder*; Reinert, *How rich countries got rich*. Classics in development include Hamilton, *Report on the subject of manufactures*; List, *Das nationale System der politischen Ökonomie*; Albert O. Hirschman, *The strategy of economic development* (New Haven, CT: Yale University Press, 1958); Alexander Gerschenkron, *Economic backwardness in historical perspective: a book of essays* (Cambridge, MA: Belknap, 1962). But see the polemic by Deirdre N. McCloskey and Alberto Mingardi, *The myth of the entrepreneurial state* (Great Barrington, Massachusetts: The American Institute for Economic Research, 2020).

56 Reinert, *How rich countries got rich*, Ch. 3; A.P. Thirlwall and Penélope Pacheco-López, *Economics of development: theory and evidence*, 10th edn (London: Bloomsbury, 2017).

57 List, *National System of Political Economy*, 1841, Ch. 6.

58 Rössner (ed), *Philipp Wilhelm von Hörnigk's Austria supreme (if it so wishes)*.

59 Jochen Hoock, 'Frankreich 1650–1750', in Wolfram Fischer et al (eds), *Handbuch der europäischen Wirtschafts- und Sozialgeschichte*, Vol 4: *Europäische Wirtschafts- und Sozialgeschichte von der Mitte des 17. Jahrhunderts bis zur Mitte des 19. Jahrhunderts* (Stuttgart: Klett Cotta, 1993), pp 476–93, at p 479.

60 Hoock, 'Frankreich 1650–1750', 481. See also a vivid depiction of this manufactory in Braudel, *Civilisation and Capitalism*, Vol II, pp 329–42.

61 List, *National System*.

62 Elisabeth Mikosch, 'The manufacture and trade of luxury textiles in the age of mercantilism', *Textile Society of America Symposium Proceedings* 612 (1990), 56–8.

63 Hoock, 'Frankreich 1650–1750', 487; Charles W. Cole, *Colbert and a century of French mercantilism*, 2 vols (New York: Columbia University Press, 1939).

64 Mikosch, 'The manufacture and trade'.

65 E. Reinert, *How rich countries grew rich, and why poor countries stay poor* (London: Constable, 2008), Ch. 3

66 Isenmann, 'War Colbert ein Merkantilist?'. See also the interesting interpretation of Colbert and mercantilism in Jacob Soll, *Free market: the history of an idea* (New York: Basic Books, 2022), Ch. 7.

67 Rössner, *Freedom and capitalism*.

68 Rössner, *Scottish trade in the wake of Union 1700–1760*, Ch. 2, Appendix on British customs duties after 1707.

69 Isenmann, 'War Colbert ein Merkantilist?'; Soll, *Free Market*, Ch. 7.

70 Gottmann, *Global trade, smuggling, and the making of economic liberalism*, p 130. Apart from Cole, Colbert and Philippe Minard, *La fortune du colbertisme: Etat et industrie dans la France des Lumières* (Paris: Fayard, 1998), the current state of the art is Isenmann, 'War Colbert ein "Merkantilist"'; Isenmann, 'From privilege to economic law'. Both papers are based on Isenmann's unpublished *Habilitationsschrift* (University of Cologne, 2016), pp 115ff., and pp 126ff. on industrial policy, which puts Colbertism in a new perspective. See also Arthur John Sargent, *The economic policy of Colbert* (London: Longmans, Green, 1899), Ch. 3; Thomas J. Schaeper, *The French council of commerce, 1700–1715: a study of mercantilism after Colbert* (Columbus (Ohio): Ohio State University Press, 1983), p 179; Jacob Soll, *The information master: Jean-Baptiste Colbert's secret state intelligence system* (Ann Arbor: University of Michigan Press, 2014); Isenmann, 'Égalité, réciprocité, souveraineté. The role of commercial treaties in Colbert's economic policy', in Antonella Alimento and Koen Stapelbroek (eds), *The politics of commercial treaties in the eighteenth century – balance of power, balance of trade* (Basingstoke: Palgrave Macmillan, 2017), pp 77–103.

71 Charles H. Wilson, 'Trade, society and the state', in *Cambridge economic history of Europe*, Vol 4: *The economy of expanding Europe in the sixteenth and seventeenth centuries* (Cambridge: Cambridge University Press, 1967), 487–576, at p 548. On discourses about manufacturing, development and enlightened economy in 18th-century Spain, see Adriana Luna Fabritius, 'Signs of happiness: a proposal for a new Spanish empire', *History of Political Economy* 53:3 (2021), 515–32. On early modern Spain and economic policy, see also Grafe, *Distant tyranny*.

72 Schinzinger, 'Wirtschaftspolitik der Habsburger'.

73 Coenen, 'Infant industry protectionism and early modern growth?'

74 H.J. Bidermann, *Die technische Bildung im Kaiserthume Oesterreich: Ein Beitrag zur Geschichte der Industrie und des Handels* (Vienna: C. Gerold und Sohn, 1854), p 26, cited after Otruba (ed), *Österreich über alles*, p 33; Gustav Otruba, *Die Wirtschaftspolitik Maria Theresias* (Vienna: Bergland Verlag, 1963), p 29.

75 Otruba, *Wirtschaftspolitik*; Karl Pribram, *Geschichte der österreichischen Gewerbepolitik von 1740 bis 1860: auf Grund der Akten*, Vol 1, *1740–1798* (Leipzig: Duncker & Humblot, 1907); John Komlos, *Ernährung und wirtschaftliche Entwicklung unter Maria Theresia und Joseph II: eine anthropometrische Geschichte der Industriellen Revolution in der Habsburgermonarchie* (St. Katharinen: Scripta-Mercaturae-Verlag, 1994), Ch. III; Herman Freudenberger, *Lost momentum: Austrian economic development 1750s–1830s* (Cologne: Böhlau, 2003), esp. pp 61–130; Bernhard Hackl, 'Die staatliche Wirtschaftspolitik zwischen 1740 und 1792: Reform versus Stagnation', in Helmut Reinalter (ed), *Josephinismus als Aufgeklärter Absolutismus* (Vienna, Cologne and Weimar: Böhlau, 2008), pp 191–272.

76 Antal Szantay, 'Cameralism in the Habsburg monarchy and Hungary', *History of Political Economy* 53:3 (2021), 551–69.

77 Hackl, 'Die staatliche Wirtschaftspolitik', p 194.

78 Roman Sandgruber, 'Österreich 1650–1850', in Wolfram Fischer et al (eds), *Handbuch der europäischen Wirtschafts- und Sozialgeschichte, Vol 4: Europäische Wirtschafts- und Sozialgeschichte von der Mitte des 17. Jahrhunderts bis zur Mitte des 19. Jahrhunderts* (Stuttgart: Klett-Cotta, 1993), pp 619–87, at p 668.

79 Hackl, 'Die Staatliche Wirtschaftspolitik', p 198.

80 Ibid., p 199. On politics under Charles VI, see Stefan Seitschek and Sandra Hertel (eds), *Herrschaft und Repräsentation in der Habsburgermonarchie (1700–1740): Die kaiserliche Familie, die habsburgischen Länder und das Reich* (Berlin: De Gruyter Oldenbourg, 2020).

81 Hackl, 'Die Staatliche Wirtschaftspolitik', p 205.

82 Herbert Knittler, 'Die Donaumonarchie 1648–1848', in Fischer et al (eds), *Handbuch*, pp 880–915, at p 907.

83 Roman Sandgruber, 'Wirtschafts- und Sozialstatistik Österreichs 1750–1918', *Vierteljahrschrift für Sozial- und Wirtschaftsgeschichte*, 64:1 (1977), 74–83, at 77–8, 81.

84 Ibid., p 81.

85 Hans-Joachim Voth, 'Height, nutrition, and labor: recasting the "Austrian model"', *Journal of Interdisciplinary History* 25:4 (1995), 627–36, at 629–30. Cf. Reinhold Reith, 'Arbeitsmigration und Technologietransfer in der Habsburgermonarchie in der zweiten Hälfte des 18. Jahrhunderts', in Ulrich Troitzsch (ed), *'Nützliche Künste': Kultur- und Sozialgeschichte der Technik im 18. Jahrhundert* (Münster: Waxmann, 1999), pp 51–65, at p 61.

86 Roman Sandgruber, 'Marktökonomie und Agrarrevolution. Anfänge und Gegenkräfte der Kommerzialisierung der österreichischen Landwirtschaft', in Anna Maria Drabek, Richard Georg Plaschka and Adam Wandruszka (eds), *Ungarn und Österreich unter Maria Theresia und Joseph II: neue Aspekte im Verhältnis der beiden Länder: Texte des 2. Österreichisch-Ungarischen Historikertreffens* (Vienna: Verlag der Österreichischen Akademie der Wissenschaft, 1982), pp 131–45, at 140.

87 Felix Butschek, *Österreichische Wirtschaftsgeschichte: Von der Antike bis zur Gegenwart*, 2nd edn (Vienna: Böhlau, 2012), pp 90–4.

88 Roman Sandgruber, 'Einkommensentwicklung und Einkommensverteilung in der zweiten Hälfte des 18. Jahrhunderts – einige Quellen und Anhaltspunkte', in Richard Georg Plaschka and Österreichisches Bundesministerium für Wissenschaft und Forschung (eds), *Österreich im Europa der Aufklärung: Kontinuität und Zäsur in Europa zur Zeit Maria Theresias und Josephs II. Internationales Symposion in Wien 20.–23. Oktober 1980* (Vienna: Österreichische Akademie der Wissenschaften, 1985), pp 251–63, at p 263.

89 English translation: *Quintessence of capitalism: a study of the history and psychology of the modern business man* (New York: Dutton, 1915), p 148 (for both quotes).

90 Christopher A. Whatley, with Derek J. Patrick, *The Scots and the Union* (Edinburgh: Edinburgh University Press, 2008); Karen J. Cullen, *Famine in Scotland: the 'ill years' of the 1690s* (Edinburgh: Edinburgh University Press, 2010).

91 Thomas M. Devine, 'Urbanisation', in Thomas M. Devine and R. Mitchison (eds), *People and society in Scotland, Vol I: 1760–1830* (Edinburgh: John Donald, 1988), pp 27–52; updated in Thomas M. Devine, *The Scottish nation: a history 1700–2000*, Amer. edn (New York: Viking/Penguin, 1999), Ch. 8.

92 The quote relates to a phrase coined by Sir T. M. Devine, see later; Christopher A. Whatley, *The Industrial Revolution in Scotland* (Cambridge: Cambridge University Press, 1997); Christopher A. Whatley, *Scottish society: beyond Jacobitism, towards industrialization* (Manchester: Manchester University Press, 2000); Thomas M. Devine, 'Scotland', in R. Floud and P. Johnson (eds), *The Cambridge economic history of modern Britain, Vol I: Industrialisation, 1700–1860* (Cambridge: Cambridge University Press, 2004), pp 388–416; Thomas M. Devine, 'The modern economy: Scotland and the Act of Union', in Thomas M. Devine, C.H. Lee and G.C. Peden (eds), *The transformation of Scotland: the economy since 1700* (Edinburgh: Edinburgh University Press, 2005), pp 13–33; and within the same volume, Thomas M. Devine, 'Industrialisation', pp 34–70. Further studies: Henry Hamilton, *An economic history of Scotland in the eighteenth century* (Oxford: Clarendon Press, 1963); Anthony Slaven, *The development of the west of Scotland 1750–1960* (London: Routledge, 1976); Alastair J. Durie, *The Scottish linen industry in*

the eighteenth century (Edinburgh: Donald, 1979); Roy H. Campbell, *The rise and fall of Scottish industry 1707–1939* (Edinburgh: Donald, 1980); Roy H. Campbell, *Scotland since 1707: the rise of an industrial society*, 2nd revised edn (Edinburgh: Donald, 1985); Iain D. Whyte, *Scotland before the Industrial Revolution: an economic and social history c. 1050–c. 1750* (London: Routledge, 1995); Iain D. Whyte, *Scotland's society and economy in transition, c. 1500–c. 1760* (Basingstoke: Palgrave, 1997).

93 Daniel Szechi, *Britain's lost revolution? Jacobite Scotland and French grand strategy, 1701–8* (Manchester: Manchester University Press, 2017).

94 Reinert, *How rich countries got rich*; Markus Lampe and Paul Sharp, *A land of milk and butter: how elites created the modern Danish dairy industry* (Chicago: University of Chicago Press, 2019).

95 Whatley, *Scottish society: beyond Jacobitism, towards industrialization*, passim; Patrick O'Brien, Trevor Griffiths and Philip Hunt, 'Political components of the industrial revolution: parliament and the English cotton textile industry, 1660–1774', *Economic History Review*, new series, 44:3 (1991), 395–423.

96 Thomas M. Devine, *The transformation of rural Scotland: social change and the agrarian economy, 1660–1815* (Edinburgh: John Donald, 2001).

97 Hoppit, *Britain's political economies*.

98 The most recent account is Alexander Murdoch, *Making the Union work: Scotland 1651–1763* (Abingdon: Routledge, 2020).

99 Rachel, *Die Handels- und Akzisepolitik Preussens 1713–1740*, Vol 2/1, pp 305ff.

100 Thomas M. Devine and Philipp Robinson Rössner, 'Scots in the Atlantic economy 1600–1800', in John MacKenzie and Thomas M. Devine (eds), *Scotland and the British Empire* (Oxford: Oxford University Press, 2011), pp 30–54.

101 Fundamental studies are Whyte, 'The growth of periodic market centres in Scotland, 1600–1707'; Marshall, *Presbyteries and profits*, passim; Richard Saville, *Bank of Scotland: a history 1695–1995* (Edinburgh: Edinburgh University Press, 1996), Ch. 4; Whyte, *Scotland before the industrial revolution*, pp 288–90.

102 Whyte, 'The growth of periodic market centres'.

103 Marshall, *Presbyteries and profits*; W.R. Scott, *The constitution and finance of English, Scottish, and Irish joint-stock companies to 1720* (Cambridge: Cambridge University Press, 1910).

104 Watt, *The price of Scotland*.

105 Marshall, *Presbyteries and profits*; Whatley, *The Scots and the Union*.

106 For the Holy Roman Empire, see Bog, *Der Reichsmerkantilismus*.

107 *Records of the Parliaments of Scotland to 1707*, www.rps.ac.uk, last accessed 1 December 2022.

108 O'Brien, Griffiths and Hunt, 'Political components of the industrial revolution'. See Alice Dolan, *The fabric of life: linen and life cycle in England, 1678–1810*, unpublished, University of Hertfordshire PhD (2015), pp 267–8.

109 Rössner, *Freedom and capitalism*.

110 Nisbet, 'Scotland's first industrial region', quotes on p 5.

111 Parthasarathi, *Why Europe grew rich*.

112 Lennart Jörberg, 'Structural change and economic growth: Sweden in the 19th century, *Economy and History* 8:1 (1965), 3–46; Magnusson, *An economic history of Sweden*; Lennart Schön, *An economic history of modern Sweden* (Abingdon: Routledge, 2012). On Swedish politics and commerce in the age of greatness, see David Kirby, *Northern Europe in the early modern period: the Baltic world, 1492–1772* (Harlow: Addison Wesley Longman, 1990), Ch. 9; Michael North, *The Baltic: a history* (Cambridge, MA: Harvard University Press, 2016).

113 Mats Olsson and Patrick Svensson, 'Agricultural growth and institutions: Sweden, 1700–1860', *European Review of Economic History* 14 (2010), 275–304.

[114] Klas Rönnbäck and Leos Müller, 'Swedish East India trade in a value-added analysis, *c.*1730–1800', *Scandinavian Economic History Review* (2020), 1–18.

[115] K.-G. Hildebrand, 'Foreign markets for Swedish iron in the 18th century', *Scandinavian Economic History Review* 6:1 (1958), 3–52; Jennifer Newman, ' "A very delicate experiment": British mercantile strategies for financing trade in Russia, 1680–1780', in Ian Blanchard, Anthony Goodman and Jennifer Newman (eds), *Industry and finance in early modern history* (Stuttgart: Franz Steiner, 1992), pp 116–42; Chris Evans and Göran Rydén, *Baltic iron in the Atlantic world in the eighteenth century* (Leiden: Brill, 2007).

[116] Lennart Schön and Olle Krantz, 'The Swedish economy in the early modern period: constructing historical national accounts', *European Review of Economic History* 16:4 (2012), 529–54, at 542; Rodney Benjamin Edvinsson, 'Swedish GDP 1620–1800: stagnation or growth?', *Cliometrica* 7 (2013), 37–60, at 51–2; Lennart Andersson Palm, 'Sweden's 17th century – a period of expansion or stagnation?', University of Gothenburg, *Institutionen för historiska studier*, Reports (2016). On Swedish governmentality and gender, see Maria Ågren, *The state as master: gender, state formation and commercialisation in urban Sweden, 1650–1780* (Manchester: Manchester University Press, 2017).

[117] Schön and Krantz, 'The Swedish economy in the early modern period', 542.

[118] Schön and Krantz, 'The Swedish economy in the early modern period', Table 4 and Figure 5, p 546.

[119] Wennerlind, 'The political economy of Sweden's *Age of Greatness*, pp 156–85.

[120] Kirby, *Northern Europe in the early modern period*, p 234.

[121] Wennerlind, 'The political economy of Sweden's *Age of Greatness*'.

[122] Hermann Kellenbenz, 'The organization of industrial production', *Cambridge economic history of Europe*, Vol 5: *The economic organization of early modern Europe* (Cambridge: Cambridge University Press, 1977) pp 462–548, at p 472.

[123] Murdoch, *Network north*; Evans and Rydén, *Baltic iron*.

[124] Evans and Rydén, *Baltic iron*, p 31.

[125] Evans and Rydén, *Baltic iron*, p 36.

[126] Christopher Polhem, *Christoph Polhems Commercienraths, Ritters und Commandeurs des königl. Nordsternordens Politisches Testament* (Stockholm: 1760), transl. Daniel Gottfried Schreber (Grätz [Graz]: Widmanstätterische Erben, 1761), p 2.

[127] Evans and Rydén, *Baltic iron*, pp 32–34 and passim.

[128] Magnusson, *An economic history of Sweden*, p 63.

[129] Magnusson, *Economic history*, p 69. On Polhem, see Reinert and Carpenter's chapter in Rössner (ed), *Economic reasons of state*, pp 26–53, at pp 36–9.

[130] Lars Magnusson, 'Anders Chydenius' life and work: an introduction', in Maren Jonasson and Pertti Hyttinen (eds), *Anticipating the wealth of nations: the selected works of Anders Chydenius, 1729–1803* (Abingdon: Routledge, 2011).

[131] Ragnhild Hutchison, 'The Norwegian and Baltic timber trade to Britain 1780–1835 and its interconnections', *Scandinavian Journal of History* 37:5 (2012), 1–23, at 10–11, 14.

[132] Werner Buchholz, 'Vom Adelsregiment zum Absolutismus. Finanzwirtschaft und Herrschaft in Schweden im 17. Jahrhundert', in Peter Rauscher, Andrea Serles and Thomas Winkelbauer (eds), *Das Blut des Staatskörpers* (Munich: Oldenbourg, 2012), pp 129–81, at p 131.

[133] Walde, *Storhetstidens litterära krigsbyten*, Vol I, pp 108–11, 178.

[134] On Schreber, see Johann Georg Meusel, *Lexikon der vom Jahr 1750 bis 1800 verstorbenen teutschen Schriftsteller* (Leipzig: Fleischer, 1812), Vol 12, pp 433–38, and *Neuestes Conversations-Lexicon; oder, Allgemeine deutsche Real-Encyclopaedie fuer gebildete Staende*, Vol 16, pp 293–4.

[135] Eli F. Heckscher, *Economic history of Sweden* (Cambridge, MA: Harvard University Press, 1954), pp 10–11.

[136] Koerner, *Linnaeus*.

[137] Wennerlind, 'Political economy of Sweden's Age of Greatness'; Wennerlind, 'Theatrum Œconomicum'.

[138] Wennerlind, 'Political economy of Sweden's Age of Greatness'; for an anti-statist marginal voice, Wennerlind, 'The magnificent spruce: Anders Kempe and anarcho-cameralism in Sweden'.

[139] Koerner, *Linnaeus*.

[140] After Erik Thomson, 'Swedish variations on Dutch commercial institutions, 1605–1655', *Scandinavian Studies* 77:3 (2005), 331–46, at 338.

[141] Ibid., 332.

[142] Jan de Vries, *European urbanisation, 1500–1800* (London: Methuen, 1984).

[143] Mats Morell, 'Subsistence crises during the 'Ancien' and 'Nouveau Régime' in Sweden? An interpretative review', *Histoire & Mesure* 26:1 (2011), 105–34; Magnusson, *Economic history*, Ch. 2.

[144] According to figures in Fouquet and Broadberry, 'Seven centuries of European economic growth and decline'.

[145] K. Enflo and A. Missiaia, 'Between Malthus and the industrial take-off: regional inequality in Sweden, 1571–1850', *Economic History Review* (2020), 441–48, Figures 3, 4, 6; quotation taken from p 445.

[146] Lennart Jörberg, 'Structural change and economic growth: Sweden in the 19th century', *Economy and History* 8:1 (1965), 3–46.

[147] Magnusson, *Economic history*, pp 57–61, 66–75.

[148] On timber and forestry and related processes and resources, see further L. Östlund, O. Zackrisson and H. Strotz, 'Potash production in northern Sweden: history and ecological effects of a pre-industrial forest exploitation', *Environment and History* 4:3 (1998), 345–58.

[149] Hans Brems, 'Sweden: from great power to welfare state', *Journal of Economic Issues* 4:2/ 3 (1970), 1–16.

[150] After Michael F. Metcalf, 'Challenges to economic orthodoxy and parliamentary sovereignty in 18th century Sweden', *Legislative Studies Quarterly* 7:2 (1982), 251–61, at 252.

[151] Eli F. Heckscher, 'The place of Sweden in modern economic history', *The Economic History Review* 4:1 (1932), 1–22, at 6.

[152] E.F. Heckscher, 'Swedish population trends before the industrial revolution', *The Economic History Review*, new series, 2:3 (1950), 266–77.

[153] Metcalf, 'Challenges to economic orthodoxy', at 252.

[154] Ivan T. Berend, *An economic history of twentieth-century Europe: economic regimes from laissez-faire to globalization* (Cambridge: Cambridge University Press, 2016), pp 229–30, 235–6.

[155] Volckart, 'The dear old Holy Roman Realm, how does it hold together?'; Ulrich Pfister and Hakon Albers, 'Climate change, weather shocks and price convergence in pre-industrial Germany', *European Review of Economic History* 25:3 (2021), 467–89; but see Oliver Volckart, 'Power politics and princely debts: why Germany's common currency failed, 1549–1556', *Economic History Review* 70:3 (2017), 758–78; extended introduction in Volckart (ed), *Eine Währung für das Reich*.

[156] Richard Tilly, 'The political economy of public finance and the industrialization of Prussia, 1815–1866', *The Journal of Economic History* 26:4 (1966), 484–97; collected studies in Wolfram Fischer (ed), *Beiträge zu Wirtschaftswachstum und Wirtschaftsstruktur im 16. und 19. Jahrhundert* (Berlin: Duncker und Humblot, 1971); Wolfram Fischer, 'Das Verhältnis von Staat und Wirtschaft in Deutschland am Beginn der Industrialisierung', in Wolfram Fischer, *Wirtschaft und Gesellschaft im Zeitalter der Industrialisierung: Aufsätze-Studien-Vorträge* (Göttingen: Vandenhoeck & Ruprecht, 1972), p 972; Hans-Peter

Ullmann, 'Staatliche Exportförderung und private Exportinitiative. Probleme des Staatsinterventionismus im Deutschen Kaiserreich am Beispiel der staatlichen Außenhandelsförderung (1880–1919)', *Vierteljahrschrift für Sozial- und Wirtschaftsgeschichte* 65:2 (1978), 157–216; Volker Hentschel, *Wirtschaft und Wirtschaftspolitik im wilhelminischen Deutschland: organisierter Kapitalismus u. Interventionsstaat?* (Stuttgart: Klett Cotta, 1978); Hans-Werner Hahn, *Wirtschaftliche Integration im 19. Jahrhundert: Die hessischen Staaten und der Deutsche Zollverein* (Göttingen: Vandenhoeck & Ruprecht, 1982); W.R. Lee, 'Economic development and the state in nineteenth-century Germany', *The Economic History Review*, new series, 41:3 (1988), 346–67; Sheilagh Ogilvie, 'The beginnings of industrialisation', in Sheilagh Ogilvie (ed), *Germany: a new social and economic history*, vol II: *1600–1830* (London: Arnold, 1996), pp 263–307; Hubert Kiesewetter, *Die Industrialisierung Sachsens: Ein regional-vergleichendes Erklärungsmodell* (Stuttgart: Franz Steiner, 2007). On the industrial heritage of Europe, see Jordan Goodman and Katrina Honeyman, *Gainful pursuits: the making of industrial Europe 1600–1914* (London: Arnold, 1992).

157 Lee, 'Economic development and the state', 350; Sidney Pollard, 'Industrialization and the European economy', *Economic History Review*, 2nd series, XXVI (1973), 636–48; Sidney Pollard (ed), *Region und Industrialisierung: Studien zur Rolle der Region in der Wirtschaftsgeschichte der letzten zwei Jahrhunderte* (Göttingen: Vandenhoeck & Ruprecht, 1980).

158 Drawing on outdated literature, Andre Wakefield, 'Silver thaler and Ur-Cameralists', in Mary Lindemann and Jared Poley (eds), *Money in the German-speaking lands* (New York: Berghahn, 2017), pp 58–73.

159 Kaufhold, 'Gewerbelandschaften'; Stromer, 'Gewerbereviere und Protoindustrien'.

160 Safley, *Family firms and merchant capitalism in early modern Europe*; Von Stromer, *Oberdeutsche Hochfinanz 1350–1450*, 3 vols.

161 Heinz Schilling, *Aufbruch und Krise: Deutschland 1517–1648* (Berlin: Siedler, 1988); Richard Dietrich, *Untersuchungen zum Frühkapitalismus im mitteldeutschen Erzbergbau und Metallhandel* (Hildesheim: Olms 1991); Ian Blanchard, *The international economy in the 'age of the discoveries', 1470–1570: Antwerp and the English merchants' world* (Stuttgart: Franz Steiner, 2009); Blanchard, *International lead production and trade*; Harreld, *High Germans in the Low Countries*. See the illustrated flagship work of the GDR historians' collective: Autorenkollektiv (Laube, Steinmetz and Vogler), *Illustrierte Geschichte der frühbürgerlichen Revolution*.

162 See especially the new work by Pfister, 'The timing and pattern of real wage divergence in pre-industrial Europe'. As Tilly and Kopsidis argue, 'German states that successfully centralized power in the post-1648 period at the expense of particularistic interests would have a clear advantage in creating swiftly the institutional framework of a modern market economy after 1800'; Tilly and Kopsidis, *From old regime to industrial state*, p 25.

163 Joseph A. Schumpeter, *Capitalism, socialism and democracy* (New York: Harper Perennial Modern Thought, [1942] 2008).

164 Rössner, *Deflation*, p 295; Rudolf Palme, 'Überblick über den Stand der Forschungen zur Bergbaugeschichte Tirols unter besonderer Berücksichtigung der Krisen und Konjunkturen', in Christoph Bartels and Markus A. Denzel (eds), *Konjunkturen im europäischen Bergbau in vorindustrieller Zeit: Festschrift für Ekkehard Westermann zum 60. Geburtstag* (Stuttgart: Franz Steiner, 2000), pp 23–36, at pp 33–4.

165 Palme, 'Überblick', p 35.

166 Joseph von Sperges, *Tyrolische Bergwerksgeschichte* (Vienna: Trattner, 1765), p 5.

167 Mokyr, *The gifts of Athena*.

168 For Saxony at the time of the Reformation, I have discussed this in Rössner, *Martin Luther on commerce and usury*, Ch. 2.

[169] The economic implications are discussed in Dittmar and Meisenzahl, 'Public goods institutions, human capital, and growth'.

[170] Agricola, *De Re Metallica*, Book VI; Westermann, *Montanregionen*.

[171] Sidney Pollard, *Marginal Europe: the contribution of marginal lands since the Middle Ages* (Oxford: Clarendon, 1997); Westermann, *Montanregionen*.

[172] Palme, 'Überblick', p 31.

[173] Ekkehard Westermann, 'Silbererzeugung, Silberhandel und Wechselgeschäft im Thüringer Saigerhandel von 1460–1620: Tatsachen und Zusammenhänge, Probleme und Aufgaben der Forschung', *Vierteljahrschrift für Sozial- und Wirtschaftsgeschichte* 70:2 (1983), 192–214.

[174] Ekkehard Westermann, 'Das 'Leipziger Monopolprojekt' als Symptom der mitteleuropäischen Wirtschaftskrise um 1527/28', *Vierteljahrschrift für Sozial- und Wirtschaftsgeschichte* 58:1 (1971), 1–23, at 3.

[175] Ibid.

[176] Most recently, Heller, *Birth of capitalism*; Banaji, *A brief history of commercial capitalism*.

[177] Schumpeter, *Capitalism, socialism and democracy*.

[178] Agricola, *De Re Metallica*, transl. Hoover, p xxv–xxvi.

[179] Karin Zachmann, 'Kursächsischer Merkantilismus', in Günter Bayerl and Wolfhard Weber (eds), *Sozialgeschichte der Technik: Ulrich Troitzsch zum 60. Geburtstag* (Münster: Waxmann, 1998), pp 121–30, at pp 127–8.

[180] Zachmann, 'Kursächsischer Merkantilismus', p 128, quoting Forberger, *Die Manufaktur in Sachsen*.

[181] After Rachel, *Die Handels- und Akzisepolitik Preussens 1713–1740*, Vol 2/1, p 328. A list of protectionist and prohibitive measures can be found in Vol 2/2: *Aktenstücke und Beilagen*, pp 277–83.

[182] Rachel, *Die Handels- und Akzisepolitik Preussens 1713–1740*, Vol 2/1, p 367; Rössner, *Scottish trade in the wake of Union*, statistical appendix and discussion in Chs. 4 and 5.

[183] Rachel, *Die Handels- und Akzisepolitik Preussens 1740–1786*, Vol 3/2 (Berlin: Parey, 1928), p 601.

[184] Most recent urbanization figures in Philipp Robinson Rössner, 'Das friderizianische Preußen (1740–1786) – eine moderne Ökonomie?', *Vierteljahrschrift für Sozial- und Wirtschaftsgeschichte* 98:2 (2011), 143–72; Ulrich Pfister, 'Urban population in Germany, 1500–1850', CQE Working Papers 9020, Center for Quantitative Economics (CQE), University of Münster (2020), pp 21–3, Figure 3.5; on taxation, see Gustav Schmoller, *Umrisse und Untersuchungen zur Verfassungs-, Verwaltungs- und Wirtschaftsgeschichte besonders des Preußischen Staates im 17. und 18. Jahrhundert* (Leipzig: Duncker & Humblot, 1898), p 180 (table); more recently, Spoerer, 'The revenue structures of Brandenburg-Prussia', pp 781–91; discussion in Schui, *Rebellious Prussians*.

[185] Otto Hintze, *Die Preußische Seidenindustrie im 18. Jahrhundert und ihre Begründung durch Friedrich den Großen*, Vol 3 (Berlin: Parey, 1892), pp 103–35; Ingrid Mittenzwei (ed), *Hugenotten in Brandenburg-Preußen* (Berlin: Akademie der Wissenschaften der DDR, 1987); Erik Hornung, 'Immigration and the diffusion of technology: the Huguenot diaspora in Prussia', *American Economic Review*, 104:1 (2014), 84–122.

[186] Rachel, *Die Handels-, Zoll- und Akzisepolitik Preußens 1740–1786* (Acta Borussica Abt. C Vol 3/2) (Berlin: Parey, 1928), pp 364s.

[187] I have used the annotated edition in Burkhardt and Priddat, *Geschichte der Ökonomie*, pp 143–80.

[188] Summarized in Whaley, *Germany and the Holy Roman empire*, Vol 2, pp 270–7, at p 282. See also Burkhard Nolte, *Merkantilismus und Staatsräson in Preußen: Absicht, Praxis und Wirkung der Zollpolitik Friedrichs II. in Schlesien und in westfälischen Provinzen (1740–1786)* (Marburg: Herder, 2004).

[189] Hintze, *Preußische Seidenindustrie*, p 1; Karl Heinrich Kaufhold, 'Preußische Staatswirtschaft – Konzept und Realität 1640–1806. Zum Gedenken an Wilhelm Treue', *Jahrbuch für Wirtschaftsgeschichte/Economic History Yearbook* 35:2 (1994), 33–70; Toni Pierenkemper, 'Ideen und Erfolge staatlicher Merkantilpolitik im Deutschland des 17. Und 18. Jahrhunderts', *Acta Oeconomica Pragensia,* roè. 16, è. 1 (2008).

[190] David Blackbourn, *The conquest of nature: water, landscape, and the making of modern Germany* (London: W W Norton, 2007).

[191] Hans-Joachim Uhlemann, *Berlin und die Märkischen Wasserstraßen* (Berlin [East]: Transpress, 1987), pp 10–1, 21–3, 34–8.

[192] Otto Wiedfeld, *Statistische Studien zur Entwickelungsgeschichte der Berliner Industrie von 1720 bis 1890* (Leipzig: Duncker & Humblot, 1898), pp 17–21.

[193] *Acta Borussica*, 3/2, p 422.

[194] Detailed discussion in Rössner, *Scottish trade in the wake of Union*, Ch. 3.

[195] Lars Behrisch, *Die Berechnung der Glückseligkeit Statistik und Politik in Deutschland und Frankreich im späten Ancien Régime* (Ostfildern: Thorbecke, 2013); Deringer, *Calculated values*.

[196] Kaufhold, 'Schwerpunkte des preußischen Exportgewerbes', at p 243; Jacob von Klaveren, 'Die Manufakturen des *Ancien Régime*', *Vierteljahrschrift für Sozial- und Wirtschaftsgeschichte*, LI (1964), 145–91, at 185; Kaufhold, 'Manufakturen im Alten Reich. Aspekte einer vorindustriellen gewerblichen Betriebsform', in Meyer and Popplow (eds), *Technik, Arbeit und Umwelt in der Geschichte*, pp 41–52; Wiedfeld, *Statistische Studien*, p 63.

[197] Hugo Rachel, *Das Berliner Wirtschaftsleben im Zeitalter des Frühkapitalismus* (Berlin: Rembrandt, 1931), pp 130–1, 141–4; Hugo Rachel and Paul Wallich, *Berliner Grosskaufleute und Kapitalisten*, Vol 2: *Die Zeit des Merkantilismus 1648–1806*, new edn (Berlin: De Gruyter, 1967), p 276.

[198] Karl Heinrich Kaufhold, 'Wirtschaftspolitik in Brandenburg-Preusen im europäischen Vergleich', in *Preussen 1701: Eine europäische Geschichte*, Vol II: *Essays* (Berlin: Deutsches Historisches Museum, 2001), pp 101–8, at p 104; Karl Heinrich Kaufhold, *Das Gewerbe in Preußen um 1800* (Göttingen: Schwartz, 1978) is still the state-of-the-art survey; but see Erika Herzfeld, *Preußische Manufakturen: Großgewerbliche Fertigung von Porzellan, Seide, Gobelins, Uhren, Tapeten, Waffen, Papier u. a. im 17. und 18. Jahrhundert in und um Berlin* (Bayreuth: Verlag der Nation, 1994); Frank Hoffmann, *'Ein den thatsächlichen Verhältnissen entsprechendes Bild nicht zu gewinnen': Quellenkritische Untersuchungen zur preußischen Gewerbestatistik zwischen Wiener Kongress und Reichsgründung* (Stuttgart: Franz Steiner, 2012); Zhao, 'Public happiness through manufacturing and innovation'.

[199] Behre, *Statistik*, p 403.

[200] A measure of capacity equalling roughly six tons.

[201] Rounded figures after Behre, *Statistik*, 229.

[202] Siemaszko, *Das Oberschlesische Eisenhüttenwesen*.

[203] Kaufhold, *Gewerbe*.

[204] Rössner, 'Das friderizianische Preußen', tables.

[205] Wolfram Fischer, 'Germany in the world economy during the nineteenth century' (Annual Lecture of the German Historical Institute, London) (London, 1984), 3–30; Richard Tilly, 'German industrialization and Gerschenkronian backwardness', *Rivista di Storia Economica*, new series, 6:2 (1989), 139–64; Hubert Kiesewetter, 'Competition for wealth and power. The growing rivalry between industrial Britain and industrial Germany 1815–1914', *Journal of European Economic History* 20:2 (1991), 271–99; Jan de Vries and Ad van der Woude, *The first modern economy: success, failure, and perseverance of the Dutch economy, 1500–1815* (Cambridge: Cambridge University Press, 1997).

[206] Douglass C. North and Robert Paul Thomas, *The rise of the Western world: a new economic history* (Cambridge: Cambridge University Press, 1973); more recently, Acemoglu et al,

'The rise of Europe'. On the economics of *Gutsherrschaft* (manorial or serfdom economy), see Kula, *An economic theory of the feudal system*; Boldizzoni, *The poverty of Clio*, with a critique especially of Douglas C. North's interpretation of the manorial economy.

207 Spoerer, 'The revenue structures of Brandenburg-Prussia, Saxony and Bavaria', p 790, Tab. 1.

208 On Schröder, see, most recently, Keller, 'Happiness and projects between London and Vienna'. On the classification of economic bestsellers and Schröder's work, see Reinert et al, '80 economic bestsellers before 1850', *The Other Canon Foundation and Tallinn University of Technology Working Papers in Technology Governance and Economic Dynamics* 74 (2017).

209 John Brewer, *The sinews of power: war, money and the English state, 1688–1783* (Cambridge, MA: Harvard University Press, [1988] 1990); Michael North, 'Finances and power in the German state system', in Bartolomé Yun-Casalilla and Patrick K. O'Brien (eds), *The rise of fiscal states: a global history, 1500–1914* (Cambridge: Cambridge University Press, 2012), pp 145–63, at pp 148–52.

210 Based on a limited number of partially outdated works, Messina, *History of states and economic policies*, pp 198–9.

Epilogue

1 Holt, *When money talks*.

2 Prasannan Parthasarathi, 'State formation and economic growth in South Asia, 1600–1800', in Rössner (ed), *Economic growth and the origins of modern political economy*, pp 189–203; Lieberman, *Strange parallels*, pp 329–34, 565–75; Irfan Habib, 'Potentialities of capitalistic development in the economy of Mughal India', *Journal of Economic History* 29:1 (1969), 32–78.

3 Spufford, *Money and its use in medieval Europe*; Sargent and Velde, *The big problem of small change*; Desan, *Making money*.

4 Samuel N. Eisenstadt (ed), *The origins and diversity of axial age civilizations* (New York: State University of New York Press, 1986).

5 Von Rohr, *Einleitung zur Staats-Klugheit*, pp 237–8.

6 David Graeber and David Wengrow, *The dawn of everything: a new history of humanity* (New York: Farrar, Straus and Giroux, 2021).

7 Stuart Lasine, 'Samuel-Kings as a mirror for princes: parental education and Judean royal families', *Scandinavian Journal of the Old Testament: An International Journal of Nordic Theology* 34:1 (2020), 74–88, at 84–5.

8 Tilly, *Coercion, capital, and European states*; Scott, *Seeing like a state*; Michel Foucault, *Security, territory, population: lectures at the college de France, 1977–78*, new edn (Basingstoke: Palgrave Macmillan, 2007).

9 Jonsson, 'The origins of cornucopianism'; Jonsson and Wennerlind, *Scarcity*.

10 James Scott, *Against the grain: a deep history of the earliest states* (New Haven, CT: Yale University Press, 2018).

11 Piketty, *Capital in the twenty-first century*; Walter Scheidel, *The great leveler: violence and the history of inequality from the Stone Age to the twenty-first century* (Princeton, NJ: Princeton University Press, 2017); Alfani and Di Tullio, *The lion's share*; Thomas Piketty, *Capital and ideology* (Cambridge, MA: Harvard University Press, 2020).

12 Kevin Hjortshøj O'Rourke, 'Passions, interests, and hobbits', *Critical Quarterly* 59:2 (2017), 122–6, at 122; Acemoglu and Robinson, *The narrow corridor*.

13 Acemoglu and Robinson, *Why nations fail*. But see the review by Vries, 'Does wealth entirely depend on inclusive institutions and pluralist politics? A review of Daron Acemoglu and James A. Robinson, "Why nations fail: the origins of power, prosperity and poverty"'; Boldizzoni, 'On history and policy'.

[14] Mokyr, *The lever of riches*.

[15] Keynes, *Economic Opportunities for our grandchildren* (1930). I have used the online version on www.marxists.org/reference/subject/economics/keynes/1930/our-grandchildren. htm (last accessed 31 October 2022).

[16] Larry Neal and Rondo A. Cameron, *A concise economic history of the world: from paleolithic times to the present*, 5th edn (Oxford: Oxford University Press, 2016).

[17] Cf. Georg Friedrich Knapp, *Staatliche Theorie des Geldes*, 1st edn (Munich: Duncker & Humblot, 1905); Suzanne de Brunhoff, *The state, capital and economic policy* (London: Pluto Press 1978); a theme picked up again in Graeber, *Debt: the first 5,000 years*.

[18] Jevons, *Money and the mechanism of exchange*.

[19] For example, Robert Brenner, 'Agrarian class structure and economic development in pre-industrial Europe', *Past & Present* 70 (1976), 30–75; Dobb, *Studies in the development of capitalism*; Ellen Meiksins Wood, *The origin of capitalism*, revised edition (London: Verso Books, 2002); Heller, *The birth of capitalism*; Henry Heller, *A Marxist history of capitalism* (Abingdon: Routledge, 2018); Banaji, *A brief history of commercial capitalism*; Yazdani and Mohajer, 'Reading Marx in the divergence debate', pp 173–240.

[20] Werner Sombart, *Der moderne Kapitalismus*, 3 double vols (Munich: Duncker & Humblot, 1921–27).

[21] Braudel, *Civilisation and capitalism*, Vols 2 and 3.

[22] The literature on the origins and unfolding of the British Industrial Revolution is large. Game changers include Deane and Cole, *British economic growth*; a view later modified, inter alia, by N.F.R. Crafts, *British economic growth during the Industrial Revolution* (Oxford: Oxford University Press, 1985); T.S. Ashton, *The Industrial Revolution (1700–1760)* (Oxford: Oxford University Press, 1975); David Landes, *The unbound Prometheus: technological change and industrial development in Western Europe from 1750 to the present*, new edn (Cambridge: Cambridge University Press, 2008); Pat Hudson, *The Industrial Revolution*, new edn (London: Bloomsbury Academic, 2014). A recent synopsis is provided by Vries, *Escaping poverty*. There was a commercial revolution that preceded the industrialization, which is not always given much credit but see, for example, Ralph Davis, *A commercial revolution: English overseas trade in the seventeenth and eighteenth centuries* (London: Historical Association, 1967); for Scotland, I have established a quantitative framework and chronology of this revolution in Rössner, *Scottish trade in the wake of Union 1700–1760*; and for discussions of the possible connections between commercial and industrial revolution and the economic agents involved, Inikori, *Africans and the industrial revolution in England*; Nuala Zahedieh, *The capital and the colonies: London and the Atlantic economy, 1660–1700* (Cambridge: Cambridge University Press, 2010).

[23] Parthasarathi, 'State formation and economic growth'.

[24] For Scotland, Marshall, *Presbyteries and profits*.

Index

References to figures and photographs appear in *italic* type;
those in **bold** type refer to tables.

Printed and bound by CPI Group (UK) Ltd, Croydon, CR0 4YY

23/04/2025

14661023-0003